Studies in Modernity and National Identity

SIBEL BOZDOĞAN and REŞAT KASABA,
Series Editors

Studies in Modernity and National Identity examine the relationships among modernity, the nation-state, and nationalism as these have evolved in the nineteenth and twentieth centuries. Titles in this interdisciplinary and transregional series also illuminate how the nation-state is being undermined by the forces of globalization, international migration, electronic information flows, as well as resurgent ethnic and religious affiliations. These books highlight historical parallels and continuities while documenting the social, cultural, and spatial expressions through which modern national identities have been constructed, contested, and reinvented.

Modernism and Nation Building: Turkish Architectural Culture in the Early Republic
by Sibel Bozdoğan

Chandigarh's Le Corbusier: The Struggle for Modernity in Postcolonial India
by Vikramaditya Prakash

Islamist Mobilization in Turkey: A Study in Vernacular Politics
by Jenny B. White

The Landscape of Stalinism: The Art and Ideology of Soviet Space
edited by Evgeny Dobrenko and Eric Naiman

The Landscape of Stalinism

THE ART AND IDEOLOGY OF SOVIET SPACE

Edited by EVGENY DOBRENKO and ERIC NAIMAN

UNIVERSITY OF WASHINGTON PRESS
Seattle and London

This publication was supported in part by the Donald R. Ellegood International Publications Endowment.

Library of Congress Cataloging-in-Publication Data

The landscape of Stalinism : the art and ideology of Soviet space / edited by Evgeny Dobrenko and Eric Naiman.
p. cm.—(Studies in modernity and national identity)
Includes bibliographical references and index.
ISBN 0-295-98333-7 (alk. paper)
1. Communism and culture—Soviet Union. 2. Socialist realism.
3. Stalin, Joseph, 1879–1953. I. Dobrenko, E. A. (Evgenii Aleksandrovich)
II. Naiman, Eric, 1958– III. Series.

HX523.L32 2003
335.43—dc21 2003046767

The paper used in this publication is acid-free and recycled from 10 percent post-consumer and at least 50 percent pre-consumer waste. It meets the minimum requirements of American National Standard for Information Sciences—Permanence of Paper for Printed Library Materials, ANSI Z39.48–1984.

CONTENTS

FIGURES

ACKNOWLEDGMENTS

This volume received generous financial support from the Committee on Research and from the Institute of Slavic, East European, and Eurasian Studies at the University of California, Berkeley, as well as from the Institute for Russian, Soviet and Central and East European Studies at the University of Nottingham, the International Center for Advanced Studies at New York University, and the Stanford Humanities Center.

The editors wish to express their appreciation to the translators who worked on this volume: Mary Akatiff, Abigail Evans, Jeffrey Karlsen, Sonja Kerby, and Glen Worthey. The book benefited enormously from the editorial and research assistance provided by Gabriel White and from the editing of Jane Kepp. We are particularly grateful to Michael Duckworth at the University of Washington Press for his patience and continued enthusiasm for this project.

NOTE ON TRANSLITERATION

Within the text we have used the transliteration system of the Library of Congress, but have altered it slightly to render names familiar to or at least less unpronounceable for readers unfamiliar with Russian. In the notes we adhere strictly to the Library of Congress system when citing Russian sources.

Introduction

ERIC NAIMAN

While supervising an inexperienced pilot on a military training flight, a taciturn, self-sacrificing hero suddenly loses his eyesight in E. Pentslin's 1939 film *The Destroyers* (Istrebiteli). Without indicating that anything is amiss, he instructs his young charge in the procedures necessary for a successful landing. When the fledgling pilot jumps down from the front seat and protests that he was inadequately prepared, the hero gazes blankly in front of him and says quietly: "Give me your hand, Yasha, it seems that I've gone blind."[1]

This moment from an undistinguished film (thus rather typical for its time and place) might be "read" in several ways, but I have selected it to open this collection of essays because it seems to me emblematic of the plight of Soviet citizens who sought to make their way through the social and discursive space of Stalinist culture. Survival and success depended on one's skills in ideological navigation, on being able to make one's way through a world that existed on the plane of representation and imagination, a plane that exerted a kind of asymptotic and symptomatic pressure on the surface of everyday life. The provincial hero of Andrei Platonov's 1936 story "Among Animals and Plants" is initially perplexed, even stunned, by the lack of fit between ideological discourse and the emotionally barren landscape that surrounds him.[2] He is traumatized by the inaccessibility of the ideological world, irritated "that he didn't know science, that he didn't travel in trains with electricity, that he hadn't seen Lenin's mausoleum and that he had only once sniffed perfume, from a bottle that belonged to the wife of the director of section number ten." This sense of ontological impotence ends when he finally gains access to the world of record players and female parachutists by staging his own heroic event—the prevention of a railway accident. The result is not a lapse into psychotic fantasy but an invitation to Moscow and a dramatic shift of his own "reality" into closer proximity with the utopia that he has been struggling to see and hear all around him. Physically crippled as a result of his exploit, he has learned to function in another landscape, one that can be accessed by a kind of productive, imaginative vision born of a frequently intoxicating and often terrifying blindness.

The numerous maimings of Stalinist heroes in literature and art have led Igor Smirnov and Lilya Kaganovsky each to speak of the importance of masochism and symbolic filial castration in narratives that prioritize the potency of Stalin, the "Father of Peoples."[3] But one might claim that this loss is compensated for by a new, symbolic empowerment, an empowerment informed by a sense of historical development, a sense of steering through the virtual landscape of the future by projecting it onto the topography of the present. Marxism had long insisted on the priority of historically informed vision; Feuerbach's problem, Marx alleged, was that when he looked at the landscape in Manchester or Rome, he saw only what was in front of him, not the historical process of which that landscape was a part.[4] Soon after the Russian Revolution of 1917, Soviet theoreticians began cautioning Party members and sympathizers against looking at the world "with an unarmed eye."[5] The arming of the eye involved learning to see "dialectically" or, to put it another way, to see in accordance with the discursive curves of the Party's General Line. Essentially, this learning was a kind of epistemological training flight, one ending in ideological competence, disciplined blindness, and heightened vision.

Stalinist culture and Soviet ideology are often—and quite rightly—regarded as verbal phenomena. Stalin himself highlighted the primacy of speech in his own speeches; to a significant extent, his most important "works" were all metadiscursive: "Everyone is *talking* about the successes of Soviet power in the area of the kolkhoz movement. . . . What does this all *say?*"[6] For Stalin, events were primarily discursive and metadiscursive, often to a dizzying degree: "Remember the latest events in our Party. Remember the latest *slogans,* which the Party has put forward lately in connection with the new class shifts in our country. I am *speaking* about *slogans,* such as the *slogan* of self-*criticism,* the *slogan* of heightened struggle with bureaucracy and the purge of the Soviet apparatus, the *slogan* of organization, etc."[7] In Stalin's indictment of him, Bukharin's chief fault in 1928 was his failure to grasp the Party's slogans. As recently published diaries from the period reveal, the struggle for success in Stalin's Russia was in many respects akin to an effort to master a new language. Lately, historians have begun to embrace a methodological "linguistic turn" in an effort better to understand the truth (or is it "truth"?) of the Stalinist epoch.[8] The contributors to this collection do not disparage the importance of language to an understanding of Stalinist culture. They embrace the concept of discourse but focus upon that concept's spatial dimension.

What was the importance of space to the discourse of Stalinist ideology? How did one have to focus *vision* on ideological figures in order to move vigorously through Stalinist society? In approaching the importance of this category to the shaping of the Stalinist subject, we must understand space as discourse in three dimensions, discourse through which the subject *moves*. One might define ideological space as language (broadly conceived) that seeks to transform life on a poster into life on the skin. But instead of bringing a poster to life, discourse can transform life into a poster, producing subjects all too aware of the ideological inadequacy of sham three-dimensionality.

We can profitably study Soviet culture of the 1930s from any of three directions. The first approach strives for dispassionate, archaeological distance, looking at the material remnants of the 1930s or, where space is concerned, the physical transformation of the earth. From this point of view, by "straining away the mountains of verbiage," we might discover that the landscape of Stalinism was not radically different from the landscapes of other rapidly industrializing empires.[9] A second approach explores the experience of Soviet citizens as they climbed that mountain of verbiage, as they coped with material deprivation and a sense of ideological inadequacy (the inadequacy of ideology or the inadequacy of their sense of self).[10] A third approach, employed by the contributors to this book, focuses less on the consumption of ideology than on its production. The essays in this collection are studies of ideological poetics that deal with various components of a particular ideological "trick"—the shading of discourse, the projection of rhetoric, the drawing of lines simulating motion. They deal with ideology's attempt to climb into another dimension and transcend the distinction between landscape and space. The volume concerns itself with quotation marks that offer themselves as eyeglasses. Perhaps this is not a particularly eloquent image, but it captures the extent to which the essential experiential figure provided to Stalinist subjects was the mixed metaphor.

In the late 1930s, Mikhail Bakhtin formulated the theory of the "chronotope," a notion that insisted on the appropriateness of a certain conception of space to each historical era. The emergence of this critical tool, this concept of spatio-temporal specificity, in a specific country and at a specific time is often neglected, but we should recall that this was a country in which—as the following essays show—the notion of space (and of space in its ideological unfolding) was imbued with remarkable ideological prominence. Bakhtin himself, a scholar with a rich philological background, continued to seek the condensation of time and space in verbal images. The contributors to this volume logically expand the purview of his investigation as they explore in verbal, visual, and spatial constructions the chronotopes of the time and the space that produced the very idea of the chronotope.[11]

The book is divided into three parts. The first explores ways in which producers of various forms of art utilized space in the period between the first Five-Year Plan and Stalin's death, that is, from 1929 to 1953. We begin with aesthetic uses of space because, following the lead of Vladimir Nabokov and Boris Groys, we believe that Stalinism can best be understood as a lethal aestheticization of life.[12] The essays in part one consider the spatial dynamics of ideology in architecture, painting, cinema, song, and aesthetic criticism. Part two deals with aspects of the naturalization of ideological space. Taking as their focus objects as diverse as postage stamps, tourism, advertising, map making, and the Soviet musical, the authors examine how Soviet citizens were symbolically mobilized. The contributors to part three study the utopian impulse of what Emma Widdis calls "the imaginary geography of the 1930s." They show how Soviet ideology centered on spaces that seemed to be outside human history (the north, the underground), spaces on which Soviet society could inscribe itself, as if on a blank page. Even where the focus was on areas of human habitation, the impulse moved from exploration *(razvedka, uchen'e)* to mastery *(osvoenie)* and the remaking of nature in one's own image.

The contributors to this volume represent diverse backgrounds: philosophy, history, art history, and literary studies.[13] Methodologically, stylistically, and thematically they are quite heterogeneous, and in several cases the essays reach diametrically opposed conclusions. Yet while they differ in their conclusions, the contributions share several themes. The authors return repeatedly to the semanticization of space, the "saturation" (Oksana Bulgakowa) of space with meaning. Totalitarianism is distinguished by a kind of epistemological imperialism, the battle for the "symbolic occupation" (Boris Groys) of space and time. An aspect of this battle is the impulse toward the sacralizing of space (Katerina Clark); often in unexpected ways space is coded as sacred or profane. (Mikhail Ryklin argues that this dichotomy had profound temporal complications, with formerly sacred spaces both debased *and* redeemed by their contact with the historically profane.) Nearly all the contributors emphasize the paradoxical centrality of the periphery in the Stalinist landscape. The provinces and edges of the nation were continually labeled periphery, yet this insistence on distance was often paired with an affirmation that distance could be magically annihilated.

Several of the authors consider what might be called the ideology's "personal periphery." In their examination of depictions of leisure, Randi Cox, Evgeny Dobrenko, Richard Taylor, and Emma Widdis show how the home and activities of relaxation became important arenas for the assertion of ideological control. Their essays also explore important representational differences distinguishing the Stalin era from the preceding decade. Two essays, those by Hans Günther and Mikhail Epstein, take issue with the proclaimed "novelty" of Soviet space and assert continuities with the prerevolutionary past.

Many of the essays attest to the presence of an infantile narcissism at the heart of Stalinist ideology. Several authors highlight the ideological desire to transform space into a representation of oneself. Jan Plamper discusses the inescapably metaphoric relation of nature to mankind in Stalinist painting. Emma Widdis and John McCannon each describe the desire to use nature as a mirror for the Soviet project. The dynamic of *osvoenie* discussed by Widdis may be seen as the clearest expression of the desire to make nature like oneself. Epstein writes of the Russian urge to turn spaces of habitation into replications of the lonely human body. Günther treats this question in Jungian terms, seeing in mass songs of the period a continual replication of the maternal body. The collapsing of distance, a frequent theme in these essays, serves as a corollary to the utopian desire for temporal leaps and is another sign of the ideological demand for immediate fulfillment of desire.

We have placed Epstein's essay last not only because it raises to a "metaphysical" plane some of the issues in the other contributions but also because it implicitly poses far-reaching questions with which we wish to leave our readers. Epstein describes the Russian attitude toward space as one of mythological dread, the horror of a vacuum linked to "the burden of freedom." The "mythologeme" at work is thus not desire for the "blank page" but the fear of it. Or rather, Epstein's essay, read in the light of those preceding it, suggests that in the Soviet period the fear of space was conjured away by talking about space, by turning space into language, by pretending that geography could be figured in two dimensions—by a page of any sort. As Dobrenko argues, even the time-honored form of two-dimensional spatial representation—the map—was too directly linked to the three-dimensionality that it traditionally signified. Maps gave way to description, to language, in a virtually metasymbolic act of appropriation. In this volume, we explore how one-sixth of the globe was gobbled up by words. We offer readers a variety of voyages through the landscape of the Soviet ideological imagination during a time when that imagination was both tragically blind and intensely creative.

NOTES

1. *Istrebiteli,* E. Pentslin, director, Kievskaia kinostudiia, 1939.

2. Andrei Platonov, *The Portable Platonov,* trans. Robert Chandler and Elizabeth Chandler, *Glas* 20: 179–216. Complete Russian text published in *Rossiia,* 1991, no. 1.

3. I. P. Smirnov, "Scriptum sub Specie Sovietica," *Russian Language Journal* 41 (1987): 115–138; Lilya Kaganovsky, "Bodily Remains: The 'Positive Hero' in Stalinist Fiction," Ph.D. dissertation, University of California, Berkeley, 2000.

4. Karl Marx and Friedrich Engels, "The Germany Ideology," in *Collected Works* (New York: International Publishers, 1976), 5: 40.

5. G. Zinovyev, *Filosofiia epokhi* (Moscow: Moskovskii rabochii, 1925), 5.

6. I. V. Stalin, "Golovokruzhenie ot uspekhov," in *Sochineniia* (Moscow: Gos. izd., 1949), 12: 191. Emphasis added.

7. I. V. Stalin, "O pravom uklone v VKP(b)," in *Sochineniia* (Moscow: Gos. izd., 1949), 12: 11. Emphasis added.

8. The most prominent work in this vein is probably Stephen Kotkin's *Magnetic Mountain: Stalinism as a Civilization* (Berkeley: University of California Press, 1995).

9. For an interesting example of this approach, see Kate Brown, "Gridded Lives: Why Kazakhstan and Montana Are Nearly the Same Place," *American Historical Review* 106, no. 1 (2001): 17–48.

10. For pioneering work in this direction, see Sheila Fitzpatrick, *Everyday Stalinism: Ordinary Life in Extraordinary Times. Soviet Russia in the 1930s* (New York: Oxford University Press, 1999). See also Véronique Garros, Natalia Korenevskaya, and Thomas Lahusen, *Intimacy and Terror,* trans. Carol A. Flath (New York: New Press, 1995). Other important contributions include Jochen Hellbeck, "Fashioning the Stalinist Soul: The Diary of Stepan Podlubnyi, 1931–1938," *Jahrbücher für Geschichte Osteuropas* 44, no. 3 (1996): 344–73; Igal Halfin, *From Darkness to Light: Class, Consciousness, and Salvation in Revolutionary Russia* (Pittsburgh, Pa.: Pittsburgh University Press, 2000); and Golfo Alexopoulos, "Portrait of a Con Artist as a Soviet Man," *Slavic Review* 57 (Winter 1998): 774–90.

11. On the impact of Stalinism on the evolution of the concept of the chronotope, see Anne Nesbet and Eric Naiman, "Formy vremeni v 'Formakh vremeni': Khronosomy khronotopa," *Novoe literaturnoe obozrenie* 2 (1993): 90–109.

12. Vladimir Nabokov, *Bend Sinister* (New York: Vintage, 1947); Boris Groys, *The Total Art of Stalinism: Avant-Garde, Aesthetic Dictatorship, and Beyond,* trans. Charles Rougle (Princeton University Press, 1992).

13. In its subject and methodological diversity, our volume has a predecessor, *Beyond the Limits: The Concept of Space in Russian History and Culture*, ed. Jeremy Smith (Helsinki: Suomen Historiallinen Seura, 1999). The essays in that volume range from economic geography to social anthropology. Although some of the essays deal with the Stalinist period, most have a wider or later temporal focus.

Part One

Space and Art

1

Socialist Realism and the Sacralizing of Space

KATERINA CLARK

For decades Soviet and Western cultural critics bandied about the term "socialist realism" as a virtually self-evident category that applied in all creative fields. Of course some common stipulations for socialist realism were widely applicable—for example, mandatory optimism, aesthetic conservatism, moral puritanism, and *partiinost,* the last somewhat barbarously translated as "party-mindedness" and generally meaning enthusiasm for things Bolshevik. Few critics, however, addressed the question, Is there such a thing as *a* socialist realism, or did "socialist realism," in practice, have different conventions for each field, despite common factors such as those just named?

Traditionally, Soviet literature—or, more specifically, the novel—has been regarded as the cornerstone of socialist realism, and within that literature, the "positive hero" is the key element that defines the tradition. The positive hero encapsulates the cardinal public virtues, and his or her career over the course of the novel symbolically recapitulates the nation's progress toward communism, thereby legitimating the status quo and affirming that Soviet society is on the correct, Marxist-Leninist track. The hero fulfills these functions within an elaborate system of verbal signs such as motifs, plot functions, and epithets organized as a de facto code that enables the heroic biography to perform its task. Clearly, several of the arts, especially those with little or no narrative component, such as painting and architecture, but also many of the performing arts such as opera, ballet, and music, were limited in the extent to which they could find analogs for the highly elaborated verbal code of the Soviet novel.

Another common denominator is to be found in most, though not all, examples of Soviet culture that are labeled socialist realist. (This common denominator does not particularly apply to music, especially when a given composition has no thematic dimension.) At the heart of many canonical works of socialist realism lie spatial myths in which "heroes" or "leaders" function as human embodiments of, or emissaries from, a higher-order space. Even unadorned socialist realist buildings (that is, those with no clear thematic potential) could be interpreted as expressing such spatial myths. Arguably, in the novel, at the level of deep structure, the hero's mission is not ultimately his public task to build that power station, raise those economic yields, or drive out that enemy, not even *just* to grow as a communist, but to mediate between two different orders of space that might somewhat tritely be classified as the sacred and the profane. Consequently, architecture, as spatial architectonics, could be seen as the quintessential genre of socialist realism. Significantly, perhaps, in the first half of the 1930s, the very decade when the conventions of socialist realism were being established, architecture was the branch of the arts that received the greatest attention from the leadership.

Architecture's central role in Stalinist culture has its own logic in that building and spatial organization lie at the heart of Marx's account of society: the base-and-superstructure model. This potential was picked up in Bolshevik Party rhetoric about "building communism." Building also assumed tremendous importance in Stalinist culture because of the utopian aspects in the notion of living "in communism," the perfected society. By the thirties, the Russian Revolution was at least fifteen years old, and the realization of the new society still proved elusive. Yet (or perhaps consequently) in that decade building was given a privileged status in both the leadership's pronouncements and its practical programs.

At the beginning of 1931, a time of general reevaluation of the country's goals and ideals as the first Five-Year Plan wound down and leaders took stock and planned the second, Party leaders in their speeches began to use architectural models to explicate the current historical moment and its place in the overall Marxist-Leninist model of history. It was said recurrently that with the plan and its concomitant cultural revolution, the "foundation" *(fundament)* of socialist society has been laid; now it was time to construct its "edifice" *(zdanie)*.[1] Then, at the Party plenum in June 1931, a plan for rebuilding many of the major Soviet cities was announced. Thereafter, throughout the decade (as had been less true earlier), plans for particular towns and buildings were supervised closely by Party leaders, especially by the Moscow Party head Lazar Kaganovich, who in 1933 was appointed head of the supervisory body, Arkhplan. Whether as cause or as effect, in Party rhetoric the rebuilding of the Soviet city came to stand for the moral and political transformation of the entire society into a communist one. Architectural schemes and tropes became dominant sources for political rhetoric throughout this most formative decade in the history of socialist realism.

My topic in this essay is not just the centrality of architecture in socialist realism but specifically the sacralizing of space. In this aspect of the socialist realist tradition, not only Party rhetoric and official programs but also widespread intelligentsia prejudices were contributing factors. During the period leading up to the revolution and beyond, the various factions among the intelligentsia, deeply divided as they were, generally shared one prejudice: they reviled the perceived effects of a rentier-mercantilist society on culture and looked to purify it by driving out the market, a secular version of the biblical story of Jesus driving the money changers out of the temple. A particular bête noire for both Bolsheviks and the intelligentsia generally (not, after all, entirely separate categories) was the "petty shopkeepers" and their stalls *(lavochki)*—a bête noire also, incidentally, for members of the Frankfurt School.[2]

The purification or repurification of space was to prove an obsessive concern in Stalinist culture. Its centrality in the purges, for example, is not far to seek. After the revolution itself, it informed many of the rituals of iconoclasm and spatial transgression to be found in the culture of the twenties; some involved tearing down the statues of the ancien régime in order to repurify space, whereas in others, such as the mass spectacles, the central act was some spatial transgression whereby "the proletariat" or oppressed classes burst into the polluted space of the rentier-mercantilist-cum-tsarist regime, claiming that space for themselves and repurifying it by driving out the "scum."

By the thirties, however, the Soviet Union had largely passed through its iconoclastic phase and was into one of nation building. The institutionalization of socialist realism has to be seen as a key moment in this process. The Bolshevik leadership needed a culture adequate to the great new nation it had founded. It is no accident that at the same time the Soviet state was "creating" its new culture, it was also rebuilding its capital, Moscow, as the symbolic center of the renewed nation. In May 1931 Maxim Gorky returned to the Soviet Union permanently from quasi-emigration; in less than a year a single Union of Writers had been formed, with him as head, and the "new" literary method of socialist realism was proclaimed. At the Party's plenum of June 1931—only a month after Gorky's arrival—when the plan for the reconstruction of

Soviet cities was announced, it was already clear that Moscow was to get the lion's share of the funding and attention. The rebuilt Moscow, it was declared, was to function as the model *(obrazets)* for the rest of the country and for the progressive forces of the world besides.[3]

In this policy one already sees the tendency that was to be defining for Stalinist culture—the naming of a canonical model to function as a beacon toward which all lesser examples of the phenomenon in question (in this case, towns) should incline. Moscow, however, was not merely a model; it was also the seat of power. Consequently, it came to function as an extraordinarily privileged space. All other cities were limited merely to approaching it.

It will be recalled that in Russia the building of cities already, from prerevolutionary times, played a central role in accounts of national identity. Moscow and St. Petersburg were not merely rival claimants to the title of capital, but the distinctive features of the layouts of the two cities had come to stand for rival accounts of the national identity. Among those who admired St. Petersburg, its canals and embankments, "clad in granite" and presided over by grand statuary, and the city's broad streets and gridlike street plan came to stand for culture, modernization, and Westernization. St. Petersburg's detractors saw the same features as standing for soullessness and a fatal distortion of Russia's historical path. The latter group generally preferred Moscow's onion domes and narrow, higgledy-piggledy lanes, which they proclaimed not just the opposite of St. Petersburg's "rigid grid" but veritable embodiments of a more spontaneous, spiritual, and organic Russia. Moscow's detractors saw the narrow lanes and onion domes as icons of chaos, backwardness, and obscurantism.

During the reigns of the last two tsars, moreover, there had been a sort of "battle of the styles" between those who wanted architecture to be in the style of seventeenth-century Muscovy (the century when the present-day Kremlin walls were erected) and those who supported the empire style of neoclassical St. Petersburg. Both of the tsars, Alexander III and Nicholas II, preferred the Muscovite style, which they believed stood for a closer (if somewhat paternalistic) relationship between the tsar and his people. A lobby of architects—many of whom later reemerged to prominence as the principal designers of the monumental public structures commissioned in the Stalinist thirties—allied with the liberal, modernizing faction within the emerging middle class, favored the neoclassical style.[4]

Both parties in this debate were reacting against recent vogues for eclecticism and *style moderne*. Spatial purification, the redirection of architecture from the variegated toward a more consistently maintained style that predated the modern mercantilist world (associated with recent vogues), was a common aim of both schools. Those proselytizing for a return to the empire style advocated not only construction of new buildings in that style but also freeing existing examples from the clutter of the stalls and minor structures around them. Moreover, those who sought a neoclassical revival, no less than advocates of the Muscovite style, promoted specific styles not just for their surface features but for a particular nexus of attributes that essentially represented an entire weltanschauung.

When proselytizers wrote about buildings in the empire style, they praised them for the way they achieved a "harmonious" integration of the buildings' component parts, for their "wholeness" *(tsel'nost')*, and for their monumental facades. They also repeatedly invoked attributes from a common inventory: "simple" *(prostoi)*, "severe" *(strogii)*, "austere" *(surovyi)*, "restrained" *(vyderzhannyi)*, and "lucid" *(svetlyi)*. Moreover, they tended in their writings toward an isomorphy between descriptions of the architects and of their buildings: both were characteristically "simple," "stern," "restrained," and "severe."[5] Significantly, these clichés resurfaced later as the core of a standard inventory of epithets in socialist realist literature for identifying the hero as an emblem of political consciousness.

This is not to suggest that neoclassical architects and their champions influenced socialist realist literature.[6] But what appear in both instances to be descriptions of external features are in fact simultaneously affirmations of an ideological position. Thus, for example, "simple," indicating in the case of architecture that superfluous features have been eliminated in the interest of preserving the tradition's "strict" lines, is at the same time a claim that the tradition used has divined a supernal formula. In the case of socialist realism, one mandatory function of which was ritual affirmation of the status quo, art in its very formal features affirmed the ideological purity of the regime and the *extra*ordinary extent to which the leaders were diviners of the true (after all, the capsule version of Lenin called him "simple like the truth" *[prost kak pravda]*). For this reason, when the infamous "signal" article in *Pravda* in 1936, attacking Dmitry Shostakovich's opera *Lady Macbeth of Mtsensk Region*, decried the way the music's unharmonious "confusion" *(sumbur)* rendered the mandatory "simplicity" impossible, the criticism was not merely aesthetic in its implications.[7]

The entire country was organized in a hierarchy of spheres of relative sacredness, a cartography of power. It was the task of socialist realism, whether in art, in film, or in literature, to present the public with its landmarks and its route maps.

The more obvious examples of the sacralizing of space and its links to building are to be found in visual forms of socialist realism. In literature, it is largely present at the level of deep structure, as we shall see, but is sometimes quite transparent. One example of this is a passage in Vasily Grossman's classic of socialist realism, the novel *Stepan Kol'chugin* (1937–39). This novel, set in a prerevolutionary Donbas mining town, chronicles the (for socialist realism typical) progress of its hero, Stepan Kol'chugin, from callow and oppressed working-class lad to conscious Bolshevik revolutionary. Stepan, however, conceives the progress to communism in terms of building a city, as is particularly apparent in a scene in which he returns one evening from his first major encounter with a mentor figure at the factory and pauses as he contemplates the benighted workers' housing:

> The tiny houses were barely raised above the ground. Straight ahead the black industrial hill rose up before him, and on its summit a lantern shone. . . . The cottages were clustered under its slope as if driven there in a disordered *[besporiadochnuiu]* bunch. . . .
>
> And Stepan wanted to drive these little huts from the earth [against which they huddled], to make them larger and higher so that they might stand beneath that distant light on the top of the hill, that a mighty people who have dominion over fire and iron might not stoop, might not creep, coughing, into these dark and narrow burrows. Vague and dim notions *[predstavleniia]* rose up in his mind, notions that were alarming, daring, and audacious.[8]

These "vague notions," or embryonic consciousness, are thus identified with building a new, modernized city. Progress toward Bolshevik political awareness is conflated with a version of the myth of the building of St. Petersburg as a bulwark against Russian primitivism and obscurantism. The light on the top of the hill stands for the "pinnacle," or political end, to be striven toward, but it also stands for a guiding light.

The passage is also informed by that valorized spatial binary, high-low, which was to become central in the metaphorical system of Stalinist culture. This spatial hierarchy informs the choices of many of the symbolic heroes who were foregrounded in the rhetoric and ritual of the thirties, such as aviation heroes, who were said to go "ever higher," mountain climbers, and even virtuoso violinists, whose notes were said to go "higher" than those of lesser performers. It was also a central value in architectural practice. The most famous moment of Soviet architectural history is the competition of 1931–33 to design a Palace of Soviets building. The winning design, by Boris Iofan, was intended to be the highest building in the world—taller than the recently constructed Empire State Building—and crowned with a gigantic statue of Lenin.

In the passage from *Stepan Kol'chugin* one also finds a fundamental of the socialist realist system: an emphasis on the greatness of space as a guarantee of the greatness of time—in other words, of the historical record. Similarly, in socialist realist architecture, buildings are not just functional—they do not just meet practical needs—but are also monuments bearing witness to an extraordinary time. In actuality, several styles were used for Moscow's new buildings, primarily some version of the classical, but also Renaissance, Russian national, and Gothic, the latter frequently refracted via the recent architectural vogues of New York and Chicago. But whichever style was used, the crucial criteria for a building's design were that it be monumental and that it proclaim in its very style a grand pedigree.

Thus the division into two orders of space that lies at the heart of socialist realist practice implies a parallel division into two orders of time—or, more accurately, there is a division into two orders of space-time. The temporal dimension, however, is largely implicit; Stalinist culture put extraordinary emphasis on space. It is no accident that the popular hit from Grigory Aleksandrov's 1936 film *Circus* (Tsirk), "Song of the Motherland" (Pesnia o rodine), which had the singular distinction of also functioning as an auxiliary national anthem, opens with the line, "Broad is my motherland." The opening epithet "broad" *(shiroka)*, which is given greater emphasis by its placement as the first word in the song, encapsulates the greatness in the country as symbolized in its vast, almost endless horizontal sweep. In effect, "broad" functions as a metaphor for imperial might.

Although the country might have had an extraordinary spatial sweep, in rhetoric it was generally represented not as an undifferentiated horizontal but as one with hierarchical divisions. In a sense, the opposition high-low that we find in *Stepan Kol'chugin* is but a translation to the vertical axis of another, horizontally articulated one, most characteristically patterned as center-periphery. Generally, this opposition determines the deep structure of socialist realist literature; the hero progresses in the novel from "periphery" to some sort of center.

These two space-times (center and periphery) are so radically different that they must be represented as maximally cut off from each other. Consequently, when, for example, toward the end of the typical novel, the hero travels from his provincial town or collective farm for a visit to Moscow, the intervening terrain is rarely depicted. Often, he goes by airplane, so that as he bridges the gap between the two places he sees nothing but the clouds, suitable props for a liminal space. Alternatively, the intervening journey is not reported—there seemingly is no contiguity between the two places, and the one can be reached from the other only by a spatio-temporal leap. Similarly, when the journey from periphery to center occurs within a single space—for example, when a city is modernized—it is important to represent the "new" Soviet city as a total and immediate transformation of the old. Hence a cliché of literature from the early thirties is the hyperbolic claim that "all of Moscow is under scaffolding" *(vsia Moskva v lesakh)*—Moscow, as it were, is in a chrysalis from which a diaphanous butterfly will emerge, bearing no resemblance to its former, grublike state. Later, in some of the classics of socialist realism, a schematic opposition between the "new" Moscow and other sections of the country had an explicit temporal correlate—the new Moscow as the future versus some provincial location as the present or past.[9]

Despite claims that "all of Moscow" was being transformed, in actuality only some sections of the capital were rebuilt, principally those in the center. The majority of the other grandiose designs for new public buildings in Moscow went unrealized, including even the Palace of Soviets, which was intended to recenter the capital. Arguably, this was not merely because ambitions and the desire to outdo Hitler's new Berlin outran the pocketbook. So many novels and films of this time include a fleeting segment involving a vision or even the construction of a fantastic city that emerges, phantomlike, ex nihilo (or from the rubble created in an orgy of dynamiting) and is often gleaming white.[10] Such scenes had their visionary, miragelike quality because, like the grandiose plans for public buildings in Moscow, they were not so much representations of reality as proleptic rhetorical devices; they were both a promise of a great and glorious future as-yet-not-totally-realized and a template, a guiding model. As proleptic devices, they were anticipated in A. A. Zhdanov's capsule formula for socialist realism made in his keynote address to the First Writers' Congress in 1934: "A combination of the most matter-of-fact, everyday reality and the most heroic prospects" *(sochetanie samoi surovoi, samoi trezvoi prakticheskoi rabotoi s velichaishei geroikoi i grandioznymi perspektivami)*—note that "prospects" are both spatial and temporal.[11]

Architecture is in some ways the most concrete and material of all art forms, but at the same time—as the architectonics of space—it is one of the most abstract. This dual ontological status played a critical role in socialist realist practice. Sinyavsky, in his famous essay "On Socialist Realism," brought out this twofold nature, the way in which socialist realism tries both to present actuality and to monumentalize. Hallowed space is essentially outside of time; distinctions between past buildings and "the new" need not necessarily obtain. Indeed, a select few buildings from prerevolutionary times, such as the Kremlin and the Bolshoi, enjoyed this special status more than any new structure. But these mythicized structures, whether of the new Moscow or the old, had simultaneously a very real, concrete, and even banal existence.

Architecture functioned in the socialist realist tradition rather the way the icon does in Russian Orthodox culture, in that it had a simultaneous existence in two orders of reality, sacred and profane. Like Alice's looking glass, it reflected an image and yet was also a portal. But the pattern largely represented an inversion of the usual inside-outside distinctions that obtain for a sacred space. The inside of a given building might be defined largely by its mundane function (for example, as the location of a Soviet institution) while outside it functioned as a sacred monument to inspire awe and contemplation. The Kremlin, however, the most sacred space, was sacred both inside and outside.

Moscow had become the center of the nation (more so in the thirties than in the twenties), but the capital, in turn, had its own center. Because the Palace of Soviets was never built, the Kremlin remained the center of centers. The spatial hierarchy was articulated in a series of concentric circles, somewhat like a national *matrioshka* doll: the outer rim was the country at large (the periphery), the first inner circle was Moscow, and then came the Kremlin. There was also an innermost inner, Stalin's study in the Kremlin, but it was generally considered too sacred to be actually represented; it could be seen only as "the light in the window." In its stead, commonly either St. George's Hall, the place of public ceremonial and investiture, or a tower of the Kremlin functioned as that solid, innermost doll of the *matrioshka*.[12]

In visual and literary representations, the Kremlin is not normally caught in its totality. Not only are the administrative buildings and churches played down in favor of the fortress walls and towers, but often the expanse of them is not shown. Instead, a single tower, possibly with a short stretch of adjacent wall, is portrayed. This is particularly apparent in Aleksandr Gerasimov's *Stalin and Voroshilov in the Kremlin* (1938), a painting that is a candidate for *the* exemplum of socialist realist art, in that it won one of the first Stalin Prizes (in 1941), and thereafter "few civilian institutions" would fail to have a copy.[13] In this painting, a monumental Stalin and Voroshilov, in greatcoats, stand at a balustrade on a Kremlin height (see fig. 2.3). Their perpendicular form is picked up in a parallel figure, a tower of the Kremlin not far away. This arrangement is clearly not just for the purposes of composition. The isomorphism between Stalin and Voroshilov, on one hand, and the Kremlin tower, on the other, implies identification.[14]

In this painting, as was characteristic, Stalin is like a monument or a monumental building. Indeed, when Stalin appears in films, if he moves at all, it is in slow, lumbering, deliberate movements, as if he were a stone statue à la the commendatore in Mozart's opera *Don Juan*. Representations of Lenin were sometimes monumental, like those of Stalin, but more frequently he was depicted, whether in film, painting, or sculpture, leaning forward, as if straining toward the revolutionary tomorrow, or at least with lively, darting eyes to suggest a mind forever in motion. Frequently in art and film, his body is placed on a diagonal rather than a vertical, as for Stalin. In another canonical representation of him by Gerasimov, *Vladimir Il'ich Lenin* (1930), an accompanying banner flapping in the wind beside him (and arranged on a diagonal) is used to represent motion despite stasis.[15] This technique for representing Lenin did not, of course, originate with Gerasimov but can be seen in, for instance, romantic, patriotic art of the nineteenth century and in Eisenstein's 1927 film *October*.

In this respect, the most common representation of Lenin is closer to that of ordinary people, who generally appear either as a mass or (especially if a smaller group) in some sort of motion or activity, often straining muscular, seminude bodies in the performance of some task.[16] What is to be noted here is a binary, a valorized spatial division with an implicit corresponding temporal hierarchy. Whereas generally in art and film, Stalin (and, by analogy, other major leaders) is monumental, motionless, and vertical—the solo tower, so to speak—both Lenin and the people are in motion, either inclining forward or in a bustling, directionless conglomeration.[17] Lenin and the people are in a state of *becoming* (although Lenin is ahead of the people and leading them forward); Stalin is in a state of *being*.

In paintings and photomontages of the 1930s, Stalin and the other leaders are generally represented as monumental, towering figures out of proportion to the rest of the citizenry depicted.[18] They are often placed on some higher point on the frame or landscape in order to accentuate this monumentality. In films of the period, towering architecture also plays a major role in the depiction of leaders. This is particularly striking in Eisenstein's *Alexander Nevsky* (1938) and *Ivan the Terrible* (part one, 1944).[19] In both, the hero-leader, played by the tall, willowy Nikolai Cherkasov, seems to tower over his environment. But the buildings with which he is associated are also disproportionately large. In *Nevsky,* the "folk" live in underground dugouts while Alexander lives in a vast wooden structure. Indeed, there seems to be a symbiotic relationship between the hero-leader and these buildings: most of his major decisions or critical moments occur as he touches one of the monumental buildings or imitates its shape with some bodily pose.

The reification of Stalin—the leader as a statue or monumental building—was often accompanied by the anthropomorphizing of a symbolic building. Thus in Aleksandrov's musical film *Circus,* after the two heroes together compose that famous song "Broad Is My Native Land" at a grand piano in a stateroom of the Hotel Moscow, the Kremlin tower looms up, unrealistically close, at the heroine's window. Orwell got it wrong. It was not Big Brother who was watching us but a great tower of the Kremlin, which so often functioned in socialist realist art and film as a sentinel, a guardian, or a guarantor of ideological purity.

In *Circus,* the Kremlin tower also stands as the guarantor of the good life. The hotel suite in which the heroine is staying and through the window of which the tower can be seen represents the height of luxury in the new society. In a later scene, it is the Bolshoi that rears up in the background, this time as other characters eat cream cakes in the hotel's roof garden. Thus the privileged space in the symbolic system of socialist realism can have either a worldly import—luxury—or a more sacred one. Or both can be there simultaneously. It might be said that while the Soviet Union aspired, consciously or unconsciously, to achieve in its culture an imperial sublime—at the heart of which was a binary opposition between two orders of reality akin to those found in a traditional belief system—in fact it was operating in the modern, secular world. In consequence, the exalted in its culture was always in danger of devolving into something of more mundane, material value. All systems leak, and even in "totalitarian" cultures they are never implemented to perfection. Binary systems are, in the last analysis, only constructs anyway, although in a culture dominated by such a doggedly dualistic theoretical system as Marxism-Leninism-Stalinism, the binaries tend to be more consistently maintained than is generally the case.

Stalinist culture was very schematic. The identification discussed here between a leader-mentor figure and a tower or other architectural feature is possible because both are essentially abstractions. Arguably, in literature the positive hero is, though a character in his or her own right, at a fundamental level also an abstraction. His or her principal function is to mediate between the provinces (the periphery) and Moscow.

Socialist realist novels are generally set in the periphery. This is not just because it provides a pared-down microcosm for representing processes that take place in the greater arena of society at large, but also because the periphery is the space of the masses. The center is a sacralized space, the space of the great leader(s). The role of the masses is to be forever in motion, striving to attain "Moscow," to enter that extraordinary space to which an extraordinary degree of activity (speed) will transport them. But they can attain "Moscow" only figuratively, fleetingly, or tokenly. The positive hero and his mentors are virtually the only ones who can go to Moscow. They must *ritually* mediate the temporal gulf in a journey, in space, though no member of the general populace can traverse the temporal gulf in actuality. Thus when Stalin is to deal with the populace at large, he has to leave the sacred space, temporarily—to come outside the Kremlin and stand on the mausoleum to greet the people for the revolutionary holiday parades.

Of course Stalin also sees a select few in the Kremlin, generally as he gives them awards in St. George's Hall, sometimes as he extends them advice. In representations of such scenes, however, emphasis is laid on how extraordinary the spatial surroundings appear to ordinary mortals, how remote from their world. Extensive use is made of light and the color white. For example, Aleksandrov's musical *The Radiant Path* (Svetlyi put', 1940), a veritable parody of the socialist realist conventions discussed here, culminates in a series of events taking place in some extraordinary space-time. The audience is first treated to the heroine's dazed view at a reception in the Kremlin, and then, as she is taken up into the skies in an open car, it is given an aerial view of the Moscow of the future. Finally, after the heroine descends, the audience sees a series of shots of the All-Union Agricultural Exhibition (some featuring Vera Mukhina's statue *Worker and Collective Farm Woman*). In all these scenes, as is typical of the finale of an Aleksandrov film, white and shimmering light is used to a hyperbolic degree.

White, like light—as, for example, in the candelabra of the Kremlin hall or a metro station—can have a phantomlike or miragelike quality suggesting a different order of space, something sacred or eternal. But it can also palpably suggest this-worldly positives—consumerism and luxury (smart casual clothes à la the jazz age, white curtains in the stateroom, candelabra such as only the rich might have). In this aspect, white affirms the radical extent to which the quality of life has improved for the worker. It is also symptomatic of the extent to which the heroic age of Marxist revolutionism in the twenties has come to an end: realistically, a worker could not wear white because his clothing would get dirty at work; it was traditionally the engineer who wore white gloves, and he was despised for that very reason. But white (and light) are crucial as devices for representing the "suddenly" of that mind-boggling leap from provincial backwardness (often underlined with scenes of muddy roads) to the glittering, modern city.

An evanescent glitter or a blinding flash of light that may temporarily overcome the positive hero is an important convention of socialist realist practice for representing moments of encounter with the Great Leader or moments when a protagonist is in some sacred space. Those moments must be epiphanic—that is, intense—but extremely brief and not extending to later life, except as inspirational memories or moments marking an absolute transformation. They are outside time. In this particular aspect, the hero's ecstasy sometimes has suggestions of an orgasm.

Symptomatic of the extent to which "the leader" and even the most positive of heroes participate in two entirely different orders of time can be seen in the presentation of their private lives. Most Stalinist novels, and many films as well, are structured as rituals of initiation whereby a less mature figure is guided through his maturation by an older mentor and can eventually be initiated in some ritual way and enter (political) adulthood.[20] This ritual of maturation, however, only tokenly entails the hero's attaining the ontological status of a Stalin. The distance between them must be absolute, and a guarantee of this is the way they live in different temporalities. One can see this, for example, in Mikhail Kalatozov's film *Valery Chkalov* (1941), in which the extremely impetuous eponymous hero is ushered through his ritual maturation in a visit with Stalin himself at the Kremlin. The substance of this meeting is left unrepresented, and we next see Chkalov when he has married and consummated his sexual relations with a woman he had hitherto only courted with adolescent bravado; soon he becomes a father. Similarly, in Mikhail Chiaureli's *The Fall of Berlin* (Padenie Berlina, 1949), when the burly Stakhanovite hero is summoned for his first visit to the Kremlin and approaches "the Great Gardener" in its gardens, he is like a mawkish teenager and stumbles off the path onto the garden bed in his embarrassment at the sight of the great leader. Again the content of the meeting is not represented, but we next see the hero as he is romantically involved with the heroine. Before, he had been unable to express his great love to her, but Stalin had encouraged him to follow his heart.

Stalin functions in such scenes not merely as initiator on the level of political consciousness cum acquiring greater self-discipline. The meeting with Stalin may, as in tribal initiation, simultaneously serve as a kind of sexual initiation. But Stalin (or some counterpart) sends the initiate out into the world to bear children and enter the lifestream. In many films, Stalin (or his counterpart) acts as matchmaker, presiding over the moment at the film's end when the male and female positive heroes are ritually betrothed, but he presides as a figure who stands outside such moments himself.[21] Frequently, in representing such moments there is a suggestion of sexual excitation on the part of the hero, but such excitation cannot be mutual: Stalin stands beyond any situation where he could be subject to this, in a different order of time and space.[22]

A division into two orders of space, the sacred and the profane, was thus a common denominator of socialist realism. In any given work the binary could be deployed in its simple, straightforward form or in a more complex articulation, but this division was fundamental to the Stalinist cosmology, enabling the human, the aesthetic, the philosophical, and the political to be melded in the one system. The defining features of the Soviet regime and its ideological underpinnings were presented through the discourse of space and architecture.

NOTES

1. See, for example, "K. E. Voroshilov na IX s"ezde VLKSM," *Pravda*, 22 January 1931.

2. See, for example, Siegfried Kracauer, "Die Kleinen Ladenmädchen Gehen ins Kino," *Frankfurter Zeitung*, 11–19 March 1927.

3. "O moskovskom gorodskom khoziaistve i o razvitii gorodskogo khoziaistva

SSSR. Doklad tov. Kaganovicha L. L. na iiun'skom plenume TsK VKP(b)," *Pravda*, 4 July 1931.

4. Richard Wortman, *Scenarios of Power: Myth and Ceremony in Russian Monarchy* (Princeton: Princeton University Press, 1995).

5. See, for example, L. Rudnitskii's untitled lead article in *Istoricheskaia vystavka arkhitektury* (St. Petersburg, 1911), 32, 33.

6. In my book *The Soviet Novel: History as Ritual* (Bloomington: Indiana University Press, 2000), 56–64, I point to the use of similar epithets in Russian hagiography.

7. "Sumbur vmesto muzyki," *Pravda*, 28 January 1936, 3.

8. Vasilii Grossman, *Stepan Kol'chugin*, Part 2 (Moscow: GIKhL, 1939), 97–98.

9. See, for example, Aleksandr Malyshkin's *People from the Backwoods* (Liudi iz zakholust'ia, 1938), in which action takes place in three locations—Moscow, the new industrial city of Magnitogorsk, and a recently collectivized agricultural area (the "backwoods")—which represent future, present, and past, respectively.

10. An example is Sergei Iutkevich's film *The Miners* (Shakhtery, 1936), originally titled *The Gardener* (Sadovnik).

11. "Rech' sekretaria TsK VKP(b) A. A. Zhdanova, *Pervyi s"ezd pisatelei: Stenograficheskii otchet* (Moscow: Ogiz, 1934), 4.

12. See, for example, the poster by Viktor Govorkov, "O kazhdom iz nas zabotitsia Stalin v Kremle" (Stalin in the Kremlin cares about each one of us), 1940, in Victoria E. Bonnell, *Iconography of Power: Soviet Political Posters under Lenin and Stalin* (Berkeley: University of California Press, 1997), fig. 4.17.

13. Igor Golomstock, *Totalitarian Art in the Soviet Union, the Third Reich, Fascist Italy, and the People's Republic of China* (New York: HarperCollins, 1990), 224.

14. This deliberate compositional isomorphism between Stalin and some towering edifice was a commonplace of socialist realist art. As an example using an analogous technique but a different structure, consider the poster of the late Stalin era "Slava Velikomu Stalinu—Zodchemu Kommunizma!" (printed in Golomstock, *Totalitarian Art*, 267), in which the tower used in the composition is not from the Kremlin but an example of wedding-cake architecture.

15. Bonnell, *Iconography of Power*, fig. 4.10.

16. Examples are Aleksandr Deineka's *Defense of Sevastapol* (1942) and Vera Mukhina's statue *Worker and Collective Farm Woman* (1937). The latter also uses cloth waving in the breeze to suggest motion, in this case draped around the figures' bodies and fluttering behind them.

17. Note, for example, that other canonical socialist realist painting, Mikhail Avilov's *Comrade Stalin's Arrival at the First Cavalry Army*, one of the two (with Gerasimov's *Stalin and Voroshilov*) "most popular paintings" and one that "few military institutions" would not display (Golomstock, *Totalitarian Art*, 224). It shows Stalin on a cart reviewing the cavalry riding past, but he has every air of a statue being hauled rather than of a human being.

18. See, for example, Konstantin Finogenov's painting *Stalin at the Front* and Gustav Klutsis's photomontage poster *Da zdrastvuet raboche-krest'ianskaia krasnaia armiia—vernyi strazh sovetskikh granits* (1935), printed in David Elliott, *New Worlds: Russian Art and Society 1900–1937* (New York: Rizzoli, 1986), 148.

19. It is of course problematical to categorize Eisenstein's films as "socialist real-

ist." In these respects, however, he follows the tradition, though it in no way defines him.

20. Clark, *Soviet Novel,* chapters 5 and 7.

21. Examples are Eisenstein's *Alexander Nevsky* and Chiureli's *Fall of Berlin.*

22. Freud analyzed this phenomenon among charismatic leaders; see his *Group Psychology and the Analysis of the Ego* (1921).

2

The Spatial Poetics of the Personality Cult

CIRCLES AROUND STALIN

JAN PLAMPER

A visitor from the Russian provinces to the Soviet Union's Tretiakov Gallery in Moscow at mid-twentieth century would likely have been offered a guided tour with a focus on artistic representations of Lenin and Stalin. The guide might have graduated from a crash course based on the 1947 essay "Methodical Elaboration of Excursions in the State Tretiakov Gallery on the Subject: 'The Images of Lenin and Stalin in the Soviet Fine Arts'" by Vladimir Sadoven'. And this being the Soviet Union, the guide would probably have followed the Sadoven' pamphlet quite closely. It taught that the subject of Lenin and Stalin in Soviet art "is of great, exciting interest for every Soviet person." The depictions of Lenin and Stalin embodied "the best features of the Bolshevik-revolutionary and the builder of socialism, and [therefore] the tour has a great moral-political, educational goal." It went on to explain that "by invoking through the artistic images of Lenin and Stalin . . . different stages in the history of the party and the Soviet state, the tour also has great political and historical edifying value." "Because of these goals," Sadoven' warned, "the tour must be conducted in an accessible, politically accurate, and emotional manner."[1]

The tour would have started with a short introductory lecture, followed by a powerful visual salvo of two emblematic paintings, Isaak Brodsky's *Lenin at the Smolny* (1930) and Dmitry Nalbandian's *Portrait of I. V. Stalin* (1945). Only then would visitors have passed through rooms displaying a series of drawings and sculptures of Lenin by Nikolay Andreev. Interspersed adulatory quotes about Lenin and Stalin from the poetry of Mayakovsky, Lunacharsky, and Dzhambul accompanied the entire tour. To "sustain the mounting impressive impact on the viewer from the images of the 'Leniniana,'" the tour would then have glossed over a number of paintings and hurried to "subtheme Stalin"—specifically, a room exhibiting Aleksandr Gerasimov's monumental painting *Stalin and Voroshilov in the Kremlin* (1938).[2] There, visitors would have heard the tour's lengthiest exegesis:

> The picture shows comrades Stalin and Voroshilov during a walk in the Kremlin against the backdrop of the wide panorama of Moscow. The figures of Stalin and Voroshilov are given in full size in the foreground. On the second plane are the ancient towers of the Kremlin; on the third is Moscow under reconstruction. Stalin and Voroshilov are looking into the distance. They are walking along the pavement, which is still wet from the rain that has just fallen, and their figures are distinctly recognizable against the backdrop of the city and the cloudy sky with blue breaking through here and there. The subject of the picture is very simple and taken, as it were, from everyday life, from a genre painting. But the picture captivates the spectator with a feeling of elation and importance. The artist managed to create this impression both with his composition and with the harmonious, uplifting colors; he successfully used the motif of the weather, when everything seems illuminated by the recent rain, and even the color gray looks cheerful. Likewise, the artist has attained a unity of pictorial tone that enables the wholeness and forceful elation of the impression. In the appearance of Stalin and Voroshilov one can sense calm strength and vigilance. The result is an unpretentious and majestic image of the leader of the Soviet people and his closest comrade-in-arms, the People's Commissar of Defense, against the background of the great city, the capital of a new world, Moscow. They are standing in the ancient Kremlin, the heart of the city and the world, are guarding this new world, and are vigilantly looking into the distance.[3]

In this chapter I examine how space was configured in Stalin's personality cult, especially in its painted manifestations. I posit a nexus between the organization of society around a central leader *(vozhd')*, Stalin, and the spatial organization of Stalin portraits in concentric circles. The emergence of this spatial paradigm was coeval with the installment of personalized, patrimonial authority, centered in a single leader, as the dominant principle of power in the late 1920s; its pictorial representation reinforced that very principle. That not only paintings of the "great leader and teacher" but also those of other heroic figures were arranged in concentric circles points to a diffusion of the personality cult throughout Soviet society, from Stalin outward to the "cults of small leaders" *(kul'ty malykh vozhdei)*.

Following Edward Shils and Clifford Geertz, I further postulate a connection between centrality and sacredness: no place is more sacrally charged than society's center.[4] The closer a person is to the center of society, the more sacredness is attributed to that person. The person placed closest to the center of society embodies the sacred most powerfully.[5]

It was during the Great Break, between 1929 and the early 1930s, that Stalin successfully completed a process of maneuvering himself into the center of Soviet society and firmly established a system of single, dictatorial rule that was to last until his death. This principle of power came to encompass all spheres of society; in the words of Katerina Clark, "the entire country in all its many aspects—political, social, symbolical, and cultural—became unambiguously centripetal and hierarchical in its organization."[6] On the level of symbolic representations, Stalin was moved into the center, too. His person was glorified through elaborate cultural products—posters, paintings, statues, films—and a veritable personality cult developed around him.[7] In these cultural products, Stalin began to occupy center stage, and other persons and objects began to be assembled around Stalin, the center, in circles.

Centralized, sacrally charged authority had a long and highly specific tradition in Russia. Since Christianization (988), the Russian sovereign was both head of the Russian Orthodox Church and head of the state.[8] After the fall of Constantinople, the spiritual and symbolic center of eastern Christianity moved to Moscow, the "Third Rome."[9] Until the very end of the ancien régime, Moscow retained this special symbolic status, and the Russian monarch, with some modifications, to be sure, remained head of the Russian Orthodox Church.

If throughout its history the Russian state was usually centered on a single person, this pattern extended to the micro level as well. The institution of the intelligentsia circle *(kruzhok)* is a case in point.[10] Most Bolsheviks had been in or had led Marxist study circles *(kruzhki)*, each grouped around a single leader. Thus most Bolsheviks were socialized in the *kruzhok* during their formative years. During the Stalinist 1930s, textual cultural representations of the Communist Party were unabashed in placing the circle in the beginning of the Party's genealogy. Organized Russian Marxism started as a *kruzhok* and ended up as the Party, according to the *Short Course:* "The VKP(b) formed on the basis of the workers' movement in prerevolutionary Russia out of Marxist circles *[kruzhkov]* and groups, which connected with the workers' movement and brought Socialist consciousness to it."[11] Lenin himself had begun as the leader of a circle: "Lenin entered a Marxist circle, organized by Fedoseev, in Kazan'. After Lenin's move to Samara, the first circle of Samara Marxists soon formed around him."[12] Later, in St. Petersburg, Lenin reshaped many smaller circles into one larger circle, an embryonic party: "In 1895 Lenin united all Marxist worker circles (already about twenty) in Petersburg into one 'Union of the Struggle for the Liberation of the Working Class.' Hereby he prepared the foundation of a revolutionary Marxist workers' party."[13] But the reconfiguration of circles turned out to be more difficult than expected and demanded superhuman efforts from the shapers, Lenin and Stalin: "The rise of the workers' movement and the manifest closeness of revolution demanded the foundation of a single, centralized party of the working class, capable of guiding the revolutionary movement. But the state of the local party organs, the local committees, groups, and circles was so poor, and their organizational disunion and ideological differences so great, that the creation of such a party posed incredible difficulties."[14]

Let us move from Bolshevik textual self-presentation, as in the *Short Course,* to more general representations. In searching for a starting point in visual genealogy for the sacralizing of the circle, Christian symbolism would probably be a good choice. Later, throughout Europe, the quintessential court portrait *(paradnyi portret)* was centered on the courtly person or sovereign. Anton von Werner's painting of the proclamation of the German Empire on January 21, 1871, in the Hall of Mirrors in Versailles (fig. 2.1) is an interesting exception: it famously placed Bismarck, in his white uniform, in the center of the picture, despite the presence in the painting of King Wilhelm I and other members of the Prussian royal family. The artist, according to the common interpretation, centered the picture on Bismarck in order to suggest that the statesman, rather than the monarch, deserved credit for founding a German empire.

These principles of spatial arrangement applied to cities as well. Moscow can be seen as always having been concerned with circular spatial order rather than with axial or linear order, because it was organized in ring roads around the Kremlin. This was only reinforced in the "general plan" for the reconstruction of Moscow in 1935. St. Petersburg–Petrograd–Leningrad, by contrast, was organized around the axis of Nevsky Prospekt, pointing toward the Neva, which, as the "window

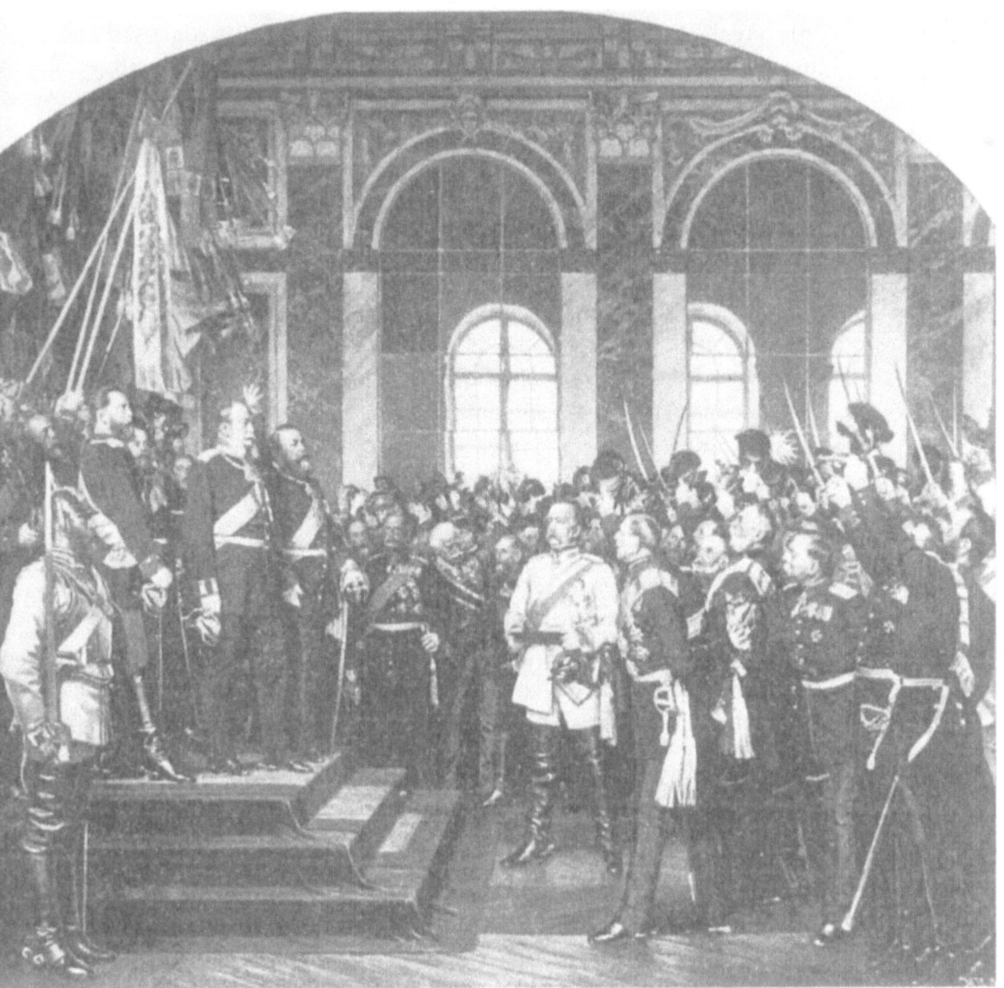

Fig. 2.1. Anton von Werner, *The Proclamation of the German Empire* (1877).

of Europe," leads out into the Neva delta and to the Baltic Sea and the world. The revolution itself was always represented as linear, forward movement.

Thus the centered pictorial representations of Stalin were but a late point in a long visual genealogy. Just as the Russian state had always been centered on a single leader, images of the Russian state, its rulers, and its religion had usually been organized in concentric circles. The revolutionary era and the period of New Economic Policy (NEP, 1921

28) were the exception rather than the rule. This is not to suggest that linear movement was banished altogether from the Stalin portrait. Stalin quite simply monopolized linear movement: his gaze came to figure as the only axis pointing outside the circular pictorial patterns.

Stalin and His Metaphors in Folklore and the Rhetoric of Art

The late 1920s saw the eclipse of the Russian avant-garde and the rise of realist art. In cultural politics this shift was signaled in 1928 by the empowerment of the organization of realist artists, AKhR, and the dethronement of the various avant-garde artist organizations.[15] As in other sectors of the arts, the organizational structure was tightened with the unification of artist organizations into monolithic unions in 1934. By that time, abstractionist painting had been all but silenced in the Soviet Union, and realism reigned triumphant.

Within realism, however, changes took place as well. One of them consisted in a reordering of the hierarchy of artistic genres: the portrait was established as the primary genre, and all other genres (landscape, still life) were devalued.[16] Excepting the nascent Lenin iconography, throughout the 1920s realist artists had operated on the principle of depicting, via the portrait of a single person, an entire social class.[17] Movie directors such as Dziga Vertov and Sergei Eisenstein, in their rejection of star actors, had adhered to the same principle of "typicality." In the 1930s the meaning of the portrait was reinterpreted. Now portraits were to depict with realist means the characteristic psychological traits of an outstanding Soviet person. The enthronement and redefinition of the portrait genre was the precondition for the surge of leader portrait painting. All the while, discussions about the "portrait" or the "image of the leader" *(obraz vozhdia),* about how to represent Lenin and Stalin, took place at artist union meetings and occupied the pages of the print media, the theoretically minded thick journal *Iskusstvo,* and the more quotidian newspaper *Sovetskoe iskusstvo.*

Stalin began to occupy center stage in other fields of cultural production, too. He engendered uncountable metaphors and became a metaphor himself. Indeed, Stalin and the Soviet Union—its nature, its topography—were locked in a loop of mutual signification. If Stalin's physical body functioned as a signifier for nature (the gaze directed into no-time and no-place—utopia), then nature functioned as a signifier for Stalin. Stalin's coming to power ushered in a toponymical revolution. Villages and cities, channels and roads, mountains and islands began to bear his name. Movement through Soviet space without encountering Stalin coordinates became impossible.

At the same time, Stalin was consistently likened to nature in the texts of writers, poets, and artists. His biographer, Henri Barbusse, wrote: "Here he is, the greatest and most important of our contemporaries. . . . In his full size he towers over Europe and over Asia, over the past and over the present. He is the most famous and yet almost the least known man in the world."[18] In the aftermath of Stalin and Voroshilov's famous meeting with three artists, Isaak Brodsky, Aleksandr Gerasimov, and Evgeny Katsman, on July 6, 1933, at Stalin's dacha, Katsman wrote to Voroshilov:

> Stalin has enchanted us all. What a colossal man! To me he seems as huge and beautiful as nature. I was on the top of Mount Tupik *[(sic!) na verkhnem Tupike]* in Dagestan during sunset. The mountains radiated like bright gems, I couldn't take my eyes off this, and wanted to remember everything for the rest of my life. Stalin is just like that: I looked at him, wanted to look at him forever and couldn't. I wanted to remember Stalin and couldn't. He very much resembles nature—the oceans, the mountains, the forests, the clouds. You wonder and are amazed and fascinated, but you know that this is nature. But Stalin is the peak of nature—Stalin is the oceans, mountains, forests, clouds, coupled with a powerful mind for the leadership of humanity.[19]

Pravda ran a photograph of Mount Kazbek's snow-covered peak in the Caucasus. "On the hillside of Kazbek's peak," elaborated the caption, "fifty-one combine operators and tractor drivers from the Azov–Black Sea Territory" had just "built, through the formation of their rows, the name Stalin" (fig. 2.2).[20] Characteristically, such glorifications liken Stalin to central points of elevation.

Another typical nature trope was that of Stalin as light or the sun. If the earth revolves around the sun, then the Soviet Union revolved around Stalin. Looking at Stalin therefore required a celestial, upward gaze. The quintessentially centralistic trope of Stalin as light or sun was especially prominent in Soviet folklore.[21] According to a quantitative textological analysis, an Armenian collection for Stalin's sixtieth birthday, *Stalin in the Works of the Armenian People,* contains 151 appellations of "great," 119 of "father," and 116 of "sun."[22] The Kazakh folklore performer Dzhambul Dzhabaev sang:

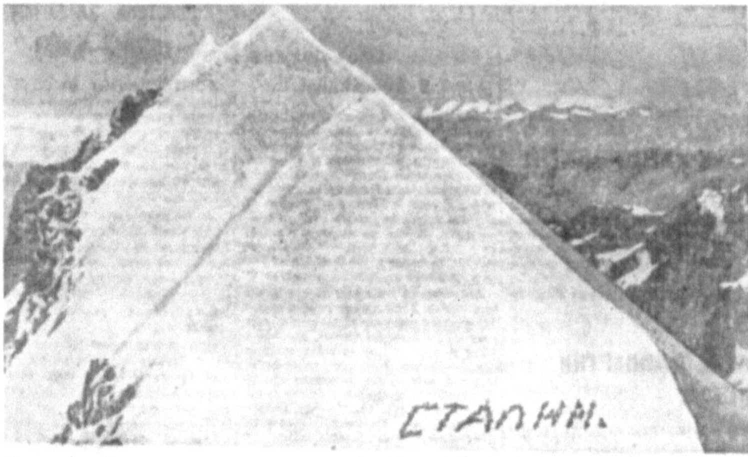

Fig. 2.2. *On the Hillside of Kazbek's Peak*, photograph published in *Pravda* (1935).

Stalin, my sun, in Moscow I realized
That the heart of wise Lenin beats in you:
On a day that shone like turquoise,
I was in the Kremlin among a circle of friends.
My eyes saw
The greatest of men.
You, whose name has reached the stars,
With the glory of the first wise man,
Were attentive, affectionate, simple,
And dearer to me than my own father.
For the joyous, fatherly reception in the Kremlin
Stalin, my sun, I thank you.[23]

Or, "Stalin, our sun, and with him, we are winning and will win."[24] Yiddish folklore also eulogized Stalin: "He has raised the big shining sun / over the earth, / has turned our land / into a blossoming garden."[25] And for the "small peoples" of the north, Stalin-sun not only brought the light of education "but also melted the fetters of ice and brought a cozy glow into the native tents."[26]

Artists echoed the image of Stalin as light or sun. In Katsman's words after the 1933 meeting of artists with Stalin: "It was as if the life of every one of us was illuminated with a particularly invigorating light *[kak by osvetilos' osobo zhivitel'nym svetom]."*[27] Light here might have had Christian connotations, but there is also the modern transmutation (of the old Christian luminary motif) of the role of light in enlightened modernity.[28] Finally, a Yiddish ditty *[chastushka]* posed the question of referentiality itself: "Stalin, what can we compare you with? You cannot be compared with anything." The conclusion of Stalin's incomparability is reached, of course, only after attempting to liken him to each of the elements of nature—sun, clouds, winds, ocean, fire, and water, in that order.[29]

Stalin at the Center

As banal as it may sound, Stalin was not born into the Kremlin or destined by right of birth to inhabit the center of the Soviet Union's cultural representations. He had to be placed there. In the case of pictorial representations, this involved concrete visual strategies directed at distinguishing Stalin from other Party leaders. Through a perusal of *Pravda* during the years of Stalin's consolidation of single power, between 1929 and 1934, some of these strategies become apparent. Stalin was distinguished from others in black-and-white photographs and reproductions of pictures by his place in the picture, his size, and the color of his clothing. His distinction was further marked by his portrayal as motionless, whereas the bodies of others were shown in a state of movement.[30] Motionlessness in general became one of the key tropes in representations of Stalin, and the words "calm" *(spokoinyi)* and "confident" *(uverennyi)* proliferated in reference to him. Objects of everyday life in Stalin's immediate proximity—the pipe in his hand, a map, a newspaper or book—also set him apart from others. His closeness in the picture to the figure of Lenin or an image of Lenin—a poster or painting on a wall—was another distinguishing marker.

The sense of Stalin's uniqueness was enhanced by setting him off against others to whom the negative side of culturally latent binary pairs was ascribed. For example, the male-female "gender code," to paraphrase Joan Scott, evoked a series of other binaries, such as strong-weak, mind-body, and reason-emotion.[31] This principle of binary definition was later extrapolated outside of the Soviet context. The cigarette or pipe stuffed with tobacco (Gertsegovina Flor was allegedly his favorite brand) came to signify proletarian class background, whereas the cigar acquired the status of the pipe's bourgeois other. Stalin's male-coded composure was juxtaposed against Hitler's female-coded hysterical fits.

Artists spoke openly about placing Stalin in the center of their paintings. Aleksandr Gerasimov stressed, on one hand, the historical accuracy of his *Teheran Conference,* painted on the premises of the 1943 meeting of the Allied powers, but on the other hand told his audience unabashedly that "it was important that the necessary person be the center of attention. In my case Stalin."[32] And about his monumental 1942 *Hymn to October*—406 by 710 centimeters in size—Gerasimov told his listeners: "This is a huge picture. Yet I must say with confidence here that, regardless of its size, regardless of the fact that the chandeliers and golden loges shine there,—the attention still falls on comrade Stalin."[33] Gerasimov achieved this effect by pointing a spotlight at the comparatively small figure of Stalin, who stands behind a rostrum at the Bolshoi off to the left of center stage, and by pointing the heads of the entire audience in Stalin's direction. Moreover, a silhouette of Stalin towers on the Bolshoi's curtain above a large Lenin sculpture. The silhouette is topped only by the Roman numerals XXV, which signify the twenty-fifth anniversary of the October Revolution.

After Stalin had been firmly established in the center of visual culture, by about 1935, pictures in mass media such as *Pravda* changed their strategies. Stalin was shown not in groups but by himself more frequently after 1936, and often he was merely invoked through a Stalin image or sculpture in the background.[34] In both the press and in easel painting, concentric circles became the dominating pattern of spatial organization.[35]

Perhaps no other painting illustrates this pattern better than Aleksandr Gerasimov's *Stalin and Voroshilov in the Kremlin* (1938; fig. 2.3), and perhaps no other painting in the Soviet Union ever attained more fame.[36] Stalin and Voroshilov are shown walking along the sidewalk of the inner Kremlin with the Vodovozny Tower in the immediate background. The Moscow River and the city of Moscow lie in the more distant background. The spatial arrangement of this painting is predicated on concentric circles grouped around Stalin, the center. Even though, technically speaking, Voroshilov's folded hands (or more precisely, his army overcoat's cuffs) occupy the picture's geometric center, Stalin takes center stage in every other respect. In perspective, he is closer to the viewer and therefore painted as the taller figure.

Closest to Stalin (in the first concentric zone) is Voroshilov—a member, incidentally, of the coterie around Stalin also known as his "inner circle" *(blizhnii krug).* The next concentric zones are occupied

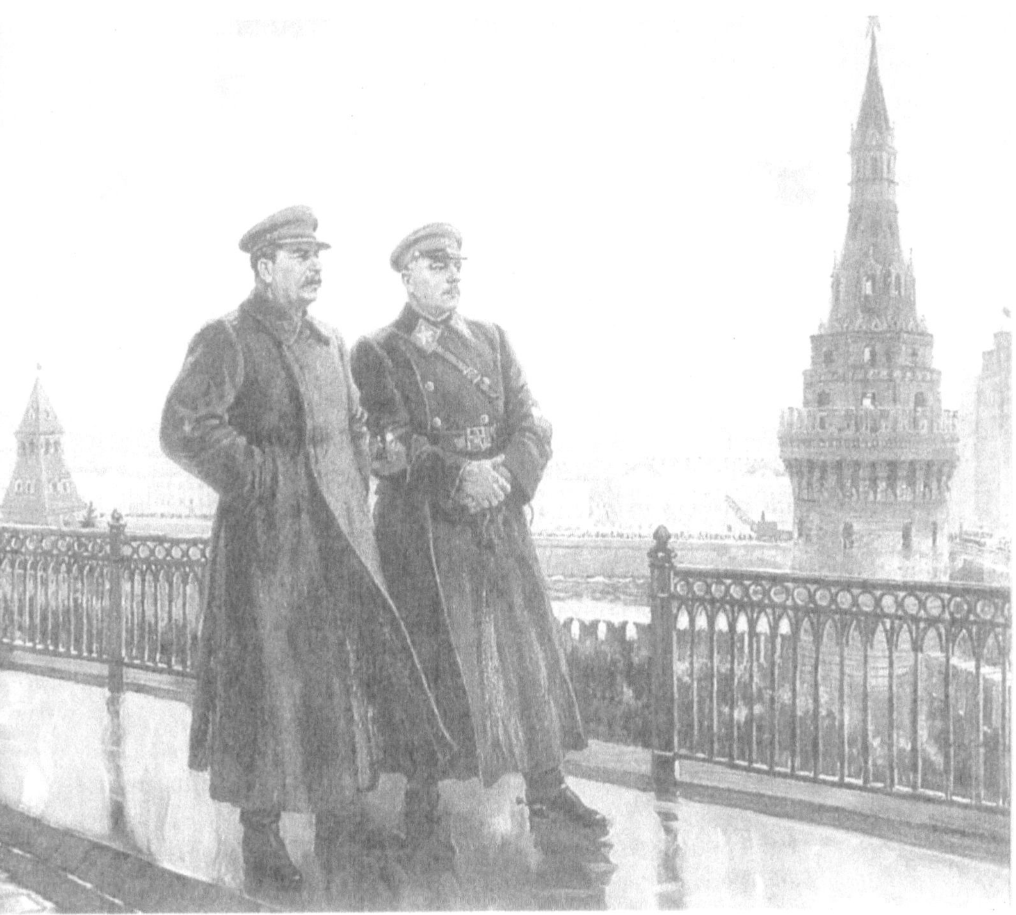

Fig. 2.3. Aleksandr Gerasimov, *Stalin and Voroshilov in the Kremlin* (1938).

by the Kremlin tower, then the Kremlin wall, followed by the Moscow River and the masses crowding along the embankment street right behind it. Finally we see the city sprawl of Moscow. The new Moscow, reconstructed according to Stalin's general plan, is signified by the "House of the Government" *(Dom pravitel'stva),* the newly built Big Stone Bridge *(Bol'shoi kamennyi most)* across the Moscow River to the far right, and the smokestacks beyond. The old Moscow, symbolized by the three cupolas of a Russian Orthodox Church, has moved to the background. The Old Russia, as it were, had been overcome. The House of the Government was specifically moved into the picture, as Gerasimov admitted, perhaps to imply the closeness to Stalin of the Party and intelligentsia elites who resided there.[37]

The circle was, I believe, the seminal Stalinist shape used to structure space. In the case of Gerasimov's picture, Stalin is the sacred center of the Soviet cosmos. Following an observation from Walter Benjamin's *Moscow Diary*, Mikhail Yampolsky noted the absence of an anthropomorphic monument inside the walls of the Kremlin.[38] Thus the sacred center of the Kremlin was uniquely freed for Stalin.[39] Stalin (and Gerasimov) did not have to fear sacral doubling by the proximity of a monument, nor was the monument threatened with sacral overcharge from Stalin's proximity. Stalin's sacredness is underlined by his size, by the immobility of his body—a center, by definition, does not move—and by his lack of ornamentation. Whereas Voroshilov bears the full insignia of a high representative of the Soviet army (the star-shaped medals, etc.), Stalin does not need these, because he is already firmly established in the collective imagination as the country's sacred center.[40] Stalin is dressed in nothing but his simple gray overcoat, his hat, and a pair of army boots. Immediately next to him is his closest guard, Voroshilov, in the closest circle. This closest circle remains open toward the viewer, who is drawn into the picture and merges with the leader.

If Stalin embodies the Soviet body politic, then Voroshilov embodies the Red Army. Thus the Soviet people, incarnated in Stalin, are protected by their army, incarnated in Voroshilov. The fence is a further symbol of defense. It is broken, jarringly and incongruously, at only one place, right behind Voroshilov, in order to show the Moscow River in more detail and, more importantly, the masses on the embankment street. The broken fence permits the creation of a visual axis between Voroshilov and the people on the Moscow River embankment. The motif of the connection between the leader, Voroshilov, and the masses is thus unmistakably present in the painting.[41] But the main theme is one of defense against outside aggression, against Fascist encirclement, a theme that also finds symbolic expression in the smokestacks that represent the preparation of Soviet industry against outside attack.

Gerasimov spoke about his picture in public on at least three occasions: in November 1938, in 1947, and in December 1949. Each time the occasion was an evening at Moscow's Central House of Art Workers, a clublike establishment where members of the artistic intelligentsia, especially actors and artists, gathered to watch plays, listen to lectures, and socialize. At the first meeting Gerasimov began by pointing out that *Stalin and Voroshilov in the Kremlin* was originally his entry in a 1937 Stalin portrait competition:

> I painted this picture for the IZOGIZ competition "Portraits of our Leaders." I could have painted Stalin . . . and other leaders with comrade Stalin, but I chose Stalin and Voroshilov because it is impossible to paint portraits from photographs, without seeing the people; it is impossible, the photograph does not render the face exactly. You have to know a person well so that he is in your visual memory as though alive. Then the photograph will help you preserve the proportion, form, and everything else you must give from yourself. I had the high honor of being at Comrade Stalin's several times. I was at Comrade Voroshilov's many times. He posed for me.[42]

From a letter to another painter, Isaak Brodsky, inviting him to participate in the competition, we can place Gerasimov's description in context and trace the conditions of the contest—and ultimately the construction and constructedness of the picture—more fully. The competition was actually called the "IZOGIZ Competition for the Best Portrait of Comrade Stalin and His Closest Comrades-in-Arms."[43] Although some portrait competitions were public and open to all, in this one only fifty select artists were invited to participate. Portraits were acceptable "in any technique—oil, watercolor, gouache, drawing, lithography, linoleum cut, etching." The painting was supposed to have a size of 50 by 60 centimeters and had to "satisfy the demands of reproduction for mass printing."[44] Upon signing the contract, the artists each received 1,500 rubles for their expenses and were allotted about half a year to finish their entries, so that the winners could be presented at an exhibit during the celebrations of the October Revolution. The jury included members of the Party elite and of the artistic and literary intelligentsia, among them Aleksey Stetsky, Platon Kerzhentsev, Dmitry Moor, and Aleksey Tolstoi. Stalin's own influence was guaranteed through the presence of a member of his personal Central Committee secretariat, Lev Mekhlis. The themes for the paintings were in fact more scripted than Gerasimov would have us believe. They included the "portrait/bust" of Stalin and images of Stalin "on the tribune of the Extraordinary Congress of Soviets," "on the tribune of the mausoleum," "with a raised arm/at the evening of the opening of the metro or at the Congress of Soviets 'Forward to new victories,'" "on the Moscow-Volga Channel," "among children, aviators, heroes of the Soviet Union," and "in the Gorky Park of Culture and Relaxation." The organizers further suggested a number of high party figures with whom Stalin might be portrayed: Molotov, Kaganovich, Voroshilov, Kalinin, Mikoian, and Ezhov.[45]

Gerasimov's statement about the deficiency of painting from photographic examples and the importance of live posing was a coded hint at the distribution of photographic and cinematic templates among the artists—an issue that was usually taboo in public discourse about art. "The publishing house is providing each participant of the competition with all the photographic records on the designated themes from its archive and is organizing the screening of the necessary films," in the words of the invitation letter for the competition.[46] Stalin, during the 1930s, never posed for Soviet artists, and the sources for their portraits of him were photographs, movies, the existing Stalin iconography, and, in the case of a privileged few, sketches drawn on occasions when Stalin spoke publicly and the artists' presence was permitted.[47]

Nonetheless, Gerasimov would have us believe that the subject of his painting was the product of his artistic inspiration alone: "I began to think about this theme [Stalin and Voroshilov] and decided that they must be painted as incarnations of the Red Army and of all peoples. And yet [they must be portrayed] in poses that convey firmness *[nepokolebimost']* and confidence *[uverennost']*. These poses are supposed to express that the peoples and the Red Army are the same, are one monolith." Here, Gerasimov perpetuated the romantic myth of artistic autonomous inspiration. He also unwittingly perpetuated the tensions that typically accompanied the continuity of this myth in Soviet Russia, where art was created according to plan, copied, and mass produced.

Gerasimov said further about his painting: "I liked the silvery gamut [of colors]. And suddenly I thought: what could be easier than to paint them in front of the Kremlin Palace, in which government meetings take place. I remember this sidewalk well. They might have come out, stood there, waited for a car or looked at Moscow. As far as the idea was concerned, it was decided. I had to do a whole number of sketches because the silvery gamut was hard for me—I am used to cheerful colors, and the gray tone is awfully difficult. There are such a great number of nuances in it that I struggled with this painting for a long time."[48]

After the war, Gerasimov gave a different gloss on his painting and claimed that he had sensed, in 1937, that the war was approaching. In his own words at a 1947 meeting at the Central House of Culture

Workers: "I painted Stalin several times, and I began the last portrait when war was already threatening on the horizon. . . . Earlier I called this painting *Guarding Peace* [Na strazhe mira]. . . . The clouds appear to sense what is about to happen. It is clear that there will be a spring thunderstorm, but the clouds will pass, it is not going to be terrible and the clear day will return. The premonition was supposed to come to a good end." He continued, "And so I ended up at the Kremlin and saw a standing person at the fence and understood at that point that this was what I was looking for. The painting went fast. The next day I had completed a sketch of the Kremlin. The Kremlin is not only the heart of Moscow but the hope of all of humanity."[49]

In 1949, Gerasimov added an interesting new detail. He asserted that Viktor Vasnetsov's *Three Warriors* (Tri bogatyria, 1898) had been his inspiration for the painting. After applauding the anti-impressionism of Vasnetsov, Gerasimov said: "I admit that this picture *[Three Warriors]* was constantly before my eyes; there are three warriors there, and here stand two warriors—our Soviet ones."[50] Vasnetsov (1848–1916), a preeminent Wanderer (Peredvizhnik), placed this picture in a cycle of illustrations of ancient Russian oral epic poems *(bylini)* about heroic Russian warriors.[51] It shows three mythical medieval Russian knights—Dobrynia, Il'ia Moromets, and Alesha Popovich—in full armor on horses in the mountainous countryside. The two to the left are looking into the distance, as if to spot the enemy. The third knight is set back somewhat and gazes in a different direction. Unlike in Gerasimov's painting, all three figures are portrayed flatly rather than in three-quarter perspective, and the two main knights look toward the viewer's left, whereas Gerasimov's Stalin and Voroshilov look to the right. Thus the gaze of the three *bylina* heroes is meant to depict the defense of the Russian land, whereas the gaze of Stalin and Voroshilov holds the dual connotation of vigilance against exterior enemies and the embodiment of history—the gaze into the socialist future.[52]

Let us now return to the circle, which serves as an organizing theme in many other paintings. One example is Vasily Efanov's *An Unforgettable Meeting* (fig. 2.4), which foregrounds a triangle of three figures arranged in circular movement: Stalin, a woman, and Molotov. The three heads indeed create the immediate visual impression of a triangle, but there are in fact more points: the three heads, the arms of Stalin and the woman, enjoined in a warm handshake (Stalin envelops the woman's hands). Together these points create a circle in the center of the picture. The remaining party luminaries, with flowers and micro-

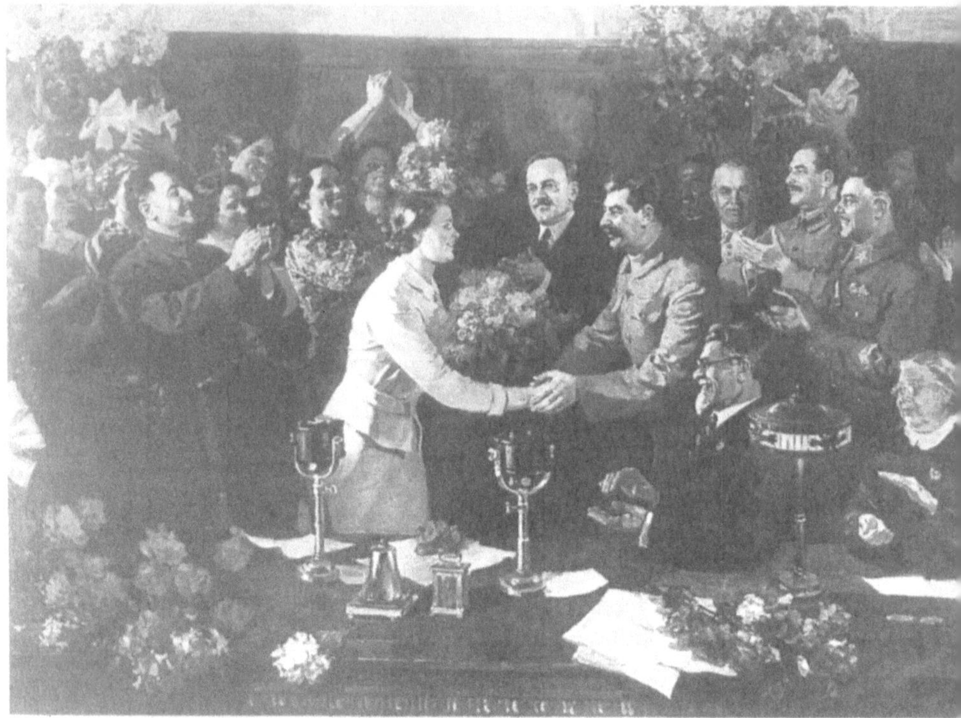

Fig. 2.4. Vasilii Efanov, *An Unforgettable Meeting* (1936–37).

phones, create a second circle around the central one. Other paintings that are quite simply arranged in circles around Stalin include Boris Ioganson's *Our Wise Leader, Dear Teacher (I. V. Stalin among the People in the Kremlin)* (Nash mudryi vozhd', uchitel' dorogoi [I. V. Stalin sredi naroda v Kremle]),[53] Iu. P. Kugach et al.'s *Glory to the Great Stalin* (Velikomu Stalinu slava),[54] Grigory Shegal's *Leader, Teacher, and Friend* (Vozhd' uchitel' i drug),[55] and David Gabitshavili et al.'s *Youth of the World—for Peace* (Molodezh' mira—za mir), in which Stalin is shown on a poster and being carried in the center of a crowd of people at a procession.[56]

The circular arrangement held wherever Stalin was, even if the painting concerned a scene from the distant past. For example, Iosif Serebriany's *At the Fifth London Congress* (Na V Londonskom s"ezde), which shows the young Stalin and the already older, bald Lenin at a London dining hall, is arranged circularly entirely around the young Stalin (fig. 2.5). Sometimes the circular arrangement was projected back

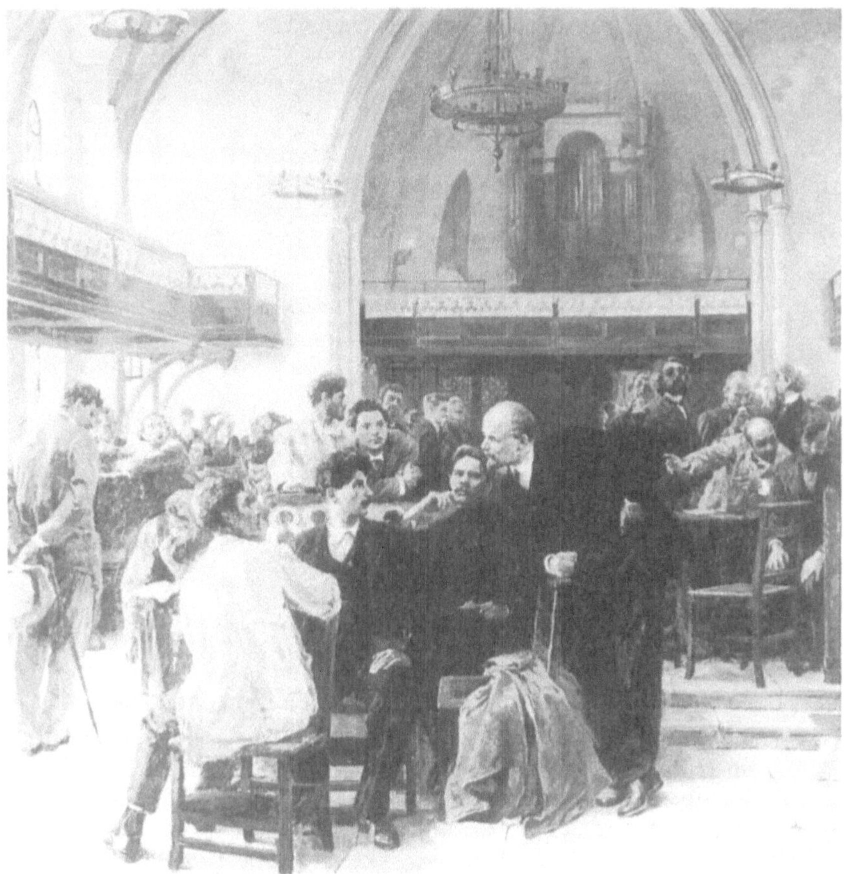

Fig. 2.5. Iosif Serebriany, *At the Fifth London Congress* (1947).

onto other spheres of society, without Stalin's being present. This practice was particularly true of the artistic intelligentsia. For example, Vasilii Efanov's picture of the theater director Konstantin Stanislavskii shows Stanislavskii in the center of a circle of people.[57]

Fedor Shurpin's 1949 *Morning of Our Motherland* (Utro nashei rodiny; fig. 2.6) shows Stalin standing in the Soviet countryside in his white postwar generalissimus uniform, carrying his overcoat. His hands are folded, his hair is grayed, the wrinkle on his forehead has become deep—this is the canonical postwar Stalin, seasoned by a world war and the loss of millions of people. The exact geometric center is the place where Stalin's heart would be beneath his uniform; this is also

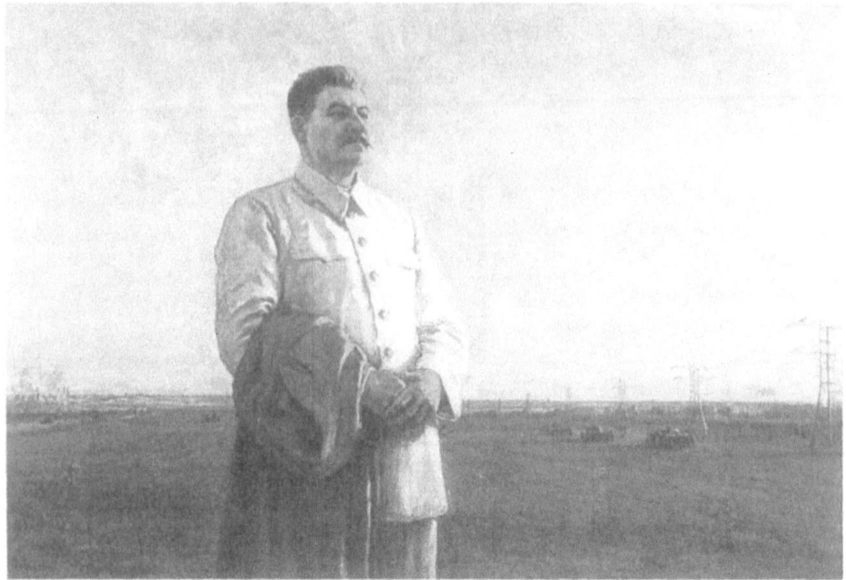

Fig. 2.6. Fedor Shurpin, *Morning of Our Motherland* (1949).

the lightest spot in the picture. Here Stalin is the immobile center of the picture. The land is already transformed and moving in no larger, metaphysical direction, only in its self-referential circles (consider the smoke of the smokestacks in the very back, the tractors, the little trees planted symmetrically behind Stalin and expected to grow to a certain height but no higher).[58] The land has been transformed through collectivization and industrialization, as is visible from the tractors and the smokestacks of the factories. There are overtones of Christian transcendence: the green behind Stalin symbolizes fertility; the white of his coat, godlike creation. The only linear movement—Stalin's gaze—is directed outward, with a vanishing point outside the picture. While the land is "utopia become real," Stalin's gaze is directed into an even brighter future.[59]

Comparing Gazes, Comparing Bodies

For heuristic purposes, it is worth contrasting Shurpin's painting of Stalin with paintings reflecting the Lenin iconography and, more jarringly and productively, with nineteenth-century American landscape painting. I begin with the second comparison and return to the first.

Albert Boime has identified "the magisterial gaze" in American landscape painting during the period of Manifest Destiny, circa 1830–65, as an "elevated viewpoint of the onlooker" that "traced a visual trajectory from the uplands to a scenic panorama below."[60] The assumption of this viewpoint, the "Olympian bearing," is deeply ideological and constitutes the discursive expression of an underlying structural disposition for key tenets of the American pioneer spirit: the subjugation of the wilderness and the concomitant destruction of the Native Americans who inhabited it, as well as the expectation of continued westward movement into a utopian paradise on earth. Boime convincingly juxtaposes the peculiarly American "magisterial gaze" with the nearly contemporaneous romantic German "reverential gaze" of a Caspar David Friedrich. In Friedrich's paintings, "his point of view moves upward from the lower picture plane and culminates on or near a distant mountain peak." According to Boime, "the reverential gaze signified the striving of vision toward a celestial goal in the heavens, starting from a wide, panoramic base."[61] It is perhaps best to further illustrate the American pioneer stance with one of Boime's readings of a specific picture. About Thomas Cole's *River in the Catskills* (1843; fig. 2.7) he writes:

> [A] young farmer standing in for the spectator leans on his axe and gazes from a hilltop foreground across the wide vista below. The foreground is strewn with thickets and storm-blasted trees symbolizing the undomesticated landscape that the farmer prepares to clear. We follow his gaze from the boundary of the wilderness across the river to the cultivated middle-ground zone and the farm dwellings. Moving perpendicularly to the youth's line of vision is a train in the middle distance crossing a bridge. The line of vision extends into the remotest distance, where smoke arises from scarcely seen manufactories on the horizon. Cole's picture tells us that the future lies over the horizon, with time here given a spatial location. . . . Of course, in actuality, the farmer would be facing in the opposite direction, away from the boundary of civilization toward the forest wilderness to be cleared. I see this reversal, however, as a metaphorical mirror of the pioneer's vision of the future prospects awaiting him. In looking backward, the farmer declares from the edge between wilderness and savagery on the one hand, civilization and order on the other, that progress moves along a timeline of the landscape.[62]

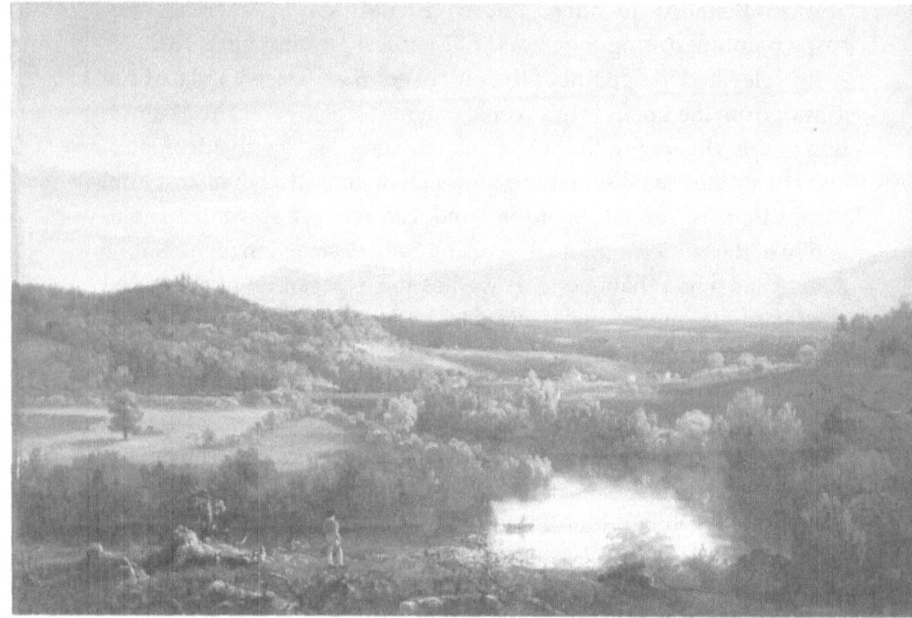

Fig. 2.7. Thomas Cole, *River in the Catskills* (1843).

Shurpin's *Morning of Our Motherland,* by contrast, features a fundamentally different perspectival arrangement. The onlooker does not assume the place of Stalin and follow his gaze but rather looks at Stalin frontally. Whereas the viewer of Cole's *River in the Catskills* is proffered, by following the gaze of the young farmer—whose face remains invisible—a pictorialized idea of the utopian future lying ahead, our only hint at the Soviet future is Stalin himself and his gaze. In the American case, landscape itself embodies utopia. In the Soviet case, Stalin embodies the bright future.

Moreover, Boime wrote about Asher Durand's *Progress* (1853; fig. 2.8) that "the diagonal line of sight is synonymous with the magisterial gaze, taking us rapidly from an elevated geographical zone to another below and from one temporal zone to another, locating progress synchronically in time and space. Within this fantasy of domain and empire gained from looking out and down over broad expanses is the subtext of metaphorical forecast of the future. The future is given a spatial location in which vast territories are brought under visual and symbolic control."[63] One reading of *Morning of Our Motherland* might likewise posit an encoding of the temporal line—progress—

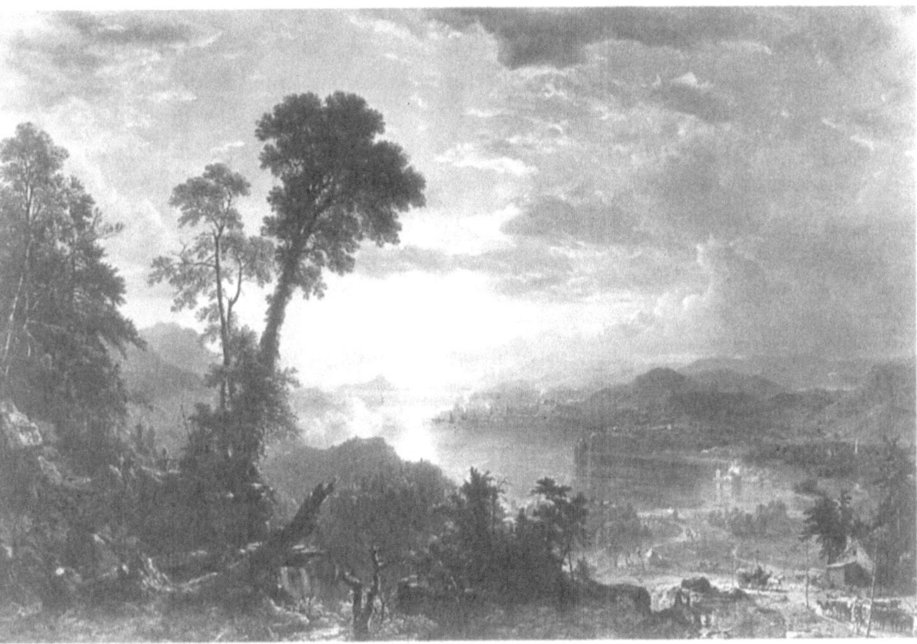

Fig. 2.8. Asher Durand, *Progress* (1853).

in the painting via the tractors moving in the background, the trees growing, and the rising smoke of the factories. But another reading is possible: the dominant encoding of progress in this painting is via Stalin's gaze, which is foregrounded; the tractors, trees, and smoke-stacks are marked by cyclical movement in self-referential circles. They are but the backgrounded achievements of the foregrounded Stalin, who can claim these as his very own achievements, as lying "behind" himself. If, in the iconography of industrial construction during the first Five-Year Plan, progress was inscribed in the portrayal of construction itself, then during the postwar era Stalin has consummated a monopolization of progress.

One could claim that *Morning of Our Motherland* cannot be compared with the American cases because Cole, for example, belongs to the genre of landscape painting, and Shurpin to portraiture. Yet the dividing line between these genres is in fact quite blurred, and both paintings feature a mixture of portrait and landscape components. More importantly, Stalinist landscape painting from the 1930s onward, as Mark Bassin has recently observed, differed from American landscape painting in its attempted reconciliation of the innate elementalism *(stikhiinost')* of nature and the Soviet people's mastery over precisely this elementalism—witness the hydroelectric plants and the industrial construction sites. "The result," writes Bassin, "was an entire category of artistic production, the individual examples of which were all united by the deliberate effort to demonstrate how Soviet reality was actually achieving the utopian goal of preserving the unique elemental splendour of the natural world at the very time that it was transforming this same world into something completely different and incalculably superior."[64]

Turning to a comparison of Shurpin's image of Stalin with the Lenin iconography, it is noticeable that the latter features a Lenin who is entirely in motion. In Viktor Tsyplakov's 1947 *V. I. Lenin (Lenin in Smolny)* (fig. 2.9), for example, Lenin's gaze into the future is echoed not only by his body, which is in dynamic motion, but also by the bayonets of the soldiers around him and by the bodies of the soldiers as well. Gerasimov, a painter who created pictorial representations both of Lenin and Stalin, spoke of his differential approach to movement and immobility with regard to the two leaders: "The Gorky Museum commissioned a large watercolor portrait [of Stalin] with a stretched-out arm," he recounted:

> I wanted to convey the loving face of Iosif Vissarionovich [Stalin], this gesture of reaching out to the audience. There is no audience in the picture, because I had been ordered to paint a portrait only. Here all my methods are opposed to the technique I used when I did a portrait of Comrade Lenin. There we have an impetuous pose, the expression of the face matches [the pose], there's the cry of the revolution, the cry for the revolution. Here in all my pictures the image of Iosif Vissarionovich is calm confidence *[spokoinaia uverennost']* in the position of the cause that he leads, complete trust in his powers *[polnaia uverennost' v svoi sily]*, nothing harsh, and calm, convincing speech *[nichego rezkogo, spokoinaia, ubeditel'naia rech']*.[65]

At another point Gerasimov asked rhetorically, "Why is V. I. [Lenin] shown talking in this portrait? Because," he answered, "this was the moment of the revolution." By contrast, in his portraits of Stalin he wanted to show "in his poses and gestures a different stage of the revolution. Then there was struggle, but here we have construction—not without struggle, to be sure, but nonetheless, this is not the kind of strug-

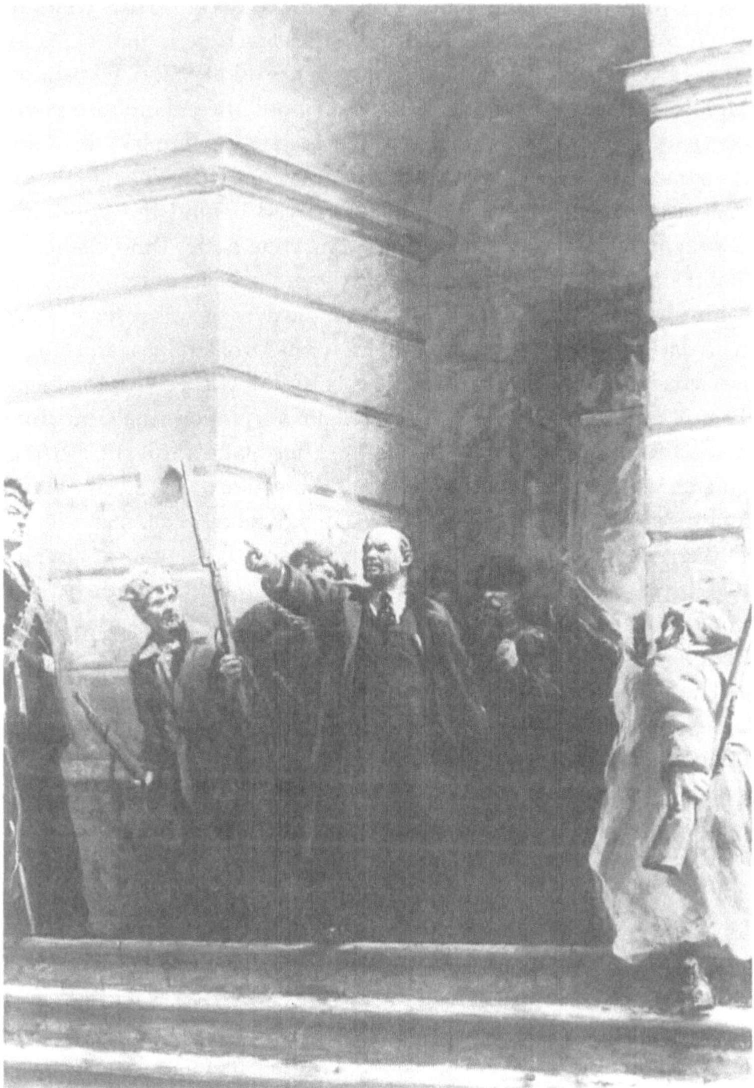

Fig. 2.9. Viktor Tsyplakov, *V. I. Lenin (Lenin in Smolny)* (1947).

gle when the fate of the revolution was still up in the air." Finally, for Gerasimov, Stalin "embodies calm, certain power," hence "the always calm gesture, the calm and utterly convincing manner of speaking."[66]

The topography of Stalin's face furthermore doubled the topography of the Soviet Union. The central site in Stalin's face is usually his eyes, which are also the point of origin for his gaze. Artists continually focused on the eyes in their discussions and descriptions of Stalin. At the 1933 "Fifteen Years of the Red Army" exhibit, Stalin, Voroshilov, Molotov, and Ordzhonikidze (all in all, about fifteen Politburo members and others) came to visit. A crowd of artists (Bogorodsky, Brodsky, A. Gerasimov, L'vov, Merkurov, Modorov, Perel'man, Shegal', the art historian Mashkovtsev, and others) moved behind the Politburo. "Everyone carefully studies Stalin. Everyone noticed the beauty of Stalin's face, the harmony of proportions, the beautiful posture, the calmness, the courage, the self-control, the eyes of amber *[piva]* color with dark outlines, around the eyes his wrinkles of kindness and laughter, which run downward from the eyes and upward on his forehead. That is a very characteristic trait of Stalin's. A rather small, medium nose, and pleasant, tanned hands."[67] After Stalin's July 1933 dacha meeting with Gerasimov, Brodsky, and Katsman, the last wrote about Stalin's eyes: "During lunch we came to talk about Lenin, and Stalin said with a warm and tender look on his face: 'He is unique, after all *[On ved' u nas edinstvennyi].*' In my mind I painted Comrade Stalin's portrait, admiring his eyes, in which his entire genius is expressed, and I felt his expressive and strong look on me."[68]

The eyes were also the point of origin for connecting axes between the leader and his people. The sculptor Nikolai Tomsky said of a meeting of Stakhanovites with Stalin that

> when one of Leningrad's best Stakhanovites spoke—a metalworker of the Kirov Factory—I had the fortune to watch Iosif Vissarionovich [Stalin] very closely, and as an artist I naturally tried to capture every gesture, every expression of his face. And when the metalworker, Kardashov, if I remember his name correctly, began to speak about the achievements of the factory, about the new people of the factory, the eyes of Iosif Vissarionivich began to shine with some inexpressible light[;] it seemed to me, thanks to the fact that his eyes are very close to one another—I am saying this as an artist—that a single radiant star shone through the entire room. At that point I understood what kind of living power, what continuous threads connect our worker, our man, with Comrade Stalin *[kakie nepreryvnye niti sviazi mezhdu rabochim, mezhdu nashim chelovekom i tovarishchem Stalinym].*[69]

In his sculpture *Stalin's Oath,* Tomsky "wanted to find in this oath the continuous bond of the Soviet people with its great leader." The gaze

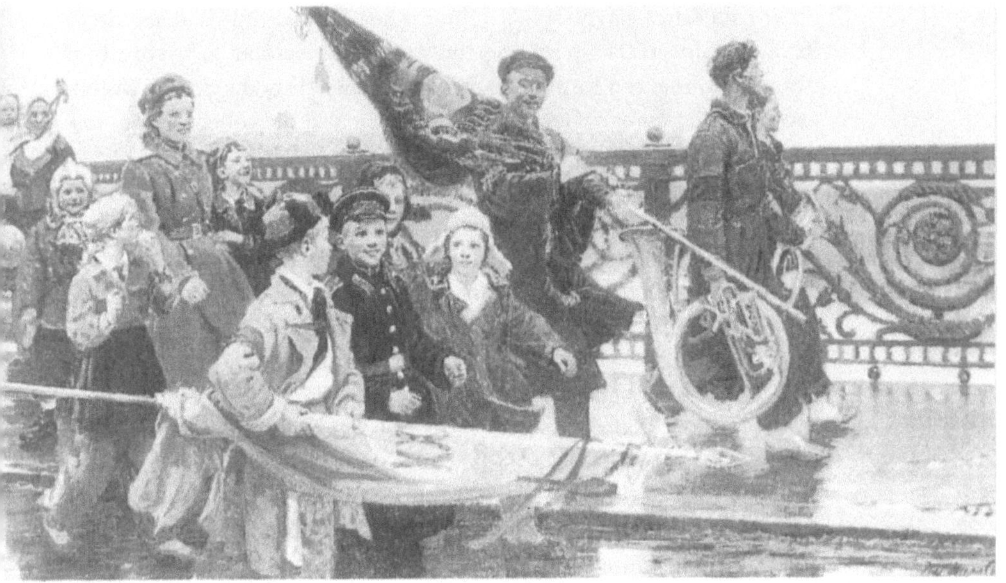

Fig. 2.10. Dmitri K. Mochalski, *After the Demonstration (They Saw Stalin)* (1949).

between Stalin and his people is mutual. Tomsky also professed to see his objective in "finding the closest bond of our people, the bond of the peoples, whose looks are fixed on comrade Stalin."[70]

Conclusion

If, in the early 1930s, visual culture was preoccupied with establishing Stalin as the center of representation, then by 1948 his apotheosis had reached such proportions that he was sometimes represented indirectly, without showing his physical appearance at all. A painting by Pavel Sokolov-Skalia, *The Voice of the Leader,* shows a group of soldiers and others gathered around a radio listening to a Stalin speech.[71] Here, Stalin is present only on the faces of his attentive listeners. In Dmitry K. Mochalsky's *After the Demonstration (They Saw Stalin)* (1949; fig. 2.10), a group of boys is returning from an event, probably a parade, where they have seen Stalin. Apart from the subtitle of the painting, Stalin is visible only on the boys' enlightened faces.

Stalin, the center, was now everywhere. When Stalin, in Mikhail Chiuareli's 1949 movie *The Fall of Berlin,* descended from his plane in the East German capital, it was as if he had never left Moscow. The jubilating crowds were interchangeable, and East Berlin, just like the other East European people's democracies, by that time had acquired its own Stalin cult, with Stalin poetry in the vernacular, to be sure, but ultimately oriented to the center in Moscow. Thus the Soviet Union exported its power system and necessarily also the concomitant paradigm of spatial organization.

When Stalin consolidated his dictatorial rule in the late 1920s, he set off a process for the reshaping of Soviet society in strictly centralized fashion. By reorganizing Soviet society centripetally, the socialist state unwittingly reconnected with a pattern of sacrally charged central authority that had prevailed before the revolution and that is, according to sociologists such as Edward Shils and anthropologists such as Clifford Geertz, nearly universal. The centripetal organization of society was at the same time reflected and bolstered by symbolic representations, namely, those of Stalin's personality cult, the beginning of which was marked by the celebrations of his fiftieth birthday in December 1929. Stalin portraiture is a prime example of a genre of cult products that exhibited the principle of circular, centered representation as depictions of other figures and landscapes began to be arranged in concentric circles around Stalin, the center. Stalin's gaze is also important in these paintings, for it is always directed at a vanishing point in the distance outside the painting. Stalin, as the sacrally charged embodiment of the Soviet state, looked into the future that this state would soon enter—the future of communism.

NOTES

I owe a great debt to Chad Bryant, Stephen Kotkin, Eric Naiman, Irina Paperno, Ingrid Schierle, and Yuri Slezkine for their thorough readings and incisive criticisms of this essay.

1. V. V. Sadoven', "Metodicheskaia razrabotka ekskursii po GTG na temu: 'Obrazy Lenina i Stalina v sovetskom izobrazitel'nom iskusstve'" (1947). See Otdel Rukopisei, Gosudarstvennaia Tret'iakovskaia Galereia (OR GTG), f. 8.III, d. 926, ll. 1–2.

2. Ibid., ll. 14, 16.

3. Ibid., ll. 16–17.

4. See Edward Shils, *Center and Periphery: Essays in Macrosociology* (Chicago: University of Chicago Press, 1975), 3, 5; Clifford Geertz, "Centers, Kings, and Charisma: Reflections on the Symbolics of Power," in *Local Knowledge* (New York: Basic Books, 1983), 146, 124.

5. On this see the widely influential formulation by Ernst Kantorowicz, *The King's Two Bodies: A Study in Medieval Political Theology* (Princeton: Princeton University Press, 1957), and the literature it engendered.

6. Katerina Clark, *Petersburg: Crucible of Cultural Revolution* (Cambridge, Mass.: Harvard University Press, 1995), 278.

7. "Personality cult" *(kul't lichnosti)* has had various meanings, occasionally overlapping, at different times. In Stalinist rhetoric it carried the negative meaning of single leadership and was juxtaposed with the ideal of collective leadership by the Party's Central Committee or Politburo. During Khrushchev's de-Stalinization it became a pejorative blanket term for authoritarian rule, the aberration from the good Leninist path, mass repression, and the glorification of Stalin through the "personality cult" proper. In the West this last meaning of the term has since been applied to all deifications of single leaders via modern mass media, including Mussolini, Hitler, Mao, Kim Il Sung, and Saddam Hussein. I use "personality cult" to connote the organization of society around a single person and the symbolic expression of this organization through cult products in multiple modern media.

8. See Michael Cherniavsky, *Tsar and People: Studies in Russian Myths* (New Haven, Conn.: Yale University Press, 1961); Frank Kämpfer, *Das russische Herrscherbild von den Anfängen bis zu Peter dem Großen: Studien zur Entwicklung politischer Ikonographie im byzantinischen Kulturkreis* (Recklingshausen: Bongers, 1978); Nicholas Riasanovsky, *The Image of Peter the Great in Russian History and Thought* (New York: Oxford University Press, 1985); Richard Wortman, *Scenarios of Power: Myth and Ceremony in Russian Monarchy*, 2 vols. (Princeton, N.J.: Princeton University Press, 1995–2000).

9. On Moscow as Third Rome, see, for example, Wilhelm Lettenbauer, *Moskau, das dritte Rom: Zur Geschichte einer politischen Theorie* (Munich: A. Pustet, 1961); Nina Sinitsyna, *Tretii Rim: Istoki i evoliutsiia russkoi samoderzhavnoi kontseptsii* (Moscow: Indrik, 1998); Ruslan Skrynnikov, *Tretii Rim* (St. Petersburg: Dmitrii Bulanin, 1994); Boris Uspenskii, "La perception de l'histoire et la doctrine 'Moscou-troisième Rome,'" in *La royauté sacrée dans le monde chrétien*, eds. Alain Boureau and Claudio-Sergio Ingerflom (Paris: Edition de l'Ecole des Hautes Etudes en Sciences Sociales, 1992); Marshall Poe, "Moscow, the Third Rome: The Origins and Transformations of a 'Pivotal Moment,'" *Jahrbücher für Geschichte Osteuropas* 49, no. 3 (2001): 412–29.

10. On the wider phenomenon of the *kruzhok* see, among other sources, the ground-breaking work of Barbara Walker, "On Reading Soviet Memoirs: A History of the 'Contemporaries' Genre as an Institution of Russian Intelligentsia Culture from the 1790s to the 1970s," *Russian Review* 59, no. 3 (July 2000): 327–52.

11. *Istoriia vsesoiuznoi kommunisticheskoi partii (bol'shevikov): Kratkii kurs* (1945; reprint, Moscow: Pisatel', 1997), 3.

12. Ibid., 17.

13. Ibid., 18.

14. Ibid., 31.

15. The Assotsiatsiia Khudozhnikov Revoliutsionnoi Rossii (AKhRR) was founded in 1922 and was renamed the Assotsiatsiia Khudozhnikov Revoliutsii (AKhR) in 1928. I use the second acronym to designate both.

16. One specialist in socialist realist art noted that "portraits dominated the AKhRR exhibitions; the 1923 Red Army show was three-quarters portraits; the critic A. Mikhailov, reviewing the tenth AKhRR exhibition, counted 121 portraits out of 283 works." See Matthew Cullerne Bown, *Socialist Realist Painting* (New Haven, Conn.: Yale University Press, 1998), 101. For a view that landscape painting constituted a central genre in Stalinist art—that "the depiction of nature was a major preoccupation of Socialist Realism"—see Mark Bassin, "'I Object to Rain That Is

Cheerless': Landscape Art and the Stalinist Aesthetic Imagination," *Ecumene* 7, no. 3 (July 2000): 313.

17. "The 'social portrait,' according to Lunacharskii, was one in which the artists should 'in a particular face, in a particular individual see and show us a whole layer of society.'" See Bown, *Socialist Realist Painting*, 101.

18. Henri Barbusse, quoted in *Stalin: K shestidesiatiletiiu so dnia rozhdeniia* (Moscow: Pravda, n.d. [1939 or 1940]), 75.

19. Rossiiskii Gosudarstvennyi Arkhiv Sotsial'no-Politicheskoi Istorii (RGASPI), f. 74, op. 1, d. 292, ll. 92–92ob. (dated 15 July 1933).

20. *Pravda*, 5 October 1935, 6.

21. On Soviet folklore, sometimes called fakelore, see Frank Miller, *Folklore for Stalin: Russian Folklore and Pseudofolklore in the Stalin Era* (Armonk, N.Y.: M. E. Sharpe, 1990); Felix Oinas, *Essays on Russian Folklore and Mythology* (Columbus, Ohio: Slavica, 1985); Alma Kunanbaeva and Izaly Zemtsovsky, "Communism and Folklore," in *Folklore and Traditional Music in the Former Soviet Union and Eastern Europe*, ed. James Porter (Los Angeles: Department of Ethnomusicology, UCLA, 1997), 3–44; Ursula Justus, "Vozvrashchenie v rai: Sotsrealizm i fol'klor," in *Sotsrealisticheskii kanon*, eds. Evgeny Dobrenko and Hans Günther (St. Petersburg: Gumanitarnoe agenstvo 'Akademicheskii proekt,' 2000), 70–86.

22. See Levon A. Abramian, "Tainaia politsiia kak tainoe obshchestvo: Strakh i vera v SSSR," *Etnograficheskoe obozrenie* 5 (1993): 38. The quantification of Stalin appellations in the 1939 volume *Stalin v tvorchestve armianskogo naroda* was undertaken by L. Dzhrnazian in 1988.

23. Stalin, solntse moe, ia ponial v Moskve: / Serdtse mudrogo Lenina b'etsia v tebe. / V den' siiaiushchii, kak biriuza, / Byl v Kremle ia v krugu druzei. / Uvidali moi glaza / Velichaishego iz liudei. / Ty, ch'e imia dostiglo zvezd / Slavoi pervogo mudretsa, / Byl vnimatelen, laskov prost / I rodnei rodnogo ottsa. / Za radushnyi, ottsovskii priem v Kremle, / Stalin, solntse moe, spasibo tebe. Quoted in Abramian, "Tainaia politsiia," 38.

24. Excerpt from Dzhambul, quoted in I. Eventov, "Kazakhskii geroicheskii epos i pesni Dzhambula," *Sovetskii fol'klor* 6 (1939): 70–85 (82).

25. See "Shein is das Leb'n," in G. von Poehl and M. Agthe, *Das Judentum: Das wahre Gesicht der Sowjets* (Berlin: Otto Stollberg, 1943), 83. The transliterated original stanza reads: "Er hat die groijße scheine Sunn / Op der Erd' arofgebracht, / a bliehendik'n Garten / Fun unser Land gemacht." This Soviet Yiddish Stalin folklore is from a Nazi propaganda publication, eager to prove the alleged "Judeo-Bolshevik" connection. For the Nazi volume, Yiddish ditties *[chastushki]* dedicated to Stalin were extracted from Dobruzhin, *Jiddische Volkslieder weg'n Stalinen* (Moscow: Der Emes, 1940). I am grateful to Frank Grüner for sharing this source with me.

26. Yuri Slezkine, *Arctic Mirrors: Russia and the Small Peoples of the North* (Ithaca, N.Y.: Cornell University Press, 1994), 298.

27. Rossiiskii Gosudarstvennyi Arkhiv Literatury i Iskusstva (RGALI), f. 2368, op. 2, d. 36, l. 16.

28. Hans Blumenberg and Martin Jay, among others, have identified as typical for modern discourse the privileging of the sense of vision and the frequency of luminary metaphors. See Hans Blumenberg, "Light as a Metaphor for Truth," in *Modernity and the Hegemony of Vision*, ed. David Levin (Berkeley: University of

California Press, 1993), 30–62; Martin Jay, *Downcast Eyes: The Denigration of Vision in Twentieth-Century French Thought* (Berkeley: University of California Press, 1993).

29. See Poehl and Agthe, *Das Judentum*, 85–86.

30. Katerina Clark is among the many scholars to have noted Stalin's immobility; see Clark, *Petersburg*, 302, and her essay in this volume.

31. For the vitality of "gender codes" in "naturalizing" power relations, see Joan Wallach Scott, *Gender and the Politics of History* (New York: Columbia University Press, 1988), 48.

32. RGALI, f. 2932, op. 1, d. 344, l. 11. Gerasimov gave this speech at the Central House for Art Workers on the occasion of Stalin's seventieth birthday, during an evening devoted to "The Image of Iosif Vissarionovich Stalin in Works of Art."

33. Ibid.

34. By counting Stalin's image on the front page of *Pravda*, James Heizer demonstrated the rise of Stalin's single appearance after 1936. See his "The Cult of Stalin, 1929–1939," Ph.D. dissertation, University of Kentucky, 1977, 133.

35. See Katerina Clark's essay in this volume.

36. I have benefited greatly from an unpublished, in-depth art historical interpretation of a painting by Deineka that can be classified as occupying the stylistic borderline between the avant-garde and socialist realism. See Diana Leslie Cheren, "Recovering Uncertainty: An Interpretation of Aleksandr Deineka's *The Defense of Petrograd*," master's thesis, History of Art, University of California, Berkeley, 1995. Otherwise, socialist realist painting so far seems to have resisted interpretation with conventional art historical methods.

37. At a 1938 meeting at the Central House of Art Workers, Gerasimov was asked, "The landscape for the portrait *Stalin and Voroshilov* is completely painted from life or changed?" He answered, "It is painted from life, but for the composition I had to move closer two characteristic houses *[dlia kompozitsii mne prishlos' dva kharakternykh domika priblizit']*." See RGALI, f. 2932, op. 1, d. 701, l. 33.

38. Mikhail Yampolsky, "In the Shadow of Monuments: Notes on Iconoclasm and Time," trans. John Kachur, in *Soviet Hieroglyphics: Visual Culture in Late Twentieth-Century Russia*, ed. Nancy Condee (Bloomington: Indiana University Press, 1995), 93.

39. True, the Lenin Mausoleum on Red Square, right outside the Kremlin walls, can be regarded as an anthropomorphic monument. As Lenin's successor, celebrated as "Lenin today" from the late 1920s to the mid-1930s, Stalin drew legitimating power from the presence of the dead leader in the mausoleum.

40. Interestingly, the Soviet star on Voroshilov's belt can be seen as being linked through a diagonal axis with the red star on the Kremlin tower.

41. The leader, however, is always in the center, and the masses remain in the periphery; see Clark, *Petersburg*, 306, and this volume.

42. RGALI, f. 2932, op. 1, d. 701, l. 25. The painting was first exhibited at the 1938 *Twenty Years of the Red Army* exhibition (see OR GTG, f. 8.II, d. 994, l. 59).

43. RGALI, f. 2020, op. 2, d. 6, l. 4. It appears that two rival publishing houses, IZOGIZ and Iskusstvo, conducted Stalin portrait competitions during the same year, 1937, on the occasion of the twentieth anniversary of the October Revolution. Both were closed competitions, meaning that only select artists were invited to participate (open competitions were publicized widely and garnered more contributions).

The IZOGIZ competition was financially even more rewarding than that of Iskusstvo: a first prize received 20,000 rubles, whereas Iskusstvo paid 15,000 rubles. For Iskusstvo's competition, see RGALI, f. 652, op. 8, d. 112.

44. RGALI, f. 2020, op. 8, d. 6, l. 3.

45. Ibid., l. 3. To be sure, the participants also had "the right to suggest their own theme to the publishing house, as long as it [did] not diverge from the purpose of the competition." See ibid., l. 4.

46. Ibid., l. 4.

47. There are stories of Stalin posing after the 1920s, but they might well be apocryphal. During the 1930s, Stalin supposedly sat for the painter Dmitrii Sharapov, who "had specially come from Leningrad to Moscow to portray Stalin. After two sessions he was arrested because Stalin disliked the way in which he had been portrayed." Matthew Cullerne Bown, *Kunst unter Stalin: 1924–1956* (Munich: Klinkhardt and Biermann, 1991), 116–17. The source for this (116 n. 35) is Roi Medvedev, "O Staline i stalinizme," *Znamia* 3 (1989): 156. Bown also claims that Stalin posed for "the sculptor Boris Iakovlev" during the 1930s, only to end up unhappy with this portrayal (116). But there was no sculptor by the name of Boris Iakovlev, only a painter Boris Iakovlev and the more famous painter Vasilii Iakovlev. (Even in Bown's own *Socialist Realist Painting*, 118, Boris Iakovlev is called a painter, and several of his landscape paintings are reproduced. Bown's *A Dictionary of Twentieth-Century Russian and Soviet Painters, 1900–1980s* [London: Izomar, 1998] lists the painter brothers Boris Nikolaevich Iakovlev [1890–1972] and Vasilii Nikolaevich Iakovlev [1893–1953], 352–53.) After the war, Stalin allegedly attempted to get Vera Mukhina to fashion his sculpture. Mukhina resisted by demanding that Stalin pose for her, "which request, she knew, Stalin would not submit to" (Bown, *Socialist Realist Painting*, 234). For variations of the Mukhina story see Bown, *Kunst unter Stalin*, 92, 257. Nowhere does Bown cite the source for this story.

48. RGALI, f. 2932, op. 1, d. 701, ll. 26–27.

49. RGALI, f. 2932, op. 1, d. 776, l. 5. An *Iskusstvo* article about Stalin Prize winners ("Prazdnik sotsialisticheskoi kul'tury," *Iskusstvo* 2 [1941]: 6), published shortly before the German attack on the Soviet Union in World War II, claimed that the title *Na strazhe mira* was not Gerasimov's invention but of popular origin: "Not surprisingly, the viewer gave the group portrait *I. V. Stalin and K. E. Voroshilov in the Kremlin* a different name: *Guarding Peace* (Na strazhe mira)."

50. RGALI, f. 2932, op. 1, d. 344, l. 9.

51. On the Peredvizhniki, see Elizabeth Valkenier, *Russian Realist Art: The State and Society. The Peredvizhniki and Their Tradition* (Ann Arbor, Mich.: Ardis, 1977); idem, *Ilya Repin and the World of Russian Art* (New York: Columbia University Press, 1990); idem, *The Wanderers: Masters of Nineteenth-Century Painting. An Exhibition from the Soviet Union* (Dallas Museum of Art, 1990).

52. One critic suggested in 1939 that Stalin's and Voroshilov's gazes were retrospective and venerating rather than utopian: "Stalin and Voroshilov are standing on the Kremlin mountain, gazing to the place where a grandiose monument in honor of V. I. Lenin is being erected—the Palace of Soviets." See I. S. Rabinovich's introductory article to *Stalin i liudy sovetskoi strany v izobrazitel'nom iskusstve: Katalog vystavki* (Moscow: Izdanie Gosudarstvennoi Tret'iakovskoi Gallerei, 1939), 7.

53. See illustration in Hubertus Gassner and Alisa Liubimova, eds., *Agitatsiia za schast'e: Sovetskoe iskusstvo stalinskoi epokhi* (Bremen: Edition Temmen, 1994), 103.

54. See illustration in ibid., 102. Also see V. I. Vikhtinskii et al.'s *Vo imia mira (Podpisanie dogovora mezhdu Sovetskim Soiuzom i Kitaiskoi Narodnoi Respublikoi)*, illustration in ibid., 107; and D. A. Nalbandian's *Dlia schast'ia naroda: Zasedanie Politbiuro TsK VKP(b)*, illustration in ibid., 100.

55. See illustration in ibid., 101. Significantly, in Shegal's picture of 1937, Lenin is still of overlife size in the back as a huge sculpture, about three times as large as Stalin. In Nalbandian's 1949 picture, Lenin appears only in a small picture in the back on the wall; Stalin himself had become so much the center that he no longer needed any sort of legitimacy from the older leader, Lenin.

56. See illustration 276 in Bown, *Socialist Realist Painting*, 253.

57. See illustration in Gassner and Liubimova, *Agitatsiia za schast'e*, 104.

58. The competing metaphor here is that of Stalin, the gardener. For Stalin's applications of this metaphor to himself, see Jochen Hellbeck, "Laboratories of the Soviet Self: Diaries of the Stalin Era," Ph.D. dissertation, Columbia University, 1998, 64–66.

59. Soviet art critical discourse itself noted the direction of Stalin's gaze. The newspaper *Sovetskoe iskusstvo* (14 February 1947, 1), for example, wrote that "the gaze of the great leader and military commander" in a Stalin sculpture to be erected at the White Sea Baltic Canal "is directed into the distance." At times the gaze into the "bright future" became so overpowering that it overshadowed conventional strategies of pictorial composition. In P. Rozin's picture *V. I. Lenin and I. V. Stalin at the Bay* (V. I. Lenin i I. V. Stalin v razlive) (1950), Lenin and Stalin are saying farewell and should be looking af each other. Instead, their respective gazes do not even meet and are both directed into the distance. See *Sovetskoe Iskusstvo* 6 (20 January 1951): 1.

60. Albert Boime, *The Magisterial Gaze: Manifest Destiny and American Landscape Painting, c. 1830–1865* (Washington, D.C.: Smithsonian Institution Press, 1991), 1.

61. Ibid., 21–22.

62. Ibid., 9–10. In his 1836 "Essay on American Scenery," Thomas Cole wrote: "Where the wolf roams, the plough shall glisten; on the gray crag shall rise temple and tower—mighty deeds shall be done in the now pathless wilderness." Boime commented on this passage: "Here is the textual delineation of his graphic rendition of the idea of futurity and the overcoming of the human and material obstacles to this progress. It is this challenge to the Euro-Americans that makes the civilizing process so basic to their idea of advance—carried out with the sense of a God-ordained mission." See ibid., 53 (same page for the quote from Cole).

63. Ibid., 75–76.

64. Bassin, "'I Object to Rain That Is Cheerless,'" 334.

65. RGALI, f. 2932, op. 1, d. 344, l. 11.

66. RGALI, f. 2942, op. 1, d. 133, l. 43ob. The occasion of these remarks was a March 4, 1939, meeting of the Moscow Sculptors' Union dedicated to the subject of "the image of V. I. Lenin and I. V. Stalin in sculpture."

67. RGALI, f. 2368, op. 2, d. 36, l. 12. This statement is by Evgenii Katsman.

68. Ibid., l. 16.

69. RGALI, f. 2932, op. 1, d. 344, ll. 21–22. The fixation on eyes had a long cultural heritage. In romanticism, for instance, eyes were considered "windows of the

soul." Richard Wortman describes the cultural significance of the eyes of Russian monarchs as expressing the tsar's character more than any other part of his body. He cites a number of contemporary memoiristic impressions of Alexander II's weak gaze, in comparison with the domineering eyes of his father, Nicholas I. See Wortman, *Scenarios of Power,* 2: 22–23.

70. RGALI, f. 2932, op. 1, d. 344, ll. 21–22.

71. For an illustration, see *Sovetskoe iskusstvo,* 22 May 1948, 1.

3

Spatial Figures in Soviet Cinema of the 1930s

OKSANA BULGAKOWA
Translated by Jeffrey Karlsen

Patterns of spatial representation are essential for establishing the styles of different authors or schools, especially in film, where segmentation of space has been crucial to the development of filmic narration based on montage. The introduction of the close-up at the beginning of the twentieth century changed cinema's conception of spatial representation, which had hitherto in its short history been shaped by compositional principles of painting and of theatrical mise-en-scène, with its two-dimensional front plane of the stage. These tableaux were oriented toward the camera, which acted as a mirror or an impersonal eye. The close-up ruptured the integrity of this space and shaped the understanding of spatial representation as dependent on a character's point of view. The character's approach toward and retreat from an object (performed literally or understood figuratively as the concentration of the gaze) provided the justification for disrupting the spatial continuum and reassembling its segments. Dreams and visions often served as the plot devices needed to motivate the juxtaposition of different places. D. W. Griffith resorted to such patterns to impart a metaphysical dimension to the spiritual intimacy of characters supposedly separated by great distances.

At the start of the 1920s, the leading Russian directors experimenting with montage—Lev Kuleshov, Dziga Vertov, and Sergei Eisenstein—established a new canon of spatial representation. It responded to the tenets of architects who, like El Lissitzky, declared, "We no longer want space that will be understood as the painted coffin for our bodies."[1] Cinematic space was understood first and foremost as virtual, constructed space. The narrative canon and the camera angle were not supposed to be motivated by an individual's point of view. In the 1930s, this representational system was substantially revised. The change was brought about by the same directors who had developed the spatial canon of the 1920s. Tracing this shift in the conceptualization of the spatial canon becomes all the more fascinating when we discover that behind purely professional decisions lay a new system of opinions, indicating a change in cultural paradigms.

Creative Geography, Total Vision, and Cubist Pulverization of Space

One of Kuleshov's first montage experiments, in 1920, involved "creative geography." A woman (Alexandra Khokhlova) walks along Petrovka Street past the Mostorg store, and a man (Leonid Obolensky) walks along the Moscow River embankment. These places are about two miles apart in the real world. Kuleshov describes their movement in cinematic space as follows:

> They see each other, smile, and begin to walk toward one another. Their meeting is filmed on Prechistenskii Boulevard. This boulevard is in an entirely different section of the city. They clasp hands, with Gogol's monument as a background, and look—at the White House!—for at this point, we cut in a segment from an American film, *The White House in Washington.* In the next shot they are once again on Prechistenskii Boulevard. Deciding to go farther, they leave and climb up the enormous staircase of the Cathedral of Christ the Savior. We film them, edit the film, and the result is that they are seen walking up the steps of the White House. When we showed this film fragment, everyone understood that Mostorg is on the banks of the Moscow River, that between Mostorg and the river is Prechistenskii Boulevard, where Gogol's monument is located, and that across from the monument is the White House.[2]

One of Vertov's first montage exercises was similarly connected to the annihilation of geographical fixedness: "You are walking down a street in Chicago now, in 1923, but I force you to bow to the late Comrade Volodarsky, who is walking along a street in Petrograd in 1918 and who responds to you with a bow."[3] But Vertov did not follow Kuleshov's practice of using narrative continuity to foster a unity of space by having the hero move from one place to another: "The coffins of popular heroes are being lowered into their graves (filmed in Astrakhan in 1918), the graves are covered (Kronstadt, 1921), a gun salute (Petrograd, 1920), eternal remembrance, people doff their hats (Moscow, 1922)."[4]

Proceeding along this course, Vertov created a montage of a universal city made from documentary segments of Moscow, Kiev, and Odessa. The freedom with which montage brings together spatial segments suggests a *total vision*, a *"panoptic,"* in tandem with the ideology of a "cine-eye" endowed with microscopic, telescopic, and X-ray vision and with the ability to alter perception by varying the speed of shooting and by disintegrating motion. Motion is then recomposed as a cinematographic entity: compressed, extended, stopped, fragmented, multiplied in numerous exposures and in the superimposition of multidirectional movements. This cine-eye sees everything inaccessible to the ordinary eye and is not bound by the old model of perception. It allows the new society to free itself from the old canon of representation and to shape a new one along with new body language and new living spaces.

Eisenstein, who completed an intensive editing seminar with Kuleshov (and was accused by Vertov of plagiarizing Vertov's montage structure), understood this film technique as a perfection of the radical cubist and futurist painterly practice based on deformation, fragmentation, discontinuity, simultaneity, and penetration of space. In his debut film, *Strike* (1924), he used 379 seams per film reel instead of the usual 40 to 60. A scene lasting about 5 minutes now contained 100 shots ranging in length from 15 frames to 1.5 meters. In filming a scene he would lightly shift the camera angle and assemble these "shifted" perspectives to produce a cinematic version of cubist, scattered, "pulverized" space with multiple viewpoints unfolding on one surface.

At first these changes of camera angle within a single scene and Eisenstein's juxtaposition of different places seemed, to his surprised viewers, unmotivated, particularly when, in the film's finale, Eisenstein jumped from shots of an ox being slaughtered to the massacre of striking workers. The audience did not grasp the connection between these shots and responded in traditional fashion by mentally "assembling" the segments in one space. Many viewers thought the massacre was taking place in the slaughterhouse. Others guessed that hungry strikers were storming the slaughterhouse. Eisenstein had combined the gunning down of a demonstration (a fictional representation, mostly in long shots) with the authentic slaughter of an ox (broken up into fragments, closing in with each shot, ending with a close-up of the ox's wide-open eye). He sought to transpose the physiological horror experienced in the real slaughter (and real death) onto the scene of the human massacre—no actor could create the same gruesome total effect.

The desired impact was not based on a logical comparison of the slaughterhouse to the massacre. Instead, the transfer of emotional impact from one scene to the other was designed to organize the sequence as a combination of stimuli that would train social reflexes such as class hatred and class solidarity. In this way Eisenstein constructed not a new space but a new causality that would produce an *intellectual "panoptic"*—a comprehensive look at a chain of events from the viewpoint of a Marxist understanding of historical development.

This overt consciousness of a distinction between real and cinematic space—the latter understood as a "creative," virtual space, constituted only in the spectator's perception—in no way undermined the notion of the "documentary" in Soviet filmmaking. These concepts were connected, on one hand, to an understanding of what comprised cinematic (photogenic) material (only real buildings, no sets) and, on the other, to the question of how to investigate the surface of this material through lighting and cinema optics. Directors' exploration of the texture of filmed surfaces that were often wet, rough, or uneven followed stylistically in the tradition of constructivist painting, with its appreciation of the materiality of things (from collage to counterrelief). In cinema, a particular, somewhat paradoxical effect was created: a heightened, textured impression of reality contributed to the construction of virtual space.

At this very time, German cinema was building whole cities in the studio. Whether born of the tradition of expressionist painting, as in *The Cabinet of Doctor Caligari,* or of the "new objectivity," as in Joe May's *Asphalt,* these cities ultimately became nightmares, spaces of the hero's inner vision, and the materiality of their hollowed-out constructions was unmasked as the reality of an unreal, unstable world. Both nature and the city were created in the studio and turned into fantasy spaces. Architecture and lighting were used with enormous virtuosity in this play between the real and the spectral, the material and the cinematic. But Soviet cinema of the 1920s seemed to manage without production designer and art director; the reality of filmed locations (cinema without sets) was one of the main postulates of the Russian school.

In the 1920s, Vertov, Kuleshov, and Eisenstein did not recompose prefilmic reality—that is, reality as it exists before being recorded by the camera—but produced a postfilmic one. A decade later, their attention switched back to prefilmic space, which was created in the studio as a simulacrum of reality. The plan of Eisenstein's unrealized film about Moscow (1933–47) reveals a radical shift in the director's understanding of what kind of space could become cinematic material and what kind of texture could be acknowledged as photogenic. Kuleshov, in the half-forgotten film *Siberians* (1941), provided a means of understanding this kind of art—an art that works to erode the border between dream and reality, a process supported by a camouflaging of the distinction between painted sets and real "nature." Only Vertov kept working with montages of documentary filmed segments. He no longer focused on renewing perception, however, but on establishing a hierarchy of meaning. In *Three Songs of Lenin* (1934) he created a set of iconic signs that facilitated the transformation of real locations on a map of the country into semantic topoi, sacred spaces.

Vertov's Bench, or How Iconic Discourse Is Created

In 1946, André Bazin understood the sacred message of a crucial scene in a film called *The Vow.* He described the descent of Lenin's holy spirit onto the new Moses, Stalin, who is standing in front of a snow-covered park bench in the Gorki estate outside Moscow.[5] Today, this scene is incomprehensible. Why a man, in the middle of a long walk along a footpath covered with snow, would stop at precisely this bench is a question that seems answerable only in terms of an arbitrary whim of the director, Mikhail Chiaureli. For us the bench is a sign whose significance has been erased, like the woman with a sword who signified virtue in medieval heraldry. But back then—both in 1946, the year *The Vow* was released, and twelve years earlier, upon the release of Dziga Vertov's *Three Songs of Lenin*—the bench was still "legible"; the spectator had been schooled in this language of objects.

The cinema in the 1930s created its own iconography, which lent meaning to concrete spaces and profane objects. This meaning became increasingly less intelligible to the uninitiated. Some icons, such as the Masonic star, have long traditions. The park bench, however, was a "new" object. It was able to achieve hieratic status only because it could benefit from an already existing orientation toward the production of ideological icons. Like the French Revolution, the Russian Revolution was adept at recoding and employing the methods of previous mythologies.

In *Three Songs of Lenin,* Vertov gave form to one version of that orientation. In this film he compiled a new folklore of the nations of the Soviet East, seeming to appropriate this mythological consciousness and to visualize its rhetorical clichés. In selecting oral literature and focusing on marginal regions, Vertov was responding with striking rapidity to several tendencies in the literary environment of the time. Oral literature had been offered, by Lelevich, for example, as one of the possible models for the development of the canon of socialist realism.[6] The choice by the constructivist Vertov of precisely this literary matrix for his second sound film appears paradoxical. Why is cinema, a medium connected with modernity, pressed into service for the visualization of an archaic poetics? In this film the incongruity between the object of representation and the metaphorical allusions is also paradoxical: the process of modernization (electrification, the emancipation of women) is interpreted in forms of thought that preserve the concept of cyclical time and exclude individual initiative, for individual freedom is constrained by the norms of a collective canon of behavior.

Vertov brings oral tradition to the screen but simultaneously reveals the oxymoronic character of oral literature in the age of writing and, even more, the oxymoronic character of cinema based on this literature. The speaking body of the performer, from which the affective voice issues, is transformed and formalized in his film, which, incidentally, is nearly silent. One does not see the singer or understand the words of the song, which are in a foreign language. Song—the very title of the film—implies voice, but voice is transferred in the film to a different plane: the graphic, the title. And into another language: Russian. This substitution introduces the strategy of the film as a whole: it is constructed on an endless series of substitutions, of transitions—voice to word, word to picture, picture to letter. Voice is replaced by script, and sound gives way to vision, a more intellectualized mode of perception.

A film presumably should provide the visual equivalent of literary symbolism. If, however, one takes visual representation to be cinema's primary element, then a film should translate objects, actions, and spaces into a set of symbolic images. In this film, Vertov carried out the work of a "primary maker of symbols," imparting a sacred character to objects of everyday life (a bench, a lightbulb, a newspaper, the body of the dead Lenin) and to concrete geographical spaces (part of a park in a certain estate near Moscow, Red Square, the power station Dneproges on the Dnieper). In this way he created for his epoch an iconic discourse that was later to be used by Soviet cinema as its common property, although Vertov's representation of Stalin in the same style in his next film, the "fourth song," *Lullaby,* would not be approved.[7]

The film about Lenin consists of three songs. The first begins with a title that enumerates the transformations that become the plot of the film: Lenin is "a woman who has thrown off the chador," "water in the desert," "an electric lightbulb," "the illiterate who have become literate."[8] Vertov attempts to broaden the semantics of the image through a title, following the technique of his films of the 1920s, in which the concrete event, such as a dinner party, signifies the bourgeoisie in general. Nevertheless, despite a certain similarity of montage devices, there are significant differences between the early films, such as *A Sixth Part of the World* (1926), and this one.

Vertov employs a set of disparate pictures for the visualization of tropes borrowed from oral literature. He pays no attention to the fairly primitive connections between title and shot (they follow the logic of illustration) but rather unfolds a chain of substitution for which the word of the title serves as stimulus. For instance, a title gives the text of the song: "My face was in a dark prison." A woman under a chador is shown objectively. In the next shot the camera imitates her perspective by assuming a limited field of vision (the camera under a chador). "I was blind" (the title): a blind woman is shown objectively, and the next shot becomes blurry (the camera imitates her blindness).

But the unfolding sequence is then emancipated from the titles, and the juxtaposition of shots produces a new semantic. In alternating montage, we see women without chadors going to school and sitting in classrooms, men praying in a mosque, and Young Pioneers marching along a riverbank. The sequence parallels actions produced in different spaces at different times but possessing identical rhythmic patterns (praying men bow repeatedly, women repeat the teacher's syllables, pioneers march first from right to left, then from left to right), facilitating a supplementary semanticization. One ritual action (bow) is replaced by another (march). The women have found a new saint, and he is Lenin. For him, a new dwelling space is created: the school, which has replaced the mosque. The world consists of subjects and objects, which can replace each other, allowing metaphorical meaning to be established as the common one for all actions. The rhythm of repetition facilitates the understanding of a concrete image as a metaphorical one: taking off the chador and going to school as "recovery of sight" and "enlightenment."

Vertov uses such juxtapositions within the montage sequence

throughout the film and applies the same technique to the pattern of spatial representation. Space here loses its fixed concreteness and becomes a general symbol: "my state farm" equals "my country," which ultimately leads to the destruction of notions of distance, depth, and location. Such simple points of reference as far and near, above and below, right and left, real and painted, and seen and imagined lose their meaning entirely.

Pioneers are filmed in a shady forest (a Russian landscape?). The woman who "sees them" is walking through an old Eastern city. An old man comes to a halt in the desert, and in the next shot his gaze fixes on Red Square. Montage technique, which through point-of-view shots freely connects in one space the glance of the looker and that which he or she sees, here does not support the impression of spatial continuity (on which the clash of two levels—the looking and the seen—is usually constructed). The principle of spatial continuity guided Vertov's and Kuleshov's experiments in the 1920s, but now, in 1934, Vertov does not strive toward the concrete suggestion of a determinate space created on the level of visual perception. Rather, he effaces the opposition of far and near in thought, transgressing the frames of purely cinematic comprehension. The contrast between the deserts and Red Square, separated from each other by two thousand to three thousand kilometers, is not essential; that distance thus loses its concrete characteristics. The space of the whole country is drawn together and filled by semantic unity.

The most frequent shots in the first song are those of women who have gathered in a semicircle around newspapers or radios, imitating the mise-en-scène around the performer of oral literature. Then we see a woman at the printing press observing the printing of Lenin's writings. The sign of what is printed is simple: a portrait on a binding (the letter has now been replaced by the image). The women who have gathered around one newspaper or radio illustrate the unity of the entire country (female), which is created thanks to the word (male), uttered and printed. The scene with the newspaper is illustrative, yet it demonstrates not that women read newspapers but rather that the word serves as the foundation of spatial unity. This new patriarchal unity encompasses the entire Soviet Union, which organizes bodies in spatial, semantic, and gendered figures.

The uttered word (although it is not literally audible in the film) comes from Moscow, from Red Square. Shots of a parade replace inaudible speech. Into this idyllic circle of women, united by a man, Lenin, who has become woman (remember the first title—Lenin is "a woman who has thrown off the chador") and who represents the spiritual father, Vertov introduces the successor, again through a title: the Party's steel hands, which guide and lead the women, a dual paraphrase of Stalin. Stalin is absent from this film, present only in metonymic indicators. Here Vertov follows Islamic tradition: the prophet is present everywhere, but he is invisible.

The first song is based on the transformation of sex (man-woman, woman-man), on the effacing of concrete spatial characteristics, and on play with the difference between the semantics of a single frame and the montage series that produces another meaning. The second song is organized on the same principle of inverted dichotomy: the opposition of motion and immobility collapses, as does the barrier between death and life. Vertov juxtaposes shots of Lenin's immobile body in its casket with the organized motion of the masses that compensates for the immobility of the single body. In the third song the series of substitutions broadens. Not only does an illiterate woman become literate, but the desert blossoms and the water of the Dnieper turns into light. The oppositions dry-moist, sterile-blossoming, and fluid-radiant describe a change of state and prepare for the main transformation: the dead Lenin is proclaimed the most living, and this "living dead man" conquers (and so creates the semantic unity of) the whole world. The end of the film shows an expansion of movement, both to the deserts of the south and the frost of the north, both into the air (airplanes) and under the earth (in mines). The movement of masses spreads beyond the boundaries of Soviet space—into Germany, China, and Spain. The integration of this "foreign" space into "Soviet" space is a result of the same semantic unification: around Lenin, or rather around the name written on the poster. Or by means of a still more characteristic substitution: "Er führte uns!" stands on the banner of the German demonstrators—"He led us!"

In the first two songs Vertov used photographs of Lenin and documentary footage. The third song shows his profile assembled from electric lights and several slogans; the portrait is replaced by the schematized sign and the shining letters. The songs, which are intended to unfold Lenin's biography before the spectator, serve as a vita, as a parable about a prophet who visited Earth and produced a series of magical transformations. That Vertov works with primary elements (water, light, the letter) underscores the shift from the documentary to the allegorical. He transforms electrification itself into an archaic magical act. He films the construction of dams like an old constructivist, but the final act of this construction leads to the magical transformation of water into light. Lenin, who in the first song *enlightened* women who had recovered *sight,* here simply imparts *light* and penetrates into every home as a "little light *[lampochka]* of Il'ich." The montage sequence does not strive to create synthetic space (the universal city) or new causal continuity; rather, it builds a system of juxtapositions that facilitates the transformation of meaning: the profane object becomes sacred, the literal action is interpreted metaphorically. Light means the little bulb, word means the newspaper, and finally, Mecca means the park bench.

The bench—an utterly banal object—becomes the refrain of Vertov's film. The first and second songs begin and end with the continuity of three shot scales: the estate in Gorki (frontal, long shot, neutral, objective), a view of the bench from Lenin's room (medium shot, diagonal composition, suggestion of his last glance, subjective), and a medium close-up of an empty bench (the impersonal eye) (fig. 3.1). These three scales are given in multiple repetitions, through iterative exposition. A photograph of Lenin sitting on a bench is included once in this montage sequence, but the empty bench is repeated, filmed in summer, winter, and spring. The repetitions are not accidental; the bench is not simply a compositional suture. The concrete place is meant to fix semantically the basic figure of collapsed dichotomy on which the film is constructed: presence-absence, life-death. It is fixed verbally in the formula "dead but alive" and should find spatial shape in the figure "present in absence." Before us is not a bench from a museum, with a "do not sit" sign hung on it, but rather a space for the presence of the absent prophet, a holy place.

It was therefore possible for Mikhail Chiaureli to use this bench in his 1946 film as a ready-made sign. The episode of Lenin's death is constructed thus: while Bukharin and Kamenev share power, Stalin goes off in solitude toward the bench. There he is to listen to the mystical voice of the prophet. A voice, however, would be too concrete. Stalin raises his eyes to the sky; a ray of sun breaks through the clouds and, as Bazin notes, strikes the new prophet. Everything is in place—"even the flames of fire."[9]

Vertov's work is one of symbolizing and synthesizing. His early film compiled heterogeneous material (archival shots, filmed scenes, live interviews, news footage) and created a new, virtual filmic space. The space of *Three Songs*—despite its extension to various ends (south, north, west, east, underground mines, heights above the clouds)—is centri-

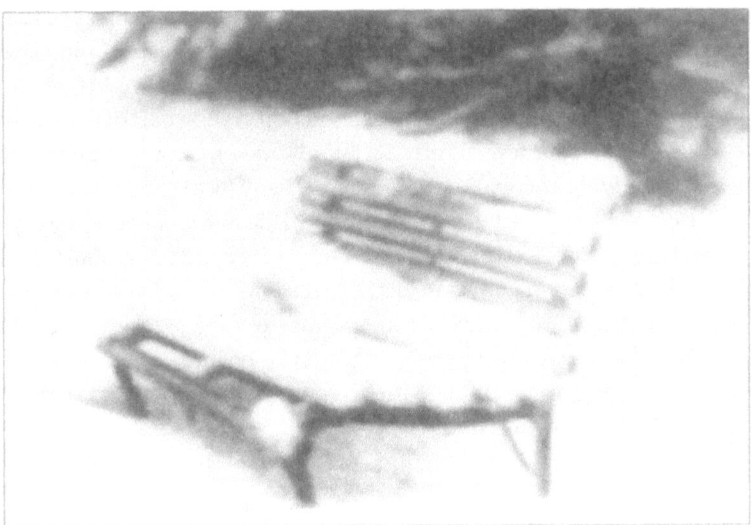

Fig. 3.1. Frame showing the bench in Dziga Vertov's *Three Songs of Lenin* (1934).

petal, saturated with "meaning." Space is stratified and decomposed in accordance with significant and insignificant elements. This is not a landscape; it is a medium for the communication of a sacred message, and it uses montage and a unifying name to suture *space.* Vertov completely erodes the border between the documentary and the fictive, between the concrete and the metaphorical. The synthetic space of this film is cinematically "extraspatial." It is to be constituted by the spectator not as a spatial but as a semantic structure.

In the 1920s Vertov's work revolved around a central dichotomy: nearly the entire world (of capitalism) versus one-sixth of the globe (socialism). In the 1930s this opposition was replaced by a new one: center versus periphery. The rise of a political, economic, cultural, and symbolic center, Moscow, changes the parameters of spatial perception. This change is dictated and amplified by the means of communication: radio, telephone, airplane, and train.[10] Vertov still understands the cinema as the medium of the total gaze, as a "panoptic" encompassing both the center and the periphery, which see and recognize each other at a glance without having, as it were, ever met. In a sense different from the one meant by Heidegger in *Being and Time,* Vertov renders *Entfernung,* distance, as *Ent-fernung,* undoing of distance: he shows distance as enormous, unencompassable, and, simultaneously, collapsing. This is not the simultaneity and disregard of distance that we find in modernism, when new technologies of transportation and communication converge to create the impression of an implosion and loss of space.[11] In Vertov's spatial construction, a sixth part of the world is compressed to a few signifying topoi, even to a single object, in which signifying energy is concentrated as a mystical image. The entire space of industry is reduced to Dneproges, the entire space of the capital to Lenin's mausoleum, all of "Mecca" to the bench. A spatial figure becomes an emblem and an object, a part standing for the whole. This rhetorical feature is characteristic of the mythological thinking in which Vertov seemed to be absorbed. But was he imitating this mythological thinking by adapting to the screen a truly synthetic Soviet folklore, or was he creating it himself?

Eisenstein, or the Unbuilt Sets for Moscow

Vertov's film points to a shift in the conceptualization of "creative geography," of the spatial continuity established through montage. A film planned by Eisenstein marks a change in the understanding of what is cinematic. His project was founded upon his fascination with spatial illusions created in the studio, with copies, mock-ups, and distortions, with imitation of the world in a cardboard box—all this in striking opposition to his style of the 1920s.

In June 1933 Sergei Eisenstein was assigned a film about Moscow. The plans for the general reconstruction of the capital entailed not only a concrete restructuring of the city but also the realization of a new philosophy in an easily legible, symbolic urban form. Cinema was expected to assist in the creation of a new architectural alphabet. The choice of Eisenstein, who had once trained as an architect, to direct a film about the reconstruction of the city was highly emblematic. There was no other director in Soviet cinema who could so skillfully transform architecture into a meaningful text. The storming of the Winter Palace in his film *October* (1927) was staged as an occupation of the symbolic forms of the old power. Its signs—architecture and statuary of imperial St. Petersburg—were demythologized as objects; the objects of a new power—armored vehicles, flag, telephones, maps—were transformed into fetishes. *October* had cemented the image of Petrograd as the city of revolution and as Lenin's city.

Now Eisenstein was supposed to capture the birth of Stalin's Moscow in effective film images. He was supposed to teach the ignorant audience how to read the new symbols and create a correspondence between the film and the state's utopian architecture. In reality the new Moscow would be obliged to preserve the historic radial, ringed structure, with movement outward from the Kremlin, but the history of the city, set in architecture, was to be recoded anew: the center was to be displaced from the Kremlin to the Palace of the Soviets on the other side of the river, and a string of edifices possessing symbolic form was to be erected along the Garden Ring. One of these would be the Soviet Army Theater, built in the shape of a five-pointed star.

Eisenstein started to work on *Moscow in Time* in June and July 1933, before dropping the project for a number of years. He came back to it in 1946, when, after being awarded the Stalin Prize for the first part of *Ivan the Terrible*, he was invited to work on a trilogy about Stalin: *The Caucasus, Moscow,* and *Victory*. Finally, he conceived *Moscow* as one of his last projects, now *Moscow 800*, a film for the anniversary of the city's founding, incorporating several of the 1933 *Moscow*'s motifs and developing them in accordance with his ideas on color dramaturgy. The last draft is dated September 30, 1947. Despite the brevity of the surviving notes, Eisenstein considered this project important in the elaboration of a new poetics; the film would present a total reconceptualization of cinematic space and texture. Planning the film, he announced: "I'm starting to learn all over again. . . . We're at the beginning of a new era in film development. In *Moscow* I shall endeavor to combine the methods of *Potemkin* and *October*."[12] In the film, Eisenstein wanted to translate the principle of Mexican cinema onto the Russian screen, to portray history through urban architecture, and to present the story of an individual as the history of a class. The film was conceived as a kind of synthesis of all of Eisenstein's previous cinematic achievements.

Although his work on *Moscow* began pursuant to a government order, Eisenstein's repeated return to this project over the course of twelve years is symptomatic. Still more so is the context in which the project arose. Eisenstein made notes for the script during the first ten days of June 1933, during which time Moscow was supposed to host an international congress on city planning. But the Soviets unexpectedly canceled it at the last minute. Preparations for the congress had been extensive; international architects had aspired to express during the debates an opposition to the architectural line triumphant in Moscow. The elites of the architectural world were indignant about the plans for reconstructing the Soviet capital. Many internationally acclaimed architects, such as Walther Gropius, Le Corbusier, and Hans Poelzig, had participated in a competition to design the new Palace of Soviets, which was to replace the demolished Church of Christ the Savior. All of their proposals had been rejected. Sigfried Giedion, secretary of the Association of International Architects (CIAM), wrote a letter to Stalin in their name, expressing their bewilderment over socialist classicism. Giedion's letter probably led to the cancellation of the congress. (The architects instead met aboard a ship sailing from Marseilles to Athens. They analyzed thirty-two modern cities and adopted the "Athenian Charter," conceived by Le Corbusier and proclaiming his vision of the new, decentralized "Radiant City.")

Eisenstein presumably knew of the dramatic events surrounding the architecture congress, because he had participated in a discussion of proposals for the Palace of Soviets in the spring of 1933. That he sketched his first ideas for the film at this time is hardly a coincidence. He certainly knew of the reconstruction projects, for his film was to illustrate Moscow's new understanding of architecture. The city was being rebuilt according to Stalin's general plan, presented by Lazar Kaganovich in a 1931 speech, much as peasant Russia had been rebuilt according to Stalin's General Line—the subject of Eisenstein's previous film of 1926–29. Stalin's plan rested on the ideology of an absolute center: a city that materialized the utopian dream of the nation's future. Grandiose architectural plans for building a subway, canals, and skyscrapers tested the limits of depth, height, length, and breadth. Moscow, a northern city without access to the sea, was declared the capital of five seas and built like a southern Mediterranean metropolis. When the heroes of Grigory Aleksandrov's *Volga-Volga* (1938) reach Moscow, they enter it as if it were Venice, sailing through wide canals on steamers, boats, skiffs, and yachts, and even by swimming. Moscow greets the arriving Siberian in Ivan Pyr'ev's *The Party Card* (1936) as a city on a river, the site of a magnificent fireworks display (again Venice).

But in the 1930s the real Moscow—with its narrow, twisting streets, its low, wooden, chaotically arranged houses—was still far removed from this grand vision. On every big square, monasteries and warehouses blocked the view and bore little correspondence to the new city's ideal vision. As a result, Moscow is virtually absent from the films of those years. Automobile rides through 1930s Moscow in the films of that time (for example, Konstantin Iudin's 1936 *A Girl of Character*) are brief: a quick glance at Manège Square, now cleansed of old buildings, and Tverskaia Street, now being repaved. Moscow is reduced to several emblematic landmarks that migrate from film to film: Red Square, the "Moscow" Hotel, and the Bolshoi Theater. The inclusion of these selected motifs was meant to create the appearance of a city that did not yet really exist, because it was under construction: narrow streets are widened, one-story buildings are replaced by high-rises, wooden buildings are dressed in thick coats of stone, plaster, marble, and granite. Still more often, the real Moscow was replaced in film by a painted backdrop or sets, as in Aleksandrov's *Circus* (1936).

The first draft of Eisenstein's screenplay included three main trajectories: the history of the Russian and Soviet states, the transformation of nature, and the creation of a new urban architecture. Eisenstein's *Moscow* interpreted the state's idea as a new vision of a *Gesamtkunstwerk*, as the unity of history, nature, and art. He planned in 1947 to show the Tatar occupation, Ivan the Terrible, Napoleon, three revolutions, war, and contemporary life. He planned to use city architecture to structure history with the help of a model from Elizabethan theater. Four elements—water, air, fire, and earth—determined the plot as a geometrical figure. Historical dialectics were reduced to "the dialectics of nature"—as an alchemist would have understood them. The elements themselves became emblems of a coat of arms, on which history was supposed to materialize. But instead the reverse process occurs: *Moscow* would manage without architecture and without history. Eisenstein planned to build all the sets in the studio. The real city would not be filmed; it would be replaced by a cinema-city made of plywood.

Eisenstein's conceptualization of the film's texture underwent the same radical change. If his architectural project, *The Glass House* (1926–29), translated the metaphorical into the literal (the "comedy of situations" was resolved as a comedy of literal *situations*—of positions of the camera), then in *Moscow* the literal becomes the metaphorical. As they approach contemporary reality, material elements are transformed into tropes. Fire is material only under Napoleon; thereafter, it exists as "the flame of revolution" (Moscow did not burn in 1917), "the fiery ring of intervention," "the fire of the vow" (of Stalin). Air becomes "the air of freedom." The elements "dematerialize." In *Moscow 800* the victory of the figurative over the literal is masked by the "materiality" of colors: to the four elements are added the seven colors of the spectrum. In this way the materials of Moscow (stone, gold, wood) are understood as conventional epithets (*belokamennaia* equals "built of white stone," *zlatoglavaia* equals "gold-domed"), as colors. The four elements and the seven colors are deceptive in their materiality, leading not to a palpability of texture *(faktura)* but rather to allegorism, to fixed meaning. They transmogrify into heraldic emblems that manifest history. The play of theatrical elements is supposed to appear as the play of social forces, as the historical process. But the pattern of equating one with the other (liberation from the Tatars equals liberation from Napoleon, which equals liberation from fascism) leads to a state in which historical time stops and is eliminated as such; history is transformed into the cyclical play of repetitions. The historical performance that Eisenstein sought to stage for the real Moscow discloses its representationality as the representationality of theater sets. His Elizabethan cosmogony does not create history; it presents history as theater.

If Vertov works with metonyms and "minimalized" space, Eisenstein must create the image of a nonexistent city attainable only in metaphor. This is in keeping with the fundamental tendency of the architecture of the time, which elaborated grandiose plans that existed only as blueprints. These sketches did not respond to concrete demands; rather, they were directed by fantasy and imagination. Fantasy was aroused by images, not by already created objects. The utopian sweep of the time and its art permitted "reality" to exist only as a project that would exclude time and historical memory.[13]

It is not accidental that Eisenstein's project *Moscow in Time* remained unrealized, and in Medvedkin's film *The New Moscow* (1938), the gigantic city was shown as a miniature model.

The New Moscow: A Puppet City

Aleksandr Medvedkin's *The New Moscow* was condemned as a failure, and following its release the director stopped making feature films. But this failure is extremely symptomatic. The film's narrative—a tightly knit tale of romantic quid pro quo—ends with the happy uniting of two couples. One of the protagonists, an artist and urbanist, is unable to complete a sketch of Moscow because buildings disappear in the night, move about, and are replaced by new ones. The artist loses not only nature but also his model, a Moscow beauty who leaves him for a civil engineer in Siberia. The engineer has come to Moscow to present a mock-up of the new city—a Moscow that he has never seen in nature but has glimpsed in his Siberian backwoods more distinctly then have Muscovites themselves. He is an ideal carrier of that imaginative vision for which the architecture calls. The artist meets a new model, the engineer's traveling companion, a young woman who is breeding a new strain of pigs.

The allocation of priority between the artist and the engineer, the eyewitness and the visionary—affirmed by the beauty's choice—emphasizes what must be understood as an object of representation, as nature: the real city is replaced by the fantastic city, existing only in the imagination. Cinema acts as the medium of this imagination, as the time machine that appears at the movie's end. There, an instructional film presenting the new, reconstructed Moscow through animation of architectural drawings and models is crudely inserted into the fictional narrative. The new Moscow appears as a Soviet "Metropolis." Rapt admiration of this utopia, however, is replaced by the laughter of the audience to whom the model is shown.

Laughter breaks out twice. First, due to a technical oversight, the film prepared by the engineer is run backward: first we see documentary footage of the destroyed remains of Sukharevskaia Tower, Stranstnoi monastery, and the Cathedral of Christ the Savior; then these buildings arise from ruins, and the audience to whom this "time machine" is being shown begins to laugh. In order to create a desired reaction (the old must be connected with laughter and mockery), Medvedkin uses a simple trick from slapstick comedy—the reverse movement of the film. The destroyed monuments (churches) are recreated on the screen. The laughter of spectators is transferred from—and motivated by—one action (the film trick) to another (the resurrection of the demolished old church).

Spectators could also laugh during the second sequence of the film (and they do so today, always), which presents the new forms as models. Laughter is caused by the incoherence of proportions: the monumental forms realized as models appear like toys, as buildings for dwarves. Naturally, the spectators of the thirties could also laugh at that moment, but their real laughter was suppressed by the monumental music of the sequences, which encouraged the perception of these toys as projections of the future. Russian spectators of today know that most of the models could never have been realized. Instead of the destroyed gigantic buildings, drawings and puppet houses appear on the screen. The incongruity of textures and dimensions creates a comic effect of a different kind. And when airplanes the size of insects fly above a cardboard Palace of Soviets adorned by a statue of Lenin, the unintentional comedy reaches a peak.

Palaces turn out to be hollowed-out constructions. The precious materials of Stalinist architecture are completely profaned in the cinema. Marble, stone, and granite are transformed into painted cardboard, the monumental spectacle of power into a theater set composed only of a canvas facade. The individual is understood as a function, the performer of a prescribed role, but he moves in a theater of "dematerialized" architecture that has become a backdrop. This is a theater of metaphysical space, the space of apparition and dream. It is no accident that a frequent place for lovers' meetings in the films of the 1930s is not the traditional Stone Bridge embankment, beloved of Russian prerevolutionary cinema, but the exhibition of the achievements of the national economy, the Soviet "Potemkin village," the ideological Disneyland, a real theater set under an open sky, which would seem to present a palliative in relation to the visions of Eisenstein and Medvedkin.

Eisenstein's film was never made, and Medvedkin's bombed. These two projects were but the fullest expressions of the changes that had occurred in the understanding of the potential of cinematic space. The real was replaced by the fantastic; directors forsook the street and moved into the studio, where the horizon was replaced by a backdrop, stone by canvas, buildings by miniatures—where space was completely subjugated to the fantasy of the production designer, the cinematographer, the director. Over the course of two decades, from the 1930s to the middle of the 1950s, everything was built in studios: the desert, the North Pole, the Ural Mountains, even the Volga in several episodes of Mark Donskoi's trilogy.

Emerging from this tradition, Eisenstein's *Ivan the Terrible* can be interpreted as a claustrophobic film about a constructed, enclosed space that swallows the protagonists.

Life as Dream

Cinema offered architectural dreams as a simulacrum of reality. In this sense, the replacement of the real Moscow by the imagined city was perfectly natural. Kuleshov's children's film of 1941, *The Siberians* (figs. 3.2–3.5), attempted to provide a motivation for this substitution of the imagined for the actual, of the painted for the real. It was not the effacement of the border between dream and reality, or between painted forest and authentic nature (the taiga), that aroused criticism, but rather the director's attempt to offer a psychological motivation for this substitution.

The plot of the film is simple: two boys and a girl from a distant settlement in the Turukhanskii region, where Stalin was in internal exile, dream of Moscow, of meeting Stalin. For this dream to come true, they must undergo a series of tests (school examinations) and perform an

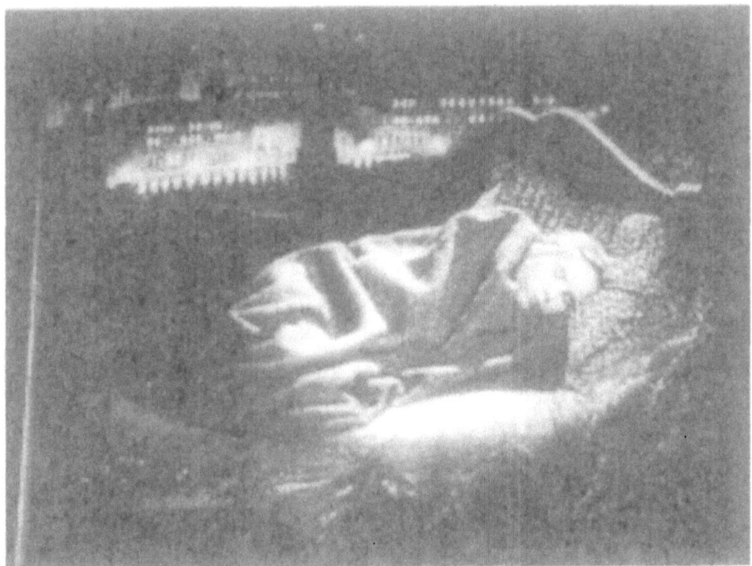

Fig. 3.2. Frame from Lev Kuleshov's *The Siberians* (1941), in which the girl dreams of the Kremlin, which illuminates her cabin like a New Year's tree.

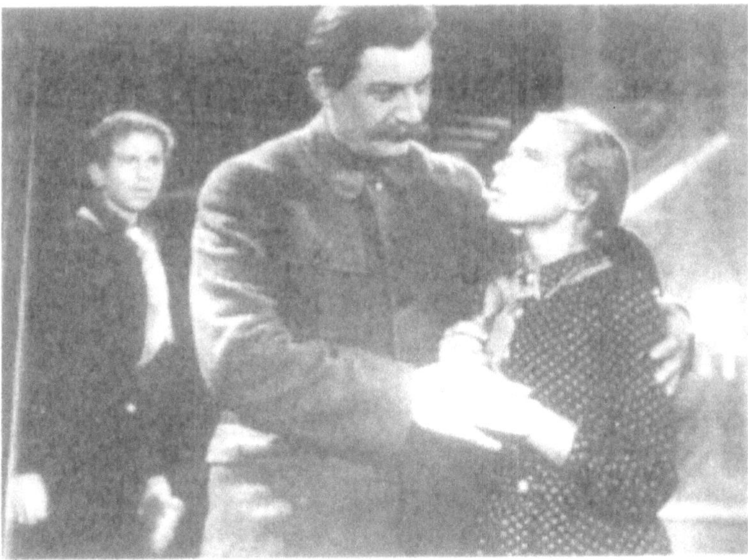

Fig. 3.3. Directly from her cabin, the girl enters Stalin's office in the Kremlin and meets Stalin in her dream.

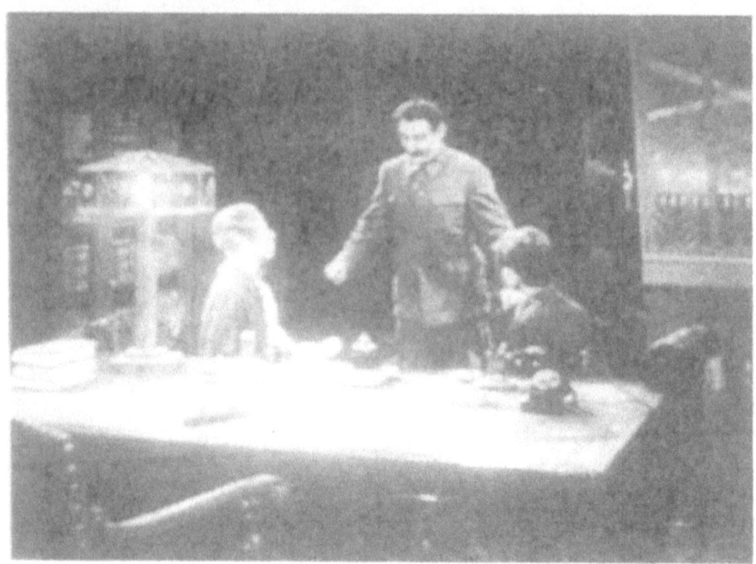

Fig.3.4. The two boys in *The Siberians* meet Stalin in his Kremlin office.

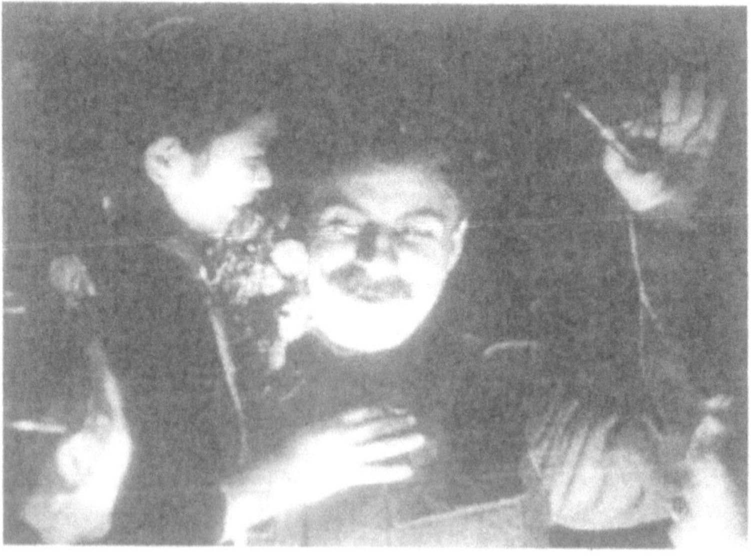

Fig.3.5. The boys give Stalin the pipe they have found—a fetish with magical powers.

unusual task. On Christmas Eve they learn from an old hunter that Stalin, during his escape from exile, gave his pipe to a certain taiga dweller. The boys decide to find it. At the end of the film the boys are on their way to Moscow. It is not they, however, but the girl who meets Stalin first and speaks to him—in a dream. The distance between the center and the periphery is covered not with the help of a "total vision" (as in Vertov) or by means of communication, but through magical transformation (telepathy, imagination, apparition). The film thematizes the effacement of the border between dream and reality not only on the level of plot but also in its set designs, which ultimately obliterate any sense of distinction between the imagined and the real, the genuine and the painted, interior and exterior.

In Kuleshov's film the protagonists' conflation of the desired and the real is motivated by the pubescent consciousness of adolescents who are striving to attract the father's love and attention. These complexes are attributed by Kuleshov to infantile neuroses (really, to the neuroses of the whole nation)—a bold step forward in the (psycho)analysis of this period's creative dreaming *(grezotvorchestvo).* Injecting this daydreaming (understood as neurosis, leading to the fusion of the desired and the real) into the children's fantasy marked its individualization, psychologization, and motivation. Similar daydreams and departure from normal perception in other films of this period (such as Medvedkin's) were not found to need analysis or justification, much less that of an infantilized, pubescent consciousness. Kuleshov's film was criticized for his insistence on the subjective aspect of vision, which he conveyed by making the camera the instrument of the character's subjective gaze.

The narrative's transitions from the real world to the dream world are conveyed through mise-en-scène, set design, camera work, and montage. The film's first shot sequence serves as an exposition of this strategy. Real nature—a snow-covered landscape, trees in long shot—narrows to a detail of ice-covered branches in close-up. Through a dissolve, these branches turn into patterns on glass (exterior becomes interior). An icy fir tree (exterior, seen from interior) is suddenly ignited by electric wreaths and the inscription "Happy New Year!" The fir tree that we have just seen from the window turns out to be located inside a room (exterior changes into interior with no motivation). The spectator no longer knows exactly where the fir tree is at all—outside or inside. Nature and sets, exterior and interior run together. In the first transition, this is eased by the use of a cinematic trick, the dissolve.

Then the director does not bother to provide motivation (not even the cinematic one) for why and how the tree seen from the window could actually be inside the room.

At the end of the film, during the girl's dreamed meeting with Stalin, this merging of boundaries reaches an apotheosis. Directly from her Siberian cabin she enters Stalin's office in the Kremlin, which emits radiance like a New Year's fir tree illuminating a cabin. The film's aesthetic leads toward a similar conclusion through long dissolves that ease and mask the transition from the real to the painted. Throughout the film, the Siberian countryside and the taiga itself stand before the spectator in various guises: as painted backdrop, as animated cartoon, as photographed nature, as studio construction with trees in pots. The texture of the landscape changes, but the transitions are camouflaged, and the spectator inadequately trained in distinguishing between nature and its imitation is constantly shaken from a position of certainty in what he sees. Similar aberrations of perception are motivated by the contrivances of the plot.

Kuleshov plays with magical metamorphoses. In school, the New Year's holiday is being celebrated. Grandfather Frost, a fairy-tale figure, appears in the company of two officials, the chairman of a state farm and a doctor. The marvelous becomes governmentalized, or, rather, the marvelous and the administrative fuse. The doctor appears as a living incarnation of the newly merged realms of science and art—he heals and sings operatic arias! The chairman of the state farm distributes gifts to the children—not, however, from Grandfather Frost, but from Stalin, who has sent these gifts from Moscow. Stalin's second deputy turns out to be the (female) teacher of the children, who is playing Grandfather Frost. That Stalin is the real Grandfather Frost the children learn immediately after the handing out of gifts, in the "red corner," the museum of Stalin. Here are painted three frescoes, three "tableaux," which are actualized (and embodied by children) at various moments of the film. At first, the boys examine the gifts against the background of a painted forest with a small hut. Framed by this painted landscape, the old hunter tells them the story of Stalin's escape. In this story, the appearance of Stalin is described as the appearance of Grandfather Frost: during his escape he falls into a river, emerges, and enters the village covered in icicles. The supreme father of the children merges with the female teacher (who played this figure during the celebration), except that he is an authentically marvelous figure, authentically covered in ice, and authentically male. But this light displacement creates the precondition for the aberration, because this real person (Stalin) performs marvelous exploits of which no mere mortal would be capable—he performs a miraculous escape and can surface from a frozen river.

In the narrative that involves the children, Stalin appears as Grandfather Frost. The teacher is but his "disguised" incarnation—in a traditional fairy-tale costume—and the chairman distributing the gifts is the real deputy. At the end of the film the aberration reaches an apotheosis: the boys are really going to Moscow, but it is the girl who meets Stalin on the screen. The film represents this meeting as dreamed, but then Stalin learns of the girl's existence "for real" and invites her to Moscow. The boundaries fade. Life is a realized dream. As the boys tell the girl of their meeting with Stalin in the same red corner, the painted Stalin (from the second fresco) extends his hand toward her from the picture—the final step in the merging of the painted and the real.

Stalin is introduced as an apocryphal figure, as a hero of oral legend and a mythical *bogatyr'*, and his enemies are designated not as political forces but as marvelous enemies—"evil folk." The pipe, Stalin's gift to the hunter who helped him escape, has magical powers; it performs miracles. It blows up a Japanese armored train, for example—the pipe is used to ignite the fuse because the matches are damp. Within this apocryphal story (oral legend is supported by the tone of the hunter's tale, a genre characterized by fabrication and exaggeration), the boys make their own adjustments. Arriving on the banks of the river, they assume poses seen in the school's third fresco: one sits like Sverdlov while the other stands like Stalin reading a letter from Lenin. Through this bodily mimicry, they appropriate the situation, deciding that Stalin's pipe was obviously a gift from Lenin. The pipe thus enters into the circle of objects from Lenin's sacred testament, a status explaining all its magical properties and heightening its symbolic value.

The pipe becomes a classic fetish, and the boys decide to find and appropriate it. They sneak past all the hunters and, finally, set off into the taiga, where the keeper of the pipe lives. The narrative employs a classic psychoanalytic model. From the exposition we know that the young teacher is romantically involved with this very hunter; the boys want to remove the pipe from a competitor, but both hurt their legs—first one falls into a trap laid by the hunter, then the other breaks his leg under the wheel of the same hunter's cart. Following this symbolic castration, the hunter presents the boys with the pipe.

In principle, none of what Kuleshov reveals in this simple plot needs motivation, which could only weaken the radicalism of the perceptual aberrations by subjectivizing them as products of an agitated, infantilized consciousness. But the replacement of objective by subjective point of view is accentuated in the film several times. The first appearance of this subjective, "displaced" view of events comes immediately after the hunter's story: the pipe is multiplied in numerous exposures, and the "ghost" pipes form a circle and spin, as if conveying the boys' vertigo—from the smoke? from the legend? from the proximity of the fetish? In a fog of euphoric delirium, the boys decide to find this pipe, which possesses a part of the official, supreme Grandfather Frost's magical strength. This scene, in a displaced, subjective key, prepares the way for their journey into the forest. The scene of their return from the forest is still more subjective: the camera takes the position of the boy lying on the cart, as he slowly loses consciousness. A pan around the whirling treetops aroused censure at the time for unnatural technique and formalism. In a review of the film, Oleg Leonidov found it unacceptable to show the world from the perspective of any character, not to mention one who is losing consciousness.[14]

This motivation of perspective explained and simultaneously trivialized the apocryphal story, removing from it the veil of solemn mystery. The introduction of a subjective viewpoint compels spectators to question what exactly they have seen. Children's fantasies about a man with a pipe? An analysis of an entire nation's infantile syndrome, in which the nation confuses the boundary between the real and the desired? Or a profanation of that syndrome? Spatial dislocation itself and the purely cinematic linking of perspective to a character's vision had become the expression of deep-seated meaning.

The Siberians and the response to it provide one more demonstration of how spatial figures were perceived as semantic in Soviet cinema of the 1930s and 1940s. This semantization of spatial perception brought together—despite the considerable variations in their individual expressions—Vertov, Eisenstein, Medvedkin, Kuleshov, and his critic Leonidov. Their reconceptualization of the conventions governing the representation of space in film—their use of montage, mock-ups, and emphatically subjective perspective as a means of representing a metaphysical, sacral, or dreamlike reality—should be seen as a fundamental unifying characteristic of the age.

NOTES

1. El Lissitzky, *Prounen Raum, G,* ed. Hans Richter (Berlin, 1923), n.p.

2. Lev Kuleshov, *Kuleshov on Film,* trans. and ed. Ronald Levaco (Berkeley: University of California Press, 1974), 52.

3. Dziga Vertov, *The Cine-Eyes: A Revolution in the Film Factory. Russian and Soviet Cinema in Documents,* eds. Richard Taylor and Ian Christie, trans. Richard Taylor (Cambridge, Mass: Harvard University Press, 1988), 92.

4. Ibid.

5. André Bazin, *The Myth of Stalin in the Soviet Cinema: Bazin at Work. Major Essays and Reviews from the Forties and Fifties,* trans. Alain Piette and Bert Cardullo, ed. Bert Cardullo (New York: Routledge, 1997), 34.

6. For an analysis of this position, see Hans-Jürgen Lehnert, "Vom Literaten zum Barden: Wandlungen im literarischen Leben der UdSSR Mitte der 30er Jahre," *Zeitschrift für Slavistik* 2, no. 36 (1991): 187–95.

7. Vertov's film was not banned, but it went practically unremarked in the press—a remarkable fact after a vigorous prerelease advertising campaign and a premiere slated to coincide with the twentieth anniversary of the October Revolution. On November 1 the film began to show, but on November 6 it was removed from theaters. There was never a written ban on its exhibition. Permission to show it was extended each year until 1950. The few published reviews were positive, but in *Pravda* the film passed unremarked, even though Lebedev-Kuzmach's song was printed there. Vertov received no awards or medals, but as he revealed in his diary, he was awarded a separate apartment (Dziga Vertov, *Stat'i Dnevniki Zamysly* [Moscow: Iskusstvo, 1996], 216).

8. The text of the title reads: "These are songs about the October Revolution: about the woman who has thrown off the chador, about the fact that all this is also Il'ich-Lenin; about the bulb that comes into the *aul* [village], about the water that comes to the desert, about the fact that all this is also Il'ich-Lenin; about the illiterate who have become literate: about the fact that all this is also Il'ich-Lenin." In *Tri pesni o Lenin,* eds. Elizaveta Vertova-Svilova and V. Furtichev (Moscow: Iskusstvo, 1971), 11.

9. Bazin, *Myth of Stalin,* 34.

10. In fiction films of the 1930s, the heroes—the "girl with character" from Iudin's film or a group of pioneers from Kuleshov's Siberians—move between these two points, the periphery and the center. Landscape is not visible in the train compartment windows, and the heroes are unconcerned with the scenes outside. They are traveling to admire the constructed space of the center, Moscow, but wind up in the fantastic space of the imagination, of sleep, of the cinema studio.

11. See Hans Ulrich Gumbrecht, *In 1926: Living at the Edge of Time* (Cambridge, Mass.: Harvard University Press, 1997), 364–72.

12. Marie Seton, *Sergei M. Eisenstein* (New York: Grove Press, 1960), 263.

13. The films of this period often tell the story of a new city arising in an empty space. This motif was not simply the reflection of the building of new cities in the first Five-Year Plans. The films about cities in empty spaces reacted to the new mythology, in which space that was unconnected with the old history affirmed its primacy over time and memory. Thus the old historical center of Moscow was radically reconstructed, and after this, in 1948, a plan surfaced for the transformation of the entire land, including the reversal of the currents of Siberian rivers and the

transformation of deserts into gardens. This radical rejection of preexisting geographical and architectural forms is reflected in films about the construction of new cities. Naturally, their construction is undertaken by young people who cannot be carriers of the old memory, as in Dovzhenko's *Aerograd* (1936), Sergei Gerasimov's *Komsomol'sk* (1938), and Vladimir Petrov's *Peter the Great* (1938), in which Peter decides to build a new capital on an empty spot where there is nothing but swamp. Correctives to this scheme were made on the eve of the Second World War and during that conflict, when films were engaged in creating a new historical memory that would rewrite the past.

14. Oleg Leonidov, "Khudozhnik i sovetskaia tema: O 'Sibiriakakh,'" *Iskusstvo kino* 1 (January 1941): 5–9.

4

"Broad Is My Motherland"

THE MOTHER ARCHETYPE AND SPACE IN THE SOVIET MASS SONG

HANS GÜNTHER

Translated by Sonja Kerby

The famous "Song of the Motherland" from Grigory Aleksandrov's 1936 film *Circus* (Tsyrk) begins with the following words:

Broad is my motherland,
Many are her forests, fields, and rivers!
I know no other such land,
Where so freely does a man breathe.

Such lines are uncharacteristic of the marches of the earlier period following the Russian Revolution of 1917; they call no one to join the class struggle or to rally the ranks around the Party banner. The key to understanding this song lies not in Marxist ideology but in earth mythology, which A. Afanas'ev described as follows: "Primitive tribes recognized Earth as a living being that functioned on its own; they equated expansive lands *[shirokie sushi]* with a gigantic body, saw its bones in solid cliffs and stones, its blood in water, its veins in tree roots, and finally its hair in grass and plants."[1] The 1936 Soviet song is unquestionably about the gigantic body of the motherland, the blood of her rivers, and the hair of her fields and forests. In this song, as in many other phenomena of 1930s culture, something new—the mother archetype—reaches beyond the bounds of the revolutionary epoch and finds expression.

Jungian theory of the archetype provides an approach that combines psychology and mythology and makes it possible to elucidate certain aspects of the profound structure of Soviet culture. Most of all, it aids in analyzing the formation of a circle of basic personages—in Propp's terminology, "dramatis personae"—of Soviet myth.[2] The image of the hero plays the leading role, and much research has already been dedicated to it.[3] The Soviet hero is in essence the man who takes heroic action; he displays outright his will and his ability to act in a great variety of ways: in the struggle, in labor, in construction, in self-sacrifice, in his ability to perfect himself, and so forth. His image is diametrically opposed to the image of the enemy,[4] who acts behind various masks and to whom is ascribed demonic traits.[5] Toward the end of the 1920s, the image of the "wise father," who stands at the head of the mythological pyramid of Soviet culture, took shape. Stalin, as the father of the Great Family, relates to heroes as to his own sons, constantly looking after them, sending them on their way, and giving them valuable directions.[6]

The model of the Great Family as the basis of Soviet myth, however, has not yet been sufficiently examined, because the family trio has lacked one important family member—the mother. Certain cultural phenomena of the thirties in no way come under either the heroic or the father archetype but belong to a third, maternal pole. I have in mind the cult of the motherland and the earth, the flowering of new genres such as the lyrical mass song and the Soviet film comedy, and the emergence of a new image of woman in the fine arts and in the architecture of abundance and fertility at the All-Union Agricultural Exhibition in Moscow.

Where is the essence of the maternal archetype to be found? By what traits can it be distinguished? And how did it enter Soviet culture? The philosophers N. Berdiaev and G. Fedotov considered motherhood the spiritual nucleus of Russian folk belief.[7] According to Fedotov, motherhood is incarnated in three hypostases: "In the circle of heavenly forces is the Mother of God, in the circle of the natural world is the earth, and in patrimonial social life the mother appears on various levels of the cosmic hierarchy of deities as the bearer of a single maternal principle."[8] The following spiritual verse points to the contiguity of a "similar, but not identical, phenomenon":

First mother is the Most Blessed Mother of God,
Second mother is the Moist Earth,
Third mother—this sorrow took.[9]

In studies of Russian religious thought, two lines of maternal principles can be distinguished: the original pagan cult of the mother moist earth *(mat' syraia zemlia)*, which is a variant of the Great Mother religion shared by many peoples,[10] and Christian worship of the Mother of God *(bogoroditsa)*.[11] When Rus' accepted Christianity, the image of the Mother of God *(bogomater')* began to transform the chthonic Mother Earth goddess, a figure that was more accessible to the folk than was masculine Christian monotheism.[12] The process of transformation was eased by the fact that in contrast to the Western church, where the accent was placed on the virginity of Mary, Byzantine tradition emphasized her role as a mother, as is indicated by certain beliefs such as that in *theotokos*, or the Mother of God.

The result is that many traits of the Mother Earth goddess were transferred to the image of the Mother of God in folk religion, though not in church dogma. "The Russian Mother of God is significantly more similar to the 'dear mother moist earth,' who loves and nurtures all of us (Mother of God as World-Spirit *[mirovaia dusha]*, Sophia), than to the historical Virgin Mary."[13] What are the most important features of the Mother Earth goddess? First, one must mention her role as the sign of fertility: "Mother Earth," writes Fedotov, "is foremost the dark bosom that gives birth, the bosom of the earth–wet nurse *[zemlia-kormilitsa]*, of the mother sower *[mater' pakhar']* that is highlighted in the perpetual epithet 'mother moist earth'—mother moist earth, breadgiver *[khleborodnitsa]*."[14] Second, among the folk there exists "an impression of the Mother of God as carnal beauty, for the most part a material beauty, a beauty that makes possible the fulfillment of Divine Logos, of Christ."[15] She signifies that indissoluble connection, which is called sophic, of the divine and the natural worlds.

Though I will not go into detail about the issue of "dual religiosity" *(dvoeverie)*,[16] I want to draw attention to the existence of two lines of the mother archetype in Russian tradition—pagan and Christian. The first pole includes elemental, material aspects (mother moist earth, nature, fertility), and the second, Christian spiritual values proper (love, mercy, intercession for the bereaved).

The introduction of the mother archetype into Soviet culture is linked with the turn to the "folk" *(narod)* and the "motherland" *(rodina)* in the first half of the 1930s. At this time the archetype underwent a profound transformation. Above all, a tendency toward displacing the Christian composition of the archetype and actualizing its folkloric-pagan aspect can be observed.

One could posit that the mother archetype became in its Soviet form the emotional-vegetative basis of life. Positive associations include—speaking in the language in which 1930s culture described itself—love, heart, laughter, joie de vivre, mirth, beauty, and happiness. The vegetative aspect includes fertility, collectivity, and spontaneity. The pathos of fertility arises, not surprisingly, in spite of the demise of real fertility and agricultural productivity after the collectivization of farmland.[17] In its organicity and "warmth," the collectivity of the thirties differed significantly from the utopian class collectivism of the period after the revolution. Folk and family, in particular, were considered organic collectives. In this sense N. Berdiaev speaks about the religiousness "of collective biological warmth" for Russians.[18] Spontaneity appears in Soviet culture in a distinctive, "tamed" form. Incidentally, the same applies even to the corporal, erotic aspects of the mother archetype, aspects that find their expression more in the visual media of the thirties than in mass song.

The scope of this essay does not allow me to trace all the implications of the multipartite process of assimilation of the mother archetype in Soviet culture. Instead, I mention here just one example: the treatment of the archetype by Sergei Eisenstein, especially his film *The General Line (Old and New)* (General'naia liniia [Staroe i novoe], 1928), in which the Christian religion and pagan fertility cults are set against each other in a polemical exchange. A procession of the cross and prayer for rain performed under the icon of the Mother of God over the withered earth turns out to be a futile, fruitless ecstasy. In contrast, Eisenstein portrays a bull and streams of milk in a dream experienced by the heroine Marfa Lapkina—an orgiastic metaphor full of pathos, a metaphor of the fertility that is the foundation of the myth of the copulation of the heavens with the earth.[19] The film, in connection with Eisenstein's essays, provides evidence of the director's intense preoccupation at that time with the problem of psychoanalysis and mythology.[20]

Let me now return to Soviet songs. The flourishing of the mass song is inconceivable without the rise of Soviet film comedies, thanks to which songs of this genre found a huge following. What usually comes to mind first in this regard is the success of Grigory Aleksandrov's 1934 musical comedy *The Jolly Fellows* (Veselye rebiata). It is worth mentioning, however, the less well-known film of the director I. Savchenko, *Accordion* (Garmon', 1934), which was adapted from a poem by A. Zharov. This film sheds light on the reasons why the mass song came into being. In it, the country boy Timosha stops playing the accordion after being chosen leader of the local Komsomol. When he understands that he must compete with the sad kulak songs played by Tosklivy ("Mournful"), he recognizes his mistake in abandoning his accordion, and in the end he gathers the other youths around him with his lively and merry songs.[21] A contemporary Soviet critic understood the usefulness of film musicals to lie in the way they answered the audience's questions and filled the vacant place formerly occupied by hack work or anti-Soviet songs. He asked, "What would a guy in a boat with his beloved sing?" His answer: "Look at those 'dark eyes.' That's what we have to get rid of, and not with administrative prohibition like the *rapmovtsy* did,[22] but with good, captivating songs, funny and lyrical."[23] New songs must be created "for every day, that is to say, for private life."[24]

The mass lyric emerges as the successor to the folk song, transforming its minor mood and motifs of sadness and despondency into intonations of joie de vivre. "The Song of the Volga" (Pesnia o Volge) neatly sums up this thought: "Before our sorrow sang, / But now our joy sings."[25] It is not surprising that the renewal of the folklore tradition—a tradition considered reactionary up until its readoption—took place immediately after the Russian countryside was destroyed by Stalin's campaign to collectivize agriculture.

A genre of song with a new composition in which traits of folk songs were united with elements of jazz songs and light, optimistic marches gained recognition only after the RAPM line on the ascetic revolutionary song had been overcome.[26] In this vein, a contemporary author criticized the "monotonous intonation, fanfare, and bombastic stamp that is so characteristic of many of our mass songs, with their incessant stilted 'heroics,' narrowness of composition, [and] lack of melodic simplicity and expressiveness, of rich and beauteous lyrics, attractive romance, good humor, etc."[27]

Beginning in 1934, such more strictly musical concerns began to crowd out ideology per se as the main principle of composition. According to Grigory Aleksandrov, the songs of Dunaevsky and Lebedev-Kumach were genuine folk songs because they expressed "the innermost feelings and thoughts" of the Soviet people.[28] The new songs focused, in the words of a contemporary critic, on "love of country, the pride of the freed masses, and the happy childhood and youth of the October generation."[29] The critic added that "the theme of nation *[strana]*, of the happy motherland, is revealed from its lyrical side and becomes, as the listener's personal song of the motherland, an emotional instrument in his consciousness."[30] These characteristics of Dunaevsky's songs in all their details support the proposition that the flourishing of the mass song reflects a profound change in the spiritual atmosphere of Soviet culture. The emergence of the mother archetype lies at the foundation of this change.

What are the special characteristics of this new genre of song? It tends toward the lyric rather than the epic, generally lacking a plot. Instead of action and a cast of characters, emotionally saturated portraiture of the motherland dominates. In the majority of instances, its lyrical "we" differs from the collective subject of proletarian poetry in that it signifies the entire Soviet people *(narod)*,[31] understood as a "common body," a "superorganism."[32]

The "we" of the mass song appears not in the form of a collective, homogeneous in class and ideology, but as a sense of community best expressed by the German term *Gemeinschaft*—something felt in the heart rather than perceived by reason. It is no coincidence that the word "heart" is encountered often in the songs of the thirties. The frequency with which this word appears points toward a phenomenon we might call (somewhat oxymoronically) the "intimate mass." In the first lyrical songs, the meaningfulness and unprecedented newness of this word is accentuated. "Heart, how good that you are like this! / Thank you, heart, for being able to love so!" (LK 253). It is not surprising that "The Song of the Heart" (Pesnia o serdtse) from the film *The Jolly Fellows* was welcomed with delight. It belongs to the genre of "songs not about one's own love,"[33] in that it is addressed not to a specific person but to the masses. The heart is that place where the personal (love, happiness) is crossed with the universal (Moscow as "the heart of the land" *[serdtse Rodiny]*). The heart is that point of view with which the collective lyrical subject regards the surrounding "native" *(rodnoi)* world.

Behind its lack of organized plot, the mass song has a kaleidoscopic structure in which the various mythic ideograms *(shifry)* are integrated into a single whole. Shifts from one unit to another in a mass song happen smoothly and imperceptibly, resulting in a structure not along the lines of montage but more as if the individual pieces were seamlessly pasted together. I use the term "ideogram" to point to the fact that the song does not unfold the myths so much as allude to them in an abbreviated manner. The ideograms introduce such topoi as the motherland, Moscow, the border *(granitsa)*, the road, the enemy, youth, the heart, happiness, and laughter. Thus, the mass song functions as a concentrated version of Soviet mythology. Besides the presence of ideograms, one is struck by the song's superabundance of emotions, which are expressed in a profusion of established epithets, such as native *(rodnoi)*, dear *(milyi)*, free *(vol'nyi)*, broad, and merry. Inasmuch as the stock of topoi and epithets is limited, one can posit that each song is in essence like the design seen through a kaleidoscope—a unique arrangement of stock clichés into a particular dominant theme.

The spatial model of the mass song repeats in general terms the structure of the myth of Soviet space. As we will see, however, it has its own specifics. In the center is the image of the motherland, which appears in various guises but is always linked to maternal principles. The motherland is an enormous female body that embodies the foundation of the life of the people *(narod)*. Isakovskii's poem "Earth" (Zemlia) directly calls to mind the mythological aspect of the motherland: "Was it not you who were imprisoned the entire century, / Birth mother, moist earth."[34] The "Song of the Motherland" from the film *Circus* (Tsyrk) goes: "Like a bride our motherland we love; / We will preserve it as our tender mother" (LK 254).

The people *(narod)* are related to the mother figure by playing the roles of heroic sons and daughters: "We go, we go, joyful friends, / Our country, like a mother, calls and loves us!" (LK 297). Brought up by the motherland, the Soviet hero is fated to eternal youth, while Stalin is always given the place of a wise "father" and "teacher."[35] This kind of infantilization goes even further in the mass song:[36] "We can sing and be daring like children" ("March of the Jolly Fellows" [Marsh veselykh rebiat]), and "Ardently we love and sing like children" ("March of the Enthusiasts" [Marsh entuziastov]).[37] Against the background of universal family happiness, lyrical regression has no limit.

Whereas looking at the motherland "from within" prevailed in songs of the 1930s, postwar songs added a curious variant to this theme when the Soviet motherland began to be regarded "from without"—though only in order to uphold its superiority once again. A song about migratory birds includes the exclamation,

I remain with you,
Forever my native country!
I need not the Turkish shore,
Nor do I need Africa! [Is. 300]

We should also call to mind the famous lines, "A nice country is Bulgaria, / But Russia is the best of them all" (Is. 247), as well as A. Zharov's song:

On holiday the warrior young
Dreams not of Carpathia beyond the border
But of the Volga, of his faraway home;
To his motherland his thoughts fly.[38]

The motherland appears to us as "boundless" *(neob"iatnaia),* "vast" *(obshirnaia),* and "enormous," and the Soviet nation *(strana)* as "broad," "large," and so forth. As D. S. Likhachev thought, "melancholia because of spaciousness" is characteristic of lyrical, drawn-out *(protiazhnye)* folk songs.[39] The mass song not only adopts from the folk song the motif of broad expanse but also gives it new meaning. This becomes especially clear when one looks at the motif of the "wide," "far" road associated with it, another motif that comes from Russian folklore.

The movement toward a faraway place characteristic of mass songs of the thirties differs from that in folk songs in that during the thirties the road is always lit up with optimism and has definite meaning and singleness of purpose:[40] "Well, how can we resist striking up a song, if all is going forward / And the road is straight and bright?" (LK 262). Here are a few more examples:

A warming of the heart begins:
It is clear and bright as far as the eye can see,
Neither is there darkness nor decay.
—from "Pour Out, Song of Mine!" (Leisia, pesnia moia!) (LK 267)

Wide and bright, before us lay
Our path, our road.
—from "Song of the Tourists" (Pesnia turistov) (LK 300)

O road, road, road!
Lead us, O road, forward!
—from "Song of the Road" (Dorozhnaia pesnia) (LK 309)

Sometimes movement across space takes on the hyperbolic proportions of fairy tale. For example, in "Dear Little Road" (Dorozhen'ka), taken down from the collective farmer P. Semenova, the motif of the road is connected to the Soviet mythology of miracle: "Dear little road bright with the dawn, bright, / It leads to the victory-miracle" (Ant. 118). Or in Isakovsky:

You march through the country. And all her roads
Before you Mother Earth opens up
As under your feet she rolls out carpets,
The broad fields of the collective farms.

The song concludes with the words:

Your road goes to the sun.
You march through the country.
And there are no barriers
That can halt your march. [Is. 113]

The Soviet slogan "forward and upward" combines with a folkloric motif that gives it a new direction. Upward movement, of course, is easily associated with aviator mythology. In "March of the Parachutists" (Marsh parashiutistov) we read:

We will go higher
To the roof of the sky,
The blue arches of the ceiling!

It continues:

And high,
A real falcon,
My motherland stands in the sky. [LK 311–12]

The country is not only limitless *(neob"iatna)* in its breadth, but the heroic deeds of the falcons also raise the "roof," the "ceiling" of the Soviet motherland.

The road without barriers easily combines with the Soviet motif of the fulfilled dream, which was already formulated in P. German's 1920 "Aviamarch": "We are born to make fairy tales reality, / To overcome space and expanse."[41] In the thirties, however, enthusiasm for technology yielded to a new lyrical spirit. Instead of the neutral "expanse" *(prostor)*, we now have the "broad expanse of the motherland" *(shirokii prostor rodiny)*. The previous era allowed for poetic images such as the replacement of the heart with a "burning motor" (by analogy with the cliché of traditional love poetry, the burning heart); in the thirties, such an image was out of place, given the new potential meanings of the word "heart" that had been opened up. Similarly, the dream motif takes a different form in songs of the thirties—for example: "What we dream and desire, we will achieve; / Straight to the sun our daring will break through!" (LK 292). "Song of the Volga" provides another example:

> We are moving both the mountains and the rivers,
> The time of fairy tales has come to life,
> And along the Volga, free forever,
> The boats are sailing to Moscow. [LK 290]

In addition, the crimson stars in "March of the Enthusiasts" are twinkling over all the lands "of fulfilled dreams" (Ant. 113).

The broad country and the open road, so dear to the songs of the thirties, express other metaphorical meanings in the language of space.[42] Mythological space carries with it a multitude of marked connotations. Dostoevsky's claim that "we are broad, broad like our little mother Russia" underlines a well-known trait of the Russian national character.[43] The words "broad" *(shirokii)* and "free" or "open" *(vol'nyi)*, which in Russian are associated with unlimited, free movement in space, spontaneity, and unbridled revelry, are both established epithets in the mass song. For example, one song describes the broad motherland "where so freely breathes man" (LK 253), and another asserts, "We grow so much broader and more free; / We go so much farther and more boldly" (LK 262).

It is no accident that "breadth" and "freedom" are often linked to the river Volga. It is so, for example, in "Song of the Motherland": "Everywhere life is free and broad, / Flows just like the full Volga" (LK 253). And in "Song of the Volga" one hears: "And, like the Volga, the powerful river, / Our free life began to flow." Let me also cite the refrain:

> Beauty of the people,
> Full of water, like the sea,
> Like the motherland free,
> Broad,
> Deep,
> Strong. [LK 290]

In these lines one can see the direct allusion to folk songs about the Volga—for instance, to the song "Hey, Let's Make a Bang!" (Ei, ukhnem!), in which the barge drivers call, "Hey you, Volga, mother river, / Wide and deep." We should recall that according to mythological understanding, a river is the blood vessel of a country, the artery through which the blood flows from the heart to various organs of the earth's body. The established attributes of the Volga glorify the spontaneous energy of the Russian people. It is no coincidence that "Song of the Volga" invokes the names of the rebels Stepan Razin and Yemelyan Pugachev.

How does the people's spontaneity expressed in the mass song coexist with the educational drive of the Bolsheviks? How is it reconciled with the Leninist need to reign in spontaneity for the good of the Party consciousness? Readopting the mother archetype results in the well-known reaccentuation whereby mythology displaces ideology to a significant extent. Ideological goals remain strong in principle, but they are held by the frame of the lyrical song only with difficulty, because they do not correspond to the song's laws of genre and archetype. The word "Party" has no place in the family model of society, and fields are rarely called "collective." Songs of the thirties are not geared toward ideological education but direct the spontaneous sources of the people's energy, which up until that time had been criticized as reactionary in the context of Soviet culture.

The feminine nature of the song genre not only contradicts the political terminology but also significantly limits the role of the father image in the mass song. Songs invoked the name of Stalin, of course, and there were songs about him ("On Stalin wise, native, and loved / A beautiful song the folk composes"), but the father archetype cannot occupy the dominant place in lyrical song and therefore often is only metaphorically or implicitly present. We find an appropriate symbolic allusion to serve as an example in "Lullaby," where the syntactic parallelism suggests that the sun is Stalin:

> The free sun warmth gives you;
> The land-mother embraces you;
> Joy awaits you, and songs, and laughter;
> My little one, you are happiest of all. [LK 270]

Similarly, the new song of the Volga "is warmed by the Soviet sun" (LK 291).

As the mother archetype predominates in the mass song, so the role of technology and machines is downplayed. Very often technical objects underlie folkloric poeticization. Tractors turn into "war" horses and "steel" horses (LK 93), planes into "steel falcons" (Ant. 127; LK 275). Pilots simply fly "as falcons" or "as eagles" in the clouds. The epithet "steel" indicates the "masculine" nature of technology, which it links to "steel" and "iron" heroes and to the firm hand of the father ("of Stalin").[44]

The striving of thirties culture toward "broad synthesis" in all spheres of life affected even the mass song. Therefore, one often meets such formulas of synthesis of feminine and masculine principles, of earth and machine, as the following: "With songs of victory thunder / The factories and fields" (Ant. 127); "My factories are being built; / My forests are making sounds" (LK 275); "And city, and factory, and plowed field— / all this is our dear and native home" (LK 298). In general, however, syntheses of this kind were less characteristic of songs than of the films and written literature of the thirties.

Attributing fertility to the earth, the Soviet song continues the cult of the mother moist earth. Corresponding to mythological presentations, "inexhaustible maternity" is peculiar to the earth,[45] which is why the earth is often considered "self-fertilizing,"[46] not requiring insemination. The mass song abounds with pictures of fertility:

Blooming are the vast
Collectivized fields. Huge, beloved,
Lies my earth. [LK 275]

Sometimes mythic parallels establish ties between people and nature:

Shining gold in the field is the rye,
Ripening;
Making merry are the youths,
Smiling. [LK 276]

Like an ear of rye, our joy ripens! [LK 292]

Not for nothing do our flowers and children grow,
And our cloudy fields of rye ear up. [LK 297]

A single time of year dominates—spring. In "Song of the Motherland" we hear that "over the country the spring wind blows; / With each day it is so much more joyful to live" (LK 254). In "Song of the

Volga" we learn that "over the country spring has bloomed," and "happiness, like May, is young" (LK 290–91). In "Katyusha" the image is "the apple and pear trees were blossoming" (Is. 154). In the motif of spring, parallelism between the general and the personal also operates. Spring, as the time of love, is associated with the blooming of nature and the entire country.

In the 1930s, Moscow became the sacred center of the Soviet motherland, continuing the centuries-old tradition of singing the praises of mother Moscow: "Moscow is mother to all cities."[47] A number of songs dedicated to the capital stress sentiment coming from "the heart." The song "Our Moscow" is about "this city dear to the heart," about how "we are all in our hearts Muscovites," and about how "everywhere we are in our hearts united with faraway Moscow" (LK 273). Moscow is "the heart of the Soviet land" (Ant. 172) and "the heart of my motherland" (LK 274). The swineherdess and the shepherd in Ivan Pyr'ev's film of that title meet, not by accident, in the capital: "And as the rivers meet in the sea, / So do people meet in Moscow" (Ant. 23). The two never forget each other, because they became friends in that particular town.

The same attributes that are ascribed to the country as a whole are ascribed to Moscow. Like the country, Moscow is young:

How old is the beauty Moscow?
They say she is seventy.
And she will never age;
She will grow young and increase.[48]

In Moscow are the same "broad spaces," but everything there is still better, still more beautiful: "City-wonder, fairy-tale city, / Our beautiful Moscow."[49] The city is always depicted in a lyrical light. In song, Moscow, as the embodiment of the mother archetype, is not the empire of the "Third Rome." The Kremlin does not even figure as a place for "the father," Stalin, but is represented purely for atmosphere. Moscow unites and reflects in itself all the best qualities of the motherland in a condensed, heightened form. The All-Union Agricultural Exhibition of 1939 provides the best proof of this; there, life pulsates "from Moscow to the very outskirts" (LK 253) and back again from the periphery to the center. If the river Volga symbolizes the "blood," the spontaneous energy, of the huge body of the motherland, then Moscow is its heart.

In contrast to the unbounded free expanse of the steppes and fields in folklore, the space of the Soviet song cannot be imagined without a clear impression of the borders that separate the "enemies" surrounding Russia from the motherland. Therefore, defense of the boundary is a holy matter. In particular, the lines separating the Soviet Union from the West and the Far East are not simply state boundaries, "they are . . . the main lines where heroism can manifest itself."[50] An entire genre of songs about frontier guards existed.[51] One song offers a greeting from Katyusha "To the Soldier at a Faraway Frontier" (Is. 154). In another, "a frontier guard marches from his post" and asks a young lady by a well for water (Is. 157). A pilot-falcon returns from the Far East "on the little road through the fields" to "his native land *[rodnaia storona]*" (Is. 159). "At the very frontier" stands a fellow who speaks "from the heart with his native lands" (Is. 170). In Pyr'ev's film *Tractor Drivers* (Traktoristy), "three tank drivers, three merry friends" arrive in the motherland from the Far East (Ant. 207). It stands to reason that in this genre, lyricism is sometimes less important than depiction of the heroic feats of the motherland's defenders.

What lies beyond the borders is unknown. It is antispace, home of the enemy, a creature without a face or with the face of a beast. Even the jolly fellows are prepared to stand up with a war song against the enemy if he "wants to snatch away our lively joy" (LK 252). In "Song of the Volga," enemies prowl the border "like hungry wolves" (LK 291), and in A. Sofronov's song "As by the Oak" (Kak u duba), the Cossacks swear, "Neither the earth nor the little grass nor this expanse of ours / Will foreign enemies remain alive to see" (Ant. 145). In pre–World War II songs the foreign enemy appears as the antagonist pitted against the border-guard hero and as a threat to the Great Family. Of the internal enemy-villain the songs say absolutely nothing. Acknowledgment of his existence would contradict the picture of universal happiness too much, as would any depiction of the "antispace" of the labor camps.

Finally, it is essential to discuss the picture that the mass song creates of itself. The intensive self-reflexivity of the mass song is striking;[52] it constantly thematizes itself and the great force it is in life. Self-reflexive statements were particularly important in the period when this new type of song was vying for the right to exist. For example, in one stanza of "March of the Jolly Fellows," they sing, "A merry song makes the heart light; / It will never make you bored." And the chorus goes:

Songs help us live and build society,
A song is like a friend, it calls us and leads us,
And the one who strides through life with a song
Will never and nowhere have to take a fall. [LK 251]

These lines are strikingly innovative in that here it is not the Party that leads and helps to build society; instead, it is the song that calls like a friend. Even work is transformed into song: "How could we resist striking up a song in a young country / Where work sounds out in song?" (LK 262). "Song of the Tractor Drivers" (Pesnia traktoristov) directly bridges the magic tie between singing and agricultural productivity:

Our strength is everywhere ripening
And when the young strike up a song,
All the wheat in the fields joins in singing;
The rye grown high too joins the song. [LK 297]

The Soviet motherland is a singing country. May "pours out songs without bounds over the beauty, Moscow," and "The entire Soviet country / sings and dances" (LK 274). In addition, "I sing a song to everyone / And each repeats after me" (LK 275). While song spreads itself across space, it is helped by the birds in spreading upward, filling the aerial space. "With the aid of a young eagle" it flies into the clouds, "with the aid of a light seagull" it skims over the water, and "with the help of a nightingale" it rings out about the native land (LK 266).

Song is always accompanied by the impression of lightness:

And the swallow song
Flies above the water,
Oh, to float easy,
Oh, to sing easy! [LK 293]

The song itself is "light," and from it one becomes "light of heart." With its joie de vivre, song lightens work, construction, all of life. Thus, the mass song expresses the entire complex of optimistic feelings that swept over Soviet culture in a wave beginning in 1934.

It was not only song that abounded in happiness and laughter; so did the poetry, journalism, and film of the time. Stalin's expression "Life has become better, comrades. Life has become merrier" became famous.

Is it possible that all these merry songs were merely responses to a new slogan? Of course, some songs were simply amplifications of some slogan or other.[53] But we must take into account that Stalin's "decree of happiness" did not come at the beginning of the wave of lyric songs; it is from his speech at the Stakhanovite congress in November 1935. We should not forget that a year earlier, the release of "March of the Jolly Fellows" provoked heated discussion, as did the appearance of any new genre in Soviet comedic film.

All of this shows how the mass song was born from a deeper stratum of the social psyche. It would be naive to think that Soviet culture grew from a foundation of ideological slogans alone. Stalin's utterances served more to express and give strength to an atmosphere that had already developed. Therefore, I have tried to explain the rise of the mass song, along with other cultural phenomena of the 1930s, in terms of its profound contribution to the psycho-mythological character of the time. A new type of lyric song sank its roots into the Russian folk tradition and became a bearer of positive emotions and vital, vegetative wealth. We can now understand it as one of the forms in which the mother archetype coming into being found expression.

Songs modeled Soviet space in a specifically lyric manner. The motherland forms the thematic nucleus of the mass song, which then spotlights the motherland from the point of view of the heart. Consequently, in these songs all phenomena turn out to be native and dear. The prevailing optimistic mood culminates in the song itself, which fills up space both outward and upward with its light voice. The motherland is a space for singing.

Furthermore, the motherland appears in the light of mythology, borrowed to a great extent from Russian folklore. The immense country is an enormous maternal body with blooming fields and deep rivers full of strength for life. The country opens up wide roads, clear to the farthest distance, roads along which young people freely stride. This entire picture calls to mind the chronotope of the idyll. Against the background of bountiful nature, where spring eternally reigns, young people—that is, people who are growing older but who love and nurture their earth mother—live free and easy in complete harmony. The young people, the earth mother, and the wise father—all of them together form the happy Great Family. An intimate connection unites people and nature. The motherland sings, and bread abounds.

NOTES

1. A. Afanas'ev, *Poeticheskie vozzreniia slavian na prirodu* (1865; reprint, Moscow: Indrik, 1994), 1:138.

2. Vladimir Propp, *Morphology of the Folktale*, trans. Laurence Scott (Austin: University of Texas Press, 1968).

3. See H. Günther, *Der sozialistische Übermensch: M. Gor'kij und der sowjetische Heldenmythos* (Stuttgart: Weimar, 1993); idem, "Russkii perevod glavy o geroiakhletchikakh pod zaglaviem 'Stalinskie sokoly' (Analiz mifa 30-kh godov)," *Voprosy literatury* 11–12 (1991): 122–41.

4. See E.M. Meletinskii, *O literaturnykh arkhetipakh* (Moscow: Rossiiskii gos. gumanitarnyi universitet, In-t vysshikh gumanitarnykh issledovanii, 1994), 36.

5. See H. Günther, "Der Feind in der totalitaren Kultur," in *Kultur im Stalinismus*, ed. Von G. Gorzka (Bremen: Temmen, 1994), 89–100.

6. See Katerina Clark, *The Soviet Novel: History as Ritual* (Chicago: University of Chicago Press, 1981), 114–35.

7. N. Berdiaev, *Sud'ba Rossii* (1918; reprint, Moscow: Sov. pisatel', 1990), 1–29; idem, *Russkaia ideia* (Paris: YMCA Press, 1971), 10, 254 (translated as *The Russian Idea* by R. M. French [New York: Macmillan, 1948]); G. P. Fedotov, *Stikhi dukhovnye* (Moscow: Progress: Gnosis, 1991), 65–78; idem, *Mat'-zemlia (k religioznoi kosmologii russkogo naroda)*, in *Sud'ba i grekhi Rossii* (St. Petersburg: Sofiia, 1992), 2: 66–82; idem, *The Russian Religious Mind* (New York, Evanston, London: Harper, 1960), 12–13, 360–61.

8. G. P. Fedotov, *Stikhi dukhovnye*, 78.

9. Fedotov, *Stikhi dukhovnye*, 78. "Sorrow" refers to the torment of giving birth.

10. See C. G. Jung, "Die psychologischen Aspekte des Mutterarchetyps," in *Gessammelte Werke*, vol. 9, part 1 (Olten: Walter, 1967), 91–123; E. Neumann, *Die Große Mutter: Eine Phänomenologie der weiblichen Gestalttypen des Unbewußten* (Olten: Walter, 1989).

11. Translator's note: Because of the distinction between the Western figure of the Virgin Mary and the Russian *bogoroditsa, bogoroditsa* is uniformly translated as "Mother of God." This is is still an approximation because it elides the emphasis that the root *-rod* places on the act of giving birth to Christ.

12. See S. Smirnov, *Drevne-russkii dukhovnik: Issledovanie po istorii tserkovnogo byta* (Moscow: Sinodal'naia Tipografiia, 1913), 264; D. Samarin, "Bogoroditsa v russkom narodnom pravoslavii," *Russkaia mysl'* 3–4 (1918): 10; J. Hubbs, *Mother Russia: The Feminine Myth in Russian Culture* (Bloomington: Indiana University Press, 1988), 99.

13. Samarin, "Bogoroditsa," 25.

14. Fedotov, *Stikhi dukhovnye*, 71.

15. Samarin, "Bogoroditsa," 19.

16. See Smirnov, *Drevne-russkii dukhovnik*, 255–56.

17. V. Papernyi, *Kul'tura dva* (Ann Arbor, Mich.: Ardis, 1985), 135.

18. Berdiaev, *Sud'ba Rossii*, 10.

19. See citations from the work of Eisenstein under the heading "Gundproblem" in V. V. Ivanov, *Ocherki po istorii semiotiki v SSSR* (Moscow: Nauka, 1976), 224.

20. See S. Eisenshtein, *Izbrannye proizvedeniia v 6-i tomakh* (Moscow: Iskusstvo, 1966), 3:74–75, 82–83; see also H. J. Schlegel, "Altes und Neues in der ideoästetischen Generallinie S. M. Eisensteins," in *S. M. Eisenstein: Schriften* (Munich: C. Hanser, 1984), 4: 27–30.

21. See R. Iurenev, *Sovetskaia kinokomediia* (Moscow: Nauka, 1964), 193–95.

22. The term *rapmovtsy* refers to members of RAPM, the Rossiiskaia Assotsiatsiia Proletarskikh Muzykantov, or Russian Association of Proletarian Musicians.

23. I. Savchenko, "Pravo zapet'. K postanovke kinooperetty 'Garmon' i 'Irinkin rekord,'" *Sovetskoe kino* 5 (1934): 59.

24. Ibid.

25. V. Lebedev-Kumach, *Izbrannoe* (Moscow: Khudozh. lit-ra, 1984), 290. Future references to this work are indicated in the text with the initials LK and the page number.

26. On the rise of Soviet song, see A. N. Sokhor, *Russkaia sovetskaia pesnia* (Leningrad: Sovetskii kompozitor, 1959), chapter 6.

27. G. Khubov, "Za massovuiu pesniu, za massovuiu simfoniiu," *Sovetskaia muzyka* 2 (1934): 4.

28. "G. Aleksandrov, I. Dunaevskii, and V. Lebedev-Kumach," *Iskusstvo kino* 6 (1938): 8.

29. M. Iankovskii, "Master massovoi pesni," *Sovetskoe kino* 6 (1934): 57.

30. Ibid.

31. Compare Sokhor, *Russkaia sovetskaia pesnia,* 181.

32. Iu. I. Mineralov, *Tak govorila derzhava: XX vek i russkaia pesnia* (Moscow: Literaturnyi in-t im. A. M. Gor'kogo, 1995), 101.

33. N. Korzhavin, "O tom, kak veselilis' rebiata v 1934 godu, ili Kak inogda oblegchaet zhizn' vysokii esteticheskii printsip: Vazhno ne 'chto?' a 'kak?'" *Voprosy literatury* 5 (1995): 52.

34. M. Isakovskii, *Izbrannoe* (Moscow: Gos. izd-vo Khudozh. lit-ry, 1950), 147. Further reference to this volume is made in the text with the abbreviation "Is." followed by the page number.

35. See Günther, *Der sozialistische Übermensch,* 179–83.

36. On infantilization, see E. Dobrenko, "Vse luchshee detiam (Totalitarnaia kul'tura i mir detstva)," *Wiener Slawistischer Almanach* 29 (1992): 159–74.

37. *Antologiia sovetskoi pesni* (Moscow: Gos. inuzykal'noe izd-vo, 1957), 2: 113. Further reference to this volume is made in the text with the abbreviation "Ant." followed by the page number.

38. A. Zharov, *Stikhi. Pesni. Poemy* (Moscow: Khudozh. lit-ra, 1964), 150.

39. D. S. Likhachev, *Zemlia rodnaia* (Moscow: Prosveshchenie, 1983), 53.

40. Regarding mass songs of the thirties, see V. Skvoznikov, "Po povodu odnogo abzatsa (o massovoi pesne 30-x godov)," *Voprosy literatury* 8 (1990): 6–8.

41. A. Shilov, ed., *Tsveti, strana sovetskaia: Pesennik* (Moscow: Izdatel'stvo muzyka, 1967), 13.

42. Iu. M. Lotman writes about how artistic space models nonspatial values in "Problemy khudozhestvennogo prostranstva v proze Gogolia" in the book of his collected articles *Izbrannye stat'i* (Tallinn: Aleksandra, 1992), 1: 414.

43. F. M. Dostoevsky, *Polnoe sobranie sochinenii v 30-i tomax* (Leningrad: Nauka, 1976), 15: 129 (from *The Brothers Karamazov*) and 6: 378 (from *Crime and Punishment*).

44. On the mythological figure of the "iron" hero, see Günther, *Sozialistische Übermensch,* 195–97.

45. M. Eliade, *Die Religionen und das Heilige* (Frankfurt: Suhrkamp, 1986), 300.

46. See Hubbs, *Mother Russia,* xiv, 54.

47. V. Dal', *Poslovitsy russkogo naroda* (Moscow: Khudozh. lit-ra, 1984), 1: 258.

48. Zharov, *Stikhi,* 288.

49. S. Alymov, *Izbrannoe* (Moscow: Voenizdat, 1953), 97.

50. Skvoznikov, "Po povodu odnogo abzatsa," 14.

51. See Mineralov, *Tak govorila derzhava,* 75–80.

52. Svetlana Boym, *Common Places: Mythologies of Everyday Life in Russia* (Cambridge, Mass.: Harvard University Press, 1994), 110.

53. Mineralov, *Tak govorila derzhava,* 97.

5

The Art of Totality

BORIS GROYS
Translated by Mary A. Akatiff

It perhaps sounds banal to assert that the main function of totalitarian ideology is a striving for totality. Nevertheless, this claim seems to be necessary when one hears and reads that the most important goals of the totalitarianism of the 1930s were the creation of societal homogeneity and the exclusion of the other. For the other was not only negated, repressed, and deemed worthy of decimation in the totalitarian ideology of that time. Mere exclusion of the other would have left something outside of totality—even if that something were just nothingness—so that the totality would have ceased being a totality. The other was the enemy and was not to be excluded but to be fought actively. By this fight, the other, the enemy, was permanently reproduced. And it was exactly this permanent struggle with the other that constituted the totality of the world for the totalitarian ideology of the time.

In the remarks that follow I consider the aesthetics of totality, focusing first on Stalinist and National Socialist painting and then on Stalinist architecture. Totality here does not mean uniformity or homogeneity of any kind but rather a total struggle of all oppositions against each other, a struggle that simultaneously unites these oppositions by making them part of a single world event. Not coincidentally, the famous "law of unity and the battle of opposites" was the central tenet of the dialectical materialism that functioned as the official ideology in Stalin's time. Political enemies were united through the permanent struggle of the material, productive forces they embodied. It was indeed this struggle alone—one that involved all oppositions and then let them fight one another—that created a total space allowing nothing outside of itself to exist.

Such visions of a totalizing, overarching struggle from which no one and nothing can exclude itself define all totalitarian ideologies of the thirties. The other became, as the enemy, a part of the totalizing whole, inasmuch as everybody was forced into the struggle. The only position truly excluded from totalitarian ideology was that of nonparticipation in the struggle—that is, a metaposition of pure contemplation. The total struggle, be it the struggle of the exploited classes against the exploiting classes or the struggle of the Aryan against the non-Aryan, could not actually be described from the outside. Nature itself could no longer be described with the neutrality of science, that is, "metaphysically," because science itself was split in two by the totalizing struggle: into a proletarian and a nonproletarian science or into an Aryan and a non-Aryan one.

History as well could no longer be understood, described, or classified into periods through the kind of neutral historical consciousness once attempted by Hegel's system. Through the battle of opposites, all periods of world history were synchronized, and the historical distance that might have made historical judgment possible was abolished: every historical description was seen as a contemporary position statement in the battle of opposites. The struggle itself was understood as the internal and continually self-reproducing engine of history.

Especially for the Soviet and National Socialist ideologies of the 1930s, every single individual was always already involved in a world-scale battle, in a world war that both defined and dominated every place on earth as well as every epoch of world history. Above all, this was a political-aesthetic struggle, in that one fought for dominion over signs—that is, for the privilege of ascribing to these signs one's own meaning. To be even more exact, this struggle took place on two different, though closely related, levels. On the first level, the struggle was to (re)claim the means necessary for aesthetic production—the artistic practices that could in no way be left to the enemy. A specific ideological significance had to be ascribed to all the images, devices, and forms found in the history of art. In turn, these ascriptions served to regulate the concrete use of art in all forms. Indeed, the battle for dominion over the historical heritage of art marks the split between the totalitarian aesthetes and the ideologies of the avant-garde, who practiced historical asceticism and were prepared to give up the entire pictorial vocabulary of the art historical tradition in order to relegate it to the past. From the perspective of total battle, however, this avant-garde ascetic position must be seen as mere defeatism. In contrast, the totalitarian aesthetes attempted to become proficient in the use of all historical art forms in order to utilize them strategically in actual battle.[1]

On the second level, the goal of the battle for dominion over signs was the conquest not only of time but also of space. The creation of any image, the erection of any building, the composition of any literary text could never be a neutral aesthetic act: it represented either victory or defeat in the battle for symbolic occupation of space. Works of totalitarian art do not describe the world—they occupy the world. The aim of totalitarian art is to fill the largest possible territory with specific signs that are identifiable as "our" signs, in contrast to "their" signs, or the signs of the enemy power. Thus, totalitarian art always makes itself present within the context of the total battle. It celebrates its victories and feels ashamed of its defeats according to the attendant territorial gains or losses. Indeed, totalitarian art is structurally incapable of reflecting on its own contextuality, in that it does not allow for a neutral worldview that would allow for such reflection.

Even when describing the enemy, totalitarian art must remain "partisan"; that is, the description always remains "our description of the enemy" and never becomes "a self-description by the enemy." Any theoretical reflection on totalitarian culture must therefore take into account the aggressive impetus behind it. The contrast between totalitarian art and other art movements is to be found not primarily on the level of the signifiers—in the form or the syntactic structure of image or text, as with the case of avant-garde art—but rather on the level of the aggressive appropriation of these signifiers and the ensuing occupation of them by ideological meaning. Only by investigating the ideological use of the artistic signifiers that have been taken from the archive of the art historical heritage can one expose the actual achievement of totalitarian art.

Painting Totality: The Painted Image as Virtual Photography

The art that was officially promoted and celebrated in the 1930s and 1940s in countries that were under totalitarian rule, such as the Soviet Union, Germany, and Italy, has remained until the present day suspect for an aesthetic consciousness raised in the tradition of modernism. Such art lacks any established position in the history of twentieth-century art. One seldom finds "totalitarian" art in present-day museums. As a rule, its authors and works are not discussed. And because recognition by the art world depends on the rules of its discourse, the very status of such pieces as works of art is rejected through this silence. Thus, the officially established art of totalitarian states presents a rare example in today's cultural context—in a world where otherwise "anything goes"—of a truly irreducible other. Only in the last few years has the situation begun to change.

The public's attitude toward totalitarian art has a certain moral motivation that would be difficult to contradict. In every totalitarian state, art was used as propaganda for the countries' respective leading ideologies, and the artists who actively participated in this propaganda took on a certain level of responsibility for the effects of these—in many ways—devastating ideologies. However, the strategies of exclusion on the part of canonized art history rest, in this instance, more on aesthetic than on ethical grounds.

Many leading artists of the twentieth century sensed their closeness to various outgrowths of communism or fascism, and many publicly admitted to such affinity. That barely tarnished their reputations. Moreover, the artists of the Russian avant-garde, who actively advertised for the Soviet powers, did indeed receive their earned place in the historical canon of art in that century. This was also the case with the Italian futurists, who demonstrated their loyalty to Italian fascism. The real problem in dealing with totalitarian art is posed by works that are held to express the seemingly premodern or antimodern sentiments of classicism, realism, or naturalism. As a rule, political dictatorships are judged more leniently when they have accelerated the history of art: we tend to forgive the tyrants of the Italian Renaissance many of their crimes because they were promoting aesthetically progressive art. We absolutely never forgive tyrants with retrograde aesthetic tastes.

Therefore, the value of totalitarian art is much more an aesthetic question than a moral one. In the end, we are dealing with the issue of how the aesthetics promoted by the totalitarian regimes of the thirties and forties should be judged in art-historical terms. Does totalitarian art, despite everything, belong to the history of modern art in the twentieth century? Crucial to such a judgment is an exact agreement about what we mean when we speak of the totalitarian in totalitarianism. For the purposes of this essay, it will suffice to establish that despite all the differences among individual totalitarian states, and despite the many possible and very diverse theories of totalitarianism, there exists a crucial similarity: for the totalitarian state, all of society represents a single vast, unified, homogeneous field of operation. Modern political subjects who see themselves as embodied in the totalitarian state want to free their actions from any form of dependence on external context. More precisely, totalitarian subjects believe themselves capable of reshaping context—in its totality—at any time and in any conceivable sense. Such a belief is extremely modern, and therefore the art that is practiced under these conditions and dictated by this belief really cannot be premodern or antimodern art.

The era of totalitarianism comes, historically speaking, after the era of the avant-garde. And the artistic avant-garde occupied itself with nothing other than the crossing and erasing of the boundaries that had traditionally split and limited the effectiveness and influence of art. In the first decades of the twentieth century, all the traditional norms of artistic production were invalidated, all taboos were broken, all conventions annulled. Artists gained the freedom to integrate any and all possible forms and processes in their work. In this way, artistic production lost its traditional boundaries: like modern technology in general, the technology of art could be applied equally well to everything in the world. Even so, a certain border remained uncrossed despite all these expansions: the border between art and reality, or, in other words, between art and its observer.

For all the influence of the avant-garde, the contexts in which art could be presented—art fairs, museums, exhibits, and so forth—remained limited. Even more importantly, this limitation, the position of the observer, remained protected and untouched. The art of the avant-garde had been emancipated from traditional tastes and traditional criteria for judgment. But as long as the public was allowed to view art from a stable, socially guaranteed external position—a position that both influenced and limited art reception—artists could not completely emancipate themselves from the public's tastes and judgments. Even after decades of artistic revolt, the whole system of art still stood under the dictatorship of consumers, critics, and spectators. And this dictatorship must have been experienced by the advanced art of its time as hostile to art itself, for the era of artistic revolution was simultaneously the beginning of the era of the mass audience, whose sentiments seemed far removed from the problematics of the avant-garde.

Rooted in this situation was a developing "hatred of the masses" among the artists of the avant-garde,[2] as well as the desire to conquer these masses, to subjugate them to their creative will, to dictate to them the conditions of art reception. The inclusion of the spectator in the work of art represents the actual project of the avant-garde—and this project itself was from the beginning totalizing or, as it were, totalitarian. The radical historical avant-garde movement can best be described as an attempt to replace the dictatorship of art consumers with a dictatorship of art producers. Artists of the avant-garde wanted to eliminate the aesthetic distance ensured by the superiority of the spectator: they wanted to create the entire context in which their work was situated. The aesthetic strategies used by avant-garde artists were many and diverse. Among them were aesthetic provocations and shocks created through radical innovation, intended to disempower and destabilize the spectator.

It is obvious that the disempowerment of the spectator cannot be achieved, in the end, through purely aesthetic means. Destabilization through innovation has its temporal limits: everything new eventually becomes old. An aesthetic dictatorship requires a political dictatorship able to realize and stabilize any given aesthetic project. In the case of avant-garde art, therefore, one sees an increasing preference for activist political theories and movements, such as Marxism, that promise to re-form life. The artist hopes these movements will newly commission him or her to work with the movement for the aesthetic re-creation of reality itself. The avant-garde's wish to abolish anything limiting the creative initiative of art is closely related to the wish of the modern political subject for absolute political freedom and the power to decide the economic, social, and other conditions of his or her own actions. Modern totalitarianism is merely the most radical actualization of this wish: the political-artistic subject gains absolute freedom by abolishing all of the inherited moral, economic, institutional, legal, and aesthetic limits that reduce the possible scope for political initiative. This fundamental affinity between the aesthetic and the political avant-garde of this era suffices to refute the claim that the official art of totalitarian states was not modern.

Even so, the image of this art in the thirties and forties hardly evokes the art of the avant-garde. In Nazi Germany, modernist art, even in its moderate forms, was pursued and combated by the state. In the Soviet Union of the 1920s, modernist art was merely tolerated. Beginning in the early thirties it was increasingly oppressed, and it was driven out of the official art world entirely in 1934, after socialist realism was declared to be the only valid artistic method. To the disappointment of many avant-garde artists of the time, in both these countries and others, the kind of art required under the domination of the new political powers seemed to be, at least visually, decidedly retrograde. It appeared to be a return to the traditional mimetic image that the international art of the era thought it had left behind. Thus there was the impression of a "straightforward return to the past" carried out by political leaders lacking in contemporary aesthetic education.

Totalitarian art's turn to the figurative, however—to the human image, to the mimesis of external reality—can in no way be interpreted as a "straightforward return to the past." Certainly, many artists who were traditional in theory and practice used the new political-ideological trend to give their art a new validity, having already felt betrayed by the avant-garde. But these artists cannot be viewed as "genuinely totalitarian." For whom or for what, then, could totalitarian art be called representative? To answer this difficult question requires a detailed examination of the artistic, ideological, and political context of the era; generalizations do not apply.

The return to the mimetic image involved an artistic use of new media images—for the most part, from photography and film—that were, of course, equally mimetic. This turn to the mimetic media image was noticeable everywhere in the thirties, and by no means only in totalitarian countries. Surrealism, magical realism, and all other realisms of the era began to access the images and techniques of the fast-growing mass media in different ways. Post-avant-garde art, including totalitarian art, began to pay attention to these images and techniques, but not only because their massive spread promised increased social-political impact. There is an inner affinity between the avant-garde image and the media image that suggests the possibility of their synthesis, and totalitarian art strove toward just such a synthesis.

It was hoped that through this synthesis the gulf between high, avant-garde, elitist culture and the mass culture that characterized modernity could be overcome. The sought-after totality of totalitarianism is essentially nothing more than an attempt to abolish this gulf.[3] The divide separating the tastes of the modern cultural elites from those of the masses (and therefore separating the avant-garde from any effective influence on the masses) had to be eliminated so that the artistic-political subject could gain unlimited freedom of sociopolitical design. It was thought possible to analyze, control, and manipulate the masses' tastes in order to redesign life in ways both foreign and partly incomprehensible to the masses. With the demise of totalitarian regimes, art finally gave up these goals, to the point that today art either satisfies or criticizes the tastes of the masses but no longer attempts to transcend or radically transform them.

As I have mentioned, there is a commonality between images produced by the avant-garde and those produced by modern media technology. Both, though for different reasons, can be understood as unconsciously produced. Photography arose through the direct effect of visual reality on film—an effect compelling for the spectator. Criticism of photography has certain limits: the spectator cannot completely deny its relationship to reality (at least when the image is not computer generated), something one can always do in the case of the traditional painted image. The partially unconscious character of photography, its results not always controlled by the artist, forces the spectator to accept the photograph's reality, thus partially renouncing his aesthetic distance.

The artists of the avant-garde, on their part, repeatedly claimed that their images were created unconsciously and manifested, as it were, a quasi-photographic imprint of a transcendental, hidden, true reality. Thus the spectator was required to accept the reality of these images as well. The reference to the unconscious serves to eliminate or, better yet, to transcend the aesthetic distance separating the spectator from the work of art. If the work is supposed to have been created unconsciously, then it attains the status of reality and thus gains a certain power over the spectator. In doing so, it manages, to a large extent, to overcome the institutional, political, or economic impotence of art. Aesthetic distance turns into an illusion that both strengthens and hides the unconscious influence of the image.

Kandinsky wrote about the role of the unconscious in this artistic seizure of power in his famous book *On the Spiritual in Art* (1910).[4] In particular, he claimed that certain forms and colors have a magical, unconscious effect on the spectator, in that they transport him into a specific mood—one could say that these forms leave an imprint on the nervous system of the observer, not unlike the imprint of images on film in photography. Indeed, only very few sensitive and, at the same time, analytical souls are able to consciously grasp and produce such unconscious effects. These chosen few are the true artists. Their images are created as the expression of an unconscious but nevertheless reflective "inner necessity." In the act of giving himself over to this inner necessity, the artist begins to explore it. The task of modern art, for Kandinsky, is found in the act of experiencing inner urgency in order to master it technically. The artist who has experienced the unconscious effect of images is in a position to control the soul of the spectator, to manipulate him, to mold him into a new and better person.[5] This ability to control and manipulate distinguishes the artist as a member of a societal elite: for Kandinsky, society is strictly hierarchical, so the majority of humanity can and should be unconsciously controlled by artistic influence.

Characteristically, Kandinsky emphasized that artistic style, innovation, and originality play no role in the inner necessity of the image. Every image, be it figurative or abstract, old or new, conveys specific moods through the unconscious influence of its colors and forms on the soul of the spectator. The common criteria of conscious art-historical judgment, through which the spectator hopes to gain control over art, are rendered invalid. For the most part, images can be distinguished from each other not along formal-aesthetic lines but rather by their unconscious effects, which can be perceived and controlled only by the artist. The spectator no longer controls the image; on the contrary, the artist controls and steers the spectator through the image.

The artist therefore becomes a magician, manipulator, and trainer whose power has a controlling effect on the spectator's unconscious. This figure—the covert manipulator of another's unconscious—captivated the imagination of the era in which the artistic avant-garde flourished: examples range from the gloomy Dr. Caligari and Dr. Mabuse of German expressionist film to the kindly Dr. Freud with his psychoanalysis and Dr. Steiner with his anthroposophy. The avant-garde artist, similarly, wanted to become a "doctor" who researched and applied the unconscious effects of colors and forms. Formal distance and effortless identifiability obviously weakened the unconscious, direct effect of the avant-garde analytic image. Out of all this derived the project that ruled the art of the 1930s and 1940s: to combine the unconscious imprint of outer reality in the form of photography with the imprint of the "inner necessity" in order to achieve the maximal effect on the viewer.

This combination was central to the artistic strategies of surrealism, magical realism, new objectivity, and other realisms of the time. The presence of the inner, hidden reality of dreams or desires was suggested by the artistic implementation of quasi-photographic modes of depiction. The result was an identification of dream with reality, of the factual with the possible, of the outer with the inner. Totalitarian art was part of this shared project of the 1930s. The use of photographs and mimetic images was combined in this art with the expression of "inner necessity." But the new artist was no longer concerned with the inner necessity of sexual desire, as the surrealists were, or with the apocalyptic vision of death common to many artists working in magical realism or new objectivity. It was the collective unconscious—of a race or of a class—that was thematized in totalitarian art.[6]

Thus the manipulative effect of the image became less visible—and so more effective. The image of totalitarian art aligned itself, above all, with color photography, and by no means with the image of traditional painting. The individual, expressive, and stylistically distinctive artistic elements of the traditional image were consistently eliminated. The artist strove for the anonymity, neutrality, and sterility of conventional photography in order to achieve maximal credibility with, and maximal effect on, the viewer. In this way, the artist evaded the standard aesthetic judgment that was presupposed by the autonomous position of the viewer: the corresponding image looked somehow "normal." The manipulative effect of the image was, at the same time, ever so much more calculated.

The presence of such calculation can be demonstrated especially clearly using the example of Paul Schultze-Naumburg's treatises, which are perhaps the most representative of the aesthetic consciousness of the Nazi era. In his book *Nordic Beauty* (1937),[7] Schultze-Naumburg attempted to define and illustrate as specifically as possible the ideal of the Nordic Aryan. He reproduced images from classical art of different periods, photographs portraying "real" people, fashion sketches, and so forth, without concern for differences of style, era, artist, or technique (painting, sculpture, or drawing). For Schultze-Naumburg, these differences were irrelevant. He was interested solely in details that, according to him, exposed racial differences: the form of the foot, the line of the shoulder, the posture of the head and neck. Distinguishing between an ancient Greek sculpture, a work by Raphael, Dürer, or Rubens, and a contemporary photograph was of no great concern for Schultze-Naumburg, because in all of those cases, he claimed, the creators of the images were unconsciously establishing and handing down specific racial features.

Moreover, Schultze-Naumburg referred to the corresponding visual material in an extremely fragmented way—a shoulder here, a foot there. Given such a presentation, the borders between high and mass culture, between classical art and modern photography, as well as between various historical epochs and aesthetic styles, were erased. The whole world of images presented to the viewer became itself a totality in which the spectator himself was included, likewise as an image. This occurred, above all, through the neutral photographic portrayal. Here the spectator lost the independent, secure, aesthetic standpoint from which he otherwise would have been able to observe and judge. He was now himself judged by these images—and possibly also sentenced. Instead of being able to enjoy Greek sculpture or the paintings of Raphael and Rubens calmly, the spectator, having read Schultze-Naumburg's book, must compare his own feet and shoulders with those he sees before him, shivering to himself all the while.

The disinterested observation of which even Kant spoke does not occur here any more. The aesthetic judgment—a spectator's means of control over the artist—is rendered powerless when the artist begins to design his images consciously in accordance with racial criteria. And indeed, the human body in art of the Nazi era looks completely neutral, extremely desexualized and anesthetized. It is less a living, "real" body than a body design that strives for the visual optimization of the Aryan appearance. Consequently, there are hardly any stylistic differences between photographs and painters' portrayals of naked models. The "photographicity" of painting is used to portray the timeless Aryan body—an ideal as incontrovertible reality—and therefore to identify its timelessness with the National Socialist present.

For Schultze-Naumburg, the reading of images against the background of their racial unconscious was by no means limited to classical art or official Nazi art. In his earlier book, *Art and Race*,[8] he attempts to build visual analogies that, in his opinion, shows ties between photographs of mentally ill people and the portrayal of individuals in German expressionism. Again, the issue is not the aesthetic positions and strategies of the respective artists but rather a comparison of the images for their inherent racial characteristics, beyond all formal-aesthetic limits. Modernity is therefore by no means excluded from the totality of the image-world that is produced. More importantly, Schultze-Naumburg was concerned with the especially dangerous potential for "degeneration" under an enemy influence—a degeneration that the observer is to avoid and fight against once he has learned of its dangers.

The naked human body played a central, if not always explicit, role in the German art of the Nazi era, in that the ideology of the racial unconscious applied most prominently to the disrobed individual. All body parts became significant and began to speak a dangerous language. In comparison, Marxist theory of the class-specific unconscious can be formulated only in the language of clothing: one's class identity is recognizable above all in the way one dresses. It is no coincidence that Mikhail Bakhtin placed "carnivalesque" individuals, who continually change their clothes, in the center of his subversive cultural philosophy, written in reference to the Soviet Marxism of the 1930s.[9] One begins to understand the vehement struggle against both nakedness and fashion in the Stalin era. This rejection of nakedness had little to do with official prudery. More importantly, the disrobed individual evaded his social identifiability—much like the person who made sure he was dressed in the latest fashion—and was therefore dangerous. The sexuality manifested in fashion posed dangers for both the separation of the races and the separation of the classes. The art of the Nazi era responded to this danger by desexualizing the body; the art of the Stalin era, by strict enforcement of a clothes ordinance.

At least from this perspective, the Soviet art of the Stalin era differs externally from the art of the Nazi regime. Other differences between the National Socialist and Communist ideologies, and between the two nations' artistic traditions, are expressed in the artistic practices of the countries at the time. Even so, a fundamental similarity is obvious, enabling us to talk about totalitarian art as a unified phenomenon: in both cases, the issue is the replacement of customary rules governing the writing of art history with a vision of a single battle. This battle penetrates the innermost part of all history. Hence, all periods are synchronized, and all places are housed in a single, total space. At the same time, this battle splits apart the seemingly homogeneous historical styles at their core. In the case of Marxism, it is an issue of class struggle; in the case of National Socialism, it is one of racial struggle. Accordingly, images from the art tradition are dealt with on the same level as mass-produced images from the media—as handouts for the ideological classroom.

This pathos of timelessness is clearly visible in those of Hitler's speeches dedicated to the role of German art in the Third Reich. He argued against the notion of the "timeliness of art," which he characterized as a "Jewish invention."[10] In this way he also established his rejection of the term "modernity." In his view, the label "modern" maliciously subjugated art to changing eras and, above all, to fashion, "for true art is not subject to the law that governs seasonally bound evaluations of the achievements of a tailor's studio."[11] According to Hitler, true art was much more than that—it was the expression of the "nucleus" of the Aryan "race," and it united the art of the German people with that of ancient Greece and Rome, as well as with all other high points of European culture, in a timeless, inner, "essential" way. Therefore, it would be wrong, according to Hitler, to search for a new artistic style for the Third Reich that could be produced on the basis of specific rules: true art comes into being spontaneously if it stems from the innermost part of those individuals who have an Aryan "genetic makeup" and hence possess the true weltanschauung.[12] Hitler thus demanded a radical rejection of all external, formal, stylistic criteria for the assessment of art. Art must lose its stylistic, aesthetic differentiability so that, in the end, just one differentiation exists: that between what is Aryan and what is non-Aryan. But this differentiation has no external criteria that can be neutrally defined. More exactly, it is the place of battle that admits no outside observer.

The official programmatic goal of Stalin-era socialist realism can hardly be differentiated in this respect from the goal of Hitler's speeches, though of course the race struggle is replaced by the class struggle. The classification of artworks according to historical, stylistic, and aesthetic criteria, as well as the characteristic positions of bourgeois, formalist critique, is rejected. The meaning of individual works of art, as well as their quality, depends much more on whether the artist identified internally with the upward-striving, progressive classes during the creation of the work or with the historically surviving reactionary classes. The high points of art history—again, ancient Greece and Rome and the Renaissance—are thus interpreted as expressions of the optimism of the historically progressive classes of their time. Because the progressive class of the twentieth century is the working class, socialist art must be the successor of this earlier progressive art, rather than separated from it by means of formal-aesthetic innovation, as the Russian avant-garde wanted. Socialist realism declared that the avant-garde falsely believed that the new proletarian art had to break with the past and take on a new formal-aesthetic look. In accordance with the famous "Leninist theory of two cultures within one culture," every cultural epoch is defined by the battle between two class cultures, one progressive and the other reactionary. But the ideology of artistic modernity homogenizes the culture of a specific historical time and in this way prevents the making of a decisive choice between the art of the progressive and reactionary classes.

In essence, the theoretical-ideological strategies of both totalitarianisms consisted in the deconstruction—if I may use that term—of the formally definable and aesthetically controllable borders that organized and structured the field of image production. This deconstruction was executed by pointing out a hidden, unconscious struggle that brought these borders into a state of confusion. Following the avant-garde discovery of the unconscious, attention was shifted from the aesthetic form itself to its unconscious effect. In this way the image-world of art was transformed into a battlefield for totalitarian power, which alone could decide what was Aryan and what was not, or what was proletarian and what was not. One can easily recognize the old avant-garde "inner necessity" in the form of the unconscious, internal battle. To be sure, avant-garde artists still dealt with the traditional task of differentiating their art from earlier art on formal grounds—and thus they created new lines of separation. It was only through the utilization of new media images, images both unconsciously produced and traditionally mimetic, that even these last borderlines were put aside. Totalitarian art proved to be thoroughly modern, even if it rejected the term "modernity" as too stylistically narrow and formally defined.

The evolution of Soviet art in the 1920s and 1930s demonstrates most clearly the transition from the avant-garde to the new mimetic image via the fresh application of photography. This transition is especially noticeable in a group of leading representatives of the Russian avant-garde such as Alexander Rodchenko, El Lissitsky, and Gustav Klutsis. In the twenties, Rodchenko professed his belief in the truth of photography—because, unlike the printed image, photography operated beyond the realm of artistic will.[13] Rodchenko, however, like El Lissitsky and Klutsis, used individual photographs over and over again as elements of consciously designed photomontages whose geometric construction tried to symbolize the rational construction of the new world.

Even when Rodchenko was not making montages but only taking photographs, his individual photographic images demonstrate the subjugation of the human figure to the logic of geometric form. This subjugation is often celebrated as sport: his photographs glorify a geometrically ordered human mass that consists of well-trained bodies formed through the help of athletic technology, reminiscent of the films of Leni Riefenstahl, such as *Triumph of the Will.* But even unathletic individuals are linked into the geometric construction, as is evidenced by Rodchenko's presenting one of the first camps of the future gulags as entirely positive—a place for the disciplining of the human body, for people's enrollment in a geometric order that grants them the majesty that their bodies obviously lack.

Although the Soviet art of the thirties was increasingly dominated by painting, it is that very painting which shows, through qualities of its own, its dependence on the photomontage of an earlier time. Images of socialist realism from the Stalin era look like color photographs, and indeed, this "photographicity" is not concealed but rather publicly admitted and celebrated. Accordingly, Boris Ioganson, one of the leading official artists of the Stalin era, claimed that the place of creativity in the art of socialist realism lay not in painting technique but in "management of the image" itself. It follows that the work of the "painting artist" was not differentiated from that of the photographer in any essential way.[14] The images of socialist realism function as virtual photographs—they had to be painted only because the technology for computer-manipulated photographs did not yet exist. This use of painting as virtual photography can be demonstrated clearly, for example, in Soviet paintings that show the masses parading before the (never built) Palace of Soviets.

The images of socialist realism display the same neutrality, impersonality, mediocrity, and lack of artistic expression found in the images of National Socialist art. In this way they differ from the images of surrealism or magical realism, both of which likewise used a quasi-photographic painting technique in order to create the effect of a virtual reality—a photograph of a dream. But the art of surrealism still complies with the traditional demand for artistic originality, whereas totalitarian art consciously strives for impersonality of expression. Completely aligned with the totalitarian aesthetic, this art avoids any stylistic or formal-aesthetic definability. At least in the context of Soviet art criticism of the 1930s, any stylistic identifiability was deemed a deficiency of the image, the regression of the artist into "formalism"—this critical reaction was always the same, no matter which style was in question. The art of the Stalin era wanted to appear indefinable, "informal," inconspicuous, in order to evade the accusation of formalism and to ensure that it did not end up in the archive of ideological control. In essence, the goal was not to stand out. The indefinability of aesthetic position is the most important prerequisite for successful ideological appropriation. Only after an image is completely immunized against the aesthetic judgment of the spectator does the image itself begin to judge the spectator; the viewer loses his outside perspective and autonomy, is transplanted into the image, and becomes part of it.

Designing Totality: Architecture as Unity and the Struggle of Opposites

The same strategy of aesthetic, art-historical anonymity was also practiced in Soviet architecture, which, unlike National Socialist architecture, had time to demonstrate its own developmental dynamics. The most conspicuous and amazing aspect of the architectural debates in the official art press of the Stalin era is that they always assumed the form of total critiques that were essentially against all sides. Far from being laudatory or even approving, the official art criticism dealt with Soviet architects harshly and uncompromisingly. All of the individual positions and achievements of these architects, of any and every kind, were portrayed as inadequate, if not completely wrong or even harmful. At the same time, architects were systematically hindered from taking the detours that might have allowed them to evade the criticism. On reading this total criticism, even today's reader is overcome by a feeling of hopelessness and frustration. One cannot imagine how anything might have been built or created in such a situation.

An example of this sort of criticism is the famous instructive essay "Against Formalism, Schematism, Eclecticism," written in 1936 by Karo Alabian, who was an architect himself. Alabian's article lives up to its title: he criticizes not only constructivism, and indeed any formal innovation, but also the imitative adoption of the classical tradition, the eclectic use of various models (old and new), and the programmatic rejection of any specific architectural form.[15] Such wholesale criticism, in the context of which socialist realism was formed, was continually repeated in the publications of the thirties. Indeed, in the same year the magazine *Architecture of the USSR* issued an editorial statement criticizing "supermonumentalism," pure virtuosity in the mastery of traditional architectural forms, slavish imitation of Palladio and of Renaissance art in general, and lifeless "addiction to stylization." For the editorial board of the magazine, this criticism did not indicate a return to the formalism of the constructivist avant-garde but rather a call to arms against any and all formalism, including the classical tradition, itself understood along formalist lines.[16]

The architecture of the Stalin era is generally associated with an emphasis on decoration and facade. But the architectural critics of that era led an indefatigable battle against "facade-ism," that is, against the fascination with decoration in architecture, arguing instead for the functionality and "livability" of buildings that were to correspond to human scale and human needs. This did not mean, however, that buildings were to look constructivist and cold, purely functionalistic and inhuman. Indeed, the idea of serving the people that was demanded of every Soviet architect also implied emotional connection: the socialist building was to look monumental but at the same time seem intimate, human, cozy.[17]

A few analysts of Stalinist culture have concluded that the demands critics made on architects were too paradoxical to be fulfilled. If they could be neither innovative nor traditional nor eclectic in building, they basically could build nothing at all.[18] Supposedly, these demands meant nothing less than the total subjugation of the architects to the tastes of the Party leadership. Both Alabian and the anonymous author of the aforementioned editorial piece from *Architecture of the USSR* praised the Moscow underground transit system as the only incontrovertible achievement of Soviet architecture; they explained this unique success as resulting from the underground's having been built under the personal direction of Lazar Kaganovich, a Party leader in close contact with Stalin. Even so, on a deeper level, Stalinist art criticism did not function as a simple justification of the then current political-aesthetic party line, although various tactically motivated attempts at justification always played an important role in it.

In analyzing individual ideological and critical strategies of the Stalin era, one must not forget that they were part of the all-embracing discourse of dialectical and historical materialism, the fundamental principles of which were doled out by the Party leadership. And the most important principle of dialectical materialism in its Leninist-Stalinist form—constituted and solidified in the mid-1930s—was, as I mentioned, "the law of unity and the battle of opposites." According to this law, two contradictory claims are valid at the same time: "A" and "Not A" are not mutually exclusive but rather are situated in a dynamic relationship. A logical contradiction, in its inner structure, dismantles the real conflict between the opposing historical forces that make up the core of life—this core is living *because* it is struggling. Therefore only those sentences that are internally contradictory are "living" and thus true. "Bourgeois" thought is criticized on the grounds that it wants to eliminate internal contradiction and attain a logical consistency that is one-sided, purely formal, and internally "dead." Indeed, the thought of the Stalin era valorizes contradictory statements over statements lacking contradiction. Whereas for "bourgeois" thought, any internal contradiction in a statement is assessed as a defect in that statement, in "socialist," Stalinist thought, the opposite is true: any lack of internal contradiction is indicative of the discourse's lack of liveliness, truthfulness, and force.

There was no more pejorative epithet in the Stalin era than "one-sidedness." Any and all more or less logical, consistent, and uncontradictory thought was considered one-sided. Dialectical materialism clearly inherited this valorization of the internal contradiction from

Hegelian dialectics. Indeed, just as in Hegelian dialectics, such internal contradictions could never be overcome historically or observed retrospectively. All contradictions were always present—they struggled against each other and always formed a unity. Anyone who insisted on a specific claim was bound to render himself guilty, because he lost sight of this crucial unity of opposites. The message of the unity of contradictory opposites forms the basic structure and the entire inner mystery of Stalinist totalitarianism.

This totalitarianism requires unification within itself of literally all oppositions. Stalinism discards nothing but rather takes on everything and finds for everything a fitting place. The only thing that is unbearable for Stalinist thought is an individual's insistence on the logical, consistent, uncontradictory nature of his own position, which excludes the opposing position. Stalinist ideology sees this as a refusal—one that could be dictated only by bad will—to commit oneself to life and to the collective. The basic strategy of this ideology functions in roughly the following way: if Stalinism has already unified within itself all oppositions, then what sense can there be in insisting on a single position? To do so could not be rational, because the corresponding, opposing position also is always already contained within the totality of Stalinist ideology. Therefore, the only basis for such defiance would be an irrational hatred of the Soviet power, a hatred personally directed against Stalin. There is no possibility of further discussion with such hate-filled individuals—unfortunately, they can only be displaced or eliminated.

This ideological basis was preserved, above all, in the public trials against opposition factions within the Party. No matter what these factions claimed, they were always told that their demands had already been met by the Party and personally by Stalin himself. One wonders why, under the circumstances, a faction nonetheless insisted on its one-sided position. The answer was clear from the beginning. The basic mistake of all opposition factions was in failing to recognize that the absolute totality that was the goal of Stalinism took away any chance of logical, noncontradictory description. Consequently, these factions resembled earlier religious heretics, who wanted, similarly, to grasp the Divine Absolute with the terms of human reason. By comparison, the orthodox position (at least in eastern Byzantium) always defined the divine through the paradoxical, the internally contradictory—that is, anything at all could be said about God, while at the same time God evaded everything that was said about him.

One striking difference between Stalinism and classical religions is that the latter attempted to characterize only God in self-contradictory terms. For Stalinist ideology, the entire Soviet Union was a totality, right down to every material subsection. Therefore, Soviet people spoke about the various aspects of everyday life the way they used to speak about God alone. They saw everywhere the unity of opposites and the attempts of troublemakers trying to destroy this unity. Above all, the concern for internally contradictory unity applied to art. There, the logical conclusions derived from internal contradiction were associated with stylistic, aesthetic consequences.

This short excursus into the teachings of dialectical materialism allows us to formulate the criterion that internally defined the artistic work of the Stalin era: the goal was to maximize the internal-aesthetic contradictions within an individual piece of art. This criterion also defined the strategies of art criticism of the time. Stalinist art critics reacted negatively every time they discovered a clearly definable, consistently represented, and nonambiguous aesthetic position within a work of art. They did not criticize the artistic position as such, because they were altogether in favor of the acquisition of the classical tradition, the respect of modern functionality, and the combining of the various "achievements of architecture." The Stalinist art commentators targeted *visible* artistic strategy and the emphasis of a specific problem with a specific solution. They reprimanded everything that was specifically and clearly defined, for the perfect building was to be absolute, total, and all inclusive. It was to look highly individual, disregarding nothing that had happened in the history of architecture. It was to be utterly modern, that is, of its time, yet it was to preserve continuity with classical antiquity. It was to serve the everyday needs of the people and at the same time generate a sense of celebration and the extraordinary.

A perfect building, however, was to be above all alive, powerful, and effective. That meant that the architect was not allowed to follow any specific aesthetic or formal principal in planning the design, for any such "abstract" principle was seen by definition as undialectical, one-sided, dead. The demand for stylistic purity, in fact, could originate only in a pluralistic, "bourgeois" society in which an architect gained recognition by doing something different from others.

In Stalinist architecture, unlike in bourgeois architecture, every architect attempted to build something total, absolute, undifferentiable, and indescribable. Every building is internally contradictory and indefinable—while the whole looks unified, with its own unmistakable style. This strategy was correctly apprehended and enunciated by Party leaders from the very beginning. In this light it is especially interesting how Nikolai Bulganin, who was close to Stalin and Kaganovich, defined the term "architectural ensemble" in a 1937 speech at the First Congress of Soviet Architects. First, Bulganin dismissed any attempt to define "ensemble" formally or aesthetically. Then he argued against the suggestion that an "ensemble" be created by having a single architect build an entire district. That, he remarked, would lead only to monotony and not to the origination of a true ensemble. Last, Bulganin gave his own definition: "Given our current conditions, the ensemble means high-quality planning, the conscious, responsible relationship between architects and planning, high-quality selection and granting of projects, and equally high-quality construction."[19]

At first glance, this definition seems void of content and meaning—as do many other ideologically related formulations from the Stalin era. But its key term is "high quality," which means something fundamentally different from the word "quality." A work is "quality" when it is good in relationship to other works. A work is "high quality" when it embodies something superlative, incomparable, total, and absolute. Thus, any building that embodies the superlative constitutes an "ensemble." The ensemble does not result from stylistic homogeneity, which, according to Bulganin, would lead only to monotony. Rather, it should reveal the internal unity of "high quality." If every building is a constructed totality, then the ensemble of these buildings is the expression of the concept of totality itself. The entire city of Moscow, and later the entire Soviet territory, was supposed to be such an ensemble of constructions, every one of which was to manifest this wholeness. Thus the strategy of Stalin-era art criticism is clarified. It demanded from every architect that every single one of his buildings be "high quality," that is, that each building represent the totality. Each building was to be functional but not adherent to functionalism; inspired by classical antiquity but not adherent to classicism; highly individual but not individualistic; monumental but geared to human proportions; decorative yet simple; cognizant of all meaningful architectural developments from history yet not eclectic; and so on.

Such "high-quality" buildings could be called "our socialist" buildings, in that the socialism of the Stalin era was understood as the living unity of all the oppositions that had previously torn society apart Only Stalin himself could "think" totality, and only Soviet socialism itself, as a whole, could embody totality. Neither an individual building nor an ensemble of such buildings would ever be able to bring about much more than an approximation of the true unity of opposites. Therefore, even a harsh criticism of the work of an architect did not mean a final rejection of his project. The most important question for the criticism of the time was that of the architect's subjective attitude to the socialist whole—whether or not he worked, in Bulganin's words, "consciously and responsibly." Another way to phrase this would be to ask whether the architect strove for totality in his work, whether he was willing to relativize his own position and make himself a medium for the unity of opposites. Or did he, on the contrary, insist on his position "one-sidedly," oppose others, and fail to contribute to a reconciliation of contradictions, thus sharpening the contradiction, destroying the unity of socialism, and placing the whole right back in the condition of the bourgeois struggle—every person against every other person? The discussion of this question led to the judgment of each artist as either a loyal, even if misled, Soviet citizen who could be helped through criticism or a troublemaker, disguised or undisguised, who had to be rendered harmless.

The concern for totality and the unity of opposites, for the living paradox that opposes dead, logically functioning reason, has its roots not only deep within the Marxist dialectic but also in Byzantine Christianity. The synthesis between Hegelian German idealism and the tradition of Russian Orthodox Christianity of Byzantine origin has dominated all of Russian thought since the middle of the nineteenth century.

Urs von Balthasar wrote about the aesthetic teaching of the most important Russian philosopher of the prerevolutionary era, Vladimir Solov'ev:

> At the end stands not only the absorption of all things into an absolute spiritual subject, but also the resurrection of the dead. Therefore, for Solov'ev, eschatology practically collapses into aesthetics. . . . Solov'ev's art and technique for the integration of all partial truths make him, along with Thomas Aquinas, perhaps the greatest ordering/organization artist in the history of thought. There is no system that does not provide him with an important building block once he has robbed and emptied it of the poison of its negations. . . . Therefore it is less the power of distinguishing between the usable and the unusable in a system that makes integration possible—though this power is both eminently available and used—but more

> the art of assigning to guests places at table, in accordance with their rank. All are united in a vast totality that severely limits the possibility of independent ideological vision.[20]

This passage actually supplies the best possible description of architecture in the Stalin period, which conceived of itself as the eschatological art after the end of history—understood as the history of the class struggle—and which allowed all historical styles and aesthetic systems to rise from the dead, providing they had been emptied of their historically necessitated negations. Stalin was especially gifted as an artist of seating assignments. And Stalinist architecture, in just this way, wanted to direct every historically founded aesthetic style to its own place in the whole. Thus Stalinist architecture became a constructed ideology.

The constructions of the Stalin era are understandable only within their ideological context and only in light of their internal project. The architects of the time always built the same building—the building of Stalinist ideology, in which everything either must find its place or be destroyed—independent of its geographical position or external function. Because of this, Stalinist architecture is simultaneously monotonous and fascinating. It constantly offers the image of the same collective effort, the same social ecstasy, the same internal paradox—and the same failure of the individual. Two things form the inner tension of this architecture: the hope for the saving unity of opposites, in which the architect wishes to be contained, and the danger of standing out as different from this unity by fault of one's own. This inner tension manifests itself in obsessive repetitions, and it is through these repetitions that it is made visible even to the outside observer.

Situating Totality: Utopia as Underground

The Moscow metro played a central role in the total project of Stalinist architecture. Its central position was certainly not coincidental, for we are dealing here with the opposition of perhaps the greatest ideological importance—that of heaven versus hell. If classical utopianism, including avant-garde utopianism, wanted to construct a heaven on earth, then Stalinist culture constructed heaven underground, that is, in mythological terms, in hell.

The topos of the metro is definitely a u-topos, even if a demonic, subterranean one. Humans do not normally live underground: living space there first has to be developed, created. In this space there can be nothing inherited, traditional, taken for granted, or unplanned. One is completely dependent on the will of those who create it. This gives the metro planner the opportunity to utterly redesign people's lives, provided they set foot in the metro. It is especially important that the entrances and exits—which link the subterranean space of the metro with normal human living space—be easy to monitor and control. At the same time, the normal denizen of the city cannot possibly imagine just how the tunnels of the metro course beneath the surface. The u-topos of the metro remains concealed forever; the path to utopia can be cut off at any time, the pedestrian passageways closed, the tunnels filled in. Although the metro belongs to the reality of the metropolis, it remains fantastic—it can only be imagined, and not really experienced.

Of course, citizens of the Western metropolis experience the underground not as a utopian space but as a mere technical convenience. The Moscow metro of the Stalin era functioned in a completely different way, and traces of this earlier utopian function are still there to be found. The Moscow metro of the Stalin era was not, first and foremost, an ordinary source of public transportation but rather the design for an actual city of the communist future. The effusive, palatial, artistic interior design of Stalin-era metro stations cannot be explained except by reference to their inherent function of communicating between the kingdom of heaven and the subterranean empire.

In building the metro, an object of prestige par excellence, no expense was spared. Only the best, costliest, and most impressive materials were to be used. The *metrostroevtsy*—the metro builders—were called the heroes of the new culture. Poems, novels, and plays were written about them. Films were made about them. Newspapers were filled with reports of the metro's progress. Delegates from the metro builders attended all important political events and received all sorts of decorations and medals. The metro became ever present in Stalinist culture—it was its most important metaphor. Its role in society was to lend an explicit form to the utopian project of establishing communism.

The conquering of hell simultaneously implies the conquering of the past. Not only the living but also the dead—who were banished beneath the earth by the logic of historical life—were to be admitted into the totality of Stalinist culture. In the same way, Christ visited not only earth but also hell, whose inhabitants he led to light. Thus the Moscow metro stations affirm the image of a never-existent, utopian, transformed, and saved past. They resemble the temples of Roman antiquity or are reminiscent of the noble palaces of old Russia from the time of the Russian Empire or the Russian baroque. Or they are quotes from the priceless architecture of the Islamic East. The metro is replete with marble, gold, silver, and other expensive materials associated with the glorious past. In the midst of all this glory are innumerable frescoes, sculptures, mosaics, and panels of stained glass that lend an atmosphere of sacredness. To be sure, the heroes of antiquity or of Russian history are not the subjects of this artwork, but rather Stalin and his loyal followers, workers and farmers, and revolutionaries and soldiers from the Soviet era. The past is thus occupied by the utopian present. In the building of the Moscow metro, all traditional artistic styles were severed from their historical ties and used in a new way. In the process, the past lost its differentiability from the present and the future. Even in the depths of antiquity all one could see was Stalin, Soviet flags, and a people who looked optimistically toward the future.

The relationship of metro visitors to this architecture is even more unusual and complex. The temple serves the purpose of silent contemplation. The palace likewise invites languorous amusement; one sits in the inner parlors, reflecting upon them attentively, and engages in a long, intellectually rich conversation with the master of the house. Nothing of the sort happens in the metro. It is almost always full of people incessantly hurrying off in all directions. One hardly has the time, desire, or opportunity to observe the glory of the metro's architecture. The individual is pushed onward by the crowd, which would be impeded by his pursuit of leisurely amusement. Most of the travelers are tired, embittered, rushed. They want only to get in and out quickly. The trains arrive rapidly and often. Because the metro lies fairly deep beneath the surface, people spend a long time standing on the escalators, without the possibility of looking around.

This incessantly in-transit mass seems not to need the glory that is offered it in the metro. Riders cannot and do not want to enjoy the art, value the precious materials, or decode the ideological symbolism in a way that would do it justice. Mute, blind, and indifferent, they hurry past the countless artistic treasures. The metro is not a paradise of silent contemplation but a subterranean hell of incessant movement. In this way, it is heir to the utopia of the Russian avant-garde, which was likewise a utopia of incessant movement. In the Moscow metro, the dream of those such as Malevich, Khlebnikov, and the De-Urbanists survives—the dream of a utopian individual who is moving continually and has no specific place or topos on earth. Only now did this dream find a suitable place to be realized: under the ground.

The dialectical-materialist utopia of Russian communism was never a classical, contemplative utopia like those of earlier eras. The dialectical individual was supposed to be in constant movement, to constantly overcome himself, bring himself further, raise himself higher—both ideally and materially. Therefore the subterranean utopian city of communism was also a place of constant movement, of constant entering and exiting. The images of the Moscow metro were not to be contemplated, understood, or admired. Rather, the images themselves observe the passengers, the masses in transit. Stalin and others, the depicted administrators of this utopian hell, continually observe and judge the behavior of the people rushing past them. And people in the metro continually sense the observant and judgmental glance that follows them. Today all the gods have fallen, but not long ago one could notice how differently Muscovites behaved when they set foot on the holy ground of the metro. Suddenly all conversations were hushed, no one spat on the ground, no one dropped garbage—one behaved "culturedly," as it was called back then. For one was being observed! One was in utopia and could find no spot in which to possibly behave "naturally" and not "culturedly."

The metro had yet another dimension that was directly linked to the utopia of the avant-garde: it was illuminated with artificial, not natural, light. The battle against the sun and moon in favor of artificial, electric light is perhaps the oldest theme of Russian futurism. Not coincidentally, a programmatic work of the Russian avant-garde, the 1912 mystery-opera by A. Kruchenykh, K. Malevich, and M. Matiushin, is called *Victory over the Sun*. The futurists understood the abolition of the sun as the final conquest of the old order. The light of reason—be it divine or human, natural light—was to be extinguished, because it was a light that had given shape to the topology of our world. In contrast, a new, artificial, utopian light was to appear that would create a completely new world. Resonances with this large theme are found in Lenin's famous formulation, "communism equals Soviet power plus the electrification of the entire country." To electrify the country meant "to conquer the sun" and create a new utopian space, beyond the cycle of night and day. The electrified night is the only true daytime of utopia. The Moscow metro is the consistent embodiment of the eternal, electrified Moscow night, in which all the times and time zones of life on earth and under the sun—past, present, and future—are united in an artificial eternity.

Conclusion

The limits of totalitarian space—for instance, the borders of the Soviet state—were so bitterly guarded and defended in their time because the aesthetic borders that divided this space from others were extremely indistinct. Everything characteristically Soviet consisted of specific, content-driven, ideological (and thus invisible) operations with signs, words, and images. These operations were not restricted to the formal-aesthetic dimension. Such a restriction would have required a neutral observer capable of differentiating between the Soviet and un-Soviet based on formal-aesthetic criteria. The total claim of Soviet ideology, however, did not allow for such an outside observer. The Soviet individual stood in the middle of a conflict over the meaning, application, and interpretation of culture that could not be decided on the basis of neutral, objective criteria. In totalitarian systems, artists are undercover agents who carry out an invisible ideological struggle for which the superficial aesthetic of their works serves only as camouflage. And this camouflage is good only when it is not especially conspicuous.

And so we return to the point made at the outset. To a certain degree, the entire strategy of modern art has its origin and teleology in the desire to escape aesthetic judgment, to bar the neutral observer, to overwhelm his competence to judge. With this goal, the artists of the avant-garde continually produced something new, in order to escape the criteria of traditional aesthetics—that is, they exhibited objects and images for which there were no criteria for judgment in the repertoire of existing art theories. It quickly became obvious that this very differentiation between old and new at best served the construction of a neutral system of differentiation and ordering that in turn served objective art-historical description. In order to escape this neutral judgment, the synchronization of all historical periods had to be completed, in place of a controllable, chronological sequence of artistic styles and periods. This synchronization thematized a single event that manifested itself in the various periods. An event such as the battle between two fundamentally opposing attitudes could no longer be comprehended through art-historical periodization and description. The totalitarian aesthetic aimed primarily at escaping art-historical description—and it succeeded in this aim to a large extent. Therefore it is difficult today, if not impossible, to describe the aesthetic space of totalitarian ideology, in that after the collapse of the totalitarian regime we have again at our disposal only the long-trusted art-historical conceptual framework for such a description.

NOTES

1. See Boris Groys, *Gesamtkunstwerk Stalin* (Munich: C. Hanser, 1988); translated into English by Charles Rougle as *The Total Art of Stalinism: Avant-garde, Aesthetic Dictatorship, and Beyond* (Princeton: Princeton University Press, 1992).

2. See John Carey, *The Intellectuals and the Masses: Pride and Prejudice among the Literary Intelligentsia, 1880–1939* (London: Faber and Faber, 1992).

3. Clement Greenberg refers to totalitarian art in the area of mass kitsch in his famous essay "Avant-Garde and Kitsch" (1939), in Clement Greenberg, *The Collected Essays and Criticism* (Chicago: University of Chicago Press, 1986), 1: 5–22. More importantly, it deals with the attempt of totalitarian art to overcome the opposition.

4. W. Kandinsky, *Ueber das Geistige in der Kunst* (1910; reprint, Bern: Benteli Verlag, 1952).

5. At the end of the book, Kandinsky speaks about the power of art that raises the artist to king and imposes on him the corresponding moral duty to raise the people to greater levels; the main topic is the moral responsibility of the artist in relationship to himself (ibid., 133–36).

6. See Rosalind Krauss, "The Photgraphic Conditions of Surrealism," in Rosalind E. Krauss, *The Originality of the Avant-Garde and Other Modernist Myths* (Cambridge, Mass.: MIT Press, 1985), 87–118.

7. Paul Schultze-Naumburg, *Nordische Schoenheit: Ihr Wunschbild im Leben und in der Kunst* (Berlin: J. F. Lehmann, 1937).

8. Paul Schultze-Naumburg, *Kunst und Rasse* (Munich: J. F. Lehmann, 1935).

9. M. M. Bakhtin, *Rabelais and His World*, trans. Helène Iswolsky (Bloomington: Indiana University Press, 1984).

10. Hitler's speech at the opening of the "Grossen Deutschen Kunstausstellung" of 1937 in Munich, in *Nationalsozialismus und "entartete Kunst"* (Munich: Prestel-Verlag, 1987), 242–52.

11. Ibid., 244.

12. Adolf Hitler, "Die deutsche Kunst als stolzeste Verteidung des deutschen Volkes: Rede vom 1 September 1933 auf der Kulturtagung des Parteitags," in *Reden des Führers: Politik und Progaganda Adolf Hitlers 1922–1945*, ed. Erhard Kloess (Munich: Deutscher Taschenbuch Verlag, 1967), 113–15.

13. Alexander Rodchenko, "Gegen das synthetische Porträt—für die Momentaufnahme" (1928), in *Die Zukunft ist unser einziges Ziel . . . Rodtchenko. Stepanowa* (catalog of an exhibit of MAK), ed. Peter Noever (Vienna, Munich: Prestel-Verlag, 1991), 232–37.

14. Groys, *Gesamtkunstwerk Stalin*, 60–62.

15. K. S. Alabian, "Protiv formalizma, uproshchenchestva, eklektiki," *Architektura SSSR* 4 (1936): 1–5.

16. "Bor'ba za masterstvo," *Arkhitektura SSSR* 5 (1936): 1–4.

17. "Stalinskaia zabota o cheloveke," *Arkhitektura SSSR* 10 (1937): 10–12.

18. See Vladimir Paperny, *Kul'tura dva* (Ann Arbor, Mich.: Ardis, 1985), 28–29.

19. N. A. Bulganin, "Rekonstruktsiia gorodov, zhilishhnoe stroitel'stvo i zadachi arkhitektury," *Arkhitektura SSSR* 7–8 (1937): 18.

20. Hans Urs von Balthasar, *Herrlichkeit: Eine theologische Ästhetik* (Einsiedelen: Johannes Verlag, 1962), 2: 651–52.

Part Two

Mobilizing the Soviet Subject

6

All This Can Be Yours!

SOVIET COMMERCIAL ADVERTISING AND THE SOCIAL CONSTRUCTION OF SPACE, 1928–1956

RANDI COX

> Imagine a theater lobby. People are milling about. [In the crowd are actors disguised as] a young man with his miss. Suddenly the girl falls in a swoon. People crowd around. The young man explains, "I promised to bring her a new saucepan from TsUM, the Central Department Store. But I didn't bring it, and she fainted."
>
> —1936 proposal for a live advertising scene

The New Soviet Man and Woman were not only engineers, Stakhanovites, and kolkhozniki; they were also shoppers, customers, and consumers. Like people in other industrialized nations, Soviet citizens struggled to balance their producing and consuming activities. Yet the shortages of consumer goods endemic to the Soviet economy, as well as the productivist bent of Soviet ideology, have encouraged historians to neglect the role of consumption in Soviet life. With this essay I hope to contribute to a growing body of literature aimed at correcting that oversight by examining images in Soviet commercial advertising during the Stalin years.

Between 1928 and 1956, Soviet advertising presented the possession of material goods as an ostensibly apolitical means to personal satisfaction. In contrast to the highly politicized advertising of the New Economic Policy (NEP), which had advocated public, revolutionary consumption, advertising designers under Stalin turned to Westernized images of public and private space in order to promote "cultured" consumption, which emphasized individual and family happiness. Their advertisements constituted a conscious attempt to shape readers' attitudes toward commodities and to determine which products they should incorporate into daily life. Designers saw themselves as educators and propagandists on a par with Soviet political agitators; advertising was to be a special form of trade and industrial propaganda that would teach citizens about the goods that would provide the physical environment for modernity. Consumption of the new things created by the growing Soviet industrial machine would lead to a new identity based on private life and private space, rather than on production and political life, as advertising during NEP had urged.

The history of Soviet advertising has a number of implications for our understanding of the Stalin years. Discussions among advertising designers became forums in which to debate the social construction of public and private space and the potential role of consumption as a politically stabilizing force in the Soviet Union. Moreover, their advertisements record the evolution of the cultural relationship between production and consumption in Soviet propaganda. The interaction of production and consumption is a central feature in determining identity in mass-producing societies, and changes in this relationship shed light on the social and cultural shift from NEP to Stalinism. During both periods, advertising specialists were conscious of the larger ramifications of their work, and they tried to direct readers' tastes in a way that would benefit the country on political, economic, and cultural levels.

Yet advertising's messages in each period were quite different. Whereas NEP advertising often emphasized the macroeconomic impact of trade patterns, during the Stalin years designers drew on the Western advertising technique of stressing the benefits and pleasures of personal consumption. This tactic comprised one thread in the larger civilizing discourse of *kul'turnost'* characteristic of that era, a discourse most recently described by Vadim Volkov as an effort to "discipline the new masses" through promises of "the possibility of a prosperous and cultured life . . . in exchange for efficient work."[1] What had been decried as bourgeois decadence during NEP was now redefined, with the help of advertising, as cultured and worthy of desire. Several scholars, including Volkov, Julie Hessler, and Sheila Fitzpatrick, have identified the mid- and late 1930s as the high point of this reinterpretation.[2] Interestingly, Soviet advertising foreshadowed this shift by presenting images of cultured consumption in the late twenties, evoking a hostile response from the more radical artists of the Cultural Revolution.

My goal in this essay is to explore the connections between the "cultured" images of advertising and Soviet definitions of public and private space. The distance between consumption and space is not as great as it might seem at first glance. Indeed, private space and public space are often distinguished by an association of private space with consumption and domesticity and of public space with production and politics. Advertising, which creates a narrative of consumption, therefore can participate in the demarcation of space. The distinction between public and private space also plays a crucial role in debates about the nature of Stalinism. Vera Dunham, one of the first scholars to recognize the Soviet phenomenon of *kul'turnost'*, argued that the state's support and even promotion of cultured consumption encouraged administrative elites to accept the Stalinist system voluntarily. This "Big Deal" meant that the state did not need to rely exclusively on terror to control this segment of the population.[3] Although Dunham was seeking to refute cold war theories of totalitarianism, her thesis can be read in a totalitarian light; it suggests that the state used consumer temptations to distract administrators and professionals from politics, from public space.

It is important to recognize, however, as Dunham did, that the matter is considerably more complicated than simple misdirection. Advertising did not simply push people out of public space and into private retreats. Dunham's Big Deal, as played out in advertising, reflects not so much a buying off of intellectuals and other elites as a division of identity that allowed production and consumption to function in different psychological spheres. In placing the private, consumer sphere over the productive sphere and redefining public space as sentimentalized leisure space, advertising indeed encouraged an identity in which politics was something conducted by other people. But this latent political diversion seems to have been a side effect of a sincere effort to create a cultured self through consumption, more akin to the (powerful) hegemonic potential of Western consumerism than to a totalitarian conspiracy.

Because advertising is an extremely privileged form of discourse in the West, the history of Western consumerism is much better documented than that of the production-oriented Soviet Union.[4] Two main concepts from the literature on the West are useful in a Soviet context. First is the idea that consumption can be idealized as the primary goal of citizens in mass-producing societies. It is this utopian faith in the fantasy of consumption that joins Soviet and Western consumerism, despite dramatic differences in real economic performance. Rosalind Williams, in her study of French mass consumption at the turn of the last century, argued that consumer culture was less a function of the actual availability of goods than the creation of desire for goods and the belief that consumption was a vital aspect of modern life: "In mass consumption the needs of the imagination play as large a role as those of the body. Both are exploited by commerce, which appeals to consumers by inviting them into a fantasy world of pleasure, comfort, and amusement."[5]

For Williams, consumption has little to do with the use-value of products; instead, she focuses on objects as sources of psychological satisfaction. Individuals perceive themselves primarily as consumers rather than producers. In this light, the perennial Soviet goods famines are less relevant to Soviet consumerism than is advertising's promotion of individualistic possession of objects as the highest goal of citizens who should no longer define themselves as socialist laborers but as cultured consumers of state-produced goods. Soviet advertising functioned in a fantasy world that was completely outside of the economy; even when the advertised goods were available, the settings depicted in advertisements were usually beyond the reach of average Soviet citizens.[6] The disconnect between fantasy consumption and actual availability of goods did not necessarily lessen the power of advertising images. On the contrary, it could actually intensify their hegemonic potential. Recent scholarship by economists, anthropologists, and historians has convincingly demonstrated the ways in which communist states used their monopolies over scarce consumer goods to force people to accept state paternalism; the only way to fulfill the consumerist fantasy was to tailor one's outward behavior so as to "earn" access to goods.[7]

The second major theme in Western consumer studies that is useful in a Soviet context is the belief in consumption as a means to "magical self-transformation."[8] Both American and Soviet advertisements stressed the potential of things to change the reader's very sense of self by re-creating the home, the workplace, and the body of the reader. What has differed over time in each country has been the desired result of that utopian transformation. Whereas NEP advertising designers focused on consumption as a means to political transformation that would build class harmony *(smychka)* and an identity based on recognition of the cycle of production and consumption (fig. 6.1), advertisements of the Stalin years encouraged personal transformation through the psychological division of consumption from production and through an identity based on the primacy of family life, leisure time, and a well-stocked household. Proper forms of consumption, as modeled by advertising, could transform rough peasants and work-

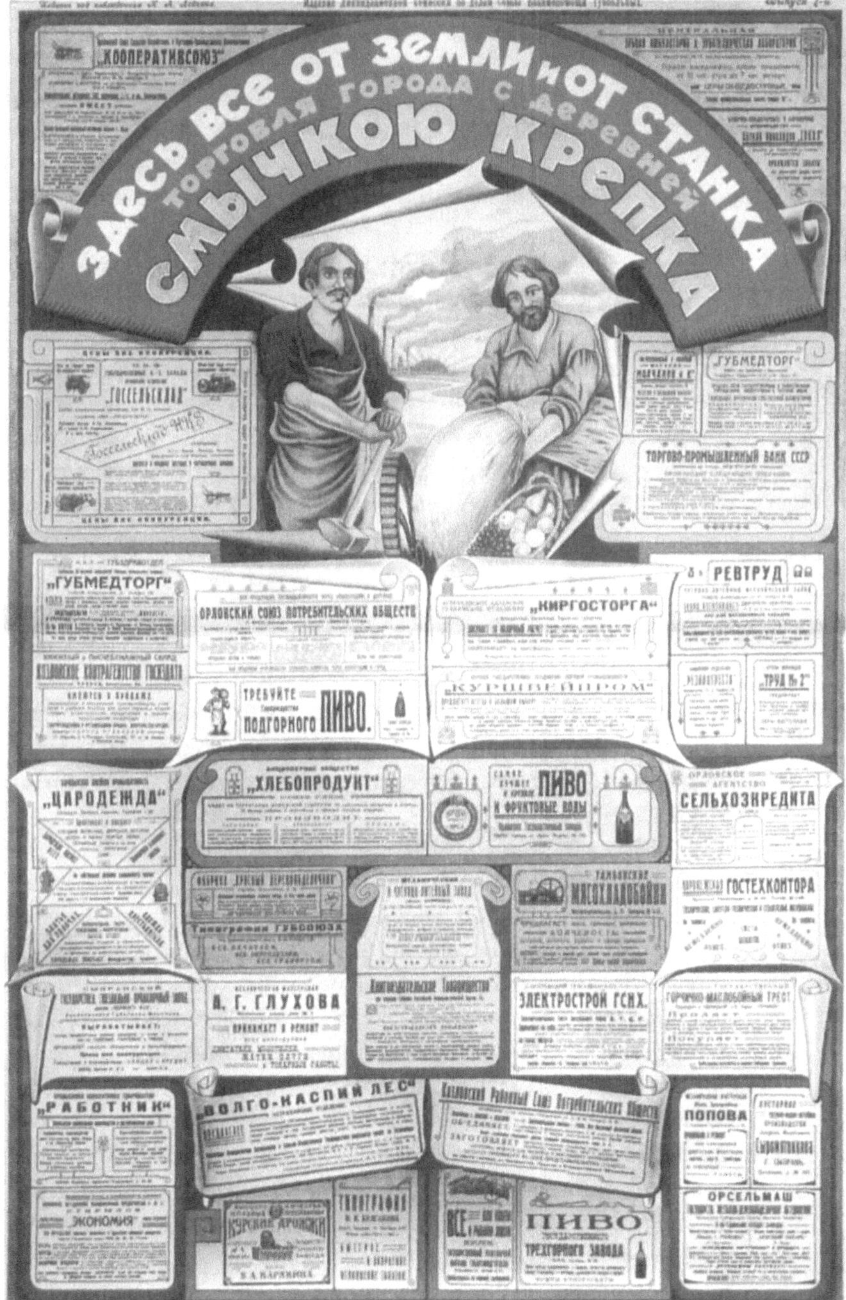

Fig. 6.1. "Here is everything from the land and the factory bench. The trade of the city and the village is strong in its unity." NEP advertisement stressing the political and economic ramifications of consumption, 1925.

ers into cultured citizens with modern, urban values.[9] In order to do this, advertising designers of the 1930s deliberately drew inspiration from American and western European advertising styles. Their goal was to extract what they saw as universal images of civilization and modernity, while leaving behind capitalist emphases on excess and self-indulgence.

Soviet commercial advertising had flourished under the New Economic Policy.[10] Several newspapers and other government bodies formed advertising agencies in order to generate revenues, and these agencies competed strenuously against one another. According to the figures of the Commissariat of the Workers' and Peasants' Inspectorate (Rabkrin), in 1924–25 these agencies earned 21 million rubles from advertising sales nationally, with 9.4 million of that coming from Moscow.[11] In 1926, however, government enterprises began to limit their advertising after Rabkrin and the Supreme Economic Council (VSNKh) warned that managers were spending too much money on advertisements that did not increase trade turnover. Decrees about "irrational spending on advertising" actually targeted only unwise practices such as advertising in publications with low circulations and running advertisements that praised the directors of a firm without mentioning the firm's products. But a press blitz on the dangers of irrational advertising and the corruption of independent agents led enterprise managers to interpret the decrees as a general ban on advertising. Sales of advertising plummeted. In January 1926 Rabkrin shut down the largest Soviet ad agency, Dvigatel' (which had operated under the auspices of the newspaper *Ekonomicheskaia zhizn'*), for corruption and unprofitability. The loss of sales in 1926–27 also prompted the closure of three of the four remaining large agencies: Transpechat', of the Commissariat of Transportation, Sviaz', of the Commissariat of Post and Telegraph, and the Central Administration of Industrial Propaganda and the Press (TsUP), under VSNKh. Their advertising operations, however, were transferred back to their parent bodies and continued to operate on a reduced scale during the first Five-Year Plan. Mosreklama, the advertising agency of the Moscow Committee on the Economy (MKKh), also remained open during the late twenties and early thirties.

In 1927, several of the major figures in NEP advertising came together to form the Association of Advertising Workers (ARR) in order to find ways to improve the performance and reputation of Soviet advertising. They called for better education for designers and more contact with Western advertising specialists. Although the largest agencies had been shut down, many of their personnel found reemployment in the advertising departments of major publications, especially *Ekonomicheskaia zhizn'*, *Pravda*, *Izvestiia*, and *Ogonek*, as well as at the publishing houses of Gosizdat, the Commissariat of Trade, and a host of smaller newspapers and journals. But Soviet advertising remained in a difficult position during the first two Five-Year Plans; rapid industrialization meant that few enterprises could afford to divert funds for advertising, and increased subsidies for central papers made them less dependent on advertising revenues. The rationing of key consumer goods from 1929 to 1935 also lessened the importance of advertising. Furthermore, the fall of the artistic-literary avant-garde, who had designed advertisements and whose work had informed earlier advertising, discredited NEP advertising styles.[12]

The end of rationing in 1935 led the Commissariat of Domestic Trade to reexamine advertising. From 1935 to 1941, Torgreklama, the advertising bureau of that commissariat, and Soiuzpishchepromreklama, under the Commissariat of Food Industries, dramatically increased their production of posters, print ads, and radio ads and even toyed with commercials to be shown before feature films. These two commissariats directly ordered their departments to place advertisements at departmental expense, and their secretariats closely monitored departmental progress in developing advertising campaigns, which were contracted out to various state art workshops. Rationing again limited advertising during World War II, but it reappeared in 1946.[13]

Soviet advertising, therefore, during the prewar Five-Year Plans, was continually looking for a way to re-create itself. The crisis in advertising in 1926 precipitated a flood of self-examination by advertisers in the press between 1926 and 1930. While they decried the ignorance of Soviet managers and the lack of training for designers, they praised American and German advertising for its creativity, technical mastery, extensive market research, and emotional effectiveness. American advertising was seen as more scientific than its Soviet counterpart, because it was based on market research and principles of psychology. Capitalist advertising fell short, however, in that its primary goal was to increase profits at the expense of telling consumers the truth, as Soviet observers saw it.

On the whole, their criticisms rang hollow. Authors might spend nearly all of an article extolling the expertise of American designers and then end with a paragraph that essentially amounted to a mournful, "If only the Americans would use their powers for good . . ." The task of Soviet designers, according to these articles, became the appropriation of American techniques without American exploitation and deception. The new Soviet advertising would be "capitalist in form, socialist in content," to paraphrase a political slogan of the day.[14] A special section of the ARR under D. I. Reitynbarg, the association's secretary, set up exchanges of research and literature on advertising with foreign organizations. The ARR also set up a library of foreign advertising literature at the House of the Press (Dom Pechati) in Moscow, and Reitynbarg wrote articles on American advertising and translated a series of articles from German ad trade publications for *Zhurnalist.* Specifically, Reitynbarg called for Soviet market research, American-style training for ad designers, and the adaptation of American advertising's stress on the psychological and emotional effect of consumption on individuals, as opposed to NEP advertising's emphasis on the use-value of products and its calls for political and economic support for Soviet enterprises by revolutionary social classes.[15]

The result was the gradual rejection of NEP styles, which had depended on class iconography adopted from Soviet political posters, in favor of Westernized images of glamour and beauty. In contrast to Mayakovsky and Rodchenko's sharp lines and geometric shapes, design styles between 1928 and 1941 turned to softer, more elegant lines to create an atmosphere of luxury or sentimentality rather than one of communist urgency. Western modernist and art deco influences show through strongly in this advertising. Whenever designers wanted to invoke images of fashion, excitement, or glamour, they turned to explicitly Western styles, an indication that the perception of the West as the ideal of beauty and modernity predominated, at least in the minds of designers. For example, beginning in 1927 Tezhe (a romantic-sounding abbreviation for the State Fats Trust) ran advertisements in which its products featured labels with French spelling. Tezhe and Lenzhet, its Leningrad subsidiary, both used French-language labels on their products during the late 1920s and early 1930s (fig. 6.2), which earned them the ire of the prominent Association of Artists of the Revolution (AKhR). In 1930 and 1931 *Iskusstvo v massy* (Art to the masses) and *Za proletarskoe iskusstvo* (For proletarian art) complained that Lenzhet and Tezhe labels should be censored because their Western motifs encouraged "petit bourgeois tendencies" and pandered to "*meshchanin* tastes," which in turn would diminish the impact of the revolution in private life.[16]

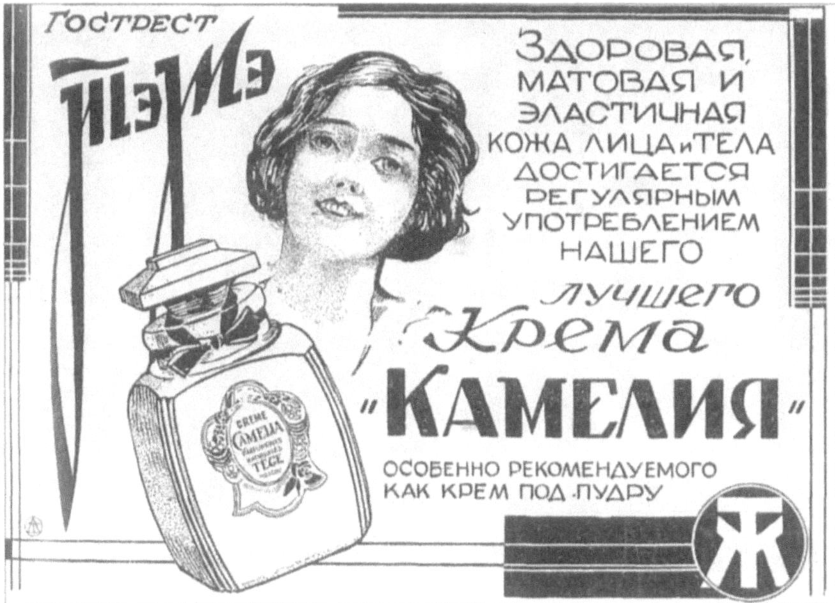

Fig. 6.2. "Healthy, resplendent, and elastic skin on the face and body may be achieved with the regular use of our best cream, *Camelia*, which is specially for use under powder." Advertisement for the Tezhe State Trust, 1929. Note the French labeling on the bottle.

Even more remarkable is a 1930 magazine advertisement in which "renowned film actress" Olga Chekhova endorses Chlorodont, a German toothpaste sold on a concession basis in the Soviet Union (fig. 6.3).[17] Chekhova also appeared in Chlorodont ads in German publications, and it is likely that Chlorodont supplied the artwork for this advertisement.[18] She looks coquettishly out at the readers of *Prozhektor* and proclaims, "My smile is the best evidence of the effectiveness of Chlorodont, which I use daily." Chekhova, a Russian actress, had emigrated to western Europe at the time of the revolution, but she gained fame during the 1920s when her films were imported to the Soviet Union, where they were very successful, especially the French-made *Moulin Rouge*.[19] Not only did this advertisement link the toothpaste to glamour and the excitement of show business, but it connected it to a star who had rejected socialism in favor of Paris and Berlin!

Despite the outcry against bourgeois specialists and the promotion of "socialism in one country" in other cultural forms during the first Five-Year Plan, advertising portrayed the West as the model of fash-

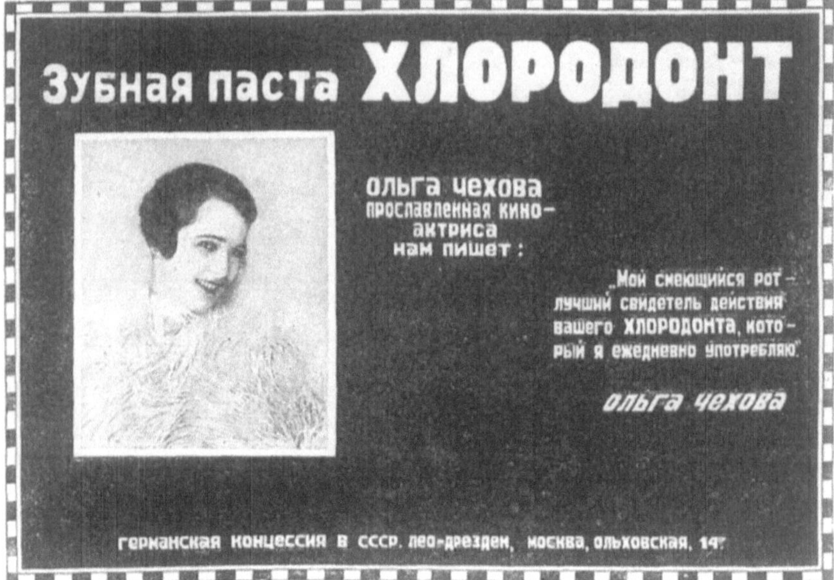

Fig. 6.3. Advertisement for Chlorodont toothpaste, as endorsed by "renowned film actress" Olga Chekhova in *Prozhektor*, 1930.

ion and modernity. As AKhR and so many others sought to isolate the Soviet Union, advertising designers looked to the West for inspiration and told consumers that they should do the same. This trend continued into the mid- and late 1930s, particularly in advertisements for Moscow restaurants and jazz clubs, which used images of the West to underscore their sophistication. Newspapers gave the name of the Hotel Savoy in Latin letters (fig. 6.4), and the Hotel Metropol' advertised "Five O'Clock Tea" in English.[20]

Advertising and Actual Space

Advertising confronted consumers in a number of locations during the Stalin period, bringing images of consumption to public Soviet space. The most common forms of advertising were shop windows, posters, and print advertisements in newspapers and magazines. After 1932, leading papers such as *Pravda, Izvestiia,* and *Krestianskaia gazeta* could afford to limit their advertising to a half page of subdued announcements, mostly for films, plays, and journals. Less politically oriented newspapers and magazines maintained advertising sections throughout the 1930s, with a noticeable increase as rationing was phased out

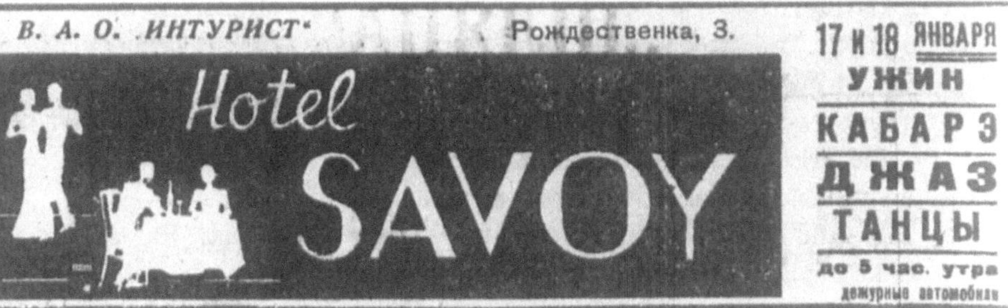

Fig. 6.4. Newspaper advertisement for the Hotel Savoy, 1935: "Dinner, cabaret, jazz, dancing."

in 1935.[21] These sections combined advertisements for films, restaurants, consumer goods, and services with classified advertising for jobs and housing. Commercial advertising disappeared during the war but returned in 1946.

Advertising sections generally occupied the last page or pages of daily newspapers. For example, before World War II, *Vecherniaia Moskva* ranged from four to seven pages in length, and the last one to three pages consisted of advertisements. After the war, papers such as *Vecherniaia Moskva, Sovetskaia Litva,* and *Zaria vostoka* (Tbilisi) devoted one-half to one page to advertisements out of four or five pages. Advertisements in magazines and journals before the war usually appeared on the back cover, the inside covers, and the last few pages of the magazine; after 1945 they appeared only on the back cover. Prewar magazine advertisements could be any size, but after the war magazines printed only full-page ads. The amount of advertising in a given issue of a newspaper or magazine appears not to have followed a pattern, either by time of year or day of the week. One issue of a publication might feature a large advertising section, the following issue might carry none, and then advertisements might reappear in the next issue. Many print ads were reprints of advertising posters.[22]

Consumers could easily evade print advertising by skipping certain pages of newspapers or by not reading them at all. Managers of advertising firms, therefore, counted on posters to reach even illiterate consumers. They urged artists to make posters as accessible as possible, with clear depictions of the product so that illiteracy would not lessen the poster's impact, although this was of less concern as the period progressed. Advertising posters, to the dismay of their critics, were displayed in a variety of public spaces, including factories, government office buildings, peasant libraries, post offices, and train stations. They decorated movie theaters, bus stops, subway cars, and trolley buses. In a speech on plans to improve Soviet advertising in February 1936, M.I. Khlopliankin, deputy commissar of domestic trade, urged artists to overlook no possible location for posters. When an audience member suggested that such extensive public advertising could become pernicious and inappropriate *(nazoilivo)*, Khlopliankin replied, "Advertising should be persistent. That's how it is done abroad. When you walk into a square, you have to close your eyes from so many ads."[23]

Outside of Moscow, local governments and publishing houses sold space on joint advertising posters to raise revenue. Joint posters featured a headline and illustration that established a common theme—generally enterprises within the same city or producing similar products—and between five and fifty small text ads, which often listed little more than an enterprise or store's name, address, and major products. This technique had been common during NEP at the major agencies, and organizations ranging from the Society of Friends of the Air Fleet to the Children's Commission and provincial city soviets had raised money by selling ad space on joint posters. The effort to revamp Soviet advertising styles led Torgreklama and Soiuzpishepromreklama to abandon this style during the 1930s, but local organizations continued to use it. Of the 25 joint posters in a sample of 211 posters dating from 1928 to 1941 that I examined, only 5 came from Moscow, and 3 from Leningrad.[24] The rest were produced in runs of 250 to 10,000 copies in cities such as Kuibyshev, Ordzhonikidze, Sverdlovsk, and Novosibirsk.[25] But whereas joint posters from the NEP years had focused on themes such as class harmony and national defense, the most common headline in the 1930s was "For cultured Soviet commerce!" A visit to any government or Party office, from the local county soviet *(volispolkom)* to the post office, or a trip on any form of public transportation, even far from Moscow, usually meant exposure to posters extolling the "culturedness" of good hygiene, family nutrition, and shopping at department stores.

Advertising designers also changed the appearance of Soviet storefronts, especially the shop windows of major department stores, during the late 1920s and 1930s. Admiration for American techniques and discomfort with avant-garde styles contributed to a Westernization of Soviet department store window displays. A two-part article on advertising in New York City by M. Mikhailov published in 1929 and 1930 provides a good example of Soviet ambivalence toward American consumerism. Mikhailov decried the images of plenty in American advertising as a sham that hid the poverty and exploitation engendered by capitalism. On the other hand, he could barely contain his glee when he described the displays at Woolworth's department store and Camel's model factory, where visitors could watch cigarettes being made on Broadway. At Woolworth's, "everything costs either five or ten cents . . . cufflinks, notebooks, books, toys, towels, socks, spoons, forks—almost everything you could want. You leave loaded down with purchases of things you need and things you don't need—after all, everything is only five or ten cents! The late Mr. Woolworth knew well the psychology of consumers, especially the psychology of American consumers."[26] The new effort during the first Five-Year Plan to adopt appeals to the "psychology of consumers" for Soviet department stores led to imitations of Western window displays, complete with scenes of well-dressed mannequins in bedrooms, dining rooms, and living rooms.

Even more than French-style labels, these new shop windows drew fire from the AKhR. It published photographs and the names of the designers of the most offensive displays. As the AKhR saw it, these windows were dangerous because they infected public space with private images. Public space should be revolutionary space, and shop windows should display agitational posters and slogans of the day; they should not be used to lure shoppers into "pornographic" celebrations of *meshchanstvo,* a petit bourgeois obsession with fashion, materialism, sexuality, and other such decadent pastimes.[27] The windows were dioramas showing scenes from banal, uncultured lifestyles, rather than guides to the new civic consciousness. It would be bad enough, argued several 1930 articles in *Iskusstvo v massy,* if these windows merely ignored politics, but they even went so far as to send anti-Soviet messages and contributed to what B. Zemenkov called "the Sovietization of *meshchanstvo.*" He criticized several stores for using busts of Lenin and other revolutionaries in their displays, where they were often surrounded by Western-style furnishings. This was inappropriate, he argued, because the stores were trying make money by using the image of Lenin to sell goods, and because placing revolutionary figures in a private context was disrespectful. An illustration accompanying his article showed a display of a dinner table set for two with fine china and crystal. The caption warned, "With this 'dining room' Mostorg agitates from its window against collective dining halls."[28]

D. Liakhovets claimed that shop windows at the Mostorg store on Petrovka Street, which featured a mannequin of a fashionably dressed woman gesturing toward a bedroom set, "teaches our consumers that a woman is an ornament for the bedroom." Such images, he criticized, encouraged people to think that women should be soft and that "labor is stupid."[29] Another author complained that stores were full of Westernized furniture, dishes, and clothing because artists had failed to come up with genuinely innovative Soviet designs. All that the "artists with names" (that is, the constructivists and other avant-garde artists) had managed to do in the twenties, he sneered, was to take the same old designs and cover them with stars, hammers, and sickles. Mostorg and other stores used Western-style shop windows to make money, like any vulgar private trader. As a result, Soviet consumers could not revolutionize their private lives, even if they wanted to.[30]

The focus of all their concerns was that shop window advertising was a violation of the proper use of public space. Mannequins decked out in the latest Paris fashions, from their bobbed hair to their high heels, and furniture arrangements designed for family (rather than collective) living space brought sexuality, leisure, and anticollective sentiments into public space and, worse yet, invited consumers to bring these sentiments home with them. The outcome, critics warned, would be a loss of revolutionary fervor and a cheapening of public space. The scenario painted by Zemenkov illustrates their fear:

> You go to a demonstration. Red banners fly overhead. You watch the march. Thoughts and steps confidently move forward. The past is irrevocably crushed. Then a dead, intent gaze falls on you. Slightly bent forward, in order to more attentively scrutinize the demonstration, and daintily holding her little finger, the window mannequin with the face of a *lishenka* points you toward the bed with its lacy blanket, to the soft easy chair, to the wall hangings. Everything is so calm and so soothing. . . .
>
> You force yourself to turn away. You walk past the window. But no sooner do you bring your attention back than you are distracted by another *lishenets* in a bowler, then another in a lady's coat. They reach out for you from the windows with their unbending hands, trying to extinguish your enthusiasm and break down your resolve. They call you to their petit bourgeois comfort of figurines, carpets, and paper flowers.[31]

Here Zemenkov assumes that the mannequins represent *lishentsy,* people deprived of civil rights due to bourgeois social origins or other connections to the prerevolutionary order. After all, "real" communists had no need for easy chairs and porcelain figurines; it was the bourgeoisie who reveled in such decadence. From his viewpoint, these shop windows were a danger, tempting communists to give up their struggle to build utopia and lose themselves in creature comforts. But his warning went unheeded, and by the mid-1930s cozy domestic scenes had become a common trope in department store windows. No longer defined as *meshchanstvo,* these dioramas of happy family settings met the standard for "cultured Soviet commerce." In each case, however, the arrangement of the environment, especially living space, had the ability to shape human identity. For Zemenkov, a comfortable interior had the power to subvert political will, to lure revolutionaries into self-indulgent isolation. The advertising and department store displays, on the other hand, suggested that such interiors elevated their inhabitants, as was appropriate now that the revolution was officially complete.

Both Amy Randall and Julie Hessler have noted that department stores of the mid- to late 1930s served as educational sites dedicated to increasing the cultural level of consumers. In this case "civilized" and "cultured" meant having an appreciation for stylish clothing, elegant furnishings, sophisticated jazz, and fine liqueurs; modernity had been conflated with Western tastes and lifestyles. Retail employees could even earn the title of Stakhanovite for developing attractive sales displays and advising customers. Model department stores in Moscow and other big cities became themselves advertisements for the newly acceptable domestic refinement as shop windows and displays provided examples of how consumers could integrate the store's wares into their lives. In 1936, one advertising designer referred to the "pedagogical task" of shop windows and argued that the windows of all the stores on each city block should be coordinated, in order to create a more effective "trade ensemble." Managers often believed that customers might be overwhelmed by the sheer quantity of goods available at the model stores and encouraged sales staff to provide guidance.[32]

Print advertisements also offered assistance. In March 1935, for example, TsUM published a store map that took up one-third of a page in the advertising section of *Vecherniaia Moskva.* The first floor had the most complicated layout, with a variety of departments, including jewelry, china, suitcases, sporting goods, photography equipment, stationery, toiletries, and carpets, among others. On the second floor were shoes, linens, ready-made clothing, toys, and a large restaurant, while outerwear, hats, more shoes and clothes, a tailoring department, and a "fashion workshop" were located on the third floor. Consumers could find silk, cotton, flannel, and other fabrics on the fourth floor. The ad encouraged readers to "clip and save" the map, because "it will help you orient yourself in the store."[33] It is worth repeating that this layout, as well as shop window scenes, was inspired at least in part by Western models. Julie Hessler has convincingly demonstrated the Western influence on model department stores during the 1930s, citing in particular deliberate emulation of the American store Macy's.[34]

Advertising artists and administrators in the second half of the 1930s proposed to turn entire cities into canvases for their work. In the 1936 edition of *Vsia Moskva,* the main city directory, a half-page ad for Mosgossvet, which produced neon signs, consisted of a drawing of a city transformed by electric advertising. "Light propaganda" decorated trams, shop windows, and rooftops.[35] Artists batted around ideas in a similar vein during brainstorming sessions at the Commissariat of Domestic Trade in February and March 1936. Khlopliankin, the deputy commissar, spoke nostalgically about his time in Paris and London, describing advertising posters near the Eiffel Tower and London skywriters who spelled out the names of firms in the sky. "But these are expensive pleasures," he sighed. "We, of course, must seek cheaper ways of influencing the psyche—words and drawings. That's where creativity, inventiveness, originality, and accessibility come in. That's where you [artists] come in."[36]

At least one artist, Ierikhonov, favored the inexpensive approach of sending actors around Moscow to play out scenes that would incorporate endorsements for various products and stores. Spectators would not realize they were watching actors; instead, they would "accidentally" witness a private moment in which ordinary people had been affected by making good, or bad, choices about where to shop. The young man at the beginning of this chapter who had forgotten to bring his girlfriend a pot from TsUM would seem to have learned an important lesson about women and consumption, which he could impart to the concerned crowd. Ierikhonov suggested another scene for use on subways and trolleys:

> Imagine yourself on a metro car. Some citizen picks up a letter from the floor and reads, "To Ipat'ev." He asks, "Who here is Ipat'ev?" Silence. Then he reads, "Dear Comrade Ipat'ev, I am alive and well.

> I received your letter, and I want to let you know that I am very grateful to you. Today I was at the Central Department Store, TsUM, and I bought a splendid cap there. My wife liked it very much." Of course, it turns out to be an actor who has brought the letter, pretended to find it, and played out this little scene.[37]

Thankfully, the other artists voted down Ierikhonov's amateurish advertising theater, so they did not have to deal with the thorny question of how to prevent travelers from seeing the same scene played out more than once on public transportation.

Advertising and Fantasy Space

In addition to transforming actual space, Soviet advertising tried to redefine the social construction of space and the roles different kinds of space should play in the formation of identity. Advertising created a fantasy that defined space "as it should be," to play on the formula of socialist realism. NEP advertising had tended to portray the entire USSR as a single unit of space engaged in a huge cycle of production and consumption. It rarely depicted consumption in a home or other private space but focused instead on scenes of peasants and workers exchanging goods or consuming a product within view of a factory or other productive location. There could be no consumption without production, and vice versa. Even when no location was discernible in an advertisement, the use of class vocabulary or the clothing of the characters immediately identified consumers as members of a class, of a producer group. Advertising from the late twenties and afterward, on the other hand, went to great pains to obscure the productive process, to identify both readers and characters in ads as private consumers, no matter whether they were consuming in public or private space. The effect was a new division of public and private space and the diminishment of public space as an arena of politics and production.

That is not to say that public space disappeared completely from these ads. Public locations portrayed in advertising, however, were sites of leisure and cultured consumption by private individuals and families; they were never sites of production. The park, the restaurant, and the department store replaced the factory and the village soviet as common settings. Following their attempt to physically change department stores, Soviet advertising designers sought in the thirties, forties, and fifties to portray such stores as exciting locales of consumer happiness. Newspaper and poster advertisements for department stores during the Stalin period featured a cornucopia of goods accompanied by sentimental images of happy children and families.

At the Commissariat of Domestic Trade, Ierikhonov dreamed of a full-length feature film, *Manon of the Central Department Store,* about the love life of a salesgirl at TsUM, "such that the viewer is left with an impression of how wonderful the goods there are and in what a civilized *[kul'turno]* manner they treat shoppers there."[38] Acknowledging the prohibitive expense of such a film, he proposed instead a series of three-minute animated films about a character named Vanichka Pokupkin (Johnny Shopper) who would visit a different department of the store in each installation. This suggestion met with greater approval than his subway idea, and designers toyed with a number of scenarios in which an ignorant Vanichka would arrive from the countryside and use advertising to find the best restaurants and a store where he could buy new city clothes. In other words, advertising would turn a peasant into a modern, urban shopper. Another designer, Agorn, suggested using Stakhanovite characters instead of a peasant. In his scenario, a woman is distraught because a strange woman has telephoned. When the caller refuses to identify herself, the wife assumes the worst of her Stakhanovite husband. But it turns out that the caller works at the delivery department of a new grocery store. The husband had sworn the clerk to secrecy because he was planning a special delivery for a surprise birthday party for his wife.[39]

Designers at the March 1936 brainstorming session at the commissariat suggested a makeover for Soviet restaurants as well. For example, the artist Ol'skii noted that many people were "living eighteen years in the past," believing that restaurants were nothing more than taverns. Advertising could point out that Soviet restaurants were instead places of "cultured leisure." Rather than "getting drunk" at home, citizens should celebrate special occasions at restaurants such as the Aurora in Moscow, where "the very best people of our country" spend relaxing evenings. One proposed commercial would star the Stakhanovite Dusia Vinogradova. After receiving her award, she would leave the Kremlin to celebrate with other Stakhanovites at a nearby restaurant. Encouraging consumers to go to restaurants, designers argued, would be a "blow against backwardness, against inertia."[40] Likewise, a print advertisement for the Aurora in April of that year included a photograph of a sumptuous interior with white columns, a mirrored bar, and tables decorated with white tablecloths and fine china (fig. 6.5). The text reminded readers that the Aurora was the "best

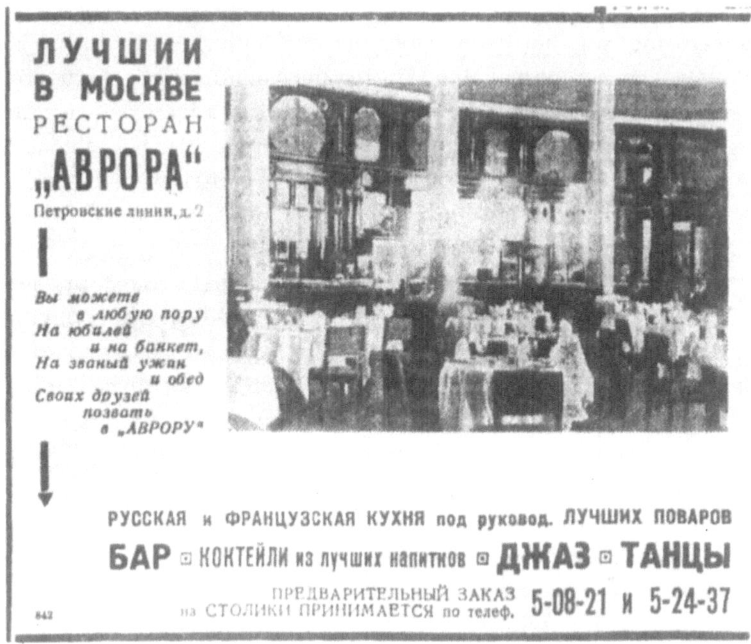

Fig. 6.5. "The best restaurant in Moscow: the Aurora." *Vecherniaia Moskva*, April 27, 1936.

restaurant in Moscow" and that it offered Russian and French cuisine, cocktails, and a dance floor. Also included was a short verse extolling the pleasures of socializing at the Aurora: "For any occasion, an anniversary, a banquet, a dinner party, or a luncheon, you can invite your friends to the Aurora."[41]

Several designers called for advertising that would target Stakhanovites, because although they were outstanding workers, they knew little about being consumers, as the designer Bel'skii put it. They suddenly found themselves with money and access to goods "of which they have absolutely no understanding." It was the responsibility of advertisers, he argued, to interpret and explain goods, "especially exotic items like oysters." All the proposed scenarios involving Stakhanovite characters took them out of a labor context, dressed them in suits and skirts, and showed them consuming in a private family setting or at a "cultured" public location such as the Aurora. Poster and print advertising rarely, if ever, identified characters as Stakhanovites; not a single example occurred in either the print sample or among the posters I studied. The point of being a Stakhanovite, in the fantasy world of Soviet advertising, was not heroic labor but developing cultured (that is, Western) consumption habits. During the commissariat's discussion of restaurants, one artist, Bolotin, suggested that advertising encourage birthday parties at restaurants, where "they are often held abroad." And at least two artists complained that the proposals were too derivative of American styles.[42]

The transformation of Stakhanovites and other Soviet citizens from rough workers into "civilized" consumers entailed a transformation of private space. Advertising provided readers with a catalog of vital goods that should fill their apartments and cottages. The standard of living portrayed in the advertising of the Stalin years, both before and after the war, was markedly urban and affluent; this tendency was particularly strong in ads for insurance companies and savings banks, whether they ran in the upscale *Finansovaia gazeta* or the more popular *Vecherniaia Moskva*. There were advertisements for furniture and housewares, but the most luxurious images of interiors appeared in bank and insurance advertising. After all, these ads did not aim to sell a specific product, which freed artists to create fantasy images of interiors far beyond the reach of most Soviet consumers.

In December 1937, for example, *Finansovaia gazeta* published an advertisement for Gosstrakh (State Insurance) that could just as easily have come from the *Wall Street Journal* (fig. 6.6). In the foreground, a well-groomed man in a three-piece suit sits at his desk in a comfortable chair, examining his new insurance policy with satisfaction. On the desk sits a lamp with a fringed shade, along with a few books, crystal paperweights, and a pen holder. To the man's left is a phonograph, and to his right, a curtained window overlooking a busy city street at least ten floors below. Behind him stands an easy chair and a grand piano. In the background, a woman, presumably his wife, hangs clothes in an armoire, and a toddler plays with blocks on a decorative carpet.[43]

One wonders what critics representing the AKhR might have made of this luxurious scene. Their insistence that domestic comfort was inherently counterrevolutionary and self-indulgent no longer carried any weight by the mid-1930s. Revolutionary asceticism had been supplanted by an entirely proper striving for a cultured life. Although the artists at the 1936 discussions of advertising at the Commissariat of Domestic Trade expressed concern that advertising could be trite or "fall into *meshchanskii* style," they also contended that the banality trap

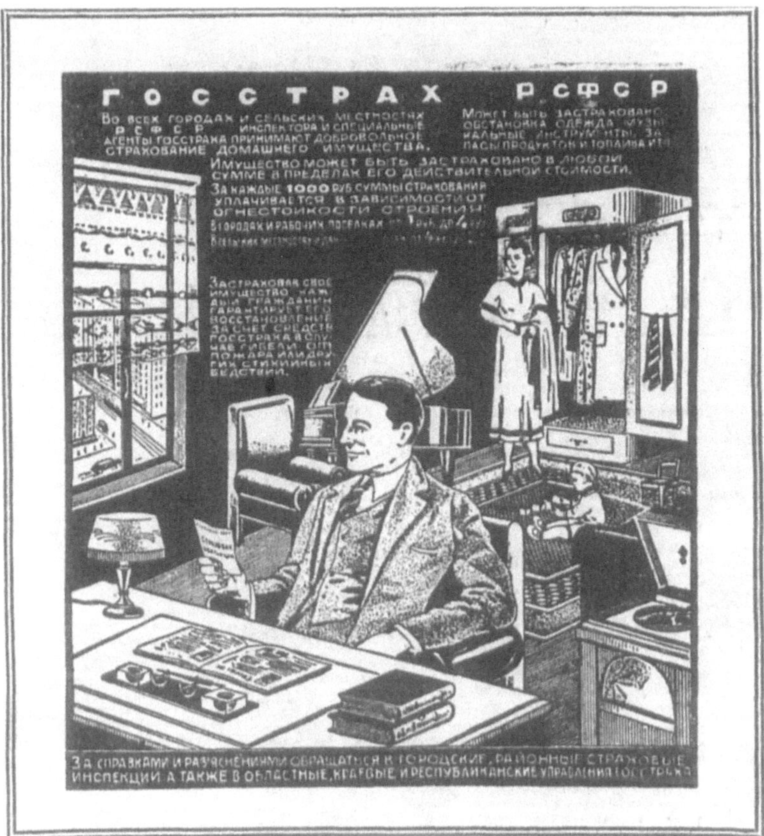

Fig. 6.6. Advertisement for Gosstrakh, the state insurance agency, *Finansovaia gazeta*, 1937.

could be avoided through "cultured," "mature," and "tasteful" designs. This distinction seems largely rhetorical, however; the artists offered no clear definition of either banality or good taste.[44]

Advertisements for banks, especially after the war, assured readers that all they needed to achieve a comfortable life was a savings account. Not only should one desire fashionable clothing, a piano, Tiffany lamps, a car, a radio, and a Black Sea vacation, but if one did not have them, it was one's own fault. Problems with the Soviet economy, the destruction caused by World War II, and hierarchical access to goods simply did not exist in the fantasy world of Soviet advertising. A bank advertisement in *Ogonek* in 1946 (fig. 6.7) made the point

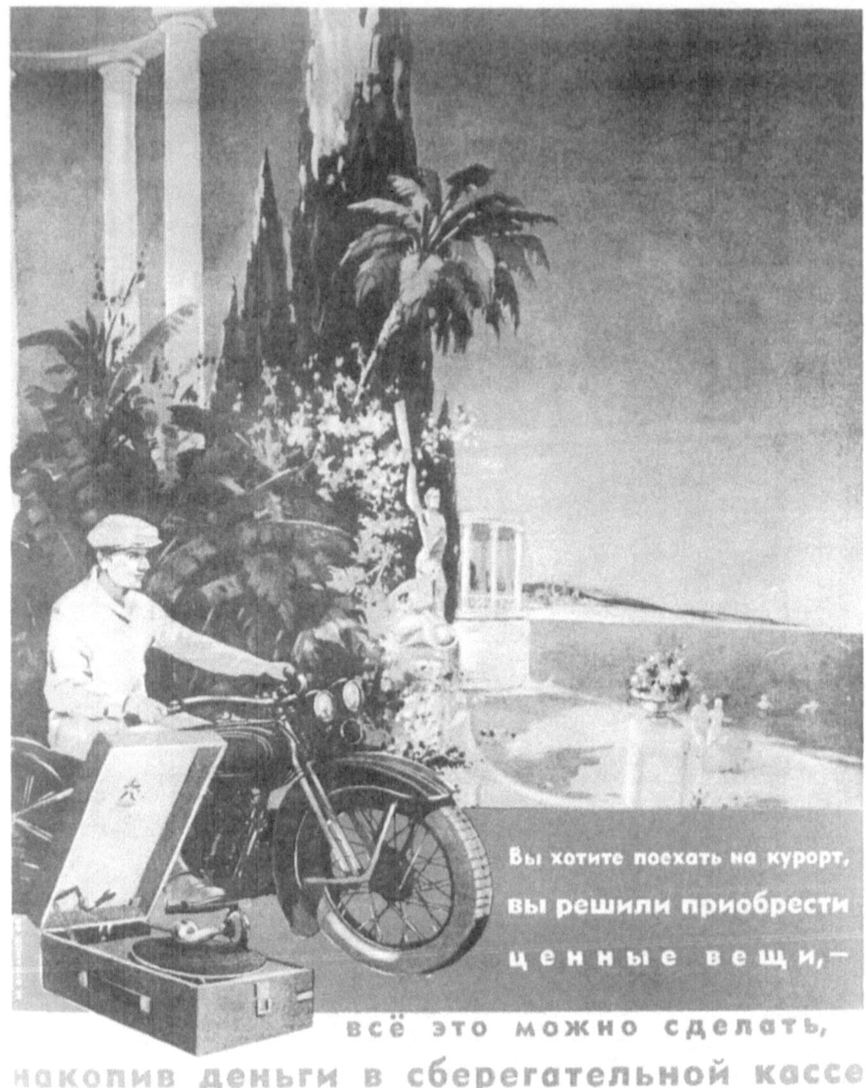

Fig. 6.7. Advertisement for a savings bank, *Ogonek*, 1946.

plain: "You want to go to a resort, you want to buy nice things—you can do all this, having saved money at the savings bank." The illustration shows a young man on a motorcycle, a record player, and an exotic Black Sea resort. A character in a 1950 ad was even more direct:

"I saved up and bought a car!" *(Nakopil i mashinu kupil!)* A few postwar ads mentioned that deposits in banks contributed to building the Soviet infrastructure, but on the whole, Stalin-era advertising emphasized the role of banks and insurance in creating and protecting urban, affluent, private space.[45]

The characters in advertisements were model consumers involved only in private life and private space. No mention is made in the Gosstrakh insurance ad, for example, of the productive lives of the characters; we know nothing about them except that they are young, urban, and affluent. Although insurance was available through the workplace, advertising did not present it as class-based aid to and from workers. Instead, men bought insurance to protect their families. Soviet advertising during the Stalin era never showed people at work, unless they were shop clerks offering a product to the reader or in some similar situation. Soviet designers told readers that the greatest source of happiness came from their role as private consumers, not as socialist laborers. The one exception to this trend was posters aimed specifically at collective farm workers, but even there the use of the politically charged word *kolkhoznik* was usually tempered with a sentimental illustration.[46]

As class faded from advertising, youth and gender became increasingly important. NEP advertising had often juxtaposed older peasants and younger (thus progressive) workers. Now, the loss of class distinctions in Stalinist advertising also meant a loss of generational distinctions, except in sentimentalized depictions of parents with young children. Even more remarkable were changes in gender images. During the 1920s, advertising designers needed to assure readers that consumption befitted Soviet ideals. They did so in part by coding consumption as male in order to overcome the revolutionary subculture's association of female consumption with frivolity and self-indulgence. In a sample of 176 posters from 1922 and 1926, 108 (61.4 percent) featured only male consumers, and 25 (14.2 percent) featured only female consumers. Mixed-gender groups appeared in 21 percent, and children appeared alone in 3.4 percent. During the Stalin era, consumption was once again coded as female, in keeping with the reassertion of traditional gender roles in that period. Between 1927 and 1929, a transitional phase from NEP advertising to Stalinist advertising, a sample of 76 posters split evenly between portrayals of men and women, with 33 posters (43.4 percent) each. Seven posters included mixed groups, and three featured only children.[47] By the 1930s, advertisers were clearly targeting women. Of the 100 posters in the sample depicting consumers from 1930 to 1941, men appeared alone in only 12 posters, whereas women appeared alone in 41. Twenty posters depicted mixed-gender groups, and 27 featured children alone, a dramatic increase that highlights the new focus on sentimental domesticity and private space.[48]

As striking as these numbers are, engendering consumption was not merely a matter of increasing or decreasing the number of men and women depicted in advertisements. The placement of images in relation to one another played a significant role in establishing hierarchical associations, a process that Victoria Bonnell has referred to as the "syntax" of the visual language of posters.[49] In the universe created by designers, Soviet men had the money and authority to purchase expensive, durable items such as cars and insurance, and women made the home provided by men more pleasant by encouraging family consumption of nutritious food, plastics, and vitamins. Although a few advertisements showed men using Tezhe toiletries or similar products, men were much more likely to be depicted as heads of households. A number of postwar bank advertisements, for example, featured men driving cars and motorcycles purchased with their savings; women never appeared as drivers.[50] Two small exceptions allowed male characters to appear in advertisements for food products. First, images of male chefs sometimes urged female readers to purchase sausages or similar goods. Second, men might appear as consumers of ice cream or beverages if they did so with women, especially if they were shown purchasing such items in a park or at a resort.[51]

Two kinds of women appeared in Stalin-era ads: the sentimentalized mother and the glamorous urbanite.[52] The latter had bobbed hair, impossibly long legs, and fashionable, if not practical, clothing. She dyed her hair and eyebrows and shaved her legs, because "the appearance of the nude body covered in hair makes an unpleasant impression, which is easily avoided with the use of our hair removal powder, Elem."[53] The magazine *Zhenskii zhurnal* called for subscriptions in 1928 with an advertisement that featured a woman with made-up lips and eyes and wearing a stylish hat and stole, while Lenzhet packaged its soaps in wrappers depicting Westernized women replete with beauty marks and mannish hair and figures.[54] Of the 211 posters in the sample from 1928 to 1941, 39 (18.5 percent) employed glamorous, Westernized images of women. However, this sexy image of women disappeared after the war.

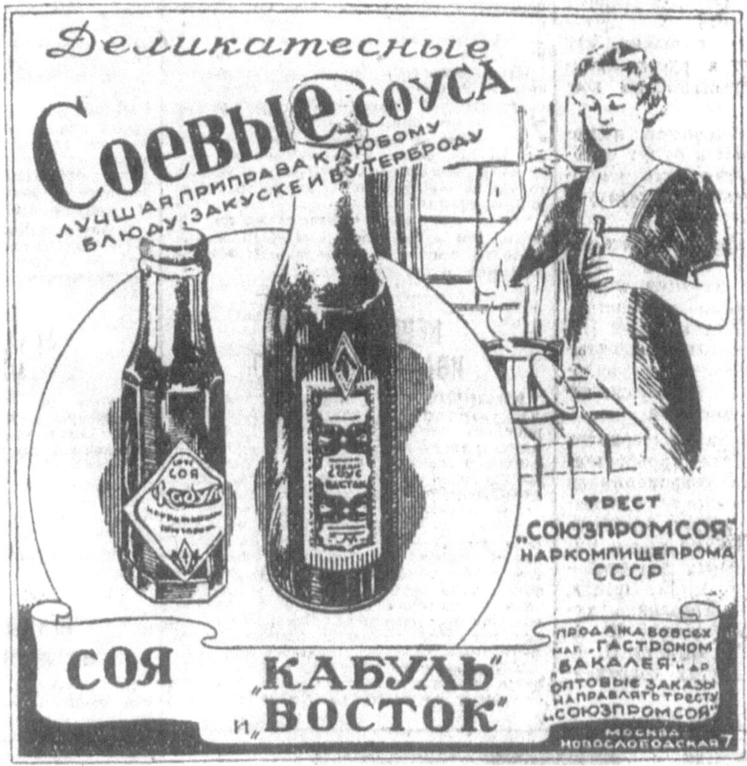

Fig. 6.8. "Gourmet soy sauces—the best spice for any dish, appetizer, or sandwich. Soy sauces *Kabul* and *East*." Poster, 1939.

More common was the sentimentalized mother. The young women who represented this image dressed fashionably and neatly, but modestly. Their features were less exaggerated than those of the glamorous urbanite, and they rarely looked directly out of the advertisement at the reader. Instead, designers placed them in poses that emphasized their nurturing relationships with others, doting on a child or husband or happily bent over food preparation for the family (fig. 6.8).[55] Advertisements for food, children's products, and household goods rarely included men, implying that Soviet women held primary responsibility for cooking, cleaning, and child rearing, in addition to their obligation to buy cosmetics and fashionable clothing in order to meet the aesthetic standards of a cultured society. A 1937 poster, for example, featured a woman bringing a jar of mayonnaise to her husband at the dinner table.

Both characters are young and well dressed, but the man is seated and the woman standing, leaning toward him with her offering. The man has a napkin tucked into the collar of his shirt, and he is posed with knife and fork over a full plate. The table is set for two, but only he is seated, because she is still busy serving the meal.[56]

The composition of the Soviet family in Stalin-era advertising reflected the nuclear family structure encouraged in the USSR as part of the discourse of cultured domesticity. When designers depicted an entire family, they drew a young father and mother accompanied by one or two children ranging in age from five to ten years. Often the children wore Young Pioneer uniforms, but these uniforms carried no political message; they appeared simply as one of the sentimentalized accoutrements of middle-class family life. The power structure in these families was clear—the father made important family decisions, the mother took care of domestic space, and children existed to be doted upon. An insurance ad from 1955 provides a good example. A family sits around a table with a male insurance agent. The father, in a suit and tie, signs the contract while everyone else looks on. The family is gathered spatially, indicating that it is a single unit led by the father. Two children sit next to him, the son wearing a tie and the daughter a Pioneer uniform. The mother stands behind them with one hand placed lovingly on the son's shoulder. She leans toward the father, watching him approvingly, but clearly in a secondary, supportive role. The room is only sparsely sketched but suggests a middle-class lifestyle with a decanter, buffet, and landscape painting.[57]

Advertising also emphasized the primacy of Russian space over non-Russian Soviet space. Characters were almost exclusively Russian in appearance, even when they were dressed in Paris fashions. Indeed, their Western clothes and hair tended to make Russian characters appear to be part of a homogenized European modernity in which consumption diminished ethnicity as a source of identity, so long as the consumer was white and light haired. Of the 125 posters depicting consumers in the sample from 1928 to 1941, only 18 (14 percent) featured non-Russian characters. And of the 151 posters with discernible locations, only 32 (21 percent) were explicitly non-Russian. Advertising distributed on a national level always portrayed Russian consumers as normative. Non-Russians appeared in only two situations: in ads aimed only at non-Russians and in designs where artists linked products to some exotic locale. In the first category was an ad from 1935 aimed at Kazakh women. The Russian-language text promised that

Tezhe hand creams and lotions "make skin soft and white"—that is, more Russian.[58]

Exotic locations and characters enhanced the desirability of products from the non-Russian areas. Stereotypical ethnic characters extolled the virtues of Georgian teas and wines, Uzbek tobacco and candies, and Caucasian spas to Russian consumers.[59] Readers should buy them not to support the growth of socialist industry in these areas but because their exotic origins made them exciting and sensual. Women in exotic ads displayed a sexuality far exceeding that of any image of Russian women; perhaps this reflected designers' own stereotypes about Caucasian and Central Asian women. It certainly played on popular and literary stereotypes of the romantic East. Also, an exotic name could make an ordinary product stand out. Tezhe, for example, manufactured a line of cosmetics under the name "Red Poppy" (Krasnyi Mak). The color red in this instance had nothing to do with communist banners; instead, posters and print advertisements for the product stressed eastern sensuality. The Cyrillic letters on the packaging seemed at first glance to be Chinese characters, and a stereotypical Chinese red tassel served as the package's handle.[60] The woman in the ad was a glamorous Russian (or at least not an Asian) made beautiful and sexual by this exotic product (fig. 6.9).

So far as Russian space was concerned, Stalinist advertising focused on urban sites as the scene of cultured consumption. Only 12 (8 percent) of 151 posters with discernible locations showed rural consumers. Seventy-eight posters portrayed scenes of urban households. Individuals and families in these advertisements gathered in urban spaces to use or purchase products, and they dressed in clothing suitable only for urban, white-collar work. Such advertisements linked consumption to an urban modernity full of escalators, cars, radios, taxis, liqueurs, and processed foods. Whereas NEP advertisements had portrayed urban progress through images of productive forces such as factories, smokestacks, and electrification, the advertising of the Stalin years shied away from presenting the productive aspects of urban society and, like Western ads, stressed instead the intangible, personal advantages of urban life, especially convenience, fashionableness, and a vibrant lifestyle.

Advertising that did show rural consumption was aimed exclusively at rural readers and offered ways to make the village more like the city. In 1950, for example, *Krestianka,* a magazine for rural women, advertised a mail-order service that offered deliveries of urban goods such

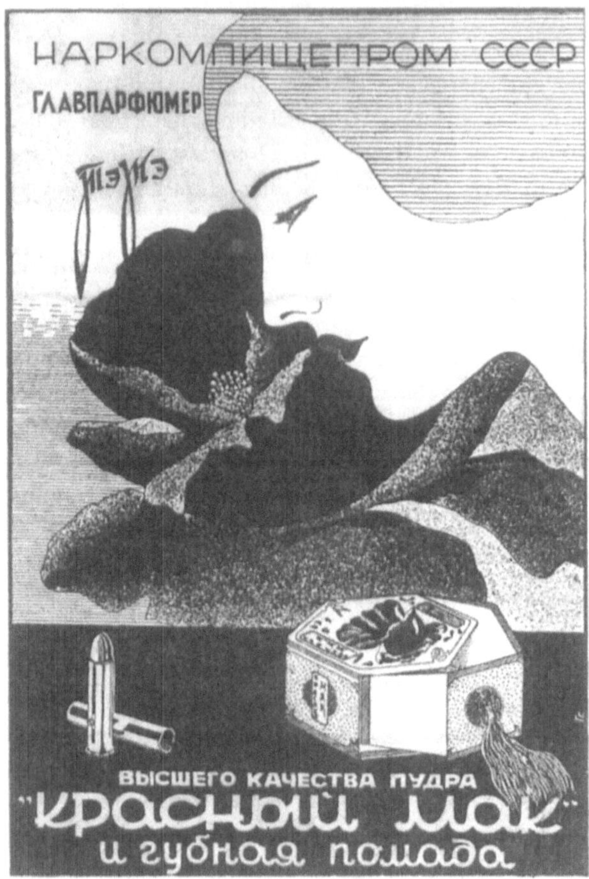

Fig. 6.9. Advertisement for Red Poppy cosmetics. Poster, 1938.

as sewing machines, radios, clocks, and cameras. In 1955 the same magazine published a bank advertisement urging readers to open an account and save money for "the purchase of valuable things" (fig. 6.10). The illustration depicts two well-dressed women adjusting the dials of a new radio sitting on a table covered with a lace cloth. Behind them, a large window opens onto a pleasant village view, including a car parked in front of a cottage. Potted plants complete the scene.[61] Given the actual conditions of the time, rural readers probably found this advertisement laughably fantastic.

But on the whole, the opposite of the city in Stalinist ads was not the village—it was the park, the resort, the sentimentalized orchard.

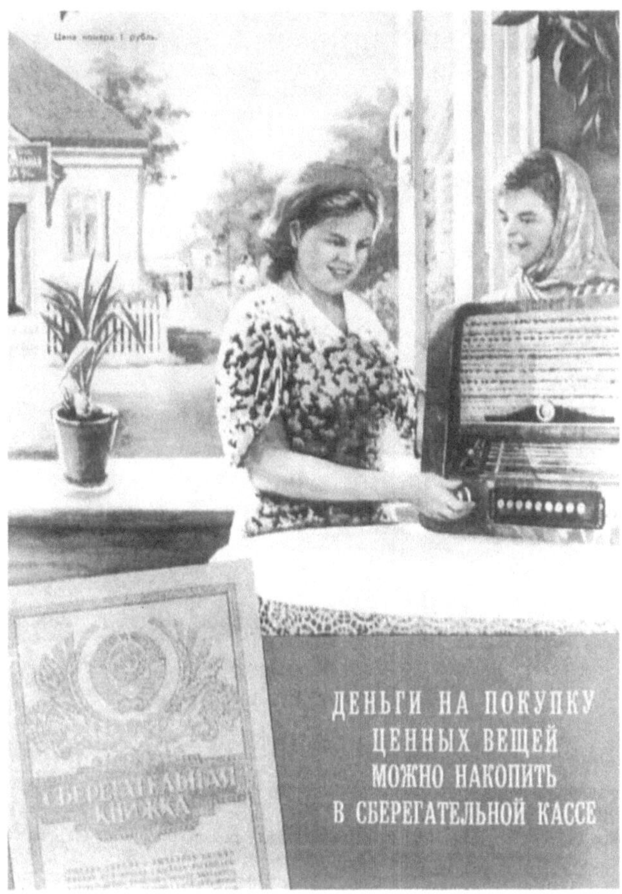

Fig. 6.10. "At the savings bank you can save up for the purchase of valuable things." Advertisement aimed at rural women, *Krestianka*, 1955.

One 1937 poster shows a mother and daughter enjoying ice cream as they stroll through a park. The text reminds readers that "it is pleasant to eat Eskimo ice cream on the street, in a park, or at home."[62] In this fantasy world the countryside became a place to go, not a place to live, as in the case of a 1952 advertisement encouraging readers to insure their automobiles, motorcycles, and motorboats (fig. 6.11).[63] The purchase of a car or vacation could allow urban consumers to escape the bustle of the city. In order to get the most out of nature, Soviet ads urged readers to bring a variety of goods with them, from rubber rafts to thermoses and crackers. And if you couldn't get away, then "natu-

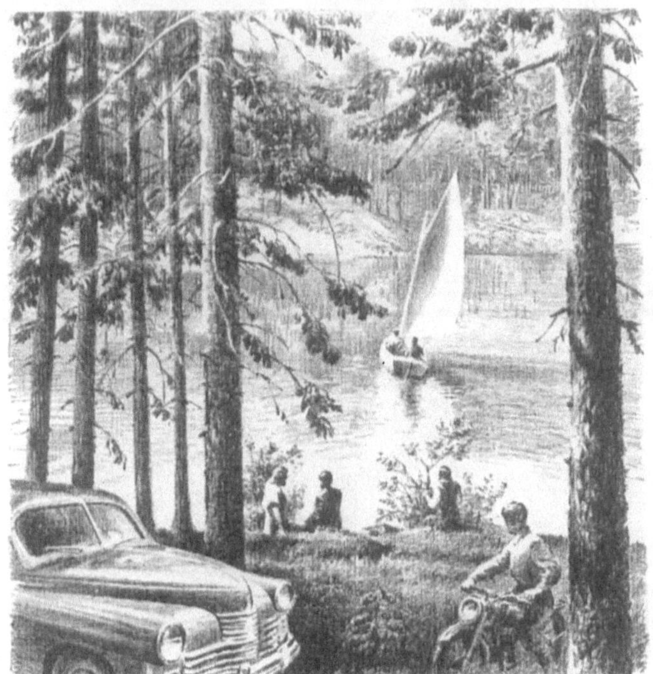

Fig. 6.11. "Automobiles, motorcycles, and motorboats that belong to citizens may be insured at Gosstrakh," the state insurance agency. *Ogonek*, 1952.

ral fruit drinks" from the Caucasus would bring the resort to you.[64] Nature, in the fantasy world of Soviet advertising, was not a place to be conquered in the name of building socialism; it was space for private leisure. The elimination of production in people's identity allowed more time for restorative play.

Sentimentalized visions of nature also made processed foods seem more natural. In one ad, boxes of frozen *pel'meni*, a kind of dumpling, repose in a Siberian pine forest (fig. 6.12), and in another, jars of jelly lie nestled in the boughs of fruit trees.[65] Designers at the Commissariat of Domestic Trade noted that Soviet consumers did not trust processed

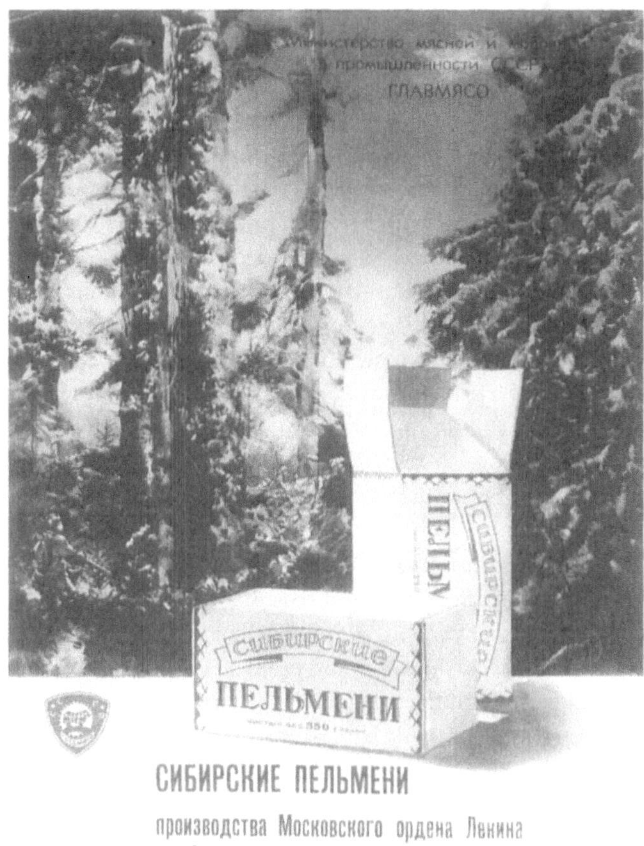

Fig. 6.12. Ready-made *pel'meni* gain legitimacy through association with nature. *Ogonek*, 1951.

and packaged foods such as margarine and candies, and by placing these foods in idealized natural settings, artists distanced the products from suspect Soviet production processes.[66] Of 73 posters from 1928 to 1941 that showed nonurban scenes, 12 featured depictions of nature as leisure space, and 17 linked products to sentimentalized nature. (Of the remaining posters, 12 showed rural consumers and 32 showed non-Russian settings; both subjects were presented in a sentimental or romantic style.) These two motifs became even more common after the war, such as in a 1946 vitamin ad juxtaposing pill boxes and flowering bushes. In the same vein, *Rabotnitsa* published a champagne ad in

1952 depicting grapes overflowing a crystal bowl with mountains and vineyards in the background.[67]

Conclusion

Commercial advertising during the Stalin period attempted to transform both actual space and the social construction of space by redefining the cultural relationship between production and consumption. This transformation, in turn, was intended to encourage a Soviet identity in which politics and class carried far less weight than family life, gender, and leisure. Advertising from the very beginning of the Stalin period deemphasized production, politics, and class and focused instead on the private, emotional effects of consumption. In doing so, it portrayed public spaces as areas for play, family outings, and cultured shopping—that is, as sources for private enjoyment. It stressed hierarchies of private over public, urban over rural, and Russian over non-Russian.

Given the prominence of Westernized images and aesthetics in Soviet advertising, one might reasonably wonder how well advertising fit with other versions of Stalinist identity offered by celebrity workers, radical literary groups, and political propaganda. Advertising did indeed clash with the militant ideals of the Cultural Revolution, and its existence at that time suggests that cultural images in public space during the first Five-Year Plan were more fluid than we generally acknowledge. It is also clear that these images, although strongly criticized at the time, established a precedent on which advertising designers could draw in the mid-1930s, when consumerism and "middle-class values" were connected to *kul'turnost'*. In this light, the use of Westernized images in advertising during the Stalin years was not necessarily a retreat from revolutionary ideals but an organic development of advertising specialists' efforts to find ways to integrate consumption into Soviet identity, consistent with the needs of the regime. During NEP, when state enterprises competed against private traders, advertising encouraged people to think of consumption of state-produced goods as part of the struggle for socialism. By the mid-1930s, when the state was the only provider of goods, advertising portrayed consumption as a means to cultural self-improvement. After the war the idea of *kul'turnost'* was fully intertwined with the official discourse of selfhood, and advertising reinforced images elsewhere in the media.

One might wonder, too, whether advertising could play a hegemonic role in Stalinist society, given the chronic deficits of consumer goods. Did it really make sense to publicize goods in an economy of shortage? At first glance it might seem that by inciting desire for unavailable products, advertising carried the seeds of destabilization; after all, few Muscovites could afford to go to the Aurora. To be sure, the most luxurious images appeared not in advertisements for things but in those for insurance and savings banks, which stressed a general level of affluence rather than suggesting the purchase of a specific product at a specific location. Still, what was the point of drawing attention to things few people could have?

The most likely explanation is that advertising did not merely incite desire; it incited desire for goods that only the state could provide. Higher incomes and access to rare goods came only by ingratiating oneself with the Stalinist order. Advertising was thus part of the disciplinary apparatus, a reminder of what could be had in exchange for appropriate performance. It is impossible to prove that this strategy was intentional on the part of trade and advertising officials, although it is somewhat implicit in the focus on Stakhanovites as model consumers. Yet deliberate or not, advertising certainly had a strong hegemonic potential. The key word here is "potential." Some readers might well have internalized the message that "cultured" goods were worthy of desire and adapted their behavior to improve, or protect, their chances of gaining access to them. Other readers, more reluctant to kowtow, might have desired advertised goods but sought them by increasing their participation in the unofficial economy. Still others might have snorted in disgust and dismissed advertising as absurd propaganda, another reminder of the broken promises of socialism.

People at all levels of Soviet society encountered advertisements in newspapers, trolleys, post offices, shop windows, and city streets. In suggesting appropriate consumer activities for different locations, advertising contributed to the demarcation of public and private space, and it helped define space in relation to selfhood. Its images, despite their Western undertones, reinforced the related prescriptions of *kul'turnost'* and loyal behavior. Advertising in the Soviet Union was not an aberration, something that fell through the cracks of censorship, or a throwback to tradition; it was a constituent part of the Stalinist discourse of self and society.

NOTES

I am indebted to the American Council of Teachers of Russian for financial support for the research of this paper. I am also grateful for comments and suggestions from Scott Bills, Eric Naiman, and the anonymous readers for the University of Washington Press, as well as comments on an earlier version of this paper from participants in the Midwest Russian History Colloquium at the University of Akron, September 15–16, 1995.

1. Vadim Volkov, "The Concept of *Kul'turnost'*: Notes on the Stalinist Civilizing Process," in *Stalinism: New Directions*, ed. Sheila Fitzpatrick (London: Routledge, 2000), 210–30 (216).

2. Volkov, "Concept of *Kul'turnost'*"; Julie Hessler, "Culture of Shortages: A Social History of Soviet Trade" (Ph.D. dissertation, University of Chicago, 1996), ch. 6; Sheila Fitzpatrick, *The Cultural Front: Power and Culture in Revolutionary Russia* (Ithaca, N.Y.: Cornell University Press, 1992), 216–37; idem, *Everyday Stalinism: Ordinary Life in Extraordinary Times: Soviet Russia in the 1930s* (New York: Oxford University Press, 1999), 89–114.

3. Vera Dunham, *In Stalin's Time: Middle-Class Values in Soviet Fiction* (Cambridge: Cambridge University Press, 1976). See also the scholars cited elsewhere in this chapter and Nicholas Timasheff, *The Great Retreat* (New York: E. P. Dutton, 1946).

4. The literature on Western consumerism and identity is enormous. For a good start, see Jean-Christophe Agnew, *Worlds Apart: The Market and Theater in Anglo-American Thought, 1550–1750* (New York: Cambridge University Press, 1986); Victoria de Grazia, ed., *The Sex of Things: Gender and Consumption in Historical Perspective* (Berkeley: University of California Press, 1996); Richard Wightman Fox and T. J. Jackson Lears, eds., *The Culture of Consumption: Critical Essays in American History, 1880–1980* (New York: Pantheon, 1983); Roland Marchand, *Advertising the American Dream: Making Way for Modernity, 1920–1940* (Berkeley: University of California Press, 1985); Thomas Richards, *The Commodity Culture of Victorian England: Advertising and Spectacle, 1851–1914* (Stanford: Stanford University Press, 1990); and Rosalind Williams, *Dream Worlds: Mass Consumption in Late Nineteenth Century France* (Berkeley: University of California Press, 1982).

5. Williams, *Dream Worlds*, 12.

6. I do not deal in this essay with actual retail trade. On that topic see Hessler, "Culture of Shortages"; Leonard E. Hubbard, *Soviet Trade and Distribution* (London: Macmillan, 1938); E. A. Osokina, *Ierarkhiia potrebleniia: O zhizni liudei v usloviiakh stalinskogo snabzheniia, 1928–1935gg* (Moscow: Izd. MGOU, 1993); idem, *Our Daily Bread: Socialist Distribution and the Art of Survival in Stalin's Russia, 1927–1941*, ed. Kate Transchel, trans. Kate Transchel and Greta Bucher (Armonk, N.Y.: M. E. Sharpe, 2001); and Amy Randall, "Revolutionary Bolshevik Work: Stakhanovism in Retail Trade," *Russian Review* 59 (July 2000): 425–41.

7. Oskokina, *Our Daily Bread*, 61–101; Lewis H. Siegelbaum, "'Dear Comrade, You Ask What We Need': Socialist Paternalism and Soviet Rural 'Notables' in the Mid-1930s," in Fitzpatrick, *Stalinism: New Directions*, 231–55; Katherine Verdery, *What Was Socialism, and What Comes Next?* (Princeton, N.J.: Princeton University Press, 1996), 24–29. Some scholars have leveled comparable charges against American advertising, suggesting that the creation of desire for goods limits the individual's ability to resist corporate power. See, for example, Christopher Lasch, *The Culture*

of Narcissism: American Life in an Age of Diminishing Expectations (New York: Warner Books, 1979), 71–77; T. J. Jackson Lears, "From Salvation to Self-Realization: Advertising and the Therapeutic Roots of the Consumer Culture, 1880–1930," in Fox and Lears, *Culture of Consumption*, 1–38.

8. On self-transformation through consumption, see T. J. Jackson Lears, *Fables of Abundance: A Cultural History of Advertising in America* (New York: Basic Books, 1994).

9. Volkov and Hessler have both commented on the transformative potential of consumption. Volkov ("Concept of *Kul'turnost*,'" 214–15) in particular has connected *kul'turnost'* with efforts to combat the "backwardness" many officials saw as peasants streamed into Soviet cities during the first Five-Year Plan.

10. For a more complete discussion of NEP advertisements, see Randi Barnes Cox, "The Creation of the Socialist Consumer: Advertising, Citizenship, and NEP" (Ph.D. dissertation, Indiana University, 2000). On NEP advertising and the Soviet avant-garde, see Mikhail Anikst, ed., *Soviet Commercial Design of the Twenties* (New York: Abbeville, 1987); and Christina Kaier, "The Russian Constructivist 'Object' and the Revolutionizing of Daily Life, 1921–1929" (Ph.D. dissertation, University of California, Berkeley, 1995), especially chapters 2 and 3.

11. B. A. Roizenman, "Summary Report, February 20, 1926," Gosudarstvennyi Arkhiv Rossiiskoi Federatsii (henceforth GARF), Moscow, f. 374, op. 12, d. 1125, ll. 23–24.

12. There is a vast amount of scholarship on the effect of the first Five-Year Plan on art and literature. For a good summary, see Richard Stites, *Revolutionary Dreams: Utopian Vision and Experimental Life in the Russian Revolution* (Oxford: Oxford University Press, 1989), 225–44. For a fuller discussion of the institutional history of Soviet advertising during the 1920s, see Cox, "Creation of the Socialist Consumer," Part 1.

13. The institutional records of advertising organizations during the 1930s and 1940s have been preserved less often than those of the 1920s. All too often I found documents in the archives stating that a meeting of such-and-such advertising committee had taken place but that minutes had not been taken. For this chapter I have relied heavily on Rossiiskii Gosudarstvennyi Arkhiv Ekonomiki (RGAE), f. 7971, op. 1, d. 247, and to a lesser extent on *dela* 240, 427, and 428.

14. I am grateful to David Ransel for suggesting this phrase.

15. "Sredi reklamnykh rabotnikov," *Zhurnalist* 5 (1927): 64; D. I. Reitynbarg, "Konkurs na gazetnuiu reklamu," *Zhurnalist* 2 (1926): 64–67; idem, "Psikhologiia reklamy v Amerike," *Zhurnalist* 8–9 (1926): 63–67; "Iarmarochnaia gazeta v Amerike," *Zhurnalist* 5 (1926): 73–74; Al. Kuntsin, "Pora nachat' izuchenie," *Zhurnalist* 7–8 (1928): 38; M. Mikhailov, "Reklama v S.-A.S.Sh.," *Zhurnalist* 22 (1929): 700–703 and 1 (1930): 22–25.

16. For examples of the Tezhe and Lenzhet ads and labels, see Department of Graphic Publications, Russian State Library, Moscow, R4 II7/2B, 1931; *30 dnei*, 1927 and 1928, back covers; and Anikst, 130–31; O. Kuz'ma, "Za novuiu etiketky," *Iskusstvo v massy* 2 (1930): 31; E. Atsarkin, "Etiketki i obertki pod khudozhestvenno-politicheskii kontrol'!" *Za proletarskoe iskusstvo* 11–12 (1931): 40–41.

17. *Prozhektor* 15 (1930).

18. Gerard Sherayko has commented on celebrity endorsements in Weimar adver-

tising and cites Chekova's Chlorodont ads as an example. Gerard F. Sherayko, "Selling the Modern: The New Consumerism in Weimar Germany" (Ph.D. dissertation, Indiana University, 1996), 233.

19. Jay Leyda, *Kino: A History of Russian and Soviet Film* (New York: Macmillan, 1960), 118.

20. *Vecherniaia Moskva*, 17 January 1935, 4; ibid., 23 January 1936, 4. Both of these hotels frequently ran advertisements using this technique throughout the mid- and late 1930s.

21. Angus Roxburgh and Lynne Attwood each mention advertising briefly in their studies of the Soviet press. Lynne Attwood, *Creating the New Soviet Woman: Women's Magazines as Engineers of Female Identity, 1922–1953* (New York: St. Martin's, 1999), 28, 67, 132; Angus Roxburgh, *Pravda: Inside the Soviet News Machine* (New York: George Braziller, 1987), 28–29, 35–36.

22. For this study, print advertisements in journals were taken from complete or nearly complete runs of *Krasnaia niva, Krasnaia nov', Krestianka, Ogonek, Prozhektor, Rabotnitsa,* and *30 dnei.* Random samplings were taken from the newspapers *Ekonomicheskaia zhizn'/Finansovaia gazeta, Izvestiia, Krestianskaia gazeta, Pravda, Sovetskaia Litva, Vercherniaia Moskva,* and *Zaria vostoka.* Newspaper-style advertising was also taken from *Vsia Moskva* for 1929 and 1936.

23. "Stenograma soveshchaniia u Zam. Narkoma, Tov. M. I. Khlopliankina, s rabotnikami pechati i iskusstva po voprosu o reklame," RGAE, f. 7971, op. 1, d. 247, ll. 10–11. It is difficult to assess the effect on consumers of advertising posters in public space. From an economic standpoint, Soviet enterprises did not keep statistics that linked sales to advertising. In 1925, *Zhurnalist* published the results of a survey in which participants were asked to name two advertisements that they could think of without effort. Twenty-seven percent of the responses named not commercial advertisements but political posters. This suggests that at least some readers saw commercial advertising as just another kind of Soviet agitation. See D. I. Reitynbarg, "Nigde krome . . .," *Zhurnalist* 10 (1925): 59–60.

24. The main source of advertising posters for this chapter is the collection at the Department of Graphic Publications (henceforth OI) at the Russian State Library in Moscow. The sample of 211 posters, dating from 1928 to 1941, included all the available advertising posters in the following categories: food, tobacco, household goods, hygiene products, clothing, department stores, transport, insurance, and "cultural goods" (musical instruments, sporting goods, toys, etc.). Because my interest in advertising grows out of an interest in consumption, the sample did not include posters promoting films, books, travel, or special events such as plays and circuses.

25. OI, folders R4 I, R5 I, and R6 I (reklama obshego kharaktera). See especially OI, R5 I/1U, 1935; OI, R5 IV1/1Z, 1936; OI, R5 I/1S, 1937; and OI, R5 IV1/1Z, 1937.

26. Mikhailov, "Reklama," *Zhurnalist* 22 (1929), 701.

27. The term *meshchanstvo* is a rather complicated one. It implied self-centeredness, lack of civic consciousness, vulgar materialism, Western tastes, and sexual carelessness. It was a common epithet hurled at those suspected of harboring materialist, Western, or prerevolutionary tendencies. See Svetlana Boym, *Common Places: Mythologies of Everyday Life in Russia* (Cambridge, Mass.: Harvard University Press, 1994), 66–72; Dunham, *In Stalin's Time,* chapter 2; and Sheila Fitzpatrick, "'Middle-Class Values' and Soviet Life in the 1930s," in *Soviet Society and Culture: Essays in*

Honor of Vera S. Dunham, eds. Terry L. Thompson and Richard Sheldon (Boulder, Colo.: Westview, 1988), 20–38.

28. B. Zemenkov, "Udarim po agitpunktam meshchanstva!" *Iskusstvo v massy* 2 (1930): 29–30.

29. D. Liakhovets, "Krovat' v ideologii," *Iskusstvo v massy* 2 (1930): 30–31.

30. V. S. [author identified only by initials], "Oformlenie byta, proizvodstvennye organizatsii ne raskachalis'," *Iskusstvo v massy* 4 (1930): 22–23. Svetlana Boym (*Common Places,* 35–37) describes a similar campaign against consumerist *meshchanstvo* in domestic space in *Komsomol'skaia pravda* in 1928 and 1929.

31. Zemenkov, "Udarim po agitpunktam meshchanstva!" 29.

32. Hessler, "Culture of Shortages," 309–68; Randall, "Revolutionary Bolshevik Work," 431–41. See also Amy Randall, "The Campaign for Soviet Trade: Creating Socialist Retail Trade in the 1930s" (Ph.D. dissertation, Princeton University, 2000). Quotation is from RGAE, f. 7971, op. 1, d. 247, l. 73.

33. *Vecherniaia Moskva,* 16 March 1935, 4.

34. Hessler, "Culture of Shortages," 332–37. On the design and implications of the layout of American department stores of this period, see William Leach, *Land of Desire: Merchants, Power, and the Rise of a New American Culture* (New York: Pantheon, 1993), 39–90.

35. *Vsia Moskva* (Moscow, 1936), 263.

36. RGAE, f. 7971, op. 1, d. 247, ll. 9–10.

37. RGAE, f. 7971, op. 1, d. 247, l. 40.

38. RGAE, f. 7971, op. 1, d. 247, ll. 38–39. Ierikhonov gave as his inspiration a French film called *The Poster* about a young girl whose picture appears on the label of a bottle of perfume. His comments suggest a rather unsophisticated reading of the film, in which the girl dies at the same moment that an enormous poster with her image is unfurled over a Paris thoroughfare. He noted, however, that sales of the perfume skyrocketed after the film's release, suggesting that French audiences missed the point, too.

39. RGAE, f. 7971, op. 1, d. 247, ll. 40, 45–48, 55–58. Advertisements for large urban grocers sometimes mentioned delivery services. See, for example, OI R5 IV2/3P, 1937; *Vecherniaia Moskva,* 20 February 1936, 4.

40. RGAE, f. 7971, op. 1, d. 247, ll. 48–51.

41. *Vecherniaia Moskva,* 27 April 1936, 4.

42. RGAE, f. 7971, op. 1, d. 247, ll. 48, 53, 69. On consumerism and Stakhanovites, see Lewis Siegelbaum, *Stakhanovism and the Politics of Productivity in the USSR, 1935–1941* (Cambridge: Cambridge University Press, 1988), 228–33; Fitzpatrick, "Becoming Cultured," 226–27; Timasheff, *Great Retreat,* 139–40; and Richard Stites, *Soviet Popular Culture: Entertainment and Society since 1900* (Cambridge: Cambridge University Press, 1992), 70–71, 75.

43. *Finansovaia gazeta,* 8 December 1937. For additional examples of sumptuous domestic interiors in insurance advertising, see *Finansovaia gazeta,* 4 January 1938; *Vecherniaia Moskva,* 1 July 1949; *Ogonek* 27 (1950); *Ogonek* 35 (1952); and *Sovetskaia Litva,* 25 January 1955.

44. RGAE, f. 7971, op. 1, d. 247, ll. 44–57, passim. Quoted phrases on ll. 52, 53, 55.

45. *Ogonek* 22 (1946), ibid., 48 (1950); ibid., 27 (1950).

46. OI, R5 II9b/2S, 1937. The text of this poster begins, "What every kolkhoznik

should know about sugar," but the illustration shows a woman in a delicate white scarf putting two lumps of sugar into a flowered tea cup.

47. Cox, "Creation of the Socialist Consumer," 277–84.

48. The gendered aspects of Soviet consumption in this period are discussed by Fitzpatrick, *Cultural Front*, 231–35, and Randall, "Revolutionary Bolshevik Work," 437–38 and passim.

49. Victoria E. Bonnell, *Iconography of Power: Soviet Political Posters under Lenin and Stalin* (Berkeley: University of California Press, 1997), 10.

50. *Ogonek* 22 (1946); ibid., 30 (1946); ibid., 48 (1950); ibid., 38 (1952).

51. Male chef characters appear in OI, R4 II9d/3D, 1933; OI, R5 II9/2S, 1938; OI, R5 II9a/3P, 1937; OI, R6 II9v/2K, 1938; and OI, R5 II9d/3G, 1937. Male characters courting women with goods appear in OI, R6 II9e/2N, 1938; OI, R6 II9e/2P, 1938; OI, R6 II9b/2M, 1938. In the last example, the flirting couple are actually male and female penguins; the humorous image allowed the designer to exaggerate the gendered overtones of their behavior.

52. Contrasting images of woman as vamp and woman as nurturer in American advertising of this period are described in Marchand, *Advertising the American Dream*, 179–85. See also Gerald Sherayko's analysis of gender in Weimar advertising. Sherayko, "Selling the Modern," 218–38.

53. *Prozhektor* 15 (1927).

54. *Ogonek* 1 (1928); Anikst, *Soviet Commercial Design*, 131. For additional examples, see also OI, R5 IV1/1Z, 1936; OI, R6 II9zh/3N, 1938; and OI, R6 II9e/3P, 1940.

55. See for example, OI, R5 II9g/2P, 1936; OI, R5 II9b/1K, 1936–37; OI, R5 II9b/2P, 1937; OI, R6 II9v/2T, 1937–38; OI, R6 II9v/3B, 1937–38; *Finansovaia gazeta*, 8 December 1937; *Rabotnitsa* 11 (1951); *Ogonek* 46 (1954); *Sovetskaia Litva*, 25 January 1955.

56. OI, R5 II9/2S, 1937.

57. *Sovetskaia Litva*, 25 January 1955.

58. OI, R5 II7/2B, 1935.

59. See, for example, OI, R5 II9e/3G, 1936; OI, R5 II9e/2O, 1937; OI, R5 II9b/2V, 1937–38; OI, R6 II9e/2P, 1938; and OI, R6 II9e/2V, 1938–39.

60. OI, R6 II7/2K, 1938. This poster also appeared as a newspaper advertisement in *Vecherniaia Moskva*, 19 May 1938, 4.

61. *Krestianka* 2 (1950); ibid., 11 (1955).

62. OI, R5 II9b/2P, 1937. See also OI, R5 II9b/1K, 1936–37; OI R4 II9b/2P, 1937.

63. *Ogonek* 38 (1952).

64. OI, R6 II9e/2P, 1936. See also OI, R6 II9zh/3A, 1938; OI, R6 II9b/3D, 1938–39; OI R6 II9b/2Z, 1938–39; and OI, R6 II9g/2V, 1939.

65. *Ogonek* 48 (1951); OI, R6 II9b/3d, 1938.

66. RGAE, f. 7971, op. 1, d. 247, ll. 45–46, 48.

67. *Ogonek* 24 (1946); *Rabotnitsa*, December 1952.

7

The Art of Social Navigation

THE CULTURAL TOPOGRAPHY OF THE STALIN ERA

EVGENY DOBRENKO

Translated by Glen Worthey

The notion of space is among the most stable and basic of human notions, and therefore it attains its greatest concentration in cultural products intended for automatic perception. In this chapter I look at three "topographic spaces" located on the Soviet cultural periphery, which therefore have gone relatively unnoticed in cultural history: postage stamps, a tourism journal, and popular geography. Inasmuch as these items not only reflect "habits of consciousness" but also form part of the "structures of everydayness," they should be seen as culturally significant even though their ideological consequences are less immediately apparent than those of Stalinist art itself.

The Postage-Stamp: Life in a Frame

Mama myla ramu.
Mama washed the frame.
—*Abecedarium*

The postage stamp is a double sign, a "token of postage" that carries in itself a token of space. It is a presentation of space to the world and to the country itself. It is at once both a sign of the overcoming of space and a sign that actively forms space. The stamp is the spatial equivalent of money. It gives space a symbolic dimension: exchangeability.

Stamps are of interest mostly to collectors, rather rarely to art critics, and almost never to cultural historians. But of all the visual images displayed by a culture, the stamp is the most democratic and accessible. Everyone uses the mail: workers, farmers, art critics, janitors, schoolchildren, professors. The scale of this "association with the stamp" is truly enormous: by 1957, the end of the time period of interest to us, the Soviet mails handled 4 billion letters and 80 million packages yearly, nearly all them bearing stamps.[1]

In mass circulation, the postage stamp belonged to the type of visual propaganda that is based on the automaticity of perception—for the ordinary Soviet citizen, it was of interest only perhaps in its monetary denomination. But the stamp did not immediately become an object of propaganda. As USSR Vice Minister of Communications K. Sergeichuk explained:

> The first Russian postage stamps served only as tokens of payment for postal correspondence. Their thematics were quite poor. From year to year, without fail, the seal of tsarist Russia was printed on stamps. The artistic merits of the majority of these stamps were weak. The efforts of artists and engravers were directed mainly toward imparting the qualities of government documents to stamps, so as to thwart their counterfeiting. For a span of sixty years, Russian stamps fulfilled only this narrow, special function as tokens of postal payment—all the way up to the Great October Socialist Revolution.[2]

In the sixty years preceding 1917, only thirty-seven postage stamp designs were issued—of which ten were various arrangements of the Russian Empire's coat of arms. The first forty years of Soviet rule saw the issuing of 50 billion stamps devoted to 2,150 different subjects. The vice minister affirmed, "Postage stamps have become, in the years of Soviet rule, miniature works of art that reflect the events of our epoch and that have commanded wide respect. Aside from their primary purpose—to be tokens of postage payment—the postage stamps of the USSR also fulfill the role of propagandist and agitator."[3] "Works of art" that "fulfill the role of propagandist and agitator" turn a "token of postage payment" into an object of cultural history.

The first Soviet stamps bore all the marks of revolutionary art. Stamp subjects in the first Soviet issue were founded on the idea of circulating the symbols of labor's victory over capital. The most important artists and engravers were recruited to design them. Thus the first Soviet stamp, issued in August 1921—"The Liberated Proletarian," which portrays a worker defeating a dragon, the symbol of capitalism—was implemented by the great master of classical engraving P. Ksidias. Other decorative stamps were engraved by the foremost master of Russian classical engraving, A. Troitsky, who also engraved stamps dedicated to the memory of Lenin (1925 issue) and a series dedicated to the Soviet dirigible-building industry (1932 issue). In 1922, the sculptor Shadr, author of the famous piece *Cobblestone, Weapon of the Proletariat*, created sculptural depictions of a worker, a peasant, and a Red Army soldier especially for postage stamps. Stamp designs were created by Repin's artist-student V. Svarog and by the battle-scene artist G. Savitsky, as well as by the graphic artists N. Zhukov, L. Golovanov, V. Bibikov, and many others.

The most important distinguishing characteristic of the first Soviet stamps was their allegorical, symbolical nature. It is sufficient simply to leaf through *Catalog of Postage Stamps of the USSR, 1918–1980* and read the descriptions: "Arm with Sword," "Arm with Hammer," "Emblems of Worker Labor," "Emblems of Peasant Labor," "Emblems of Science and Art," "Worker Engraving an Anniversary Date in Stone," "The Reaper," "The Sower," and many more.[4] Let us not, however, overestimate the stylistic heterogeneity of the genre, for the democratism of the stamp places significant limits on its stylistic development. As Valentin Brodskii, a historian of the Russian postage stamp, put it: "The art of the postage stamp, by its very purpose—because of its need to address a mass audience—consistently preserves concrete depictive realism as its fundamental artistic quality. Dictated by social necessity, the ruling position of this quality is consistently preserved in this art form, in spite of all the strength of influence of various artistic currents throughout all the periods of the stamp's existence."[5]

The Russian avant-garde never took root in the "postage field." In the spring of 1918, the fine arts division of the People's Commissariat of Enlightenment (Narkompros), which was led at the time by "left artists," held a design competition for the first Soviet postage stamps. Natan Altman and former "World of Art" member Sergei Chekhonin were declared the winners, and reproductions of their stamps were published in the journal *Fine Art* (Izobrazitel'noe iskusstvo) (1919, no. 1). Altman's designs, realized in the familiar suprematist manner, were pronounced especially successful; they depicted a hammer and anvil inside a star on the one-ruble stamp and ears of wheat with a sickle on the three-ruble stamp. "In these stamp drafts," writes Valentin Brodsky, "a new type of artistic realization is evident, one that departs decisively from the old standards"[6]—which was precisely what justified their ultimate rejection by the People's Postal and Telegraph Commissariat (Narkompochtel), which made the final decision. "The proposed examples were not very felicitous, and the People's Postal and Telegraph Commissariat was unable to use them," V. Karlinsky later explained.[7] Postal officials preferred to reprint a series that had been engraved by P. Ksidias from a 1917 drawing by R. Zarinsh—"an artist and an engraver who had for a long time been employed in the Expedition for the Purveying of Government Documents and who were more connected with tradition and more experienced in this sphere of artistic activity."[8] Such is the brief prehistory of the Soviet stamp.

The great change in the Soviet stamp, when it was transformed into a minipicture with a slogan, came in 1929. This transformation was related to a change in subject matter. As is not difficult to guess, "after the victorious conclusion of the civil war, the most difficult tasks laid before the Soviet people were in the areas of rebuilding the ruined economy and of bringing to life Lenin's plan for the building of socialism: the electrification of the country. Postage stamps dedicated to this theme depict the ebullient creative activity of Soviet people accomplishing this grand economic and cultural construction."[9]

Even greater changes occurred in the stylistics of the stamp. Three basic types of graphic technique are traditionally distinguished in postage stamps: the linear, which is inclined toward engraving and book graphics and displays a preponderance of clean lines and restrained shading; the decorative, which is inclined toward the silhouette and characterized by an intensity of colors, high contrast, and a laconicism of graphic resolutions; and finally the three-dimensional tonal type. The last "emphasizes the spatial character of the depiction and makes broad use of shading or tonal techniques for light-shade gradations, creating a multistepped scale of light and color distinctions. Stamps of this kind approach painting or photography in their treatment [of the subject]."[10]

Stamps bearing the three-dimensional tonal type of drawing made up, as Brodsky asserts, "the overwhelming majority of all issues up to the middle of our century."[11] He continues: "It can hardly be said that the combination of image and text in such works often results in a harmonious artistic unit or in some stylistic wholeness. Those among the best, however, include . . . pictures with a relatively large image of the object, figure, or group, not overcomplicated by small depictive elements. . . . Naturally, among the stamps realized in the three-dimensional tonal manner, the very best are frequently those in which the central place is occupied by reproductions of masterpieces of world art."[12]

Indeed, "masterpieces" do occasionally appear on Soviet stamps of the 1930s–50s—but only masterpieces of Russian art: paintings by the

Wanderers (Peredvizhniki), landscapes by Shishkin, and other subjects that were actively functional in Soviet culture. It was, however, *contemporary spatial subjects* that occupied the most important place.

The same genres are recognized in stamps as in painting: portraiture, landscape, still life, historical, and domestic (genre painting). The primary genre in worldwide philately, since the time of the famous "Black Penny," has been the portrait. The symbol appeared only after that, and later, the landscape. Even later came the domestic genre—depictions of domestic scenes, work activities, historical and military events, sporting events, modern domestic technologies, modes of transportation, and so forth. Then came the poster, and finally, commemorative stamps honoring some event or anniversary. Soviet stamps during the 1920s manifested this generic evolution in an accelerated way. At that time one could find practically all the genres just mentioned. They were all of equal value; none stands out. But a particular theme, as is well known, can be expressed in various ways. "Constructive labor," let us say, can be represented by an emblem, by an allegorical figure, by a historical composition, by portraits of workers, by a depiction of an industrial landscape. In Soviet stamps, it was the landscape that eventually prevailed.

If one were to leaf through a collector's stamp album, one would begin to see the transition from the allegorical stamps of the 1920s to the "broad canvases" of the 1930s–50s. The subjects of a stamp begin to appear, as a rule, against the background of a landscape. Depending on the relationship between the background, the figures, and the text, it is possible to differentiate between scenic landscapes, which serve primarily as background, and self-exhibiting landscapes, which are the principal subject of the stamp. The first type of landscape dominated in commemorative stamps, and the second, in stamps that were meant to showcase or exhibit the country itself.

The impetus for the development of the self-exhibiting landscape was a technological innovation: the use of photographic originals in the creation of a stamp. This technique was used for the first time in 1929 for stamps depicting the Moscow Telegraph building; after that, it was employed quite broadly. It was by this method that a 1947 series of urban landscapes was issued for the eight-hundredth anniversary of Moscow (fig. 7.1). Between these two events lay an entire era in the evolution of spatial presentation in Stalinist culture.

At the beginning, self-exhibiting space was not a subject of stamp art. The stamp depicting the Moscow Telegraph building was basically

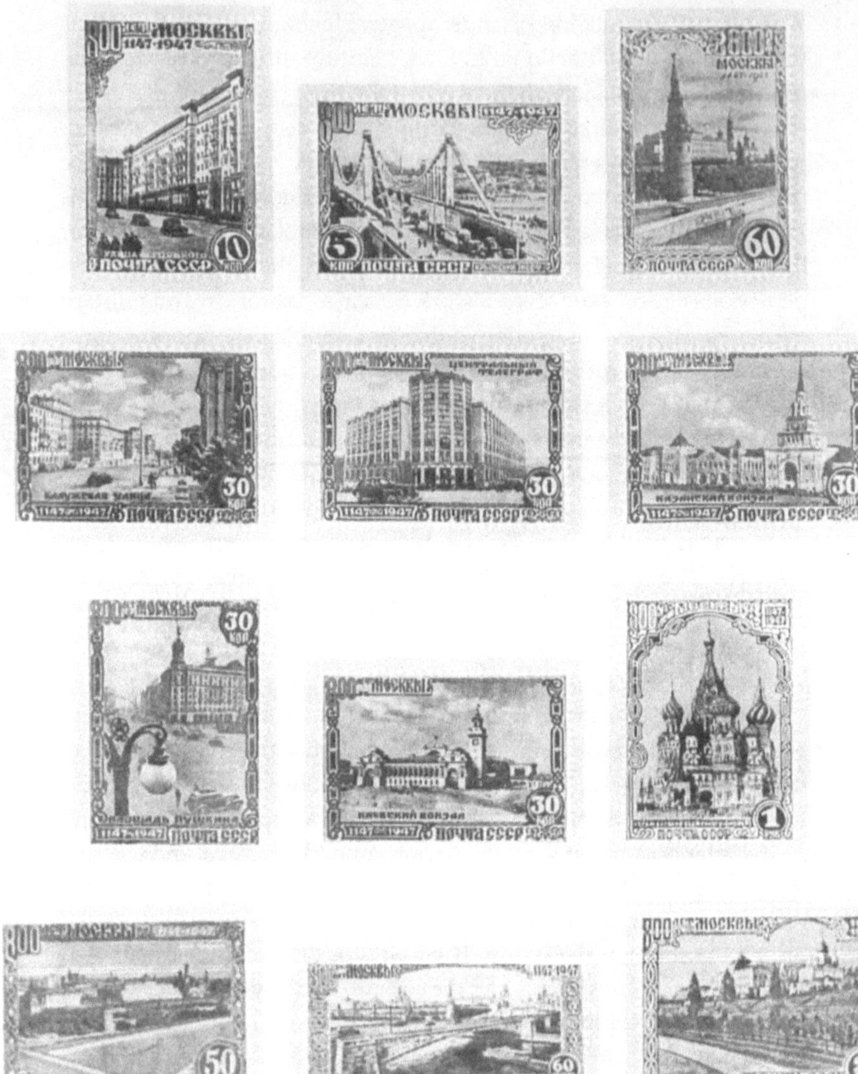

Fig. 7.1. Postage stamps commemorating the eight-hundredth anniversary of Moscow, 1947.

a display of a new building on Tverskaia Street. The series "For the Industrialization of the USSR" was similar. A stamp with the text "More metal, more machines!" depicted a factory landscape, and the stamp "Let's increase the crop capacity!" featured a column of tractors moving across a field. A year after this 1929 issue, the series "For the Early Fulfillment of the Five-Year Plan" was released, which featured a dirigible floating over a background of recent construction work. In the following year, the dirigible occupied a leading place in the two basic series of airmail stamps. It was depicted floating above the Kremlin, above fields and hydroelectric stations, above the map of the USSR and the polar ice cap, and above silhouettes of factories with the rising sun in the background.

In stamps of standard (mass) issue from the period of the first Five-Year Plan, a male worker is seen against the background of a blast furnace, and a female worker stands in front of smoking factory pipes and buildings. A peasant woman stands before sheaves of hay, and a Red Army soldier is displayed against a background of military hardware. The landscape makes significant inroads into the world of the commemorative stamp as well. The 1930 series dedicated to the ten-year anniversary of the First Cavalry depicts cavalrymen either riding across the steppe in attack formation or standing in front of a destroyed church and the corpses of White Guardsmen (or Red Army casualties?). Another series of the same year, dedicated to the twenty-fifth anniversary of the Russian Revolution of 1905, shows pictures of barricades on Krasnaia Presnia and the battleship *Potemkin* on a stormy sea.

In 1932, the landscape became the decisive champion of stamp subjects. The entire jubilee series, dedicated to the fifteenth anniversary of the October Revolution and consisting of seven stamps, is realized in landscapes: pictures of Lenin giving a speech from an armored vehicle at Finland Station, the storming of the Winter Palace, the dams of the Dnieper Hydroelectric Station, the Magnitogorsk complex, combines working in the field. The large 1932 series "Peoples of the USSR," consisting of nineteen stamps, is composed entirely of "national" scenes depicting, among others, Nenets reindeer teams, Koryak hunters, Georgian gardeners, Abkhazian sheep farmers, Lezghin craftspeople, Uzbek cotton growers, and Bashkir horse breeders (fig. 7.2). All of them are at work: in the fields, in gardens and pastures, on ice floes. Now airplanes also float above the "boundless expanses of the motherland"—above the very same ice floes, petroleum rigs, blast furnaces, and dams; above factories, kolkhoz fields, and canals. The portraits of the heroes

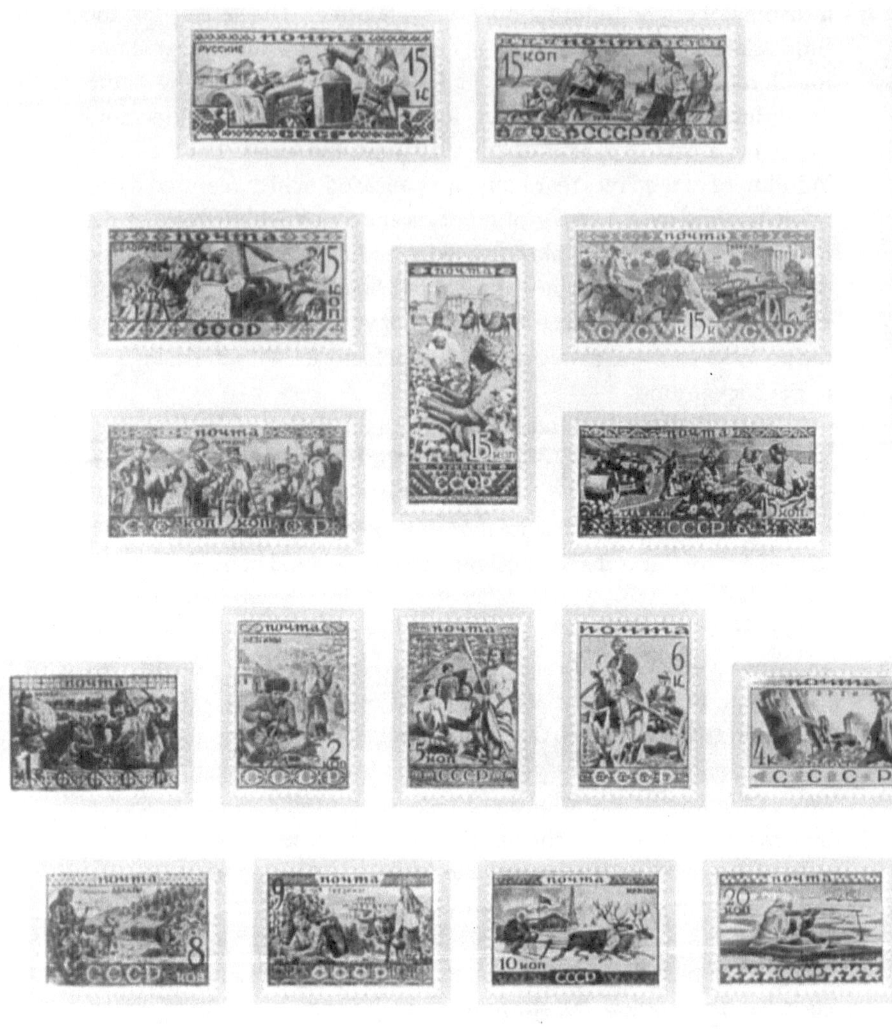

Fig. 7.2. Part of the stamp series "Peoples of the USSR," 1932.

themselves take up no more than a quarter of the space of the stamp—peripheral space is everywhere.

The mid-1930s saw a shifting of the spatial model of the country: the postal topoi became Moscow-centric. The first sign of change was a 1935 series marking the launch of the first line of the Moscow metro. The main philatelogical event of 1937 was a commemorative archi-

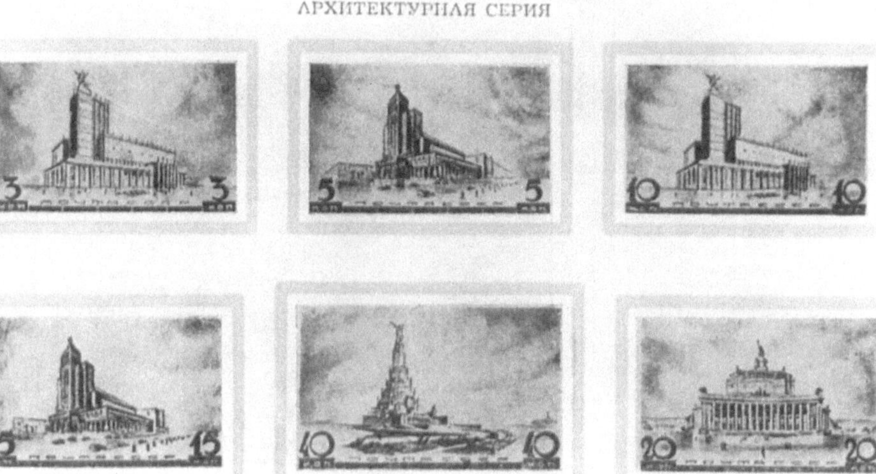

Fig. 7.3. Six stamps in a series commemorating the first All-Union Congress of Architects, 1937.

tectural series dedicated to the first All-Union Congress of Architects (fig. 7.3). It portrayed buildings planned for construction in Moscow, among them the Soviet Army Theater, the Moskva Hotel, and the Palace of Soviets. In the following year, the large series "Moscow Reconstruction" was issued, with pictures of the new Gorky Street, the House of the Soviet of People's Commisars on Marx Prospect, the Lenin Library, the Dinamo metro station, the riverboat station, and the Krymsky and Moskvoretsky Bridges. These stamps stood out because of their increased size, their decorative, contrastive style, and their minimal texts. Series after series reproduced the image of Moscow: a 1941 series of one- and two-ruble stamps with views of the Kremlin; an issue dedicated to the fifth anniversary of the Lenin Museum.

In this Moscow-centric culture, a new method of presenting the country developed. In 1939 and 1940, it took the form of pictures of the All-Union Agricultural Exhibition (VSKhV, later called VDNKh). Although the 1939 series continued to present traditional "national" motifs (Caucasian pastures, the northern fur industry, Ukrainian cattleyards, Russian grain, and Central Asian cotton fields) alongside pictures of the exhibition, the large 1940 series (seventeen stamps) consisted entirely of photographs of the republics' pavilions at the exhi-

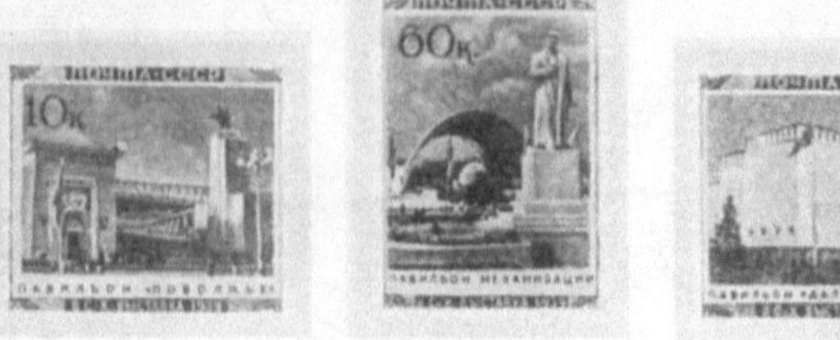

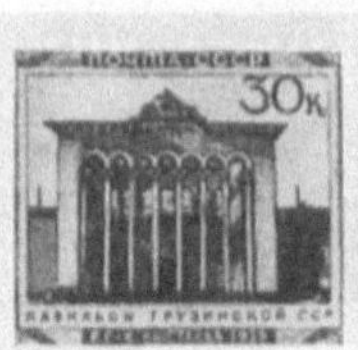

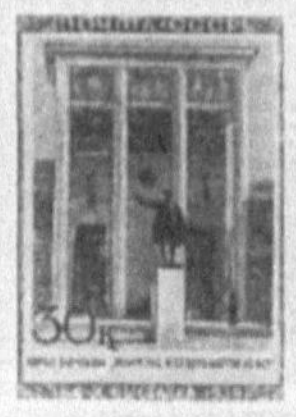

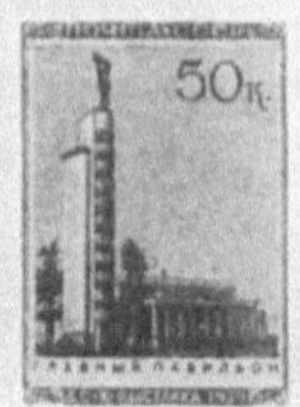

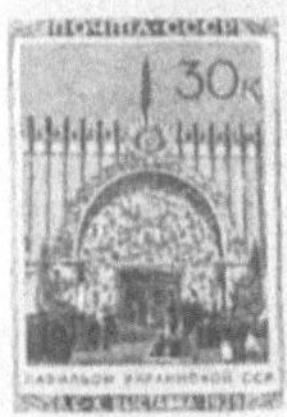

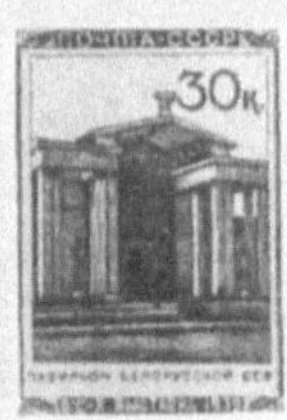

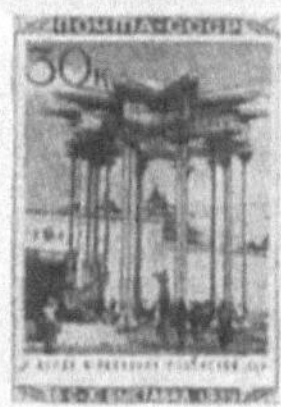

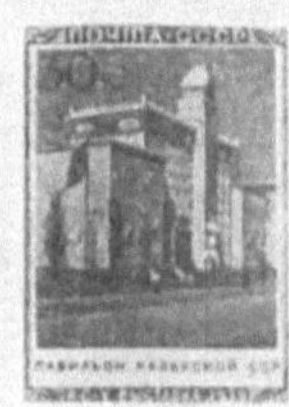

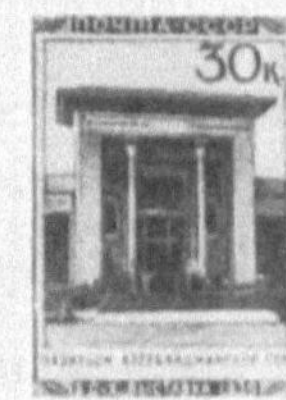

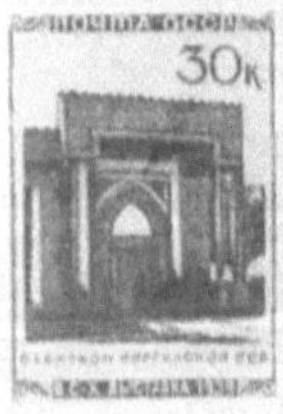

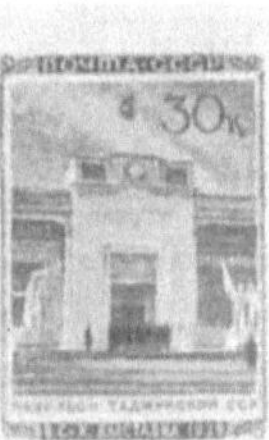

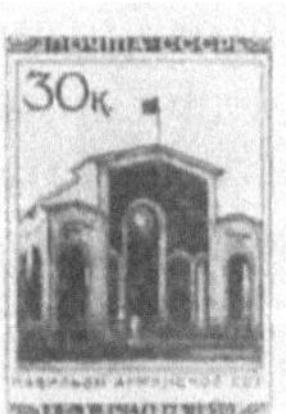

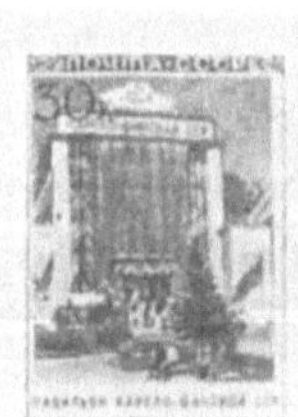

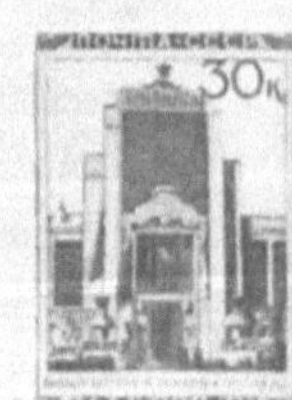

Fig. 7.4. Stamp series devoted to the opening of the All-Union Agricultural Exhibition, 1940.

bition (fig. 7.4). Industrial landscapes all but disappeared by the end of the 1930s: only the January 1941 series "USSR, the Leading Industrial Power" reminds us of this motif, with traditional visual images: a male and a female worker against a blast-furnace background, an industrial landscape, new types of steam trains, automobiles, a combine harvesting grain, the road to the Tushino airfield.

The country now has, as it were, just two faces outside the center of Moscow. One of them is the VSKhV (to some extent, part of the center itself), and the other consists of spas and resorts. The twelve-stamp 1938 series "Views of the Caucasus and Crimea" and the eight-stamp 1939 series "Spas of the USSR" consist of photo reproductions that differ little from those of the VSKhV pavilions, inasmuch as they depict either palaces or the high-culture landscapes of Yalta, Alupka, or Gurzuf (figs. 7.5, 7.6). These series definitively fixed the visual image of Soviet space in the stamp—the capital and the country's pavilions—on the eve of World War II.

The war completely changed the subjects of postage stamps, but it did not succeed in changing the established canon of their aesthetic or stylistic properties. Wartime stamp issues give us the same landscape expressions as those we saw earlier. Scenic landscapes dominate in the series "Heroes of the Great Patriotic War" (1941–42) and "Heroes of the Soviet Union" (1944), which depict the deeds of heroes such as Viktor Talalikhin, the first pilot in the history of aviation to ram his plane into an enemy bomber at night, and Major-General Dovator, commander of the Cossack corps, who earned glory with his raids behind German lines. Depictions of deeds are replaced with battle episodes in the issues of 1942–43: antitank artillery actions, spies in the German rear, signalers at the front, men carrying the wounded from a battlefield. Self-exhibiting landscape is presented in the series "Hero Cities" (1944), with views of Leningrad, Stalingrad, Odessa, and Sevastopol; in a series dedicated to the Victory Parade (1945), with views of Red Square; and in a series dedicated to the two-hundred-twentieth anniversary of the Academy of Sciences, with views of academy buildings in Leningrad and Moscow.

Stamps of the war period return us to an earlier, "precentered" spatial model of the country: once again the front (not the labor front, but the real one)—the periphery—is moved into first place, while the center, Moscow, occupies a rather humble position. The isolation of space, however, is now emphasized with a specific generic expression: Moscow and the Hero Cities are presented as self-exhibiting landscapes, whereas peripheral spaces are scenic ones. It is impossible to imagine something happening against the background of the Kremlin or some Moscow embankment, and one never encounters *pure* landscape in, for example, the middle Russian plain. Moscow is adequate unto itself; the

ВИДЫ КАВКАЗА И КРЫМА

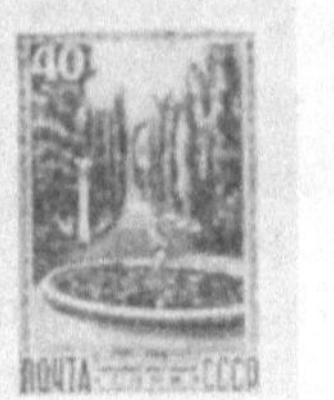

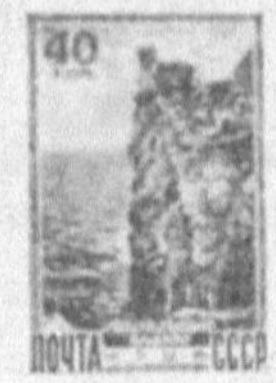

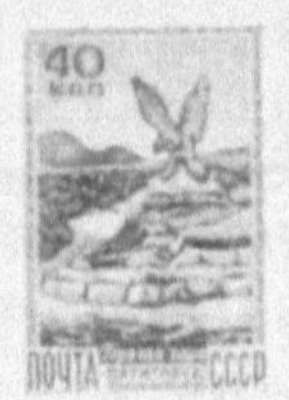

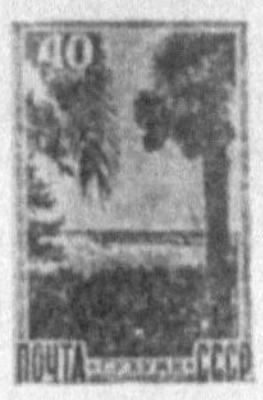

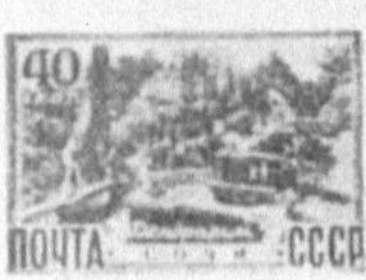

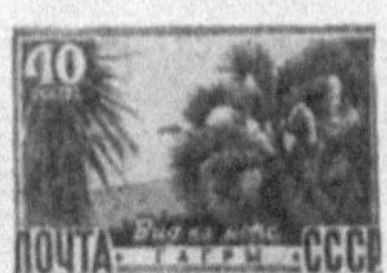

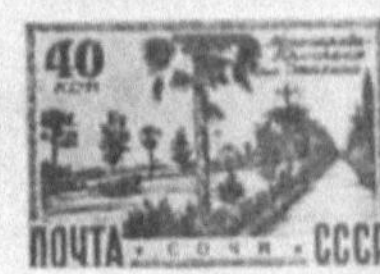

Fig. 7.5. The stamp series "Views of the Caucasus and Crimea," 1938.

КУРОРТЫ СССР

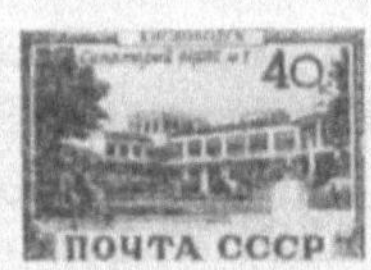

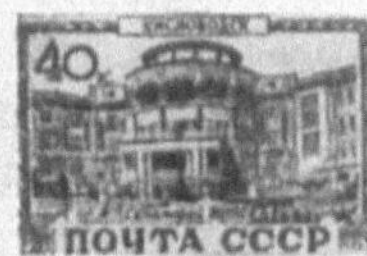

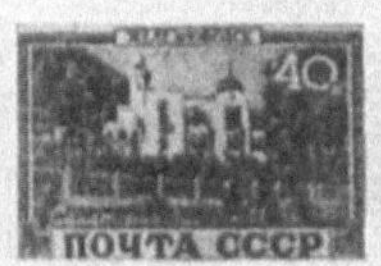

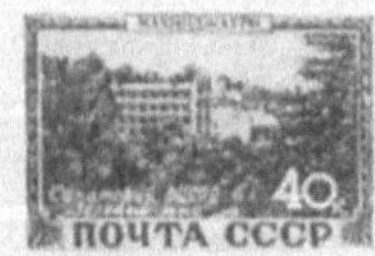

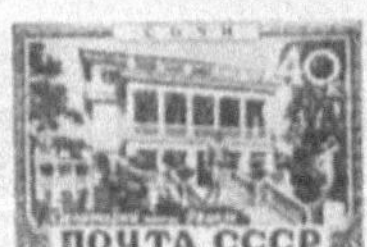

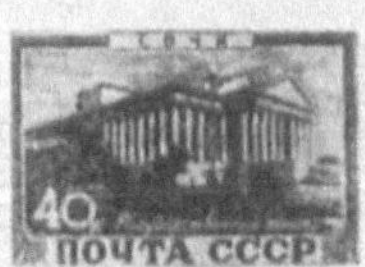

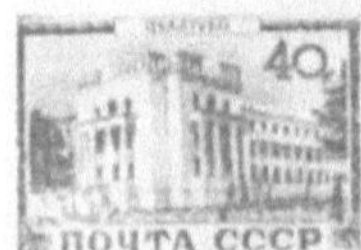

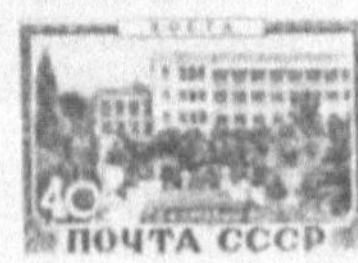

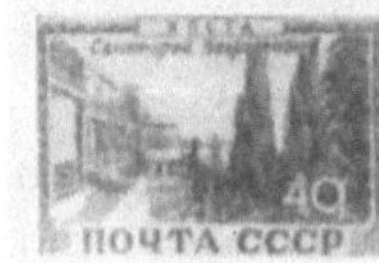

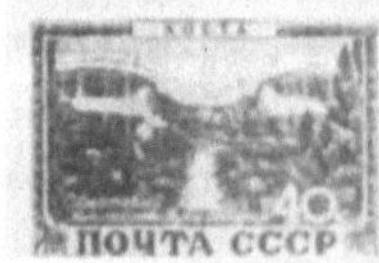

Fig. 7.6. The stamp series "Spas of the USSR," 1939.

periphery is merely a background for actions (achievements) of one kind or another.

By the postwar period it is no longer possible to find nonlandscape realizations on stamps: practically any theme is expressed by means of a "picture." In the "Pioneer Series" (1948) we see young model airplane enthusiasts launching their planes in a field, a Pioneer division making its way along the seashore, buglers, young naturalists. In a series dedicated to the thirty-year anniversary of the Komsomol (1948), we find young Komsomol members sitting in a student auditorium, driving a combine in a field, marching in an athletic parade at a stadium, highlighted by a background of blast furnaces. A 1949 series in honor of the Eighth of March (International Women's Day) depicts women in a field, in a textile factory, in a classroom, and serving on a tribunal.

It was in postwar stamps that the generic consolidation of the presentation of center and periphery was finally canonized. Moscow was presented in series that came out year after year. In "Views of Moscow" (1946), for example, four stamps out of eight display the Kremlin from various sides, two show the Bolshoi Theater, and one each shows the Moskva Hotel and the Lenin Museum. Other series titles include "The Eight-Hundredth Anniversary of Moscow," "The Thirtieth Anniversary of the Moscow City Council," "The Moscow Metro," and "The Tenth Anniversary of the Moscow Canal" (all 1947), and "Moscow Museums" (1950). The assortment of Moscow sites selected for the eight-hundredth anniversary series (see fig. 7.1) is especially interesting: the Kremlin (the Great Kremlin Palace, the Crimea Bridge, and five different views from the Kremlin embankment), Red Square (Saint Basil's Cathedral), the space adjacent to the Kremlin within the bounds of the Boulevard Ring (the Moskva Hotel, Gorky Street, Kaluzhsky Street, Pushkin Square, and the Central Telegraph), and the borders of the Garden Ring (the Kiev and Kazan train stations). This internal centering of Moscow space itself in the various Moscow series shares with the series dedicated to the republics a preoccupation with the stratification of space.

Peripheral space appears first in the "State Seal" series (1947), celebrating the twenty-fifth anniversary of the formation of the Soviet Union. The seventeen stamps—the state seal of the USSR plus those of the sixteen republics of the union—are astonishing in their use of color: an abundance of gilding and especially rich tones. The pomposity of such symbolism, however, was soon displaced by customary landscapes. In the same year, in honor of the thirtieth anniversary of the Ukraine SSR, a series of Ukrainian landscapes was issued. These included the construction of the Ukraine Council of Ministers building in Kiev, then the Dnieper Hydroelectric Station, fields, granaries, blast furnaces, and open-pit coal mines in Donbas. Three 1949 series (for the twenty-fifth anniversary of the Tajik SSR, the Uzbek SSR, and the Turkmen SSR) repeated the same model. Each opens with scenes of the republican capital cities. Next come primarily government buildings—the State House of Tajikistan, the Uzbekistan Council of Ministers building, and so forth. Of course we also see textile plants in Ashkhabad, and irrigation systems, and new construction in Tashkent, and carpet weavers at work, and the Great Ferghana Canal, but views of "government objects" are immediately highlighted by their double denomination—the reproduction of the same picture on stamps of difference prices. The internal centering of the periphery is maintained in the same, immovable canon: whereas all of the "daily life" (labor) landscapes are given scenically, as in a poster, all of the spaces of power are presented in self-exhibiting landscapes that have their generic equivalent in the "Spas of Crimea and the Caucasus" series of 1946, 1947, and 1949.

The postwar stamp altogether ceases to exhibit the periphery as such. All elements of exoticism are systematically removed: we no longer see either Chukchi reindeer teams or Nanaian yurts or Abkhazian shepherds in felt boots. Another disappearance is that of commemorative stamps in honor of all manner of heroic adventures, such as were issued in large numbers in the 1930s: the icebreaker *Malygin*'s Arctic voyage (1931), the flight of the stratospheric balloon "USSR-1" (1933), the nonstop flight from Moscow to the United States over the North Pole (1938), the polar cruise of the icebreaker *Sedov* (1940).

In March 1946, a session of the Supreme Soviet of the USSR adopted the "fourth Five-Year Plan for the restoration of the economy, 1946–50." In October, a series of stamps was issued on this theme. The series included posterlike stamps executed in a new manner: the slogan now occupies only one-eighth of the stamp's area while the rest of the space is dedicated to an industrial landscape: "Let's give the country 50 million tons of cast iron yearly!" (a blast-furnace worker against a background of furnaces); "Let's give the country 127 million tons of grain annually!" (a combine gathering the harvest); "Let's give the country 500 million tons of coal per year!" (a train carrying coal). The same sorts of landscape realizations are preserved in a 1946–47 series on the

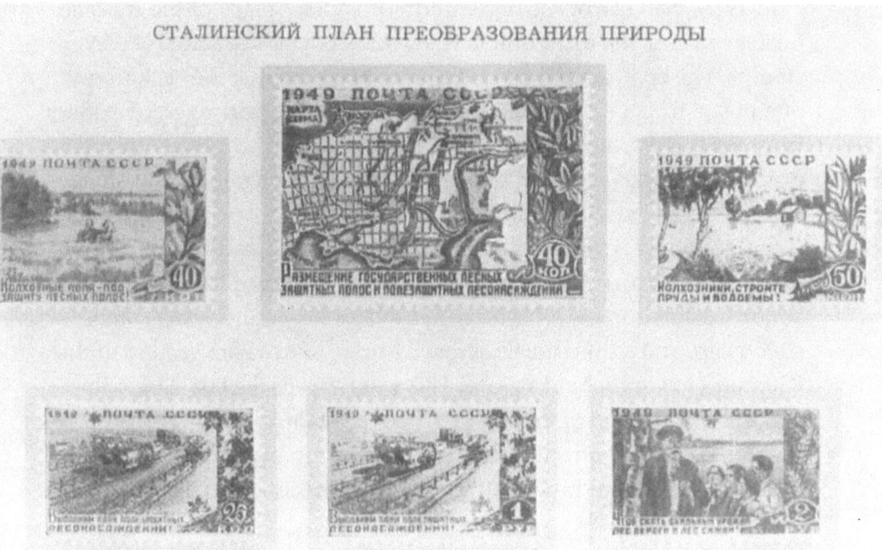

Fig. 7.7. The stamp series "Stalin's Plan for Transforming Nature," 1949.

restoration of "industry giants"—the Dnieper Hydroelectric Station, the Konstantinovsk and Makeevka metallurgical factories, the Rostov factory of agricultural machinery. In virtually all of the stamps of this series, working people and "production processes" are foregrounded against a background of industrial or agricultural landscapes.

The 1949 series "Stalin's Plan for Transforming Nature" (fig. 7.7) synthesized, as it were, the various means of landscape depiction of the previous five years. It depicted everything from "diagrams of the movement of forest preservation zones and field preservation" to landscape-illustrated slogans. In "Farmers, build ponds and reservoirs!" a pond takes up most of the stamp, with a farmer's hut on one shore and a weeping willow on the other. Another stamp, depicting birches against a field with tractors, exhorts, "Sow and make the harvest soar—Save the trees and plant some more!"

In the mid-1950s, industrial themes were replaced by agricultural topics. The 1954–56 series were completely dedicated to agriculture. Slogans urge, "Expand arable lands and increase the linen harvest!" "Let's put virgin and fallow lands to the plough!" "Grow more vegetables!" Cornfields, combines busy with the harvest, grain elevators, herds of cattle, and poultry farms all float before us.

In 1958, the year of the one-hundredth anniversary of the Russian postage stamp, the main philatelic event was a jubilee series of eleven stamps. The head stamp sported a jet airplane against the background of a postal troika silhouette; the other ten stamps portrayed episodes from the history of the mails. The stamp for the fifteenth century, for example, showed a prince's scribe in front of the Kremlin walls. Five stamps represented the Soviet period, including one picturing Red Army soldiers distributing mail to their comrades and another showing an airmail plane at the aerodrome. The climax of the series was a stamp executed in the long-forgotten symbolic manner: an airplane, a steamship, and a train hurtle across a bridge with a background of the Kremlin's towers behind a globe. This was perhaps the last "landscape" series. From the end of the 1950s, the Soviet stamp returned to the portrait genre, and the range of subjects abruptly expanded to include reproductions of paintings and other decorative art objects. Soviet symbols returned. Landscapes did not disappear entirely from stamps, but they began to occupy a decidedly peripheral place.

The stamps of the 1930s–50s reflected the transformative process of the Stalin era's spatial notions. As means of propaganda and agitation, stamps are immeasurably more accessible than paintings. Thus they not only reflect but also form a certain spatial model of culture. A stamp cannot "astonish the viewer" as, say, a painting or a film can. Yet within the automatism of perceiving a mere token of postage payment is hidden a no less powerful potential for social transformation. The purpose of deliberate influence over the masses' "habits of consciousness" in the Soviet era was to deprive the social shifts that were taking place in the country of their significance as cultural phenomena—that is, of their artificiality. Toward the end of the Stalin era, new historical and spatial realities were no longer perceived as artificially "made" but rather as wholly *natural* and therefore legitimate. The routine nature of the perception of these "framed pictures" was a certain sign that the picture proposed by them—if not of the world, then at least of the country—was a natural and normal one.

Every Soviet child knew the narrative poem "Hail to Mail," by the extremely popular children's poet Samuil Marshak. It tells the story of how a letter traveled the world in pursuit of the "addressee," with whom it was never able to catch up. The letter went from Rostov to Leningrad, from the south to the north; then postmen with "a bag on a strap" carried it around Berlin and along Bobkin Street and beneath Brazilian palms . . . But the addressee, they were always told, had already left. The letter traveled around the world and overtook its recipient only after he had returned home to Leningrad. This senseless circulation of the letter reflected the spatial model encoded in the Soviet stamp—and Marshak's verse, published in runs in the millions, was always brightly illustrated: the various stamps on the colorful covers of children's books could not fail to impress the imagination of a child.

But the Soviet stamp did not "travel the world." Its "worldly potential" lay as though dormant within it during the entire Stalin era: Soviet people sent letters neither to Berlin nor to Bobkin Street nor to Brazil. The stamp presented an image of the country that was available, almost exclusively, only to the country itself. This tautological action invites us to "read" the stamp as an iconic object. Space, as depicted on it, is fully adequate unto itself. Surrounded by a frame, it is self-enclosed, and therefore the fundamental collisions that develop in the subjects of Soviet stamps are preoccupied with relations of center and periphery. The fundamental contents of the Soviet stamp—the presentation of a topographical cultural mythology—allow us to see in it a true symbol of the new topography. Information about the country as contained in this token of postage payment is fully paid for: it is fast fixed in the Soviet mentality and sealed by history.

The Country as Image of the Country: *By Land and by Sea*

> Don't you understand? Don't you understand, kind sir,
> what it means when there is no longer any place to go to?
> Fyodor Dostoyevsky, *Crime and Punishment*

The Stalin era saw the flourishing of "mass physical education and sports" in the Soviet Union, and the leader himself was "the best friend of Soviet athletes." One aspect of the physical education movement boasted the greatest mass appeal: hiking. The number of hikers in the Soviet nation, according to data of the USSR State Committee for Physical Education and Sports, had by 1938 reached almost a million people, of whom 500,000 dedicated their vacations to so-called long-distance hiking. Another 200,000 participated in "local hiking"—that is, within the confines of their own regions of residence—and 200,000 more were "independent hikers." The last group included approximately 20,000 mountaineers.[13]

We have before us a cultural paradox. On one hand, we have an official notion that was parodied in a popular Perestroika-era song:

"Swimming forbidden here . . . Being forbidden here . . . Living forbidden here . . . You can't go here! You can't go there! You can't go anywhere!" On the other hand, we have the flourishing of hiking and tourism. This was domestic tourism, of course, inasmuch as international tourism in the 1930s was practically nonexistent. Moreover, the tourism propagandized was not of the traditional sort: "sightseeing in the capital" gave way to travel in the periphery. The "tabooing" of space, along with social mechanisms that restricted the very possibility of movement within the country beginning in the mid-1930s—the introduction of the passport system, the registration of workers in their workplaces, the impossibility of leaving the kolkhoz—was a symptom of a certain topographic paranoia. Simultaneously, the official encouragement of hiking and tourism created a peculiar topographic schizophrenia. Both of these "social diseases" were expressions of the fear of space that characterized Stalinist culture as a whole. I am speaking primarily of a cultural modeling of peripheral space: space that stands in opposition to the self-contained center.

The widely recognized "tabooing of space" in Stalinist culture was interpreted by the Soviet people as an altogether customary peculiarity of their habitat. It aroused bewilderment among foreigners, who were not allowed to take pictures of train stations, bridges, or the metro. (Characteristically, these "objects of military significance" were associated primarily with transportation—with means for overcoming space.) At the foundation of this tabooing lay a corpus of visual images of the Soviet country that were subject to constant reproduction. The very same train stations, bridges, and metro that could not be photographed were constantly reproduced in newspapers and on posters, postcards, and postage stamps. These were carefully "made" objects, however—culturally selected presentations.

But neither newspapers nor postcards give the same completeness of "work with the periphery" that we find in the pages of the immensely popular *By Land and by Sea* (Na sushe i na more), the "hikers' magazine of the USSR." The circulation of this magazine reached 45,000–50,000 copies, which exceeded the circulations not only of the "thick" literary journals but of many of the "mass" popular magazines as well. It was originally an organ of the All-Union Central Council of Trade Unions (VTsSPS) and the Central Committee of the Komsomol. After the All-Union Central Executive Committee removed tourism and hiking from the governance of the trade unions in 1936, the journal became an organ of the All-Union Committee of Physical Education and Sports, under the auspices of the USSR Council of People's Commissars (Sovnarkom). The "governmentization of tourism" was one of the measures adopted to redirect mass initiatives into "organizational channels."

The image of the Soviet hiker is ambivalent. The attributes of the hiker—a compass, a map, a mobility that turns him or her, albeit temporarily, into a person who has "fallen out" of the regime and out of the passport system—make this character suspect. First, the hiker begins to look like a "vagrant," a BOMZh, or "Person without a Definite Place of Residence," in official and labor-camp jargon. Falling out from established social space is a sign of an individual's leaving the zone of normalization, control, and visibility. Second, the hiker—a person who walks the hills with map and compass—begins to look like a spy. This ambivalence toward hikers preprogrammed, as it were, the process of creating the image of the hiker and, consequently, the process of presenting his habitat—the periphery.

When one leafs through sets of *By Land and by Sea* from the 1930s, the impression arises that one is in a decentralized country. There is practically no mention of Moscow or Leningrad. Before one's eyes (and at least a third of the magazine was devoted to photographs) are scenes of mountains, streams, and exotic vegetation and places. It would be difficult even to name all these topoi with which, it turns out, "our motherland is so generous," were it not for the "Hikers' Atlas of the USSR," which "all lovers of travel about our native country had so longed for." This atlas included "maps of only the most important tourist regions"—thirty-eight of them, from the Kola Peninsula to the Crimea, from the "Industrial Urals" to Central Asia. Hiking routes steered tourists along the upper Volga, along many other rivers, and in the footsteps of Budyonny's cavalry and Voroshilov's army.

Visual images of the country's periphery, as presented in the most important tourist magazine of the time, virtually excluded purely landscape images. More often, readers encountered landscapes with people. If a photograph showed a rushing river, then there were people in boats or canoes on it. Snow-covered mountains had backpack-laden mountain climbers making their way up in the foreground. If there were cliffs, then there were also rapellers. The pictures almost always presented images of humans fighting nature, overcoming it. Thus went the formation of the image of the Soviet hiker.

This image was altogether literary, and therefore a comparison of the magazine *By Land and by Sea* with the literary "thick" journals of the 1930s is justified. We have before us a socialist realist transformation. And just who are the heroes of the periphery? Let us acquaint ourselves with a few chosen at random:

> Nina and Zoia came to the machine-tool construction plant "Samotochka" when they were still very small—it was there that they went to school and grew, and that each attained a specialty according to her vocation.
>
> Nina Novikova, a lean, dynamic, and perky-eyed girl, became a controller in the department of quality control, and Zoia Kuzmicheva, a strong, stately girl with a decisive and willful face, chose the profession of milling machine operator.
>
> Each of them loves what she does, and each approaches her work thoughtfully.
>
> Nina, as she receives parts, never allows a product with a flaw or imprecise dimensions to get past her. She does her job with such care and swiftness that she always has free time and is often transferred to other departments to help the inspectors there.
>
> Zoia Kuzmicheva, a Komsomol member and a Stakhanovite, studied the milling machine brilliantly and mastered it like a professional. Zoia now fulfills her production plan by 160–180 percent.
>
> Aside from work in the plant, Nina and Zoia also do a lot of social work. The Komsomol Committee has rewarded the girls with tourist trips.
>
> Before 1936, neither Nina nor Zoia was involved in long-distance tourism. They hadn't seen anything more luxurious than the subtropical flora and fauna or the riches of our beautiful socialist motherland. This year they went for the first time to the Caucasus and sailed around the Black Sea on a steamship.
>
> The girls were enraptured by the comfortable atmosphere, the jovial, lively company of the tourists who had gathered from all the cities of the land, the exquisitely beautiful shore, and the snowy caps of the mountains seen from on board, sparkling in the sun.
>
> The girls decided to begin traveling in earnest, and first of all to walk the Sukhumi Military Road.
>
> Their two-week journey in the Caucasus gave the girls good exercise. They became strong, they rested, and they enriched their knowledge.
>
> Meetings with Stakhanovite tourists from other cities, conversations about Stakhanovite work methods, the new atmosphere, and

> the poetry of nature inspired in them a longing for labor and for competition.[14]

Before us is an exemplar of "transformative" socialist realist writing, beginning with a portrait—the "perky-eyed" one becomes a quality controller, and the "strong, stately" one, a milling machine operator—and ending with a plot: What will they experience on their first trip beyond the walls of their native factory? What could they see "more luxurious than the subtropical flora and fauna or the riches of our beautiful Socialist motherland"? In the end, "the poetry of nature" inspires in them "a longing for labor and for competition." Our new friends Nina and Zoia are true socialist realist characters.

We find similarly typical lyrical heroes in the magazine's innumerable essays about tourists:

> Leaving for a trip around our great country, one involuntarily wants to exclaim: "Beloved socialist motherland! How good it is to march across your boundless expanses with a backpack hanging from one's shoulders! How many new and remarkable things you will see as you float in a boat along your innumerable rivers!" The forests, the mountains, the rivers, the lakes—all this is ours. New cities, factories, machinery stations, mines, schools, canals—all this was built by us under the wise supervision of the Bolshevik Party, with the beloved leader of the workers of all the world, Comrade Stalin, at its head. You travel with pride around the world's first socialist country. What happy feelings engulf each of us upon seeing the riches, powers, and glories of the government of workers and peasants in which you are the master![15]

This romantic (in the Gogolian style) pathos merges organically with the didacticism of an editorial in 1939:

> Travels by boat, on foot, on a bicycle, or on skis develop resolute qualities; they discipline a person, inculcate him with collectivism. . . . Visual acquaintance with our motherland, with its natural riches, with the accomplishments of socialist construction, with the free and happy life of its peoples—all of this develops in the tourist a boundless love for the socialist motherland: patriotism. Healthy recreation through travel, and its emotional charge, contribute to an increase in labor productivity. . . .

> Hiking and mountain-climbing develop physically fit and resolute people. Aside from this, they alone inculcate the special knowledge that is particularly important for military activity: independent trips and mountain ascents teach skills of orienting oneself in an unknown locale, map and compass use, awareness, life on the march, overcoming of natural obstacles, techniques of moving about in the mountains, etc.[16]

And how did the tourists themselves feel? The magazine readily offered its pages to the amateur poetry of these tamers of wild rivers and of "snowy caps of mountains sparkling in the sun." For example, the tourist A. Abegauz, in his poem "When . . . ," correctly understood the significance of mountain climbing, its "importance for military activity":

> When from Elbrus and to the east
> By way of Baksan, past Adyl-Su,
> Toward its icy source
> I once again carry my pack,
> When above the foamy rapids,
> Above sea sprays, above the water's ire,
> To the fiery sunrise . . .
> Then I am met once again
> Amid the magnificence of height,
> By a calm of feeling, a clarity of word,
> And a world of dreams fulfilled.
>
> But when the enemy comes again,
> And the shadow of war torments the hills,
> O Caucasus, we then with honor
> Will defend your expanses!
> Then, with a greeting to the capital,
> Will we stand as Shkhelda on the border,
> And the rays of summer lightning
> Will reveal no fear among us.
> The snows of Elbrus confirm to me
> That only he will not turn out a coward in battle
> Who knows his way among the mountains.[17]

Just how did the country appear to the tourist and reader of *By Land and by Sea?* It was described almost exclusively along its periphery: it stretched from Kushka to the Dezhnev Peninsula, "from southern mounts to northern seas," from Brest to the hills of Kamchatka. "It lies, having spread forth its cities, covered with a net of meridians, invincible, broad, and free." The space described by the points of its extremities also broke down into internal peripheral topoi, but all of these topoi are "internal-Soviet." For example, the following is said of Baku:

> Lovers of Eastern "exoticism" now no longer need to travel to the outskirts. Everything Eastern has been transported to the central streets of the city. Chureks are sold in the bakeries and sweetshops. Shish kebab and lamb chekhakhbili are no longer roasted at a noisy Eastern bazaar but in the kitchens of restaurants and cafeterias.
>
> It is now no longer necessary to go to the "dukhan" (an Eastern tea room) in order to hear Turkish ethnic songs and music or to see dances. In clubs, palaces of culture, at the Turkish opera—everywhere ethnic art is blossoming.
>
> If you wish to become acquainted with the everyday life of the East, a museum is at your service, where you can see many paintings, marble handicrafts, carpets made by the best Eastern masters, precious utensils, and antique Eastern jewelry. . . .
>
> The Bailov Prison is easy to see from the pinnacles of an old Eastern fort. It was in this prison in 1908 that Comrade Stalin was imprisoned and wrote his "Letters from Beyond the Caucasus. Here also were imprisoned our present-day People's Commissar of the Food Industry, Com. Mikoyan, and the 26 Baku Commissars."[18]

This idea of Eastern exoticism (the very word "exoticism" is in quotation marks) is itself characteristic. *Chureks*, shish kebabs, *chekhakhbili*, and the *dukhan* (for which a special explanation is required) turn up in a completely transformed—and now properly Soviet—space: bakeries and sweetshops, the kitchens of restaurants and cafeterias. Among the sights are not monuments of ancient architecture but a prison, for it was there that Stalin and the people's commissar of the food industry (the one, no doubt, who made sure that shish kebabs and *chekhakhbili* were sold not just anywhere but in restaurants and cafeterias) had been imprisoned.

This transformed space is homogenous, as in the poem "Mother land," by the tourist Lev Chernomortsev:

The Urals, Siberia, the Caucasus, or Ukraine,
Wherever I may be, I'm always in the motherland—
I'm greeted like a native son,
Along my way are kolkhozes, villages, and cities.

Is it not because I, a citizen of the Soviets,
Walk along as a vigilant, happy hiker?
Wherever I may be—there are always words of greeting,
I'll always find discreet hospitality!

For toward the icy eagles' passes,
In the company of stars, in clouds' nomadic camps—
With good reason the broad path of the Bolsheviks
Was paved through the mountains!

Comrades! We greet with love
The country's fields, and rivers, and seas.
Our compass is true! We always march
Along the same grand route of October![19]

The most important characteristic of the space described here, just as in the texts of professional Soviet poets, is its self-sufficient closure. The Urals, Siberia, the Caucasus, Ukraine—all of these topoi are in reality but a single one ("always in the motherland"). All of these kolkhozes, villages, and cities, the country's fields, rivers, and seas, belong to an enclosed space in which, it turns out, all march "along the same grand route." That route lies along the border.

Soviet culture was a culture of inflamed borders. A border was the meeting space of two different topoi—the Soviet one and, without fail, an enemy one. The border lived its own special life, full of dangers and heroic feats, and therefore full of heroes and enemies. The hiker was fundamentally different from the enemy. He or she was almost a hero. Thus the lyrical hero of Chernomortsev's poem "walk[s] along as a vigilant, happy hiker." The simultaneity here—vigilant and happy at the same time—is significant: at any moment the hiker must be prepared to meet and disarm a spy or saboteur, because, as the magazine explained, "the use of travel for espionage has long been practiced by the intelligence services of all countries."[20]

> A collective is walking along. The column of hikers slowly climbs the pass. Breathing heavily, the people surmount the last meters of the glacial incline. And when they reach the summit of the pass . . . the leader announces a rest. Everyone takes off his or her sunglasses and sits down to rest. The sun climbs toward noon. Everyone is hungry.
>
> Breaking off into groups, the hikers take from their packs bread, sausages, sugar. Conversations begin, acquaintances are made. The hikers had left their shelters before sunrise, in the dark, and only now, for the first time, they make one another's acquaintance.
>
> A short-statured blond man seats himself in one group. He is dressed, like many hikers and mountain climbers, in knee socks and a khaki shirt, and on his feet are hiking shoes. He is a lone hiker; he came from abroad about five years before (which can easily be noted by his accent), and he works in Moscow as an electronics technician. His new acquaintances are mountain climbers on their way from a high-altitude camp to the sea. The majority of them are workers from defense industry factories.
>
> It turns out that both the fellows and the lone hiker have the same route. . . .
>
> Some time later, the short-statured blonde in knee socks and khaki shirt was sitting in the office of an NKVD investigator. He turned out to be a spy from one of the Western countries.[21]

This is how it happens . . . In a word, the border. The magazine went on to explain that

> a spy acting under the guise of a tourist—foreign or "ours"—is generally carrying out the following objectives: He is collecting information of a military character (on the production of defense industry factories, on the placement and weaponry of individual military units, on the refining of mineral resources with defense uses, etc.) and about public sentiment. He does this by means of conversation with his fellow travelers and with local residents. The spy photographs and scrutinizes the locale. He studies distinct strategic points, railroad bridges, and areas of new industrial construction.
>
> Besides this "peacetime" work, foreign intelligence agents devise and attempt to carry out various diversionary acts. They try to attract unsteady and wavering people into their ranks. For this they turn to blackmail, drink, and demoralization.[22]

Here, of course, the enemy miscalculated: one does not "demoralize" Soviet tourists. Their reactions to the "verdict of the people over the Trotskyite-Zinovyevite snakes" attest to this fact:

> Dear Iosif Vissarionovich! On August 25, at 13:30 hours, we, the wives of the commanding officers of the Stalinobad Garrison, numbering 19 persons, attained a mountaintop at an altitude of 4,150 meters in the vicinity of Gushara Kishlak. Our ascent coincided with the announcement of the verdict handed down against the enemies of the people, the Trotskyite-Zinovyevite group. By this hike we bear witness to you, dear Iosif Vissarionovich, of our readiness, along with our husbands' to stand in defense of our remarkable motherland at a moment's notice. . . . By this hike we have tested our readiness. In spite of all the difficulties of our path, which proceeded under hurricane conditions of hail and rain, in the face of avalanches and landslides, in the fierce natural conditions of mountainous Tajikistan, the indicated altitude was attained by us without stragglers.[23]

Thus our earlier misgivings that the inhabitant and subjugator of peripheral spaces—the hiker—might be somehow just as suspect as his habitat have turned out to be unfounded. Having passed through the crucible of socialist realist mimesis, this character, together with his environment, is represented as clean, reflected in the magic mirror of socialist realist writing. The result is a total transformation of a dangerous topos. The cause of this resemanticization of the periphery lies, it would seem, in the realm of the irrational. This is some sort of *spell.* The transformed topos ceases to be dangerous, and the tourist himself becomes a sort of reflection of the leading actor of the 1930s: the border guard.

And although the border, in reality, became no less dangerous, and the tourist did not cease to be suspect, these facts no longer have any cultural significance. We have before us a product created by a power that has in no way betrayed its "popular nature." This power, to use A. Piotrovskii's words, strives for "an interpretation of space . . . as a certain topographic 'reality.'" Only now that space was the very country itself, and it was the ideal image of the country that became this topographic reality. Socialist realist transformation has come full circle: the country achieves its "true" identity only in representation and discourse.

Discursive Space: *Map of the Motherland*

> I have always wanted to write geography; in this geography, one could see how to write history.
>
> —Nikolai Gogol

Among the remarkable constellation of writers whom Maxim Gorky enlisted to contribute to *Our Achievements* (Nashi dostizheniia)—the first journal he founded after his return from Italy in 1928—was the geographer Nikolai Mikhailov. The twenty-eight-year-old Mikhailov already had invaluable experience as a traveler: he had journeyed through the entire country on scientific and literary affairs, from the Kara-Kum to the North Pole. He had participated in many expeditions and hikes to the Pamirs and Tien Shan and had visited many countries of the world. On the pages of Gorky's journal, Mikhailov published articles such as "Cities That Weren't on the Map" (1933, no. 7), "The New Geography" (1933, no. 10), and "Fixing Nature" (1934, no. 2). And it was on those pages that one of the most recognized books of Soviet popular science was born: Mikhailov's 1947 *Map of the Motherland.*

Interest in the "new geography" toward the end of the first Five-Year Plan was not only related to the advertising of "our achievements" but was also a reflection of a new spatial perception by the country's citizens at the very moment when migratory processes had reached their peak. In response to this demand, the Party Central Committee issued a decree in May 1934 supporting the propagandizing of geographic knowledge among the young and acknowledging the necessity of publishing a series of books of "entertaining geography."

An earlier book of Mikhailov's, *The Face of the Country Changes,* which also began as an essay in *Our Achievements* and which came out in 1937, the year after Gorky's death, was but a harbinger. After it came *The Russian Land* (1946), *The Expanses and Riches of Our Motherland* (1946), and, finally, *Map of the Motherland,* which brought Mikhailov the Stalin Prize. (He was the only "popular science" author among the Stalin Prize laureates.) This book went through several editions and was translated into many of the world's languages. Later, Mikhailov wrote other books of the same type: *My Russia (Russian Expanses)* (1964), *In the Giant's Footsteps* (1967), and many others. But if Mikhailov had written only one book, *Map of the Motherland,* it would be enough for his name to merit mention in Soviet cultural history.

Appearing in print runs by the half-millions and continually republished in slightly changed editions ("the face of the country changes"!), Mikhailov's books truly did show Soviet people the country in which they lived. There were few maps in them, however. One could even say that there were no maps at all: *Map of the Motherland* was outfitted with contour "maps" that demonstrated, against the silhouette background of the Soviet country, the main petroleum centers ("then and now"), the main machine-building centers ("then and now"), the movement of automobile factories, examples of how industrial sites had come closer to large sources of raw materials, and so forth. Arrows showed freight routes, communications, exchanges between cities and industrial regions. Each time, we see two silhouettes: one with just a few points ("then") and another with many ("now"). Each year the maps become more cluttered with new regions and industrial objects. Yet this in no way means that anyone could ever actually have used these maps.

The traditional Soviet problem with maps is worth our attention. The map is a secret object: saboteurs, spies, and Soviet intelligence agents are somehow always hunting for a map. It is precisely in the map that the most secret information is contained—not in some technical document, not in some protocol, but in maps. Dovzhenko told the story of how he was discussing his film *Aerograd* with Stalin in his office, and how Stalin, interested in the idea of building a new city on the shores of the Sea of Japan, asked Dovzhenko to show him this newly beloved place on the map. Stalin, Dovzhenko recalled, led him through his office to a locked room where maps were hung, covered by special curtains. The holy of holies. As Khrushchev revealed in the Twentieth Party Congress, Stalin seldom left Moscow from the 1920s until his death. The Kremlin hermit ruled the largest country in the world, transforming it exclusively on maps. The map was indeed the equivalent of power, and the *real* maps were all located in Stalin's office.

But without a map, a country does not know itself—even more so a country that consists of unheard-of expanses. And if there is nothing to see, no map to look at, all that remains is to hear. Therefore, instead of a map, words are needed. It turns out that it is not at all necessary to show a map: it is quite possible to *tell* it. In addition, normal viewing of a map is useless: it does not call forth feelings; it teaches nothing. Mikhailov's books articulate the map; they teach one how to read it, and to read it in the literal sense—as history (for something is always *happening* with a map). It turns out that the map is not at all a visual image but a verbal sequence. Description is able to supplant the map. It is very selective and has a definite strategy. In essence, this descriptive strategy creates a certain virtual space, one that I call "discursive space." It is the strategy of discourse about Soviet space that will now occupy our attention.

How does geography begin? It begins with history—and the first chapter of *Map of the Motherland* is called "History's Gait." Mikhailov calls this the "'fourth dimension' of that which has opened before us: not latitude, not longitude, not altitude, but years of human effort":

> Man transforms the surface of the earth more boldly and quickly than do the play of orogenic forces, the action of water, or climatic change. He digs, drills, detonates, fills, builds. The face of the earth acquires ever newer features, which are shown on a geographic map by means of conventional symbols and colors—and the map narrates to us, in its own language, the creative labor and acts of the people. The map is responsive, like a light-sensitive cell. It records changes in the fate of nations and states. History forges its path on the map, and the map appears before us as a living witness, a wise and inspired storyteller.[24]

But it is the author who begins the story. From edition to edition the "map" in his book becomes ever more "alive." The 1949 edition begins beautifully:

> There is a geographic map on the wall. We approach it as we would an open window: through the light mesh of meridians and parallels, the country can be seen beyond the window. We have known its outlines since childhood—like our childhood home, like our mother's face. The symbol for Moscow, the branched tree of the Volga, the Urals' wrinkles, the little sickle of Lake Baikal. . . . Thought shows through the map, and before our inner eye, beyond the map's colored flatness in three-dimensional space, plains stretch out and mountain ranges tower. Little blue spots pour into broad lakes, meandering lines turn into raging rivers, small dots grow into cities filled with life. We can hear how the cold ice floes in the north scrape against the sides of a ship, and how in the south the hot sand flows in a slender stream down a dune. The window is all the way open—as though the wind has burst in from distant expanses and hit us in the face. The entire, boundless Soviet country is before us! [3–4]

All of this—open windows, raging rivers, inner eyes, and other lovely expressions—was absent in previous editions. But what always remained was the most important thing, from which the description of Soviet space begins: the border. This border is internal. It marks the map of the world from within Soviet space:

> The red line on the map tells us: a new world has arisen on the earth—the world of socialism. A state in which power belongs to the people of labor. A country where there is no enslavement of man by man. On the old map was the tsarist empire. On the new one is a socialist state, a complex organism of free governments possessing equal rights and voluntarily united. . . . The holy boundary of the Soviet land is unshakable. The red line is firmly etched on the map of the world—from Pechenega to Kaliningrad, from Kaliningrad to Izmail, from Izmail to the Kurile Ridge. This is not only the border of the greatest country in the world—this is a line that lawlessness, tyranny, and oppression cannot cross. In the countries of capital are darkness and servitude, the power of money, violence over the masses, the inflaming of wars. . . . We have here, in the Soviet land, free citizens of a free country, the happiness of peaceful, constructive labor, the great building timber of communism. . . . Our country has become a mighty power. And these historical shifts have been reflected on the map. [4–5]

As we see, it is not so much the trace, the "form," as it is the "content" that matters. Over there is an "empire," over here, a "state." The map is old only in form; it is new in content. And content must be told. Maps should be studied with the "inner eye," because they can be understood only by "reading" that which "shows through" from behind them:

> Thus we say: new cities, factories, roads, and mines are visible on the map. This, of course, is true. But neither cities nor factories arise by themselves. An economic map is a human document; it is the people's service record. The symbol for a factory also contains the heroism of the workers, and the organized talent of the leaders, and the glory of the Stakhanovites. The rectangular mass representing a field also contains the joy of collective labor, the new culture of work, new relations between the peasant and the land. The little flag that is a polar station on the shores of the Kara Sea, and the dot of the glacial obser-

> vatory in the Pamir hills—these contain modest but conscientious feats. [10]

The mystical nature of the map-reading process is in a strange way integrated with the materiality, the corporality, of the visual image "given to our perception."

The third chapter of the book, "Under the Flag of the Land of the Soviets," which tells of the expansion of the "great power," aims to let the reader feel that the "body" of the country has become, at last, unified and whole: "It wasn't immediately that our union took on those contours that we see on the map today. There was a time when millions of hapless people, our brothers by blood and language, were left beyond the borders of the great revolution." For example, "the Ukrainian land of Galicia . . . languished under the yoke of Austria-Hungary." Over the peasants of "Transcarpathian Ukraine . . . Hungarian landowners ruled." In the Baltic, "western European imperialists solidified a reactionary bourgeois regime with their armies' bayonets." Western Ukraine and western Belorussia "were tamed at the hands of Polish pani," and Bessarabia and Bukovina, at the hands of "Romanian boyars." In the east, "Japanese were lording over . . . traditionally Russian lands." Yes, "our brethren suffered long in their separation from their mother—the motherland. It was a gloomy feeling: close at hand, just beyond a not-too-distant line, lay your native country, where your own people lived, free and happy. But you labor under some foreign boss. . . . And only now have the isolated peoples been restored." It is the map of the USSR's new territories that tells of this "restoration of historical justice" (24).

And just what is the "body" of the country? A healthy body is possible only "under the conditions of our socialist reality." For example, in the West, "it is impossible to combine all private interests into a unified will" (118). But in the Soviet Union, there is

> no private ownership of the land or of the means of production, and the socialist state can easily choose the best place for construction of a power station. It can engage huge resources for the station's construction. It can use the natural energy resources in the best way possible. It can hang a power transmission line in any direction necessary. It can hook up any enterprise to that line. The choice is made by plan, and the plan originates in the interests of the people. The people work for themselves, and therefore they work well. [114]

In the face of this logic, no questions remain as to why the state is so easily able to accomplish everything, whereas nobody else is able to accomplish anything. The object lesson of the political economics of socialism turns out to be, as indeed it is supposed to be, a lesson in government. Aside from the state there are no active subjects.

If the "body" of the country is alive, that means it is changeable. Thus:

> We love our glorious, dear Volga, but we do not wish to leave it quite as it is. . . . The dams of hydroelectric stations will lock up the waters and will turn the Volga into a chain of long lakes and reservoirs of great depth. . . . The dams on the upper flow will begin retaining the spring floodwaters and releasing them during times of low water. The spring flood will be captured and distributed so that even the summer Volga will become deep and abundant in water. All of this is what is called the reconstruction of the Volga. [121]

In the same way, the Sevan Cascade will be created, which "will transform the entire Armenian economy." All of these "planned miracles," of course, are impossible under capitalism.

Everything in this country is "new." It is sufficient to glance at the chapter titles of Mikhailov's book: "New Lands on the Old Map" (ch. 4), "New Wealth of Mineral Resources" (ch. 5), "New Bastions of Socialist Industry" (ch. 6), "New Fields" (ch. 7), "New Paths" (ch. 8), "The Great Renewal" (ch. 9). And just how is it that the country changes? By what miracle is all this unseen "newness" born? This miracle is the Word. Take, for example, the creation of a "second Baku": "To prospect for oil in the middle of the country, to prospect no matter what the cost—such was the charge given by Comrade Stalin. 'Begin in all seriousness the organization of a petroleum base in the regions of the western and southern slopes of the Ural range,' said our leader. And this task was fulfilled" (65).

And thus in 1932 oil gushers spouted not only in the Urals but also on the Volga. As a result, "a new oil country was born" (65). And what if no oil had been found? Then we would have known nothing of the "directions of Comrade Stalin" on this matter. Here we have true Soviet history: its causes are told only when the consequences have justified—or when they are said to have justified—themselves. Events turn out to be just as self-sufficient as space.

Thus, the principal miracle of the map is its constant change. Transformation is the principal event in the study of the "map of the motherland." Everything changes—above all, the earth. The flora itself changes: "To change the nature of plants, and thus to remake the geography of plant biology—this is how the primary task of advanced Soviet science is formulated" (158). The goal is best served by "Michurin's biological science," which is "raised high by the distinguished Soviet scientist Academician Lysenko," in whose hands everything is miraculously transformed: winter varieties into spring varieties, late ones into early ones (159). As a result, the geography of agriculture and planting changes. "Only the creative initiative of the masses can fix the map of fruit-growing. . . . Only the people itself can create a new geography of horticulture" (191).

Indeed, a miracle is born: "Cold winters did not allow pears and apples to grow either in the Urals or in Siberia. But the Soviet people decided: wherever factories are constructed, wherever there are cities and villages, gardens can and must be laid out. And gardens were laid out" (191). Near Moscow, "vineyards . . . will become a common sight. Another common sight here will be melon plantations. This, too, is a revolution not only in the structure of field husbandry but also in the landscape: in a field alongside a northern fir or pine tree, striped watermelons or yellow cantaloupes will ripen—things that, it once seemed, could grow only somewhere near Kamyshin or Tashkent" (193).

In the miraculous Soviet country, nothing ever remains inactive—everything is moving somewhere. "Wheat is moving farther north and east," into Siberia and Kazakhstan (177). "Rice is moving north. . . . it grows near Kuibyshev, Kursk, and Ryazan, in woodland marshes . . . , in the environs of Moscow—two thousand kilometers farther north than the former rice zone." (178). Corn has been "shifted to the north," into the Siberian steppes (179). "Soviet rule has redrawn the geographic borders of cotton growing. . . . Collective cotton farms have arisen in the formerly bare steppes of the Black Earth and Azov Sea regions" (180). In a word, "after three decades of Soviet rule, our geography of agricultural crops has changed. The old 'distribution limits' have been overturned, and antiquated concepts have been crushed" (182).

Everything in these pictures is meant to astound. Visualization becomes superfluous; the picture is powerless before the word:

> These rapid and yet planned changes in the geographical landscape are unknown to people in the capitalist world. Scientists of the contemporary West lament: "Landscape is our irrevocable fate."—"No!" we say. "With our own hands, using well-considered blueprints, we

> are building our country, we are creating a new landscape." Bourgeois scientists say: "Geography is not created, but is born of itself."—"No!" we say. "Building communism, we are remaking the country with rational calculation, we are changing its geography." [7]

In this text people do not "lament" and "speak" so much by chance: only by the word is the miracle born, before which all manner of "lamentation" turns out to be powerless. It is not important what these unthinkable "transformations" were in reality; what is important is that the very sensation of reality, its *verbal* image, has changed.

For example, the author describes the draining and irrigation of land in Kolkhida, on the Kuban River, on the Irpen, in Polesie, and elsewhere. How does this occur? "People, inspired by the grandeur of the idea, create a new—a healthy and blossoming—land. The land is now being created, although its future geographic map already exists. . . . This land will exist, for it is accounted for in the socialist plan, for this is how the Soviet nation wants it to be, this is how it has decided" (207). It is impossible to learn anything of the problems connected with such grandiose tasks—but this, as it turns out, is unnecessary: we have the inspiration, a plan, an image of blossoming land.

Everything is described in the future tense. It will be thus: "Grand changes are maturing in the Turkmen Republic. Today the waters of the Amu-Darya pour into the Aral Sea in a mighty flow, while all around it deserts lie dried up under the hot sun. Tomorrow the Amu-Darya will turn toward the Caspian Sea, toward waterless lands awaiting moisture" (212). Great projects are under way: the desert is retreating; "water is washing desert regions off the map one after another" (214). These deserts have already, as it were, ceased to exist. And although it turned out, years later, that it was the Azov Sea that began to disappear, rather than the deserts, this fact has no real significance. Those who would "besmirch" the picture of creation are false, their calculations are in error, their conclusions unconvincing. The true picture lives in the word and is not subject to the erosion of reality.

The true picture of the miraculous Soviet landscape, moreover, contrasts with the picture of the capitalist West. While among "us," everything is being ennobled and improved, in America half the forests have been felled in the race for profit. "Instead of sleepy forests, all that is left are stumps." As a result, "torrents rush down in the spring, rivers splash out of their beds in destructive floods; the earth is no longer held together by the roots of trees and brush, and so it is washed away by the flowing water" (167). The prairies have all been plowed up ("without any sort of plan"!). As a result, "the soil has lost its lumpy structure, become friable, and is easily blown away by the wind" (168). In another part of the prairie, grazing lands were created, and the earth, trampled by cows, "dried up, unable to breathe, and ceased to accept moisture" (168). And later, a horrifying picture: the fertile soil has been washed away from the fields, ravines have grown, the subsoil has been exposed, and greenery has disappeared. "The wind has raised up clouds of dust, which reach tremendous heights, darken the sun, blow over thousands of kilometers. . . . Dust has penetrated into peoples' lungs, destroying their health. . . . Huge expanses of fertile soils have been turned into deserts" (168).

The description is self-sufficient. The visual range is not needed in order to depict the apocalypse. After all is said and done, why do we need a map at all? The map in Mikhailov's book is but an excuse for the narrator. His book is, after all, not only a history but also a political economy of socialism: a most mysterious science, but one still comprehensible with Mikhailov's help. Hence all the mysticism and literariness in *Map of the Motherland.*

Being of little value in and of itself, space is fused into time before our very eyes. This is some sort of self-devouring chronotope. It is for this reason that toward the end of the book the center finally begins to make itself known. Before reaching its end, readers would have said the book was about the periphery. The organization of space begins only when the book is almost finished. And it is not by chance that the spatial form most convenient for this "centralization" turns out to be urban—that is, already organized—space.

The final chapter of the book, dedicated to the cities of socialism, depicts their new aspect:

> Then: an amateur show in the merchants' club is a genuine event in the city. . . . But now in every reasonably large city there is a theater with a permanent troupe. . . . Then: a small hospital with one doctor and two sick-nurses, plus a "charitable institution." Now—an entire network of outpatient clinics, ambulatories, medical consultation offices, kindergartens. . . . Tall gates with flags, the white statue of a discus thrower, lively groups of youth: the stadium. Sounds of music, green lawns, people on yellow pathways: a culture and recreation park. [265]

The spatial axis has now fully coincided with the temporal one. The new city is turning into an ideally organized topos, a kind of model of transformation of space in its entirety. The "lived-in" quality, the rationality of the present, and the constant insufficiency of the past are reconciled in the harmony of the future.

This is how Stalingrad—which was still in ruins at the time—*will be:*

> The city, stretched out along the Volga for forty kilometers, will be a unified organism. Large, green parks will join separate regions of the city. Beautiful civic buildings will spring up on the parade grounds and main roads; they will be monumental. And all around, comfortable residential buildings of moderate height, with balconies and verandas, will be scattered among the greenery of gardens. The Volga River will be visible below in all its splendor. In the city center, the broad ribbon of Stalin Boulevard will stretch across the hills. From Fallen Warriors Square downward, the Alley of Heroes will descend, having turned green, decorated with depictions of the glorious participants of the Battle of Stalingrad. This alley will reach all the way to the Volga with its broad terraces, all the way to the embankment boulevard, which is dressed in greenery and granite. There, on the riverbanks, on Glory Square, [will stand] a grand monument in honor of the Stalingrad victory, in honor of him whose glorious name this great city, the victor city, bears. [268]

A journey, according to *Map of the Motherland,* culminates in Moscow. The "new" and "old" cities have already passed by our "inner eye." And now Moscow turns out to be not only at the spatial but also at the temporal center. The last chapter is called "The Old Moscow and the Young Moscow"—Moscow is situated at the crossroads of time. But it is also the spatial center of the country: "Here is the focus of all the best things by which progressive mankind lives. Here is the light and wisdom of our epoch. Here is the supreme authority and government of the Soviet state. Here is Stalin" (281). This "here," however, is too broad, and therefore Moscow space itself is also centered. This internal centering of the city culminates in the space of power. Its broad radius is Chinatown (Kitai-gorod), which has become the governmental center. Here are located the ministries and the directorates:

> Economic summaries and reports flow to this place from all the corners of the Union, and from here directives, instructions and requests are dispersed to all those corners of the country. Kitai-gorod, the district of central government and Party institutions, is permeated with the interests of the country, with which it lives a single life. The Kitai-gorod walls have fallen, and their disappearance proclaims: the Kitai-gorod of today is not fenced off from the people, but rather is united with them, and serves them. [284]

This centripetal motion continues toward a single point: the Kremlin. It is here that the book culminates: "The ancient Kremlin—the heart of the country and the heart of Moscow—towers over Red Square. . . . Here is the political center of our glorious motherland, the headquarters of the Soviet country. . . . The rays that bring happiness to the people radiate from here. Here, in the Kremlin, Stalin lives and works—the leader, friend, teacher, and great architect of communism" (286).

Map of the Motherland and others of Mikhailov's books, which dispense with maps and *describe* Soviet space, are in fact the most adequate presentation of Soviet topoi. Their genre is "popular-scientific geography." Mikhailov had insisted that "thought shows through the map, and before our inner eye, beyond the map's colored flatness in three-dimensional space, plains stretch out and mountain ranges tower." In fact, everything is the other way around: "thought shows through" words. Many words. So many that behind their "flatness" a map begins to appear. Simply: one must know how to describe; one must transform space into time, geography into history, the visual into the verbal. Thus, according to Mikhailov, "the fourth dimension" is born.

Truly, the world of utopia described here—ideally harmonious, aesthetically perfect, and very beautiful—requires for its presentation specific descriptive mechanisms. It cannot be presented in any other way than by means of specific "substitutes"—architectural plans, motion pictures, novels, "parks of culture and recreation," postage stamps and postcards—which stand for various kinds of descriptions. Description tends toward story; story, toward history; and history, toward myth. The mythology of space is good in every way—except that it does not work for life. One can, of course, object that nobody ever lived in this world anyway. But this is just as true as saying that it was precisely here that we did live.

NOTES

1. I. G. Papinako, ed., *Sto let russkoi pochtovoi marki: 1858–1958* [One hundred years of the Russian postage stamp] (Moscow: Sviaz'izdat, 1958), 6.

2. Ibid., 5.

3. Ibid., 7–8.

4. *Katalog pochtovykh marok SSSR: 1918–1980,* 2 vols. (Moscow: Tsentral'noe Filatelisticheskoe Agenstvo "Soiuzpechat'" Ministerstva Sviazi SSSR, 1983, 1984); D. Karachun and V. Karlinskii, *Pochtovye marki SSSR (1918–1968)* [Postage stamps of the USSR] (Moscow: Sviaz', 1969).

5. Valentin Brodskii, *Iskusstvo pochtovoi marki* [The art of the postage stamp] (Moscow: Khudozhnik RSFSR, 1967), 74.

6. Ibid., 80.

7. V. Karlinskii, "Pochtovye marki RSFSR, 1917–1921" [Postage stamps of the RSFSR], *Sovetskii kollektsioner* 4 (1966): 24.

8. Brodskii, *Iskusstvo pochtovoi marki,* 81.

9. Papinako, *Sto let russkoi pochtovoi marki,* 24.

10. Brodskii, *Iskusstvo pochtovoi marki,* 83–84.

11. Ibid., 107.

12. Ibid., 109.

13. "Sovetskii turizm (redaktsionnaia)" [Soviet tourism (editorial)], *Na sushe i na more* 6 (1938): 4.

14. D. Kuznetsov, "Stakhanovtsy-turisty" [Stakhanovite tourists], *Na sushe i na more* 8 (1936): 15.

15. B. Kotel'nikov, "Shpiony" [Spies], *Na sushe i na more* 11 (1931): 4.

16. "Zadachi sovetskogo turizma (redaktsionnaia)" [Tasks of Soviet tourism (editorial)], *Na sushe i na more* 5 (1939): 4

17. A. Abegauz, "Kogda . . . ," *Na sushe i na more* 10 (1938): 9.

18. I. Rakitin, "Baku," *Na sushe i na more* 8 (1936): 14.

19. Lev Chernomortsev, "Rodina," *Na sushe i na more* 21 (1935): 17.

20. "Sovetskii turizm (redaktsionnaia)," *Na sushe i na more* 6 (1938): 4.

21. Ibid.

22. Ibid.

23. *Na sushe i na more* 9 (1936): 4.

24. N. Mikhailov, *Nad kartoi rodiny: Izdanie vtoroe, pererabotannoe i dopolnennoe* [Map of the motherland] (Moscow: Molodaia Gvardiia, 1949), 4. Further citations of this edition are noted paranthetically in the text.

8

"But Eastward, Look, the Land Is Brighter"

TOWARD A TOPOGRAPHY OF UTOPIA IN THE STALINIST MUSICAL

RICHARD TAYLOR

A recent article by Tracy Anderson bore the title, "Why Stalinist Musicals?"[1] The manner in which the question was posed is itself significant and reflects the distorting lens through which both Western and "Soviet" scholars have historically viewed Soviet cinema, even though Anderson's article did much to refocus that lens. We nowadays take for granted that audiences in Western countries look for escapist entertainment in times of collective stress. As the British director David Lean once remarked, "Films are not real. They are dramatized reality," and, "A shop girl earning three pounds a week doesn't pay to see an exact replica of herself on the screen—she pays to see what she would *like* to be, in looks, dress and mode of living."[2] For some years we have accepted that musicals were the most popular form of entertainment in the United States and much of Europe during the Great Depression and even that during the Third Reich German audiences preferred to see musicals like *Request Concert* (1940) rather than the more obvious products of Nazi propaganda such as *Triumph of the Will* (1935) or *The Eternal Jew* (1940).[3] Why then should we not accept that, in the midst of the forced industrialization and collectivization programs of the early Five-Year Plans, in the maelstrom of the massive economic and social dislocation that these caused, in the thick of the purges and the Great Patriotic War, the Soviet people might not also have wanted something to alleviate their mass suffering and give them hope in a better future? The question I want to ask first is, why *not* Stalinist musicals?

Why *Not* Stalinist Musicals?

The distorting lens through which Western and Soviet scholars have viewed the construct known as "Soviet cinema" has been analyzed by Ian Christie.[4] There is a growing literature on Soviet popular culture, especially on popular cinema, to which a number of scholars have contributed, most notably Denise Youngblood, Richard Stites, and James von Geldern, to name only those writing in English. This literature emphasizes the continuities in Russian cultural history between the pre- and postrevolutionary periods, on one hand, and between the 1920s and the 1930s, on the other, while acknowledging the serious discontinuities and ruptures that have traditionally been the focus of research.

I have argued elsewhere that a crucial role in the establishment of a Soviet *mass* cinema was played by Boris Shumiatsky, who in October 1930 was assigned the task of creating "a cinema that is intelligible to the millions."[5] He maintained that a "cinema for the millions" required the establishment of new entertainment genres such as the musical comedy: "Neither the revolution nor the defense of the socialist fatherland is a tragedy for the proletariat. We have always gone, and in future we shall still go, into battle singing and laughing."[6]

As James von Geldern has argued, "In the mid-1930s, Soviet society struck a balance that would carry it through the turmoil of the purges, the Great War and reconstruction. The coercive policies of the Cultural Revolution were replaced or supplemented by the use of inducements."[7] The *exclusive* cultural policies of the first Five-Year Plan period (1928–32) were replaced by the inducements of *inclusive* cultural policies following the dissolution of the self-styled proletarian cultural institutions in April 1932 and their replacement by all-embracing Soviet institutions such as the new Union of Soviet Writers. The doctrine proclaimed by the latter was socialist realism, which Andrei Zhdanov, who was effectively Stalin's cultural commissar, claimed meant depicting reality "not . . . in a dead, scholastic way, not simply as 'objective reality,' but . . . as reality in its revolutionary development."[8] Anatoly Lunacharsky, in charge of Soviet cultural policy in the 1920s, tellingly remarked that "the socialist realist . . . does not accept reality as it really is. He accepts it as it will be. . . . A Communist who cannot dream is a bad Communist. The Communist dream is not a flight from the earthly but a flight into the future."[9] In official terminology, this element was called "revolutionary romanticism."

The credibility of revolutionary romanticism, the "flight into the future," was enhanced by the audience's apparent complicity in the exercise. Political speeches, newspaper articles, poster campaigns, official statistics, and, above all, cinema—which Lenin had called "the most important of all the arts"—depicted life not as it actually was but as they hoped it was becoming.[10] The media furnished what Sheila Fitzpatrick has memorably described as "a preview of the coming attractions of socialism."[11] If the Great Terror of the 1930s was to become the stick with which to modernize the Soviet Union, then entertainment cinema was to provide the carrot.

Entertainment and Utopia

The musical was in many ways the perfect vehicle for the depiction and promulgation of the socialist realist utopia. This is especially true if we bear in mind Richard Dyer's argument that the central thrust of entertainment is utopianism and that although "entertainment offers the image of 'something better' to escape into, or something we want deeply that our day-to-day lives don't provide," it "does not . . . present models of utopian worlds. . . . Rather the utopianism is contained in the feelings it embodies."[12] In fact the Stalinist musical did both: it presented models of utopian worlds (in the case of the kolkhoz musical, the "Potemkin village") while also embodying the utopian feelings that stimulated audience identification. The task of Soviet cinema in the 1930s and 1940s was to convince audiences that, whatever their current hardships, life *could* become as it was depicted on the screen: life not as it is, but as it will be. In this reel utopia, if not in everyday reality as then experienced by cinema audiences, the Stalinist slogan "Life has become happier, comrades, life has become more joyous" was made real.[13]

The reel realization of utopia was achieved by both representational and nonrepresentational signs. Dyer's observation that critics pay more attention to the former at the expense of the latter is still largely true.[14] The nonrepresentational signification in the Stalinist musical lies primarily in three areas: the use of fairy-tale narrative conventions; the music itself; and the topographical conventions of the image of utopia, all of which weakened audience resistance to the reception of the utopian model depicted on screen.

In this essay I focus on the work of the two leading directors of "musical comedies" (the word *miuzikl* was officially regarded at the time as too bourgeois), Grigory Aleksandrov (1903–84) and Ivan Pyr'ev (1901–68). Their films need to be seen in their historical and cultural context, so I also discuss the works of other filmmakers where relevant. Aleksandrov founded the Soviet musical comedy genre with *The Jolly Fellows* (Veselye rebiata, 1934) and went on to make *The Circus* (Tsirk, 1936), *Volga-Volga* (1938), and *The Radiant Path* (Svetlyi put', 1940) in the same mold.[15] Pyr'ev's first musical comedy was *The Rich Bride* (Bogataia nevesta, 1938), which established the model for the kolkhoz musical. This was followed by *Tractor Drivers* (Traktoristy, 1939), *The Swineherdess and the Shepherd* (Svinarka i pastukh, 1941), and *The Kuban Cossacks* (Kubanskie kazaki, 1949), the apotheosis of what Khrushchev was later to call the "varnishing of reality" that characterized Soviet cinema's depiction of the Potemkin village of the Stalin period.[16]

The Path to Utopia: The Fairy Tale

Maia Turovskaia has brilliantly analyzed the way in which Pyr'ev in particular used the conventions of the Russian fairy tale to project his "folklorized" vision of the Potemkin village,[17] and Masha Enzensberger has extended this analysis to Aleksandrov's *The Radiant Path.*[18] The use of these conventions enabled Soviet musicals to act, in Turovskaia's own words, "not so much as the reflection of their time's objective reality, but rather as the reflection of the reality of its image of itself."[19]

The plots of these films almost invariably center on what Russians call a "love intrigue"—but it is not "tainted" by sexual or erotic impulses. Rather, it is a "pure" romantic love based on its object's labor proficiency. In the conventions of the Soviet musical—as indeed of its Hollywood equivalent—the love intrigue is clear from the beginning when "boy meets girl." But the resolution of this "inevitable" liaison is retarded by a misunderstanding and/or by competition between two male "suitors," one of whom is "worthy" of the heroine in terms of his labor productivity, and the other of whom is not. The plot develops around the heroine's journey toward an understanding of which is which. Sometimes, as in *The Circus,* this is obvious from the beginning, and the plot therefore revolves around the heroine's discovery of the true path—the Soviet path—toward that understanding. The exceptions to this rule are the last films by each of our two directors. In Aleksandrov's *The Radiant Path,* based closely on the Cinderella story, the heroine has to prove to herself that *she* is worthy of her suitor by successfully emancipating herself through a Party-sponsored training program. In Pyr'ev's *The Kuban Cossacks,* the hero has no rival in love: his battle is with his own Cossack male chauvinist pride.

In almost all of these films, and in all the kolkhoz musicals, the central character, who eventually resolves the difficulties, is a woman. There are no fundamentally weak or evil women characters in these films. The only evil characters are foreigners, such as the Hitler look-alike von Kneischitz in *The Circus,*[20] or the forces threatening the frontiers of the USSR in *Tractor Drivers*. The weak Soviet characters are either marginalized (the bourgeois women in *The Jolly Fellows*, Kuzma and his associates in *Swineherdess*) or won over to the work ethic (Aleksei the bookkeeper—a truly bourgeois because "unproductive" profession—in *The Rich Bride*, Nazar the idler in *Tractor Drivers*). In utopia, weakness is redeemable. Evil is not, but it is externalized.

The main characters are depersonalized and universalized as in a fairy tale: they are symbolic figures, and the frequent use of choral singing helps this process of generalization. In both *The Rich Bride* and *The Kuban Cossacks*, for instance, the "battle of the sexes" is fought out in choral form. The Soviet version of the star system helped in this: all of Aleksandrov's films starred his wife, Liubov Orlova, the "prima donna" of Stalinist cinema,[21] and all of Pyr'ev's starred his wife, Marina Ladynina. Their appearance in a series of films with similar plot structures but different settings in different parts of the Soviet Union and with different casts helped audiences all over the country to identify with them more directly while broadening the appeal of the films and their message.

It must also be said that neither Orlova nor Ladynina conformed to the traditional stereotype of femininity. Although Ladynina sometimes appeared in folk costume in the kolkhoz musicals, both she and Orlova also appeared in "masculine" clothing (Ladynina in *The Rich Bride* and *Tractor Drivers*, Orlova in *The Circus*, *Volga-Volga*, and *The Radiant Path*), which desexualized them.[22] For Soviet women caught in the double bind of housework and motherhood, on one hand, and collective labor, on the other, this must have represented truly utopian wish fulfillment. The heroine is always depicted in the workplace, be it kolkhoz, circus, or spinning mill. She is shown in the home only when it, too, is a workplace, as it is for the Cinderella heroine of *The Radiant Path*. Some critics have argued that the Soviet musical heroine is a mother figure, but this is not true in the conventional sense: domesticity is absent, and there is no family but the collective as workplace in microcosm or the collective as country in macrocosm. This elision between the two is effected partly by the use of folklore and partly through the music, to which I shall return.

The characters are introduced to one another "accidentally," sometimes through the fairy-tale medium of a picture, updated as a photograph (*Tractor Drivers*, *Swineherdess*). The accident of their initial encounter reinforces the sense of the inevitability of their romance, as if it has been ordained from "on high." Often this is further reinforced by a direct or indirect "blessing" from that same source. In Aleksandr Medvedkin's *The Miracle Girl* (Chudesnitsa, 1936)—set on a kolkhoz but not a musical—the Stakhanovite heroine is summoned to Moscow, where she sees Stalin and hears him speak, as a reward for her labor achievements. In *The Circus,* the heroine "understands" her situation when she joins the May Day parade in Red Square and sees Stalin, here signified as God by the iconlike image carried at the head of the procession in the immediately preceding shot. In *Tractor Drivers,* the wedding feast finale is accompanied by toasts and oaths of allegiance to Stalin. In *The Radiant Path,* the heroine is summoned to a fairy-tale Kremlin to receive the Order of Lenin from someone whose aura reflects light upon her face: this must be Stalin, because in a Soviet film in 1940 it could hardly have been anyone else.[23]

These "unforgettable encounters" occur in numerous other Soviet films, posters, paintings, and newspaper articles of the period. They form a central thread in the fairy tale of Stalin as father of his people, as the genius who has time for everyone, who can solve everybody's problems, even when his divinity is mediated through another Party or state official such as the Soviet president Kalinin or the local Party secretary *(The Radiant Path, The Kuban Cossacks).* Stalin is the omniscient and implicitly omnipresent father of the collective Soviet family, the avuncular patriarch of the peoples.[24] Participation in this larger family sublimates the need for the heroines and, indeed, the heroes to participate in nuclear domesticity: sex is absent, and even the kissing is "innocent" *(The Jolly Fellows, Volga-Volga).* The family is the country itself,[25] in which all are equal or at least all have equal opportunity.

A central part of the fairy tale in Aleksandrov's films, though not in Pyr'ev's, is the idea that any Soviet citizen, however humble, timid, or wretched at the beginning of the film, can make a success of life and rise to the heights that socialist society has to offer. In *Volga-Volga,* the heroine, a local letter carrier, overcomes numerous obstacles to win the All-Union Olympiad of Song. In *The Radiant Path,* the heroine receives the Order of Lenin and later becomes a deputy to the Supreme Soviet, a sure sign that she has "arrived." These closures are in fact also apertures allowing the audience to participate in the action.[26]

The Radiant Path has perhaps the most interesting, and certainly the most bizarre, ending of any Stalinist musical. Following the award of the Order of Lenin, the heroine, Tania, finds herself in a Kremlin anteroom decorated only with chandeliers and a mirror. Scarcely able to believe that what is happening to her is real, she checks in the mirror.

She sees her reflection and therefore "knows" that it is real. Then she turns her face back to the camera and sings a duet with mirror images of her earlier selves. The image in the mirror then turns into Tania as fairy godmother, complete with tiara, who opens the frame of the mirror and invites the heroine's present self into the world of mirror (reel?) reality. She is thereby acquiring the necessary self-confidence to become a full-fledged participant in the construction of the Soviet utopia. The two Tanias are seated in a car that then takes off, flying over the Kremlin, then Moscow, then high mountains, and then back to Moscow to the showpiece All-Union Agricultural Exhibition (VSKhV), landing at the foot of the famous statue by Vera Mukhina, *Worker and Collective Farm Woman.* The final scene of the film takes place in the exhibition itself, where the one-time Cinderella figure, now crowned with success, reencounters her Prince Charming against a magic background of fountains and other symbols of abundance. Implicitly, now that they have established their equality in successful careers, they *may* have time for domesticity, but this is by no means made explicit.

Other films use festivals or mass scenes to draw the audience into the action and, above all, into the emotional uplift: the "storming" of the Bolshoi Theater against all obstacles by the hero and heroine of *The Jolly Fellows,* the Olympiad of Song at the end of *Volga-Volga,* the wedding feast at the end of *Tractor Drivers,* the implied weddings that conclude both *Swineherdess* and *The Kuban Cossacks.* But the device that really involves the emotions of the audience is the use of popular music in its various forms.

The Path to Utopia: The Music

The music for all of the Aleksandrov and for the first and last of the Pyr'ev musicals was written by the most prolific composer of Soviet popular music, Isaak Dunaevsky (1900–55). He received his first Stalin Prize in 1941 for the music to Aleksandrov's *The Circus* and *Volga-Volga* and his second ten years later for the score to Pyr'ev's *The Kuban Cossacks.* One of the songs from *The Circus,* "Song of the Motherland," became the call sign for Moscow radio and the unofficial state anthem of the Soviet Union until an official anthem was introduced in 1943.

The music played a crucial part because it appealed to the emotions of the audience and helped to weaken any intellectual resistance it might have had to the message of the films.[27] The scores made widespread use of choral singing, which, as I mentioned earlier, helped to universalize the characters and the situations in which they found themselves. Furthermore, the combination of catchy tunes and ideologically loaded texts (mostly by Vasily Lebedev-Kumach, 1898–1949) meant that when the audience left the cinema humming the tune, it also carried the message of reel reality into the real world outside. This helped make audiences feel that they were part of the world depicted on the screen: it elided the actual with the utopian ideal, collapsing the "fourth wall" in the auditorium.[28]

In *The Jolly Fellows,* the first verse of the theme song extolled the uplifting popularity of song, while the refrain made clear the use to which this uplift was to be put:

A song helps us build and live,
Like a friend, it calls and leads us forth.
And those who stride through life in song
Will never ever fall behind.[29]

Further verses enjoined the audience: "When our country commands that we be heroes, Then anyone can become a hero." They later warned that any enemy threatening "to take away our living joy" would be resoundingly rejected with "a battle song, staunchly defending our motherland." The idea of song as a central and necessary part of life is echoed in "Three Tank Drivers," by Boris Laskin and the Pokrass brothers, written for *Tractor Drivers:* "There they live—and singing guarantees it—As a tight, unbroken family." That family was not the nuclear family, but the motherland: the word *rodina*—deriving from the Russian verb *rodit',* "to give birth to"—was resurrected to reinforce this metaphor.[30] This was the motherland of "socialism in one country," a land whose vast size and variety were constantly extolled *(The Circus, Volga-Volga, Tractor Drivers, Swineherdess),* a land that was largely hermetically sealed against apparently hostile outside forces *(The Circus, Tractor Drivers).*

Dunaevsky's music carefully reflected the setting of each film. For Pyr'ev's kolkhoz musicals he wrote scores that were heavily influenced by folk music, Ukrainian or Russian as appropriate. The Aleksandrov musicals, on the other hand, were urban oriented, and the scores drew upon urban musical forms such as jazz, music hall, and military marches, however unlikely that combination might appear. All three are evident in *The Jolly Fellows* and *The Circus. Volga-Volga* centers on a musical civil war (the device used here for narrative retardation) between the heroine, the author of "Song of the Volga," which eventually wins the Olympiad of Song, and the hero, who prefers to rehearse classical music with his brass band. For him the music of Wagner is a sign of culture and civilization: in 1938 this was a clear indication of "false consciousness."

In these three musicals, popular or "low" culture triumphs over "high" culture. In *The Jolly Fellows,* the respectable buffet party literally becomes a "carnival of the animals," and later on the jazz band ends the film by taking the Bolshoi Theater audience, again literally, by storm. In *The Circus,* the action takes place largely within the confines of a "low" cultural form. In *Volga-Volga,* it is the popular amateur song that triumphs over professional classical music, and a child maestro who outconducts the adults. Similarly, in *The Radiant Path,* the least musical of the Stalinist musicals, it is Cinderella who outstrips her "ugly sisters." These films provided confirmation that "when our country commands that we be heroes, Then anyone can become a hero"—"and singing guarantees it!"

The texts of the songs in the Stalinist musicals tell us a great deal about the topography of utopia and clarify some of the confusions and errors committed by critics and scholars who have ignored them.

On Arrival: The Topography of Utopia

The Stalinist utopia is hermetically sealed against the outside world. The only depiction of "abroad" (the lynch mob at the start of *The Circus)* is unflattering, and other references are boldly defensive *(Tractor Drivers).* It has been argued that in this utopia, gender construction is quite straightforward: the man is identified with the city, with industry, defense, modernity, the rational, and therefore progress; the woman, by contrast, is identified with the countryside and the land, with agriculture, nurture, nature, the emotional, and therefore also with backwardness. This construction reaches its apotheosis in Vera Mukhina's statue *Worker and Collective Farm Woman,* designed to top the Soviet pavilion at the 1937 Paris Exhibition: "a syntactically symmetrical pair, but with the man wielding the mace of modernity: the industrial hammer."[31] This characterization is, however, an oversimplification. Each musical explored different parts of the Stalinist utopia, *pars pro toto.* We must therefore construct our topography of that utopia by pulling those parts together into a coherent whole.

Utopia exists in these films at two levels that may be broadly characterized as the periphery and the center. Aleksandrov's musicals are geographically centripetal, Moscow oriented. Pyr'ev's are not—but they are not, as Evgeny Dobrenko has claimed, centrifugal films in which the movement is *away* from the capital.[32] Pyr'ev's forms merely explore the periphery and validate it as part of the overall utopia.

Exploring the Periphery

The Aleksandrov musicals begin at the periphery. In *The Jolly Fellows* it is a resort in the Crimea; in *The Circus,* for once, it is overseas, the United States; in *Volga-Volga* it is the small provincial town of Melkovodsk (meaning literally "little waters"); and in *The Radiant Path* it is a small town in the Moscow region. In the course of the film the action moves to Moscow, where it ends: in the Bolshoi Theater, in Red Square by the Kremlin, in the Olympiad of Song, and in the All-Union Agricultural Exhibition, respectively. The ties that link the periphery to the center vary. The translation of the main characters from one to the other is the principal one of these links, but boats provide the principal method of interurban transport in *The Jolly Fellows* (a train is also mentioned but not seen) and in *Volga-Volga.* In the latter, the postal system is also crucial, as it is in Pyr'ev's *Tractor Drivers,* where the postman sings a song encapsulating the variety and breadth of his vast country. In *The Circus,* trains offer a means of arrival from and (interrupted) departure to places abroad, but not within the USSR itself. Telegrams act as catalysts in both *Volga-Volga* and *The Radiant Path.* In the latter film, the first link between Melkovodsk and the capital occurs when the radio announces "Moscow calling," and the last is effected through the fairy-tale mirror device described earlier. The use of radio is familiar from other films of the period, including Kozintsev and Trauberg's *Alone* (Odna, 1931) and the documentaries of Dziga Vertov and Esfir Shub. The virtual absence of aircraft and trains as means of *internal* communication and linkage, however, when they featured so strikingly elsewhere, is curious.

It is almost as if the periphery is in some ways "living in the past," a past that was present reality for most audiences of the time. The presence of the bourgeois women early in *The Jolly Fellows* strengthens this interpretation. Surely Aleksandrov is making a visual reference to the women in *October* (Oktiabr', 1927): Eisenstein's women stab a Bolshevik workman to death with their parasols, while Alexandrov's "spike" the "wrong" artiste with theirs. In *The Radiant Path,* the heroine, Tania, is employed as a domestic servant, as is Aniuta in *The Jolly Fellows*—a most un-Soviet occupation even if still widespread in the 1930s. Both liberate themselves from this drudgery as the plot develops. Similarly,

Melkovodsk in *Volga-Volga* is initially depicted in an unflattering light: the ferry breaks down, the telephones do not work, the telegram from Moscow "slows down" when it arrives in the provinces, and the people of the town seem to spend their time either petitioning the local bureaucrat Byvalov (a name meaning "nothing new" and a role played hilariously by the leading comic actor Igor Il'insky) or practicing their music.[33]

Yet this backwardness is itself depicted as a caricature: although Byvalov, who regards his recent posting to Melkovodsk as a mere staging post on his long career track to journey's end in Moscow, claims that "there can be no talent in such a dump," Strelka ("little arrow") the letter carrier insists there is "no lack of talented people" and goes on to prove her point by singing Tchaikovsky and reciting Lermontov. It is, however, the delayed telegram from Moscow announcing the "socialist competition" of the Olympiad of Song that breaks the logjam of stagnation. And in a deliberate irony, it is through Strelka's efforts that Byvalov, despite his own efforts to obstruct her, eventually arrives with the entire local musical talent in Moscow.

In Pyr'ev's films, the kolkhoz is largely a self-sufficient microcosm, a closed world of "social claustrophobia," to use Dobrenko's term.[34] In *Tractor Drivers*, the hero does, it is true, enter from outside, but he comes from the fighting in the Far East, which is therefore no longer peripheral but strategically significant (compare films such as Dovzhenko's *Aerograd*, 1935). Furthermore, while in transit to Moscow, this time by train, he chooses to travel to the Ukrainian kolkhoz *rather than to the capital*. In *The Kuban Cossacks*, the outside world hardly intrudes either, although it is referred to obliquely, as is the war, fought less than a decade previously on this very terrain. The plot in all three films is characterized by what became known as "conflictlessness" *(beskonfliktnost')*. In other words, it is confined to microcosmic personal rivalries expressed in differing personal labor contributions rather than developed in terms of macrocosmic forces such as class conflict or war, which were all too evident in other Soviet films of the period.

The leading characters in the periphery are almost invariably women. It is they who organize and produce, they who resolve the love intrigue by recognizing, albeit somewhat belatedly, the production achievements of the hero and therefore his suitability as a partner in labor and love. The exceptions are in Aleksandrov's *The Jolly Fellows*, where it is the hero who effects the resolution through his talent for improvising in the most adverse circumstances, and in Pyr'ev's

Swineherdess, where the heroine weakly accepts her fate at the hands of the deceitful locals while the hero has to ride like a knight on horseback to rescue her at the eleventh hour. One reason for the privileging of women in the countryside was the need to encourage them to play a greater part in collective, as opposed to domestic, labor in the light of male migration to the cities and the consequent labor shortage in rural areas. Another factor influencing gender roles was personal: these musicals were made by male directors to showcase the acting, singing, and dancing talents of their wives. Finally, the films emphasized that in Russia, women were equal. Independent women served to underline the superiority of the Soviet way of life. For these reasons women were never villains: the villainous characters were always men, but they could be cured of their villainy by the intervention of women, unless they were hostile foreigners, like von Kneischitz in *The Circus.*

Exploring the Center: Moscow

Moscow constituted the fairyland at the heart of the Stalinist utopia. It was where unusual, even magic, things happened: the triumph of the jazz band in *The Jolly Fellows,* the journey to understanding of the heroine in *The Circus,* the victory in the singing competition in *Volga-Volga,* the translation of Cinderella into the fairy princess in *The Radiant Path,* and the labor of love cum love of labor that blossoms in *Swineherdess.*

It was to Moscow that characters went to improve their lives and to be rewarded with recognition for their achievements. Within Moscow, the Kremlin and the newly opened All-Union Agricultural Exhibition played significant and separate roles. The Kremlin is the seat of government and can be seen as a synonym for Party and state power and thus for Stalin. Sometimes this is explicit *(The Circus, The Radiant Path;* compare *The Miracle Girl),* although the general context of contemporary propaganda images rendered such explicitness unnecessary. The role of the exhibition is more complex. It features prominently in both *Swineherdess* and *The Radiant Path.* Dobrenko argues that in the first of these, "the exhibition represents not Moscow but the 'country.'"[35] I believe this is an oversimplification. In both films the exhibition offers a dual representation: to the periphery it represents Moscow, whereas in Moscow it represents the country in all its diversity.

In *Swineherdess,* the hero and heroine sing "The Song of Moscow," which opens:

Everything's fine in spacious Moscow,
The Kremlin stars shine against the blue sky,
And just as rivers meet in the sea,
So people meet here in Moscow.

The refrain includes the lines, "I shall never forget the friend, Whom I have met in Moscow." Moscow is therefore special. We must remember that most Soviet citizens had never visited Moscow: internal passport controls and sheer cost made the journey impossible except as a special, officially sponsored reward. Most people "knew" Moscow only from screen images, and for propaganda reasons only parts of the "great stone city" were shown:[36] the Kremlin and/or Red Square, because of their historical and political associations; the exhibition, because it was very much a "preview of the coming attractions of socialism"; and new construction projects such as the Moskva Hotel *(The Circus)*, the river station *(Volga-Volga)*, and the showcase metro *(The Circus)*. As Oksana Bulgakowa points out elsewhere in this volume, "the real Moscow was [often] replaced by a painted backdrop, or sets." This applies to *The Jolly Fellows, The Circus,* and Medvedkin's *New Moscow* (Novaia Moskva, 1937), and it increased the air of unreality for those familiar with the city from personal experience. But most of the audience had nothing real to compare to this reel image, and that enhanced its magic power.

Conclusion

The purpose of this essay has been to sketch the basic outlines of the topography of the Stalinist musical, focusing on four films each by the fathers of the genre, Aleksandrov and Pyr'ev. Because these are preliminary remarks, my conclusions can be only tentative. These films were popular, and the image of the country that they created, although not "real" in any objective sense, became real in the minds of contemporary audiences. The "Potemkin village," the small town, the capital city of this reel reality created a powerful Soviet equivalent of the "Russia of the mind."[37] By entertaining the mass audience with glimpses of utopia, the Stalinist musical promoted the illusion encapsulated in popular songs not only that "Life has become better, comrades, life has become happier" but further that "We were born to make a fairy tale come true."[38] As Stalin—who, as "Kremlin censor," was in a unique position to know—once remarked, "Cinema is an illusion, but it dictates its own laws to life itself."[39]

NOTES

I am indebted to Emma Widdis, Cambridge, whose as yet unpublished Ph.D. thesis first alerted me to the literature on this subject, and to Julian Graffy, London, for reading an earlier draft of this essay and for supplying numerous relevant materials. An earlier version of this piece was published in *One Hundred Years of European Cinema: Entertainment or Ideology?* eds. D. Holmes and A. Smith (Manchester: Manchester University Press, 2000), 11–26. I am grateful to both editors and publishers for their permission to publish this slightly amended version here. In the title of the essay I have reversed the concluding line of the poem "Say Not, the Struggle Nought Availeth," by Arthur Hugh Clough (1819–61). The second stanza, even though written in the middle of the nineteenth century, could stand as a summary of the message of the Stalinist musical and of much socialist realist art in general: "If hopes were dupes, fears may be liars; / It may be, in yon smoke concealed, / Your comrades chase e'en now the fliers, / And, but for you, possess the field."

1. T. Anderson, "Why Stalinist Musicals?" *Discourse* 17, no. 3 (1995): 38–48.

2. D. Lean, "Brief Encounter," *Penguin Film Review 4* (London: Penguin Books, 1947), 29, 31.

3. R. Taylor, *Film Propaganda: Soviet Russia and Nazi Germany,* 2d ed. (London: I. B. Tauris, 1998), 162–86.

4. R. Taylor and I. Christie, eds., *The Film Factory: Russian and Soviet Cinema in Documents, 1896–1939* (London: Routledge and Kegan Paul, 1988), 1–17.

5. R. Taylor, "Ideology as Mass Entertainment: Boris Shumyatsky and Soviet Cinema in the 1930s," in *Inside the Film Factory: New Approaches to Russian and Soviet Cinema,* eds. R. Taylor and I. Christie (London: Routledge, 1991), 193–216.

6. B. Shumiatskii, *Kinematografiia millionov* (Moscow: Kinofotoizdat, 1935), 239–40.

7. J. von Geldern, "The Centre and the Periphery: Cultural and Social Geography in the Mass Culture of the 1930s," in *New Directions in Soviet History,* ed. S. White (Cambridge: Cambridge University Press, 1992), 62.

8. A. Zhdanov, speech to the First Congress of Soviet Writers, in *Pervyi Vsesoiuznyi s"ezd sovetskikh pisatelei 1934: Stenograficheskii otchet* (Moscow: Khudozhestvennaia Literatura, 1934), 4.

9. A. Lunacharsky, "Synopsis of a Report on the Tasks of Dramaturgy (Extract)", in Taylor and Christie, *Film Factory,* 327.

10. V. I. Lenin, "Of all the arts . . ." (1922), in Taylor and Christie, *The Film Factory,* 57.

11. S. Fitzpatrick, *Stalin's Peasants: Resistance and Survival in the Russian Village after Collectivization* (Oxford: Oxford University Press, 1994), 262.

12. R. Dyer, "Entertainment and Utopia," *Movie* 24 (1977), 2–13.

13. Stalin, in a speech to the First All-Union Conference of Stakhanovites on 17 November 1935, cited in K. V. Dushenko, ed., *Slovar' sovremennykh tsitat* (Moscow: Agraf, 1997), 341.

14. Dyer, "Entertainment and Utopia."

15. A less traditional but better translation than *The Jolly Fellows* for the title *Veselye rebiata,* without the old-fashioned class associations for the British reader, would be *The Happy Guys.*

16. N. S. Khrushchev, speech to the delegates of the Twentieth Party Congress in

February 1956, translated in *The Secret Speech* (Nottingham: Bertrand Russell Peace Foundation, 1976).

17. M. Turovskaia, "I. A. Pyr'ev i ego muzykal'nye komedii: k probleme zhanra," *Kinovedcheskie zapiski* 1 (1988), 132. Cf. F. J. Miller, *Folklore for Stalin: Russian Folklore and Pseudofolklore of the Stalin Era* (Armonk, N.Y.: Sharpe, 1990).

18. M. Enzensberger, "We Were Born to Turn a Fairy Tale into Reality," in *Stalinism and Soviet Cinema,* eds. R. Taylor and D. Spring (London: Routledge, 1993), 97–108.

19. Turovskaia, "I. A. Pyr'ev," 132.

20. L. Mamatova, "'Model' kinomifov 30-kh godov," in Mamatova, *Kino: Politika i liudi (30-e gody)* (Moscow: Materik, 1995), 65.

21. S. Nikolaevich, "Poslednii seans, ili Sud'ba beloi zhenshchiny v SSSR," *Ogonek* 4 (1992): 23.

22. *Pace* Enzensberger.

23. These observations are based almost entirely on the versions of the films now available, either from Polart and Facets in the United States or on off-air recordings from Russian television. These are the versions restored and de-Stalinized in the 1960s and 1970s. A tantalizing sequence from the original version of *Tractor Drivers* was included in Dana Ranga's film *East Side Story* (1997).

24. H. Günther, "Wise Father Stalin and His Family in Soviet Cinema," in *Socialist Realism without Shores,* eds. T. Lahusen and E. Dobrenko (Durham, N.C.: Duke University Press, 1997), 178–90.

25. H. Günther (Kh. Giunter), "Poiushchaia rodina: Sovetskaia massovaia pesnia kak vyrazhenie arkhetipa materi," *Voprosy literatury* 4 (1997), 46–61.

26. Anderson, "Why Stalinist Musicals?" 38–48.

27. Ibid.

28. Ibid.

29. Cf. J. von Geldern and R. Stites, eds., *Mass Culture in Soviet Russia* (Bloomington: Indiana University Press, 1995), 234–35.

30. Günther, "Wise Father Stalin" and "Poiushchaia rodina."

31. R. Stites, *Russian Popular Culture: Entertainment and Society since 1900* (Cambridge: Cambridge University Press, 1992), 84.

32. E. Dobrenko, "Iazyk prostranstva, szhatogo do tochki', ili estetika sotsial'noi klaustrofobii," *Iskusstvo kino* 9 (1996): 109.

33. M. Turovskaia, "*Volga-Volga* i ego vremia," *Iskusstvo kino* 3 (1998): 59–64.

34. Dobrenko, "Iazyk prostranstva," *Iskusstvo kino* 9 (1996): 108–17, and 11 (1996): 120–29.

35. Ibid., 9 (1996): 112.

36. Much was made in the 1930s of the reconstruction of Moscow as a symbol of the modernization of the country as a whole. The capital is presented as "the great stone city" in Vertov's *Three Songs of Lenin* (Tri pesni o Lenine, 1934).

37. O. Figes, "The Russia of the Mind," *Times Literary Supplement,* 5 June 1998, 14–16.

38. Von Geldern and Stites, *Mass Culture,* 237–38, 257–58.

39. D. Volkogonov, "Stalin," *Oktiabr'* 11 (1988): 87.

Part Three

The Blank Page

To Explore or Conquer?

MOBILE PERSPECTIVES ON THE SOVIET CULTURAL REVOLUTION

EMMA WIDDIS

Skore-e-e-e-e-e-e-e-e!
Skoreoskorei
Ei, gubernii,
snimaites' s iakorei!
Za Tul'skoi Astrakhanskaia,
za makhinoi makhina,
Stoiavshie nepodvizhimo
dazhe pri Adame,
dvinulis'
i na
drugie
prut, pogromykhivaia gorodami[1]

—Vladimir Maiakovsky,
"150 000 000: Poema"

In an unfinished article of the 1940s, Mikhail Bakhtin suggested that during the 1920s, Vladimir Maiakovsky had sought to reformulate the Soviet *krugozor* (horizon), recognizing that "the age and the masses demand a new range, very distant or very close, just not medium-range, not domestic."[2] In Maiakovsky, then, Bakhtin identified an urge to reposition the individual in a new spatial context, to discover a new viewing position from which to understand and experience the transformed world of postrevolutionary Russia. But his insight reaches far beyond the revolutionary young poet and into the broader spectrum of Soviet culture in the first decades after the revolution. Any revolutionary transformation of society is predicated upon the transformation of the world-picture of that society, on a reenvisaging of social and national space, and on the reshaping of the relationship between the individual and space. In Soviet Russia, with its vast, amorphous territory, this task was particularly urgent. In this respect Maiakovsky's verse, written in 1919 and placed at the head of this essay, provides a useful temporal and thematic point of introduction. In its command to "raise anchors" *(snimaites' s iakorei)*, it is a clear summons to mobility and exploration. It is a hymn to movement for its own sake—*skore-e-e!* (fa-a-a-ster)—and a call to energize the whole Soviet space.

The horizon, the *krugozor*, assumed a new ideological significance during the early Soviet period. As the limit of visible space, the horizon was a point of focus, that toward which to strive. Just as the revolution had overcome history, so it would overcome space. The vast Soviet *neob"iatnyi prostor* (boundless territory) was pictured as a rich terrain that must be discovered. In the imaginary map of the 1920s, the *neob"iatnyi prostor* was not a hostile, resistant natural force to be tamed by heroes or by the expansion of might from a dominant center. It was a land ripe with possibility, the raw material from which a new world was to be shaped. Exploration, movement across the map, and the creation of new routes and networks of communication were clearly articulated and urgent tasks.

The roots of this trope of exploration were as much pragmatic as ideological. There was an urgent need to map the space of the new regime, to create for it an imaginary geography. Throughout the 1920s, infrastructure projects such as electrification and the construction of new railroads were, in a sense, acts of *surveying*—the transformation of space (the unknown) into territory (the known and mapped). Toward the end of the decade, the beginning of collectivization and rapid industrialization in 1928 marked the start of a period of particularly intense spatial exploration, what Katerina Clark has called a "dash to the periphery."[3] Spatial and geographical mobility was a practical condition for the fulfillment of the targets of the first Five-Year Plan. Moshe Lewin's description of Russia during this period as *Rus' brodiazhnaia*, a country of vagrants or nomads, goes some way toward characterizing the chaotic mobility of the age.[4]

Looking principally at cinema, I examine in this essay the implications of the "mobile perspective" at two levels. First, I sketch the aesthetic and philosophical shift that reenvisaged space as decentered and mobile. Second, I explore the implications of this shift in the development of a new cinematic genre—the "film expedition." Examining how film was enlisted in the geographic and ethnographic study of the Soviet Union, I trace the ways in which cinema was used both to reveal and to create the new imaginary map. Identifying the exploratory momentum of the 1920s, I seek to challenge some commonly accepted ideas about Soviet attitudes toward the territory.

The roots of the "landscape of Stalinism," of the imaginary geography of the 1930s, are located in the preceding decade, and particularly in the period of spatial exploration that characterized the Great Leap Forward *(velikii perelom)* of 1928–32. *Osvoenie,* the conquest or mastery of space, is the term most frequently used to define both pre- and postrevolutionary attitudes toward the uncharted vastness of the space: the transformation of the unknown and untamed into the known and enlightened. According to this model, space—the vast uncharted territories of the Soviet Union—was to be conquered and staked out. The aesthetics of "conquest," or *osvoenie,* predominant during the period of "high" Stalinism from the mid-1930s onward pictured a space that was essentially static and hierarchically organized around a dominant center (Moscow) that extended radial lines of influence.[5] It might be understood as a version of Foucault's panoptic model of the organization of power, in which a radial structure creates conditions of visibility that secure control from the center.[6] It produced a vision of the Soviet territory as known and mapped, a vision in which relations between center (Moscow) and periphery provided the key axis.[7] All roads led to and from a central, nodal point; the periphery was dependent upon the center.[8]

The complexities of Stalinist *osvoenie,* however, demand further consideration.[9] My purpose in this essay is to suggest that the model of *osvoenie* may neglect some of the ambiguities expressed in representations of Soviet space during the earlier period. To clarify this, in opposition to *osvoenie* I posit the term "exploration" *(izuchenie* or *razvedka)* and suggest that the screening of the territory during the late 1920s and into the first Five-Year Plan (1928–32) may be usefully considered in terms of these two models. If *osvoenie* is understood as an assimilative attitude toward the periphery, in which the periphery is subject to a structure of control from the center, then *exploration* describes a more decentered, nonassimilative investigation of space in which difference is emphasized over sameness and the quest for information is differentiated from control. I investigate the rhetorical claims that underpinned the trope of exploration during the 1920s and into the first Five-Year Plan. My principal hypothesis is that during this period the Soviet periphery—its borders and its vast, uncharted open spaces—had more significant resonance than the center in the imaginary geography of the nation. Soviet film of the 1920s and the first Five-Year Plan pictured the Soviet Union as a decentered and dynamic space.[10]

This focus on the periphery was at once thematic and stylistic, metaphorical and actual. In addition to their pragmatic advantages, decentralization and mobility were conceptual and aesthetic imperatives of the 1920s. Ideals of mobility and dynamism grounded a rethinking of the nature of perception in Soviet avant-garde aesthetics, finding urgent and practical resonance in the political realities of the 1920s and 1930s. They were means of liberating vision and, by association, experience, from the static, hierarchical control of bourgeois civilization. The center (the city), as both concept and reality, was contaminated by prerevolutionary associations. In the early postrevolutionary period, for example, a group of artists who collected around Grigory Kozintsev and Leonid Trauberg in Leningrad named themselves the Factory of the Eccentric Actor (FEKS).[11] Between 1924 and 1929, FEKS produced five films under the banner of *Ekstsentrizm,* as defined by its manifesto in 1922.[12] *Ekstsentrizm* described a multileveled rejection of all that was "central"—that is, of dominant social and cultural forms. The decentering dynamic was implicit in the very term "eccentric," or excentric, specifically expressed as the creation of alternative spatial "axes." The film historian Naum Kleiman suggests that "ex-centrism" might be understood as displacement from the center. For FEKS, he says, "the shift of axes from the former center guarantees self-propelled movement—not only of art but also of reality."[13]

Kleiman understands Eccentrism, as did FEKS itself, in largely metaphorical terms. Inherent in his conception of the "shift *(sdvig)* from the center," however, is a spatial model that is of use in our project of exploring the cultural representations of space during the 1920s. The FEKS movement was part of a broader movement in 1920s culture, and particularly in cinematography, in which decentralization and destabilization were key aims, seeking to establish a new spatial-temporal environment. In 1919, Roman Jakobson wrote that "the overcoming of *statics,* the discarding of the absolute, is the main thrust of modern times."[14] In similar terms, Kozintsev, one of the cofounders of FEKS, described in his memoirs the conception of its third film, *Chertovo koleso* (The Devil's Wheel, 1926), as based on the belief that in film, "everything must be active." The opposition between background and action was considered irrelevant and outdated—in Kozintsev's words, "on the screen there are no 'places for action' but 'acting places' [playing on the term for dramatis personae, *deistvuiushchie litsa*]."[15] This statement makes clear the mobile dynamic, which sought to transform the relationship between actor and set and, implicitly, between man and material world.

This question of the relationship between the acting body and the world underpins the cinematic remapping of Soviet space during the 1920s. For the committed revolutionary Dziga Vertov, the camera was explicitly a means of liberating vision and an instrument for the exploration of a new space. The mobile, dynamic vision of Vertov and the documentarists used movement—the physical experience of space—to capture the dynamic and decentralized space of the Communist International. Other filmmakers, such as Boris Barnet and Friedrikh Ermler, in the second half of the decade especially, created *bytovye* (everyday) comedies that focused on the microspaces of the everyday during a time of immense change. In doing so, they sought to represent the space of experience of the ordinary man or woman.[16] All these very different cinematic movements shared one important feature: the refusal of "dominated" space, as defined by the French Marxist Henri Lefebvre.[17]

Lefebvre's term "dominated space" describes ideologically constructed space, structured according to power, from the center out. It is space that works against the individual and, by extension, against the community. Space that is "appropriated," by contrast, is space in concrete and productive interaction with everyday life.[18] This distinction can be otherwise expressed as the differentiation of *place* and *space*. For another French theorist, Michel de Certeau, it is the subject's dynamic negotiation and appropriation of place (geographically mapped and "dominated," in the Lefebvrian sense) that creates space.[19] Space, for de Certeau, is place *mobilized* and "appropriated" by practice. During the 1920s and into the early Stalin years, I suggest, Soviet filmmakers removed space from the hierarchical map of place and recreated it as dynamic, interconnected, and experiential. Their *appropriation* of space must be distinguished from the *osvoenie* of the Soviet 1930s. Although *osvoenie* is often translated as "appropriation," the *appropriation* discussed by Lefebvre and de Certeau is radically different from the Soviet use of the term to describe the extension of power from the center out, the transformation of the unknown and untamed *prostor* (expanse) into a territory (and a people) both known and enlightened. The currency of Lefebvre's and de Certeau's definition of "appropriation" has led me to translate *osvoenie* as "mastery" or "conquest."

For the avant-garde, film's unique role was to reflect the transformation of the present moment. In 1923, Dziga Vertov's *Kinoki* (Cine-eyes) manifesto called for film to render unmediated the immediacy and dynamism of the revolutionary period, the destabilized and decentered space and time of late 1920s. As Vertov described it: "I emancipate myself henceforth and forever from human immobility. I am in constant motion."[20] During the first years of Soviet power, the cinematic obsession with the train and with rail travel is testament to this ideal of mobilized perception. Early Soviet film abounds in trains, train wheels, and tracks. Although the Lumière brothers' film *L'arrivée d'un train en gare de la Ciotat* (1895), first shown in Russia in 1896, is the origin myth of Russian cinema, just as it is in the West, Russian cinematography as a whole came to the train later.[21] It was really in the 1920s that the train entered Soviet film in its full force as cultural myth and practical necessity.

During the civil war, trains served as transportation, carrying propaganda films to the front and, reciprocally, taking film images made at the front to the center. This continued through the 1920s and into the first Five-Year Plan. The role of cinema (Lenin's "most important of all arts") as integrator was dependent upon rail transport. It was not alone: the railway was a key mechanism for the abolition of spatial hierarchies, overcoming the divide between town and country, center and periphery. The laying of rail lines became a symbol of *smychka* (joining), the political and economic ideology of interconnection and codependence between town and country, worker and peasant. The construction of the Turksib railway, linking Siberian grain and timber with the cotton fields of Turkestan, is a good example of this. Its opening in 1930 provoked a storm of documentary films, press eulogies, and literature in celebration. The most famous and successful of these films was Viktor Turin's *Turksib,* in part scripted by the formalist critic and theorist Viktor Shklovsky.[22] In it, and indeed in most representations of Turksib, the steppe—the *neob"iatnyi prostor*—is pictured as resistant to "conquering," as an intransigent space. The "first Soviet railway" thus functions both as industrial enabler and as social integrator: "Through the unbounded expanse of Kazakhstan . . . across mountains and rock faces . . . steel paths have been forged."[23]

The ideology of the Soviet railway needed, of course, to be symbolically differentiated from the "colonization" of imperial and capitalist rail expansion. For the Soviets, the train was proclaimed as enabler and not subjugator: "Now the first ever republic of Soviets in the world, born on the expanses of the Russian Empire, is completing another major project: the Siberia-Turkestan railway, a project that has quite different aims and is based on a new premise."[24] Thus the railway, so crucial to imperial industrialization during the late nineteenth century, was appropriated as a fully Soviet myth. The final scenes of *Turksib,* for example, showed the railway integrated into the everyday life of the Kazakh horsemen of the steppe and blending with nature as a lone camel grazes around the rails: technology is appropriated.

The symbolism of the train suggested more than the ideological message of integration, however. For Dzigą Vertov, whose "train of revolution" in the twenty-first *Kinopravda* (Film Truth) was at the center of the Soviet train myth, the train functioned as an expression of a liberated and mobilized experience of seeing.[25] The experience of train travel offered a new vision of the Soviet space, one that was accessible to all. The train was the means through which the territory was to be explored—and appropriated. One of Vertov's most famous train sequences appears in his 1929 film *Chelovek s kinoapparatom* (The Man with a Movie Camera), in which the eponymous cameraman crouches on the rails in front of an approaching train in a life-threatening attempt to capture the dynamism and energy of the hurtling vehicle.

Vertov's "man with a movie camera" was the filmic counterpart of the "man with a suitcase," who was a key figure in Soviet culture—and reality—during the 1920s and into the first Five-Year Plan. The film, perhaps the most fully developed manifesto of Vertov's "film-eye" aesthetic, may be considered as part of the decentered, mobile vision of space that I seek to reveal. It has been much studied and correctly identified as a complex reflection on the nature of cinematic vision; Yuri Tsivian and Vlada Petric in particular have produced frame-by-frame analyses that unpack the dense network of meanings that the film carries.[26] For Petric, *Chelovek s kinoapparatom* is a formal representation of the machine aesthetic of constructivism, in which vertical and horizontal movement is juxtaposed to explore "abstract patterns of movement."[27] Although Petric's analysis of these patterns of movement is convincing, I suggest that the film does not construct abstract patterns of movement in a *geometrical* sense, where the frame becomes a canvas on which patterns of movement are explored. Rather, Vertov's juxtaposition of vertical and horizontal movement across and between frames offers a mapping of a new kind of perception—and of space—that is liberated from logical and accepted constraints and that reproduces the perceptual experience of the revolutionary body moving in space.

In his filming of a Soviet city and the activities of a man with a camera in that city, Vertov produced an image of space without a center. Space is decentered and, perhaps more significantly, centerless. In the first place, the city is unmapped—that is, it is not named or located within a geographically known Soviet space. Fragments of monumental architecture, parts of landmarks that identity different cities appear but are never articulated relationally or geographically, such that the city becomes, instead, an abstract composite of physical experiences as the camera, and the cameraman, moves through the space. The cityscape is fragmented into a series of isolated and partial shots, and montage reconstructs a playful vision of a city that cannot be mapped. Throughout the film, arteries predominate as city scenes are crossed by trams, roads, and pedestrians. Further, the arteries themselves are always crossed, because the intersection of vertical and horizontal shapes constructs the frame. In place of a map, therefore, Vertov offers a vision of space as fragmented and *peripheral.* According to de Certeau's opposition between place and space, Vertov's city is not a place: it is reconfigured as space. It exists outside a controlled or known structure of the national space. All coherent axes are refused; they are replaced by a dynamic of flux in which space can be remade according to alternative principles. The film offers a vision of the *experience* of the physical world, through the camera.

Chelovek s kinoapparatom was made in 1929, at the beginning of the first Five-Year Plan, and its principal role was to serve as a realization of Vertov's cinematic aesthetic. It was, one might suggest, the culmination of almost ten years' work in the production of the *Kinopravda* series and of other "nonplayed" (documentary, nonfeature) films. These earlier films reveal much of Vertov's "imaginary geography." In 1926, in particular, the *kinoki* produced two films, *Shagai, Sovet!* (Forward March, Soviet!) and *Shestaia chast' mira* (Sixth Part of the World).[28] The former is a center-focused eulogy to the achievements of the Soviet state, defined by the clearly articulated image of Moscow. *Shestaia chast' mira,* by contrast, is an internationalist, decentered vision of Soviet space. For it, Vertov and the *kinoki* organized a series of expeditions across Soviet territory, collecting an enormous amount of documentary, ethnographic material. *Shestaia chast' mira* explicitly seeks to create an imaginary map of the Soviet Union.

This imaginary map is constructed through a long montage linking the diverse republics and areas across the vast Soviet space. Vertov uses the possibilities of editing to construct a single "sixth of the world": film need not respect the spatial and temporal limits that separate and

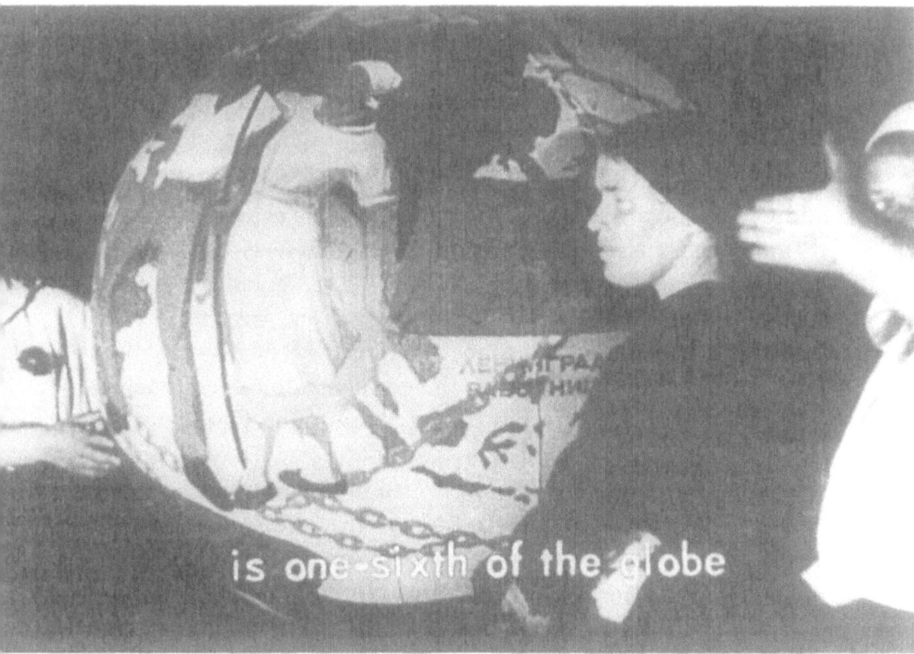

Fig. 9.1. Frame from the final scene of Dziga Vertov's film *Shestaia chast' mira*, 1926.

divide; the "created geography" of montage constructs an new, revolutionary unity.[29] The film presents ethnographic images of everyday life in far-flung regions, from the Siberian taiga to Dagestan. The final scene shows a globe presented to a group of men, women, and children, with the title "A sixth of the world is in your hands" (fig. 9.1). This implicitly global vision of Soviet space differs significantly from the ideological map of later Stalinism. Although certainly implicated in the colonization process of the formation of the Soviet empire, the film seeks to present a vision of the consolidation of a new kind of empire—one that is decentralized and socialist. Vertov's description of the film's aims is suggestive here: "We were supposed to present a marathon race along the chain of the Gostorg [state trade organization] apparatus."[30] The Gostorg "chain," as represented in *Shestaia chast' mira*, links the republics of the Soviet Union as contributing areas of national production. It has ideological implications: the use of the word "chain" to describe the Gostorg apparatus is explicitly contrasted, by Vertov, with the *okruzhenie* (encirclement) of capitalism, thus opposing a linear structure of interconnection with a circular, enclosing one.

All parts of the system are equal in the "chain." The grid, or network, predominates over the radial model of *osvoenie,* which situates the urban center at the head of an implied spatial hierarchy.

This vision of national particularity emphasized scientific interest and ethnographic learning over "local color." Through the rapid pace of its montage and the insistent beating of its intertitles ("You!"), which address and involve the spectator, the film seeks to avoid exoticism. Its montage focused on the specificity and difference of all the cultures represented as part of the Soviet Union. Regions were represented as independently functioning parts of the greater totality of the state. Unlike many later films, in which the center is seen reaching out to educate and integrate the periphery, to create sameness, *Shestaia chast' mira* portrays a spatial organization that is not centripetal: nothing either ends or begins in Moscow. These peripheral spaces are not connected by road or rail to a symbolic center. They belong instead to a supranational Communist International, a "sixth of the world." The very opposition between center and periphery implicitly evaporates.

This vision of Soviet territory reflects the politics of the period in relation to the non-Russian nationalities. As Yuri Slezkine has argued, the "Great Transformation" of the first Five-Year Plan was an "extravagant celebration of ethnic diversity," a genuine attempt to foster *raznoobrazie* (diversity) and *svoeobrazie* (particularity) within the new Soviet state.[31] Between approximately 1924 and 1930, the process of state formation for the Union of Soviet Socialist Republics involved the identification and designation of the non-Russian national republics and in some cases their creation as clearly defined national groups.[32] The first all-Union census, in 1926, sought to identify the key determinants of "nationality" in the Soviet Union, claiming, as Francine Hirsch states, "that this formal registration of nationality would guarantee each people *(narod)* the right to 'establish its life in its own way' *(ustraivat' svoiu zhizn' po svoemu).*"[33] Ethnography was perceived as a natural companion to the state-sponsored exploration of the territory that was an urgent task for the new regime: mapping and identifying the constituent parts of its space. In this context, *Shestaia chast' mira* is indicative of a key moment in Soviet spatial imaginings: a rush to the periphery and exploration of the specificity and difference that constituted Soviet national space. Vertov's "sixth part of the world" was an imaginary Soviet space in which hierarchy was abolished. In this, cinema was an enabler: in Vertov's words, "the Kino-eye means the conquest of space, the visual linkage of people throughout the entire world based on the continuous exchange of visible facts."[34]

Vertov's idea of film's "visible fact" links him with a larger, state-sponsored quest for ever more knowledge and information about the country's vast territory. Cinema had a key part to play here. *Shestaia chast' mira* was one of the first of a large number of cinematic "explorations" of the periphery that began to proliferate during 1926 and 1927. In April 1927, the influential journal *Sovetskoe kino* produced an edition boldly entitled "We need to know our country," an impassioned call for film to engage with the problem of "the study of the ethnography of the USSR."[35] This was not, the editorial suggested, to be a romantic vision of exotic otherness, but rather a "precise documentation of the everyday life, labor, and folklore of the peoples of the USSR." Cinema, it continued, had a duty to study and not merely to "show," to inform and not merely to entertain. In another article in the same edition of *Sovetskoe kino*, the head of the Moscow Musei Narodovedenii (Museum of Study of the Peoples), a Professor F. Sokolov, called for cinema to discover "authentic" ethnographic material and not to filter its ethnographic images through the material available in his museum.[36] Cinema, he claimed, had a unique ability to "capture the genuine dynamic of life, just as the museum is unavoidably static"—that is, cinema had the ability to escape from a fetishized, implicitly colonial vision of ethnic particularity into a genuine understanding of the real life of the national republics. It is surely significant that, in Professor Sokolov's words, this "genuine understanding" would be not static but dynamic and mobile.

Cinema, then, was to be drafted into the broader state project of ethnographic research. During the early years of Soviet power, ethnography seemed a natural companion to the state-sponsored exploration of the territory that was such an urgent task for the new regime. In 1925 and 1926 alone, for example, 633 "scientific" expeditions were organized with the aim of gathering "historical and ethnographic" material about the various component regions of the new state. The explosion of local museums in the first decade of Soviet power is similarly testament to the state's ideological investment in ethnographic and geographic information about the national space. Between 1918 and 1923, 270 new museums were created, and of these a startling 193 were local *kraevedcheskie* (local knowledge/study) museums.[37] This growth continued through the 1920s. *Kraevedenie*, which had been identified as a national imperative as early as the Eighth Party Congress in January 1918, became a significant movement, involving notable party members such as Krupskaia, Lunacharsky, Krzhizhanovsky, and Kalinin, together with academics and historians.[38] The number of *kraevedcheskie* organizations, dedicated to local research in geological, ethnographic, and historical areas, increased tenfold between 1917 and 1927, from 155 to 1,688.[39]

In the new, equalized space of the Soviet Union, cinema had a unique task: "In no other country can there be such a vital need for cinema to work at acquainting us with the authentic everyday life of those nationalities that populate our Soviet Union, the only place in the world where the many peoples are in the unique position of total equality."[40] The debate in *Sovetskoe kino* marked the beginning of explicitly ethnographic film in the Soviet Union. Statistics published in 1927 showed that of fifty-eight *kulturfil'my* (cultural-educational documentary films) produced by Sovkino (the state film organization) in 1926, seventeen had an explicitly "ethnogeographic theme." This was the single largest category, and the call went out to increase it. A state-sponsored project of 1926–27 organized film expeditions in the Urals, Siberia, and the Far East that encompassed various articulated aims, both geographical and "ethnographic."[41]

The rhetoric of this debate promised a search for an elusive form of "objective," socialist representation, which the camera lens (the *ob"ektiv*) seemed uniquely placed to offer. Two apparently conflicting aims can be identified in the description of the intention of these film expeditions: scientific study, on one hand, and intervention (to encourage the building of socialism), on the other. The limits and contradictions of the claim to objectivity are thus evident. In these early articulations of the ethnographic and travel imperative, however, we can trace a greater focus on science: travel motivated by scientific curiosity was seen as valuable for its own sake, and the scientific expedition was an important part of the cult of exploration.

The aim to acquaint center with periphery, with the "real, working life of the peoples of our Union," was, and remains, a complex ideological issue and a problem that has been explored in recent anthropological debate among Western theorists and practitioners such as James Clifford and George Marcus.[42] Knowledge, recent anthropology has claimed, is itself inevitably implicated in the colonizing process: it is an assertion of power, part of the drawing of boundaries, the constitution of self and other that sustains and objectifies the imperial structure. In Russia, the heritage of this colonizing cartography reached far back beyond the revolution: the earliest expansion into Siberia, during the reign of Peter the Great, was accompanied by intense cartographic and geological research that sought to "map" the region at a number of levels.[43] It is clear that the Soviet state recognized the need for information as a prerequisite for solid state-building: "In the tenth year of revolution we must have an authentic scientific picture." The Soviet ideological apparatus during the 1920s, however, was at pains to differentiate itself from the construction of empire as *osvoenie.* Knowledge was consistently articulated as the means of liberating the nation from repressive imperial structures and building an equal society: "The equality of the nationalities, achieved by the October Revolution, by definition excludes the possibility of even the slightest inattention or carelessness in relations with those nationalities."[44]

However spurious this distinction between knowledge and control may appear, the significance of the debate should not be underestimated. "Authentic" ethnographic detail was presented as a prerequisite for the genuine equality of the peoples. An awareness of the objective thrust of this exploratory urge offers a more nuanced understanding of the process of *osvoenie.* It was not uncommon throughout the 1920s and into the early 1930s, for example, to encounter a similar differentiation of Soviet exploration and imperial colonization. The Soviet version of the adventure journal *Vokrug sveta* (Around the world), founded in 1861 by M. O. Vol'f as a "magazine of physical geography, natural sciences, the most recent discoveries, inventions and observations," differentiated itself from its imperial predecessor by a somewhat tendentious definition: "The bourgeoisie sought to know the earth in order to exploit it. In our magazines we tell how the victorious proletariat is changing the earth so that it will carry the joyful beacons of socialist cities."[45] The victorious proletariat, then, will not exploit the earth but rather inhabit it and "know" it, in a newly productive relationship between humans and the physical world.

The 1928 film *Krysha mira: Ekspeditsia v Pamir* (The Roof of the World: An expedition to Pamir), by the director and critic Vladimir Erofeev, reflects and problematizes the ethnographic urge of the early period. Erofeev was much interested in the connections between cinematography and scientific ethnography and was at the center of the debate of 1927.[46] As a director, he made twenty-five documentary films in thirteen years, of which at least eight were explicitly of the national ethnographic-travel genre.[47] *Krysha mira,* his first *kino-ekspeditsiia,* was the product of an expedition jointly organized by Sovkino and the

Geological Committee. Its aim was "to capture the nature and everyday life in the heights of Pamir . . . which are of significant scientific interest."[48]

Extracts from Erofeev's travel journal were published in *Sovetskoe kino* in association with the ethnographic push of 1927–28 and in other periodicals such as *Vecherniaia Moskva* (Moscow in the evening).[49] In 1929 he published his account of the journey as a book, *Po "kryshe mira" s kino-apparatom: Puteshevstvie na Pamir* (On the "Roof of the World" with a movie camera: A journey to Pamir). The book was published as part of a series by *Molodaia Gvardiia* entitled "A contemporary library of travel, local lore, adventure, and science fiction," which included accounts of the construction of the Turksib railway as well as the encouragement of "national tourism"; it was promoted as offering a "focus on the most distant and least known corners of our country."[50] The book was positioned explicitly between science and entertainment, as part of the broad *nauchno-popularnyi* (popular-scientific) genre developing in the second half of the decade, in which exploration and adventure were reformulated as scientific expedition.

In the foreword to his book, Erofeev emphasized that the diary would be composed only of facts; it would fill in those details that the camera could not show. For him, the camera was neither omniscient nor neutral. Indeed, throughout his written accounts of this first expedition, Erofeev directed attention to the problems of representation and the role of the camera as intrusive observer. In a curious reversal of roles, he and his colleagues, the "expedition," are stranger, more "other," than those whom they have come to film. Women, for example, refuse to be filmed, and a scandal ensues in which the filmmakers are demonized by the local community.[51] Further, in the film Erofeev consistently emphasizes the materiality of transportation—from the train at the beginning of the film, which carries the expedition from Moscow to Pamir, through the trucks and donkeys that take them on the more difficult parts of the journey. Obstacles to travel, such as the wheels of a truck stuck in mud, serve similarly to emphasize the role of the expedition as interloper. "The expedition" itself is the key protagonist of the film, which functions as a self-reflexive document of exploration that explicitly problematizes the role of the viewing camera eye. By stressing the contingency of representation, Erofeev constructed a reciprocal dynamic between center and periphery in which the camera eye was clearly represented as subjective. Ethnography, here, is not a neutral exercise.

This contingency was echoed at a stylistic level in the finished film. Erofeev was one of the earliest Soviet directors to use panoramic shots consistently, initiating a cinematography of long takes and mobile panoramas. His camera eye is a mobile eye, but it is explicitly the eye of a traveler and explorer. *Krysha mira* features long tracking shots that emphasize the scale of the territory to be traversed, making explicit the frailty of the camera in relation to the totality of the landscape it seeks to reveal. Throughout the film, Erofeev stressed the limits of representation, emphasizing as much what the camera could not show as that which it could. In doing so, he revealed an acute awareness of his own role and that of his team as observer-participants in the world they filmed.

Although at first glance it would appear that Erofeev's panoramas and slow editing contrast sharply with Vertov's dynamic montage, in fact there are marked similarities between the two filmmakers. As Vertov's aesthetic foregrounded the experiential limitations and possibilities of vision, so Erofeev took this awareness into his early travel films. Erofeev's geologists with a camera (the presence of the camera is made explicit throughout the film) recall Vertov's man with a camera, exploring the extent to which the camera reveals new aspects of the world. They reject monumental, static images in favor of a contingent vision.

In this, his first travel film, Erofeev emphasized nonideological exploration as motivation: "Both film and book," he wrote, "can convey only weakly the feeling of the traveler, placed face-to-face with nature, sensing directly a surprising, diverse life, full of as yet unknown pleasures."[52] This traveler was explicitly not colonizing: he confronted "nature" directly, and this confrontation, enabled by the cinematic eye, was to permit a clearer apprehension of a world that was crucially *mnogoobraznyi* (diverse). Feeling *(oshchushchenie),* accessible through experience, is here prioritized over message, such that the role of the film is simply to communicate to a wider audience the experience of the travelers. Similarly, although there are sections of the film in which the enlightening influence of Soviet power is shown to be transforming and modernizing ("They already know Lenin here"), this integration does not provide the dominant dynamic of the film. In its place is a representation of exploration that is not integrational but that emphasizes the imperative of mobility and experience. Perception and understanding are rooted in the physical experience of travel.

An objective urge to map and understand coexists in *Krysha mira* with the more experiential model of travel. The need to mark routes through the territory is clear in Erofeev's film, just as it is refused in Vertov's. The route of the expedition is clearly mapped from Moscow, and an animated map reoccurs throughout the film to confirm and reconfirm the position of Pamir in the Soviet Union. A larger-scale map of the region itself charts the progress of the expedition through the area. Thus the film is mapped at two levels. Further, the scientific objectivity of the expedition is emphasized through the figures of two geologists who accompany the filmmakers.

Vladimir Erofeev's oeuvre demonstrates marked shifts in its representation of landscape and traces a turn from the aesthetics of exploration toward those of conquest. In this sense, *Krysha mira* can be interestingly contrasted with a film he made four years later, entitled *Daleko v Azii* (Far away in Asia, 1931). Together these two films provide an index of shifts in attitude toward the periphery during the Cultural Revolution. *Daleko v Azii,* made in collaboration with the documentarist Roman Karmen as cinematographer, is a similar *kino-ekspeditsiia* in which Erofeev and his crew travel to Uzbekistan. Compared with *Krysha mira,* this film makes explicit in its very title a view that originated in Moscow: it is "far away" in Asia. Although it continues the technique of *Krysha mira* in problematizing its own status as representation and the role of the filmmaker as intruder and voyeuristic eye, the film nonetheless presents a clear vision of a backward Asiatic world transformed by the arrival of Soviet enlightenment. Soviet machinery accelerates the harvest, otherwise held back by the primitive laziness and even foolish superstition of the local people. The cinematic eye is implicitly linked with the modernizing vision of the Soviet center. The map from Moscow, only nascent in *Krysha mira,* becomes the dominant axis around which *Daleko v Azii* is structured.

The fate of Soviet *kraevedenie* is similarly rooted in transformations in the Soviet ideological map in the mid-1930s and reveals a shift from exploration to assimilation in Soviet attitudes toward the territory. In its original formulation, *kraevedenie* was explicitly local in origin and orientation: it focused on the dissemination of local knowledge to a local population. In 1937, however, *kraevedcheskie* organizations were officially liquidated, and a decree in 1938 declared that practitioners of *kraevedenie* were enemies of the people. Henceforward, the work of the *kraevedy* was to be carried out by central organs of *prosveshchenie* (enlightenment/propaganda). This policy change marked an end point in a progressive shift in the ideological emphasis of territorial exploration and information gathering. *Osvoenie,* the extension of power radially, substituted the imperative of enlightenment for that of exploration. The end of *kraevedenie* signaled, I suggest, the end of the period of mobility and decentralization that I have identified. Other indicators abound: in 1933, Sergei Ordzhonikidze condemned the "suitcase mentality" of the first Five-Year Plan, and the reintroduction of the imperial *propiska* (internal passport) system on December 28, 1932, restricted mobility by insisting on the registration of the population. *Propiska* was an unambiguous move to control this mobility and to restratify the national space.

I have suggested, then, that the cinema of the 1920s and of the early Stalinist period was characterized by an imperative of mobility that pictured the vast Soviet territory as a space to be explored. The folkloric *put'* (journey) was reconfigured, not as progression to an elusive but significant goal but as the dynamic process of transformation itself.[53] The development of the travel film genre during the second half of the 1920s demonstrates, in practical terms, the symbolic weight of the *put'*. It is defined by a double objective: to obtain "authentic" knowledge about the territory and to "experience" the world afresh. Erofeev described the extraordinary *oshchushchenie* (feeling—the term incorporates both sense and sensation) offered by his film expedition, echoing Vertov's call for film to offer a new, cinematic *oshchushchenie* (feeling) of the world.[54]

Film, then, did not just offer views of the new space of Soviet Russia; it articulated a relationship with that space. In this respect, the predominance of the train in film of the 1920s and early 1930s can be usefully contrasted with the cinematic adulation of the airplane that emerged in the later 1930s in films such as Dovzhenko's *Aerograd* (1935), Iury Raizman's *Letchiki* (1935), and Pentslin's *Istrebiteli* (1939), among others. The use of aerial shots in Soviet cinema of the 1930s paralleled the emerging ideology of *osvoenie.* In real terms, the airplane overcame distance, transforming the vast spaces of the Soviet Union into a controllable territory. In parallel, the aerial shot expresses control over the landscape, rendering it tame.

The aerial shot provides a very different spatial perspective from the horizontal view offered by the train. Where the train window creates a linear, experiential vision of space *as it is traversed,* the airplane (the aerial shot) offers a controlling gaze that maps and orders. It is a gaze that abstracts and frames the landscape. In 1925, Viktor Shklovsky described the aerial perspective in precisely these terms: "The land, seen from above, is single-faceted and geometrical."[55] Sergei Tret'iakov expressed a similar sense of shock at this transformed space, viewed from the air: "The landscape is nature in the eyes of a consumer."[56] For Tret'iakov, the relationship of consumer to landscape was explicitly non-Soviet, a relationship of possession. Furthermore, "you start to long for knowledge." The aerial view, he suggests, removes the spectator from the experiential "knowledge" of the space that was the crucial characteristic of the Soviet vision of exploration.[57]

Much more recently, Michel de Certeau pointed to a similar distinction between views from above (the aerial shot) and horizontal-experiential views when he wrote in the 1980s of viewing New York City from the top of the World Trade Center. The view of the city from a height, he suggested, "transforms the bewitching world by which one was 'possessed' into a text that lies before one's eyes. It allows one to read it, to be a solar eye, looking down like a god."[58] The aerial view, then, is one of control but not of involvement. It creates a relationship of separation. In opposition to this scopic totalization, de Certeau situates "practice": the *appropriation* of the city by the act of walking through it. The "knowledge" that Tret'iakov seeks corresponds, I suggest, to this experiential knowledge of space, produced by practice, by movement through the space.

In a sense, it was precisely the totalizing aspect of the aerial perspective that Vertov sought to break down in his own early use of the technique. In the fourteenth *Kinopravda,* for example, the camera films an airplane as a distant speck in an empty sky before implicitly assuming its viewpoint and exploring the cityscape from above in a series of precarious, highly mobile tracking shots. In the eighteenth *Kinopravda,* the ground seems to rush up from below the carriage of a rapidly descending airplane. In these early films, then, the aerial shots reproduced the destabilized, mobile viewpoint that was at the center of the *kinoglaz* aesthetic. Vertov united cinematic vision with exploration; the camera was a privileged means of reenvisaging space. The constructivist critic and theorist Aleksei Gan wrote a descriptive interpretation of the experience of viewing Vertov's thirteenth *Kinopravda:* "And we see airplanes, and at the same time watch from them the earth below, but the earth is running, as streets, houses, and newspapers shift to another perspective."[59] As Gan makes clear, in these early films Vertov refused the monumentality of the aerial perspective in favor of a horizontal and dynamic vision.

The aerial view of the late 1930s portrays the territory as "landscape"—it begins to construct the "landscape of Stalinism." There was,

I venture to suggest, no "landscape" of the 1920s and no "landscape" of the first Five-Year Plan. The emergence of "landscape" traces a shift from exploration toward the aesthetics of "conquest," or *osvoenie*. In his discussion of the chronotope, through which he interrogated the spatio-temporal dimensions of texts as an index of context, Mikhail Bakhtin suggested that the appearance of "landscape" in cultural texts marked a point of rupture between space and action: "Then nature itself ceased to be a living participant in the events of life."[60] Nature is reduced to "picturesque remnants."[61] It is transformed: "Then nature became, by and large, a 'setting for action,' its backdrop; it was turned into landscape."[62] A parallel phenomenon can be traced in the representation of space in Soviet film of the 1920s and 1930s. Films of the 1920s had eschewed landscape in favor of representing a physical experience of space, the "appropriation" of that space. In the later period, the "space" of exploration and experience was reconfigured as knowable and controllable. It became a "view."

NOTES

This essay draws on and elaborates material from my book, *Visions of a New Land: Soviet Film from the Revolution to the Second World War* (New Haven, Conn.: Yale University Press, 2003).

1. "Fa-a-a-ster . . ./ FasterFaster / Hey, provinces / Raise your anchors! / Astrakhan, follow Tula/ one *makhina* [large, bulky thing] after another/ Standing immobile / Even in Adam's day / have now moved / and are shoving / others, rattling / their cities." Vladimir Maiakovskii, "150 000 000: Poema," *Polnoe sobranie sochinenii*, 13 vols. (Moscow: Khudozhestvennaia Literatura, 1956), 2: 119.

2. M. M. Bakhtin, "K voprosam teorii romana, k voprosam teorii smekha, 'o Maiakovskom,'" *Sobranie sochinenii*, 7 vols. (Moscow: Russkie Slovari, 1996–), 5: 48–63 (55).

3. Katerina Clark, *Petersburg: Crucible of Cultural Revolution* (Cambridge, Mass.: Harvard University Press, 1995), 281.

4. Moshe Lewin, "Society, State, and Ideology during the First Five-Year Plan," in *Cultural Revolution in Russia, 1928–1931*, ed. Sheila Fitzpatrick (Bloomington: Indiana University Press, 1978), 41–78.

5. Vladimir Papernyi, in *Kul'tura dva* (Moscow: Novoe Literaturnoe Obozrenie, 1996), offers a rich analysis of Russian culture from the viewpoint of horizontal and vertical axes, in which Stalinism is characterized by vertical spaces. The model of *osvoenie* that I describe could be understood within this framework of horizontal and vertical. It is my intention, however, to expand and challenge the restrictions of Papernyi's framework.

6. Michel Foucault, *Discipline and Punish: The Birth of the Prison*, trans. Alan Sheridan (New York: Vintage Books, 1995), 195–229.

7. See my article "Borders: The Aesthetic of Conquest in Soviet Cinema of the 1930s," *Journal of European Studies* 30, no. 4 (December 2000): 353–460.

8. This is a familiar trope of Stalinist film and literature, where the narrative telos is the triumphant finale of the "journey to Moscow." See, for example, *Volga-Volga* (Grigorii Alexandrov, 1938) and *The Swineherdess and the Shepherd* (Ivan Pyr'ev, 1941).

9. Evgeny Dobrenko, in "Do samykh do okrain," *Iskusstvo kino* 4 (1996): 97–102, explores cinematic images of the periphery in feature films of the 1930s, arguing convincingly that the periphery is an active and self-sufficient space.

10. See Widdis, *Visions of a New Land.*

11. FEKS is the acronym for Fabrika Ekstsentricheskogo Aktera. The early FEKS consisted of Kozintsev and Trauberg with Sergei Yutkevich and Georgii Kryzhitskii.

12. These films were *Pokhozhdeniia Oktiabriny,* (1924), *Chertovo koleso* (1926), *Shinel'* (1926), *SVD (Soiuz Velikogo Dela)* (1927), and *Novyi Vavilon* (1929). After 1929, Kozintsev and Trauberg's next film, *Odna* (1931), marked an aesthetic transition that Kozintsev himself described as a shift toward the representation of a "hero of our time," leading eventually to the Maksim trilogy. Grigorii Kozintsev, *Glubokii ekran: Sobranie sochinenii,* 5 vols. (Leningrad: Iskusstvo, 1982–86), 1: 364.

13. Naum Kleiman, "Eksentricheskoe i tragicheskoe," *Kinovedcheskie Zapiski* 7 (1990): 132–35 (133).

14. Roman Jakobson, *Language in Literature,* eds. Krystyna Pomorska and Stephen Rudy (London: Belknap Press, 1987), 30.

15. Grigorii Kozintsev, *Glubokii ekran* 1: 91.

16. For further discussion, see Widdis, *Visions of a New Land.*

17. Henri Lefebvre, *The Production of Space,* trans. Donald Nicholson-Smith (Oxford: Blackwell, 1974), 164.

18. Ibid.

19. Michel de Certeau, *The Practice of Everyday Life,* trans. Steven Rendall (Berkeley: University of California Press, 1984), 117.

20. Dziga Vertov, "The Film Eyes: A Revolution," in *The Film Factory: Russian and Soviet Cinema in Documents, 1896–1939,* eds. Richard Taylor and Ian Christie (London: Routledge and Kegan Paul, 1988), 89–94 (93).

21. For a discussion of the train myth in early Russian cinema, see Iurii Tsivian, *Early Cinema in Russia and Its Cultural Reception* (London: Routledge, 1994), 137–47.

22. *Turksib* (1930), directed by Viktor Turin, screenplay by Aleksandr Macheret, Viktor Shklovskii, and Iakov Aron (Vostokkino). See also *Pervomaiskii podarok trudiashchimsia strany* (1930), a second film with the title *Turksib* (1930), directed by Ermolaev, and *Turksib otkryt: Kino-ocherk* (1930), directed by G. Room (Vostokkino). Vostokkino was a regional studio organized on March 26, 1928, to provide films in eastern republics.

23. *Turksib* (1930).

24. "Beg Paravoza," *Vokrug sveta* 26 (1928): 20.

25. Dziga Vertov, "Za stoprotsentnyi kinoglaz," in *Istoriia stanovleniia sovetskogo kino* (Moscow, 1986), 64.

26. Yuri Tsivian, "*Man with a Movie Camera,* Reel One: A Selective Glossary," *Film Studies* 2 (2000): 51–77. Subsequent issues of *Film Studies* continue the analysis.

27. Vlada Petric, *Constructivism in Film: The Man with the Movie Camera, a Cinematic Analysis* (Cambridge: Cambridge University Press, 1987), 7.

28. *Shagai, Sovet!* directed by Dziga Vertov, with Svilova, Beliakov (Kul'tkino, 1926); *Shestaia chast' mira,* directed by Dziga Vertov, with Svilova, Kaufman (and three *kino-*

razvedchiki: Aleksandr Kagarlitskii, Il'ia Kopalin, Boris Kudinov) (Kul'tkino, December 1926). The latter was made on order from Gostorg, the state trade organization, to promote Soviet trade.

29. The term "created geography" was coined by Lev Kuleshov as part of his experiments in film editing. See Lev Kuleshov, *Sobranie,* 3 vols. (Moscow: Iskusstvo, 1987), 1: 171.

30. Dziga Vertov, "Iz istorii kinokov," in *Stat'i, Dnevniki, zamysly,* ed. Sergei Drobashenko (Moscow: Iskusstvo, 1966), 116–20 (116).

31. Yuri Slezkine, "The USSR as a Communal Apartment, or How a Socialist State Promoted Ethnic Particularism," *Slavic Review* 53, no. 2 (1994): 414–52.

32. For a detailed study of the "ethnographic" identification of "nationality" between 1925 and 1940, see Francine Hirsch, "The Soviet Union as a Work in Progress: Ethnographers and the Category *Nationality* in the 1926, 1937, and 1939 Censuses," *Slavic Review* 56, no. 2 (1997): 251–79.

33. Ibid., 257.

34. Vertov, "Ot 'kinoglaza' k 'radioglazu' (iz azbuki kinokov)," in *Stat'i, dnevniki,* 109–16 (112).

35. "Nam nuzhno znat' svoiu stranu," *Sovetskoe kino* 4 (1927): 1.

36."Etnografiia i kino," *Sovetskoe kino* 4 (1927): 12–13 (12).

37. L. N. Gordunova, "Organy upravleniia museinym delom v SSSR, 1917–1941gg.," *Muzeinoe delo v SSSR: Muzeinoe stroitel'stvo v SSSR, Sbornik nauchnykh trudov* 19 (1989): 13–42 (27).

38. From 1921 it was coordinated by the TsBK (Tsentral'noe Biuro Kraevedeniia), established by the first All-Russian Conference of Kraevedenie.

39. A. V. Ushakov, "Nauchno-issledovatal'skaia rabota muzeev istoricheskogo profilia, 1917–1959gg.," *Muzeinoe delo* 19 (1989): 45–71 (46).

40. *Sovetskoe kino* 4 (1927): 12.

41. L. Sukharebskii, "Nauchnye kino-ekspeditsii i ikh zas'emka," *Sovetskoe kino* 4 (1927): 13–14. Statistics from the Moscow department of Sovkino (Soviet Film Organization).

42. See in particular James Clifford, *The Predicament of Culture: Twentieth-Century Ethnography, Literature, and Art* (Cambridge, Mass.: Harvard University Press, 1988), and *Writing Culture: The Poetics and Politics of Ethnography,* eds. James Clifford and George E. Marcus (Berkeley: University of California Press, 1986).

43. J. L. Black, "Opening up Siberia: Russia's 'Window on the East,'" in *The History of Siberia: From Russian Conquest to Revolution,* ed. Alan Wood (London: Routledge, 1991), 57–68 (61–62).

44. "Etnografiia i kino," 12.

45. *Vokrug sveta* 4 (1931): 1.

46. Vladimir Erofeev, "Kino-industriia v Germanii," *Sovetskoe kino* 4 (1927): 80–81.

47. These eight were *Za Poliarnym krugom* (1927), *Krysha mira* (1928), *Serdtse Azii* (1929), *K schastlivoi gavani* (1930), *Daleko v Azii* (1931), *V Ussuriiskom Taige* (1938), *Geroicheskii perelet* (1938), and *Liudi moria* (1939). Erofeev also made a film in honor of the opening of the Volga-Moscow canal, *Put' Otkryt* (1934), and two films of Moscow parades that emphasize national unification: *Olimpiad iskusstv* (1930) and *Stalinskoe Plemia* (date unknown). *Za poliarnym krugom* (Beyond the Polar Circle, 1927) was a montage of footage produced during an expedition in which he did not take

part. See *Vladimir Alekseevich Erofeev (1898–1940): Materialy k 100-letiiu so dnia rozhdeniia*, ed. A. Deriabin (Moscow: Muzei Kino, 1998), for filmography.

48. Vladimir Erofeev, *Po "kryshe mira" s kino-apparatom (puteshestvie na Pamir)* (Moscow: Molodaia Gvardiia, 1929).

49. Vladimir Erofeev, "Iz dnevnika Pamirskoi ekspeditsii," *Sovetskoe kino* 2–3 (1928): 19. Also, *Vecherniaia Moskva*, 24 March 1928.

50. Erofeev, *Po "kryshe mira"* advertisement, *Molodaia Gvardiia*, inside front cover.

51. Erofeev, *Po "kryshe mira,"* 110.

52. Ibid., 185.

53. See Mikhail Bakhtin, "Forms of Time and the Chronotope in the Novel: Toward a Historical Poetics," in *The Dialogic Imagination* (Austin: University of Texas Press, 1981). Bakhtin is one of many theorists who have indicated the significance of the road, or journey, in Russian folklore. The journey acts as the narrative structure of the tale. It is this emphasis on process over defined aim that I wish to indicate here.

54. Dziga Vertov, "Kinoki. Perevorot," in *Stat'i, Dnevniki*, 50–58 (54).

55. Viktor Shklovskii, "'Velikii Perelet' i kinomatografiia," in *Za 60 Let: Raboty o kino* (Moscow: Isskustvo, 1985), 76–77 (76).

56. Sergei Tret'iakov, "Skvoz' neprotertye ochki," *Novyi LEF* 9 (1928): 20–24 (20).

57. Ibid., 23.

58. Michel de Certeau, *The Practice of Everyday Life*, trans. Steven Rendall (Berkeley: University of California Press, 1984), 92.

59. Aleksei Gan, "Kino-pravda: Trinadtsatyi opyt," *Kinofot* 5 (1922): 6–7.

60. Bakhtin, "Forms of Time," 217.

61. Ibid., 144.

62. Ibid., 217.

10

Tabula Rasa in the North

THE SOVIET ARCTIC AND MYTHIC LANDSCAPES IN STALINIST POPULAR CULTURE

JOHN MCCANNON

During most of the 1930s, the Soviet Union experienced a fascination with Arctic exploration that can be described only as a national craze. Excitement about the Russian North mounted steadily after the early part of the decade, when the Stalinist regime launched a battery of polar expeditions that, in scope and ambition, were unprecedented in the history of Arctic exploration. In 1932 the icebreaker *Sibiriakov,* in an expedition headed by Professor Otto Shmidt, the prime mover behind the USSR's great campaign in the North, became the first vessel to cross the entire northern coast of Russia—the famed Northeast Passage—in a single navigational season.[1] Two years later, when the *Cheliuskin,* a vessel carrying Shmidt along with 104 other men, women, and even children, developed a crack in its hull and sank to the bottom of the Chukchi Sea, Soviet polar aviators staged one of the most daring aerial rescues of the century by evacuating the stranded passengers from the drifting ice.[2] In 1937, the banner year for the USSR in the Arctic, Soviet pilots captured the world record for long-distance aviation twice in succession by soaring over the North Pole from Moscow to the United States. The first was Valery Chkalov, dubbed by the Soviet press "the Greatest Pilot of Our Time"; the second was Mikhail Gromov.[3] That same year, during the famed *Severnyi polius*-1 (SP-1) expedition, an extravaganza planned by Otto Shmidt, the USSR became the first nation in history to land aircraft at the Pole itself. In the course of the operation, the Soviet Union also became the first country to establish a scientific outpost there, a four-man station headed by Ivan Papanin.[4]

The Arctic was a key element in Stalinist propaganda and popular culture of the 1930s.[5] Polar exploits were featured almost endlessly in the mass media, and the pilots and explorers themselves became national celebrities of the first magnitude. The vast cultural output associated with Arctic heroics—hereafter referred to as the "Arctic myth"—fit well into the framework of socialist realism, which, with its themes of technological progress, patriotism, the glorification of Stalin, and above all heroism, was emerging as the dominant idiom for cultural expression in Stalin's Russia. In short, the USSR's Arctic myth was immensely important as a cultural phenomenon, and it reveals much about the official Stalinist worldview of the 1930s: how the Soviets viewed the natural world, how they understood their country and its place in the world, and how they conceived of the relationship between the individual and the state.

As a result, the Arctic became something of a reflective lens for the Soviets, in which their self-image took form even as they formed images of their northern frontier. As one historian of exploration has noted, terra incognita serves as "a mirror for the habitual."[6] For the USSR, the Arctic was the country's last terra incognita, its final blank space on the map. Therefore, the language used metaphorically to fill in that space reveals as much about Soviet attitudes concerning the USSR itself as it does about the polar world. Conveyed to a public audience by means of carefully manipulated words and images, the Arctic became a vital part of Stalinist Russia's mythic landscape.

In this essay I examine the Arctic's place in the USSR's modern cosmography. I focus first on the symbolic relationship between Moscow and the Arctic, which were portrayed as diametrical opposites. Then I turn to the topic of how the Arctic was used to demonstrate the Soviet Union's ability to bring the light of civilization and culture to the deepest recesses of the wilderness. Finally, I discuss how Soviet settlement of the Arctic was presented as a model of the society that the USSR was to become in the future.

The Antipodes: Moscow and the Arctic

According to the cultural geography mapped out by the socialist-realist worldview, Moscow was both the physical and the spiritual center of the universe. For the Soviet nation and the Soviet people, it was the *axis mundi* around which the USSR turned. At the very center was the Kremlin, the sacred sanctuary in which Stalin himself sat enthroned in glory. Stalin, the great Father of Nations, remained hidden from ordinary eyes, but his love and concern radiated outward from the Kremlin to every man, woman, and child in the *rodina*, the socialist motherland.[7]

The Arctic stood in complete contrast to Moscow. In the metaphoric sense, it was as far from the capital as one could get: it was the "essential elsewhere" in the Soviets' "mythical wilderness."[8] Uncivilized and unknown, the Arctic was the most distant part of the Soviet Union's periphery, the very edge of the world. It was the ultimate battleground in the Soviets' great "struggle against the elements" *(bor'ba so stikhiei).* It was also the ultimate enemy in that conflict, personified by Stalinist discourse into a tangible, anthropomorphic opponent.[9]

Because the Arctic was so extraordinary as a metaphoric landscape, depictions of it often approached the hyperbolic. Triumphs in the Arctic were translated into victories of almost cosmic significance. A headline celebrating the North Pole landing of 1937 boasted that "we have conquered time and space!"[10] When the last of the Cheliuskinites were rescued from their camp on the frozen Arctic seas, *Izvestiia* trumpeted that "technology has conquered nature, man has conquered death."[11] In a somewhat less dramatic case, the citizens of one Arctic community explained to a visiting *London Times* reporter why they operated on Moscow, not local, time:

> "Never mind the sun, comrade. If we took any notice of it, we should not be living here at all. We cannot accept all the moods of the Arctic. After all, it's we who are the bosses here."
>
> So that was the law in Igarka! Men decided to live here and they are bending Nature to their command. They do not even abide by the mills of time![12]

The heart of the Arctic, the North Pole itself, had its own special qualities. It was often referred to as a "magical pillar."[13] It represented the literal and figurative top of the world—the highest of high grounds, strategic or sacred.[14] The pole was also the earth's most jealously guarded secret: an icy, faraway stronghold. The North Pole was thus a great fortress, the "polar citadel," containing within it a hidden prize akin to the Holy Grail.[15] The state-sponsored "folklore" of the high Stalinist period often rendered the Pole as the castle of the evil "Tsar of the North," guarded by his "whirlwind-ministers" and their chairman, "Red-Nose Frost."[16]

With all this, it is no surprise that the metaphor of mutual aggression permeates the language used publicly to describe the Arctic. The exploration of the North was presented consistently as a great military campaign, fought by the nation's "army of polar explorers" *(armiia poliarnikov).* Newspapers and propaganda films spoke of the "Arctic front" and celebrated every attack *(ataka)* and assault *(nastu-*

plenie) on that front; they urged the country on to the final conquest *(zavoevanie)* of the Arctic. Finally, upon the success of the USSR's polar landing in 1937, the newspapers cried, "The Arctic and the North Pole Have Been Conquered by Us!" as if the Pole had indeed been a fortress under siege.[17] This image provided a concrete link between the Arctic and the words of Stalin himself: "There are no fortresses which the Bolsheviks cannot capture." The continuous exhortations to "storm the Arctic" *(shturmovat' Arktiku)* echoed Stalin's famous slogan. The Soviet Union's multiple victories over the Pole throughout the decade constituted its most striking fulfillment.

This was, then, dangerous territory, and it was here that the civilizing influence of Moscow could be expected to be at its nadir. This was especially the case when the metaphysical aspects of the Arctic landscape were taken into consideration. Speaking of the magical geography of fairy tales, the folklorist Jack Zipes says of the enchanted forest that it is part of the interior lives of ordinary individuals: it "possesses the power to change lives and alter destinies. . . . it is there that [people] lose and find themselves."[18] Unconsciously, the Soviets made of the northern periphery an enchanted forest of sorts. A number of the scientists and explorers writing about the region depicted it as a psychological wilderness that affected the mind just as much as it did the body. As Rudolf Samoilovich, chief of the All-Union Arctic Institute, commented to a U.S. journalist, "the Arctic does strange things to men."[19]

The most obvious of the Arctic's psychic effects were typically felt during the polar night. Explorers could stand the hellish cold, the arduousness of their work, and the sense of isolation from their homeland. But the grim darkness that descended during the winter months enervated them with its atmosphere of gloom and despair.[20] On the other hand, the Arctic also beckoned and beguiled. The aviator Mikhail Vodop'ianov, who participated in the *Cheliuskin* rescue and the North Pole landing, writes that "the North calls" to him: "All a pilot needs is one flight to the polar regions and he's hooked." He will be "pulled there by an irrepressible strength," and the "fever of the North" will burn in his veins.[21] Ivan Papanin, head of the SP-1 outpost, tells a journalist from *Pravda* that "the grim North, the endless icy waste, has bewitched me."[22] The transpolar pilot Sigismund Levanevsky heard the call as well. He speaks of the Arctic as "my element" and remarks that "the Arctic has long had a hold on me."[23]

Travels into the Arctic also brought on episodes of psychological, crisis-driven insight. Being by oneself in the frozen starkness of the North was the ultimate in bleakness: it brought the individual into contact with absolute nothingness and forced one to face oneself and one's place in existence. Ernst Krenkel', radioman for the *Sibiriakov, Cheliuskin,* and SP-1 missions, describing a nighttime walk he went on not long after arriving to take up his first job in the Arctic, strikingly conveys the shock of such isolation. Unable to express himself fully with his own words, Krenkel' borrows an excerpt from "The White Silence," a Jack London story, to describe the experience:

> I was surrounded by silence. To call it dead silence would be putting it mildly. Nature has many tricks wherewith she convinces man of his finity—the ceaseless flow of the tides, the fury of the storm, the shock of the earthquake, the long roll of heaven's artillery—but the most tremendous, the most stupefying of all, is the White Silence. All movement ceases, the sky clears, the heavens are as brass; the slightest whisper seems sacrilege, and man becomes timid, affrighted at the sound of his own voice. Sole speck of life journeying across the ghostly wastes of a dead world, he trembles at his audacity, realizes that his is a maggot's life, nothing more. Strange thoughts arise unsummoned, the mystery of all things strives for utterance. And fear comes over him.[24]

In his memoirs, Krenkel' leaves no doubt that this episode was an epiphany—a formative, even life-changing, moment in his career.

On the whole, it was with a sense of unease that official discourse admitted so readily to nature's powerful psychological effects on humanity. It was one thing for Soviet men and women to be toughened by the war against the elements, as in the following remark by Veniamin Kaverin, author of *The Two Captains,* one of the key fictional works in the Arctic canon: "The hero of *The Two Captains* gets his tempering by struggling against nature. He is typical of all polar explorers. The North gave my hero his strength, and it is back into the North that he is returning it all. In peace he extended the borders of civilization; in war he is defending those borders."[25] But to discuss openly any deeper transformation was relatively rare, for a straightforward reason. If the Soviets allowed for the possibility that nature could meaningfully influence *Homo sovieticus,* then they undermined the whole discursive scaffolding they had erected to show that they held incontestable sway over the natural environment. After all, the Soviets were in the Arctic to change it, not to be changed by it. And so, as much as possible, the Arctic myth downplayed the notion that the North had any real psychological impact on the Soviets who lived and worked there. Instead, it chose to emphasize how the region was being dominated by the Soviets—in other words, how Moscow was able to extend its controlling hand even to the farthest reaches of the USSR's mythic universe.

The Advance Posts of Culture: Civilizing the Arctic Landscape

When the Soviet Arctic pavilion opened its doors at Moscow's All-Union Agricultural Exhibition (precursor to the more famous Exhibition of the Achievements of the People's Economy, or VDNKh), it adopted the following motto, attributed to the Leningrad Party boss Sergei Kirov: "There is no land that Soviet power cannot transform for the good of mankind."[26] This was perfectly consistent with the deeper meaning of the Arctic culture of the 1930s. One of the central messages of the Arctic myth was that no matter how remote or hostile a fastness the northern periphery might be, the civilizing influence of Moscow could make itself felt there. Consequently, in the language of the Soviet media, the USSR's polar communities, research installations, and expeditions became "advance posts [*forposty*, an explicitly military term] of culture" in the Arctic wilderness.

Much effort was taken to demonstrate the ability of Soviet explorers and scientists to transplant everyday modes of existence to the frozen tundras and open expanses of the North. Polar stations and Arctic settlements were portrayed as top-of-the-line workplaces and ideal living environments. The men and women who staffed them were praised as model Soviet citizens. Arctic outposts were said to be stocked with film collections, libraries, and other entertainments. In 1935, the first "polar theaters"—troupes of actors, dancers, and musicians who made circuits throughout the Arctic—began performing in small towns, at mining complexes, on icebreakers, and so forth. The English journalist Harry Smolka spotted several local jazz bands and operas during his visit to the Soviet Arctic.[27] In 1935 and 1936, Soviet polar stations were said to have been supplied with the following miscellaneous items: 430,000 rubles' worth of books; 175,000 rubles' worth of bicycles; 42,000 rubles' worth of toys; 700 Victrolas, along with 21,000 records for them; 550,000 rubles' worth of sports equipment; 800,000 rubles' worth of musical instruments; and, on top of that, ten pianos and enough assorted trumpets and horns to fit out five full brass bands.[28] With respect to more practical matters, the Soviets claimed to have a first-rate network of hospitals in the North, staffed by the nation's finest doctors and nurses.[29] Much was also made of the fact that by 1937, 1.5 million rubles were being put aside each year for the schools serving the 2,176 children who lived on or near polar stations.[30]

The Arctic myth developed this theme in more abstract ways as well. While in the northern wilderness, Soviet explorers replicated life as it was back in "civilized" Russia as best they could. They faithfully observed the niceties of Stalinist ritual by celebrating every holiday in the modern calendar of the USSR, from New Year's Day and May Day to Stalinist Constitution Day, with as much grandeur as their circumstances allowed. They held Party cell meetings and political education sessions. The technological marvel of radio enabled them to follow soccer tournaments, Supreme Soviet elections, and show trials as if they were home on the mainland. Standards of cleanliness and hygiene were maintained without fail. When members of the SP-1 expedition placed a sign reading "Wipe Your Feet!" at the North Pole, it was only partly a matter of humor.[31] This is also why Soviet explorers were nearly always depicted as clean shaven. A smooth face showed that no citizen of the USSR would even consider allowing the rigors of the wilderness to overcome his cultured behavior. The pilot Vasily Molokov refused to let any man with an unshaven face aboard his airplane during the final flight to the North Pole in 1937. A dispensation was made for Otto Shmidt, because, as Molokov explained, "the whole world knows and loves his beard."[32] In all of these ways, the Soviet presence in the Arctic was used to reinforce the notion that the USSR was, more than any other nation in the world, capable of establishing order in the midst of chaos. As Maxim Gorky declared, when asked during an interview to comment on the *Cheliuskin* rescue, "In the darkness of the polar night, the sun of human intellect now shines brightly."[33] And there was no doubt that by "human," Gorky really had it in mind to say "Soviet."

The ultimate source of this civilizing capacity was, of course, the city of Moscow, which acted as a metaphoric beacon for explorers and aviators throughout the Arctic. As Sigismund Levanevsky remarked, Moscow was to him a "powerful magnet" that guided his flying in the empty wastes of the North (and, by implication, stood in direct contrast to that other "powerful magnet," the North Pole).[34] More specifically, it was the unparalleled genius and force of personality of Stalin himself that animated the entire Soviet presence in the Arctic, including the efforts of the explorers and scientists to impose socialist modernity there. Accordingly, Stalin's name and image were inextricably woven into the narrative history of every heroic episode that took place in the North. It was Stalin's brilliance that inspired and masterminded each of the country's glorious feats in the Arctic. Films and newspapers showed him as the driving force behind the *Cheliuskin* rescue. He was said to have designed the SP-1 expedition to the North Pole. It was Stalin who was supposed to have plotted the flight paths taken by the transpolar pilots of 1937, as reflected in the poem "The Stalin Route," by Perets Markish. In it, Chkalov and his fellow crew members tell Stalin:

> By your hand will be traced
> The swift path above the wintry peaks!
> At the behest of our Leader, with the support of our people,
> We will blaze a path from Pole to Pole.[35]

Later, during their flight, Chkalov and his comrades, aloft in the tempest-tossed Arctic skies, invoke the name of Stalin once again, almost as if in prayer:

> Their lips quietly whispered:
> "Leader and Friend, guide us from afar!
> Against these storms and winds,
> Above these deserts of eternal ice!"[36]

Stalin's ubiquity in the Arctic myth was rhetorically linked to broader questions of authority. In a speech to the Eighteenth Party Congress in 1939, for instance, Ivan Papanin compared the Soviet Union to a massive icebreaker, with Stalin as its steely captain.[37]

In keeping with the socialist realist vision of Soviet society as a pyramidally patriarchal "Great Family," Stalin was also portrayed repeatedly in the Arctic myth as the symbolic father of polar explorers and Arctic pilots, just as he was depicted as the father of all Soviet heroes and, ultimately, the "Father of Nations."[38] During the greater part of the 1930s, Arctic heroes were among the favorite sons in Stalin's "Great Family." They were his fledglings *(pitomtsy)*, reared with infinite care and love.[39] As they grew and matured, Stalin bestowed fatherly wisdom upon them, tempering their heroic energies with discipline and concern. In all ways, he supported them and made their heroic exploits possible. And he stood by his sons even in death. In the event of an Arctic hero's demise, Stalin called upon the entire nation to mourn and planned for him a funeral service suitable for the greatest of luminaries. For their part, of course, the Arctic heroes returned Stalin's love with a fierce and devoted filial affection. In the Soviet universe, there could be no stronger bond than that between the heroic son and his father-leader. As the transpolar pilot Valery Chkalov wrote in "Our Father" *(Nash otets)*, a famous essay that appeared in *Izvestiia:* "He is our father. He teaches us and rears us. We are as dear to his heart as his own children. We Soviet pilots all feel his loving, attentive, fatherly eyes upon us. He is our father."[40] Of the Arctic heroes of the 1930s, Chkalov was by far the favorite "son" of Stalin (at least in the Arctic myth), but to one extent or another, the same dynamic applied to all Soviet polar celebrities.

Unsurprisingly, then, it was back to Stalin that the heroic (and civilizing) quest of the polar explorer and the Arctic pilot led in the end. Upon returning from their exploits in the remote North, polar heroes were typically invited to the Kremlin, frequently to an audience with Stalin himself, along with the USSR's other leading state officials—lesser lights in orbit around the Great Leader. These visits took on the flavor of religious pilgrimages, bringing the hero into the presence of the living embodiment of Soviet power. For the Arctic hero, an encounter with Stalin was a crowning moment in his or her career. It was a supreme rite of passage that eclipsed all others and elevated the hero into the rolls of the country's elect: the so-called best people of the USSR, the ranks of which included the finest workers, soldiers, artists, farmers, and sportsmen in the nation. Meeting the leader was also a numinous experience: being in the presence of Stalin placed the hero virtually within reach of the sacred, providing him or her with a tangible connection to the flesh-and-blood embodiment of Soviet nationhood. Such encounters symbolized the perfect joining of the Soviet family circle, in which father and child were united.

Representations of meetings between Stalin and the heroes of the Arctic are steeped in the air of ritual.[41] The encounters take place in a variety of ways: heroes appear with Stalin in Red Square; they are summoned to Stalin's offices to discuss the logistics of their projects; at times, they receive the highest of honors and are invited to be Stalin's guests at the Kremlin or a dacha. When Stalin appears, he is simultaneously overwhelming and accessible. Although his presence is overpowering, attracting the attention of all present, Stalin is never distant or remote. Memoirs and personal recollections consistently refer to him as informal and modest, attentive and warm.[42] Being near Stalin is, more than anything else, comforting and nurturing: heroes lucky enough to meet him inevitably come to feel that they have always known him. And of course they have, for Stalin is their spiritual father. Whether the hero receives a handshake or a slight nod of approval from Stalin, stands near him on Lenin's mausoleum, looks at the night sky with him in a Kremlin courtyard, or enjoys a game of billiards with him, he or she is instantly reminded of this kinship. This happy knowledge remains with its recipients forever, giving them strength wherever they go and whatever they do.

And so the journey of the polar hero turned full circle: from Moscow to the Arctic, then back from the most remote wilderness to the center of the world. In the process, Moscow's pride of place was reaffirmed. Such was the theme of a light verse by Viktor Gusev, "The Cheliuskinites Are Coming," written in 1934.[43] Gusev tells how the various cities of Russia vie among themselves for the attentions of the Cheliuskinites, who have just been rescued and are traveling from Vankarem across the country. Each city, personified as an actual character, pitches its woo to the new heroes, trying to convince them to visit and stay a while. Vladivostok curses like a sailor when the Cheliuskinites bid it farewell; Viatka calls to them in the wooden whisper of the forest; Tashkent extends its invitation in the seductive, tender tones of the East. And so on, until a veritable cacophony of pleas and entreaties breaks out. Suddenly, the voice of Moscow, quiet but firm, cuts through the din, silencing the quarrel. The capital city declares that its interminable patience has been exhausted and that it is eager to welcome its sons and daughters home. The Cheliuskinites are whisked to the city with lightning speed. When they arrive, they are wrapped in the warm, all-nurturing embrace of all that is best about their homeland. Gusev's poem, like so much else in the Arctic myth, is a clear reflection of what the Soviets' great goal in the Arctic was, cosmographically speaking: to link the antipodes to Moscow, binding up everything in between into a unified whole. This was the intention boldly stated by the polar pilot Mikhail Vodop'ianov in his article "A New Year's Dream," which appeared in *Pravda* on New Year's Day, 1938: "The world will revolve upon a Bolshevik axis."[44]

The Land of Tomorrow: The Arctic as the USSR of the Future

More than once, Norway's Fridtjof Nansen—who was, hands down, the foreign polar explorer most admired in the Soviet Union—called

Siberia and the Russian North "the land of tomorrow." Not surprisingly, the Soviets eagerly took his words to heart. Their descriptions of the Arctic helped to shape a concrete picture of what the Soviet Union of the future was supposed to be like. The Arctic was an especially good geographical space for which to construct such images: the vast polar expanses served as the perfect blank slate—a discursive tabula rasa—on which the Soviets could inscribe their visions of the new socialist world they were purporting to build. The popular culture of the 1930s depicted the Arctic as a land of gleaming new cities and settlements, sparkling under the glow of the northern lights, untainted by any vestige of the old, corrupt tsarist order. Steel and concrete began to rise rapidly from the ice and snow in what the press called "A Region Born of the Five-Year Plan."[45]

Strictly in terms of Marxist ideology, of course, this sort of metaphor represented either a logical fallacy or the boldest of claims. Was it possible to say that Soviet "socialism" could be established in the midst of nothingness, when, according to Marxian doctrine, socialism, then communism, must grow dialectically out of earlier stages of social and economic development? Were those who designed the Arctic myth deliberately asserting that the Soviets had somehow found in the North a place—and a way—in which to bypass the normal strictures of historical materialism? Or had they, caught up (like so many others) in the rhetorical excesses of socialist realism—not to mention the innate flashiness of Arctic imagery—unconsciously generated this absurdity? Given the way socialist realism was riddled with internal ideological contradictions of all types, the latter seems more likely. Either way, everything being built in the North was depicted as brand new, as a harbinger of what the government and Party planned to do throughout the entire Soviet Union.

One of the brightest jewels in this Arctic crown was the young city of Igarka, on the banks of the Yenisei River. Established in 1929 as a center for the logging industry, Igarka became one of the state's favorite symbols of expansion into the polar wilderness. Igarka repeatedly attracted the attention of the Soviet media. In 1938, the coverage was amplified by the publication of a popular book entitled *We Are from Igarka.*[46] The volume was produced by Maxim Gorky (before his death in 1936), along with the children's author Samuil Marshak. It comprised a collection of letters written by the boys and girls of the town, describing their lives on the Arctic frontier. The portrait that the children paint is uniformly robust and positive. As bleak as its physical surroundings might be, Igarka lacks for nothing. It has a growing, happy population. The local administration is effective and attentive; its local newspapers, schools, and hospitals are of excellent quality. The city has a network of libraries, theaters, and cultural centers.[47] Most important, Igarka radiates the camaraderie, vibrancy, and freshness that can be gained only by *building* civilization, rather than merely enjoying its benefits. As the children themselves wrote, "Soviet power has made the North unrecognizable. . . . Igarka is not only a town or a port. It is an advance post of culture."[48] The press had already concluded much the same. As *Pravda* wrote, "The Good Life in Igarka" was a synecdoche for the "good life" that the whole country was meant to be striving for: Soviet socialism at its best and bravest, which would carry the entire nation forward, into the future.[49]

Portraits of the major expeditions to the Arctic carried with them the same message. *Pravda,* for instance, called the icebreaker *Sibiriakov* a "floating republic" as it made its way along Russia's northern coast.[50] Even more famous was the carefully designed image of the Cheliuskinites' camp on the ice, which was presented as a miniaturized USSR in the wilderness.[51] When the *Cheliuskin* sank in February 1934, the members of the expedition had only two hours to abandon ship. Having been aware for several weeks that their vessel might break up, they had prepared for an emergency evacuation and were thus able to offload clothing, food, tools, construction materials, and, most importantly, radio equipment before the ship went down. Their situation was perilous in the extreme: 104 people, including 10 women and 2 children, were left stranded on ice floes in the midst of a polar winter. Still, the Cheliuskinites had with them the basic tools for survival, and they constructed a makeshift outpost that they named "Camp Shmidt" in honor of their leader.

Camp Shmidt was home to the Cheliuskinites for two long months, until mid-April, when the last members of the group were finally airlifted. In the meantime, it also became the subject of one of the most utopian subsets of the Arctic myth, by means of officially sanctioned images that were glamorized and contrived. The camp was depicted as the "perfect Bolshevik collective," kept alive and functioning by the "iron discipline" and "nurturing goodwill" of Shmidt himself. The castaways did not merely survive by huddling on the ice and passively waiting for rescue but diligently carried on with their scientific work and devoted their energies to building and maintaining the camp. The Party members in the group "published" a handwritten wall newspaper called "We Shall Not Surrender!" (the final issue, left behind by the last of the group to be evacuated, read, "We Did Not Surrender!"). The Cheliuskinites ceremoniously celebrated Red Army Day (February 23) and other major events in conjunction with the rest of the country. The ship's artist raised spirits by turning the supply depot into the Red General Store—"Everything You Need for Life on the Ice!" He also sketched a series of cunning and amusing cartoons to buoy his comrades' mood.

The stranded Soviets played soccer and volleyball during the day, then gathered in the evenings for songs (there was even a gramophone, complete with records), dominoes, and poetry readings (the Cheliuskinites had managed to save four books from their sinking ship, including a volume of poems by Pushkin).[52] Shmidt entertained his fellow castaways with a series of dazzling lectures. His vast range of knowledge (as editor-in-chief of the *Bol'shaia Sovetskaia entsiklopediia,* Shmidt had a reputation as a polymath) allowed him to speak authoritatively about astronomy, analytic geometry, modern history, Freud, Russian monasticism, and a variety of other topics. On one occasion, Shmidt refused to answer a radio call from the mainland because he was in the midst of explaining the intricacies of dialectical materialism to an enraptured audience.

Obviously, the colors used to paint this picture came from a palette that was overly bright. Accounts of everyday life at Camp Shmidt are, almost without fail, optimistic and positive. Reading the memoirs and diary entries of the expedition members is enough to give anyone the impression that the Cheliuskinites were on a grand vacation, roughing it in the wild for fun and relaxation rather than fighting a constant battle just to stay alive. Instances of shirking and selfishness, grumbling and complaint are mentioned rarely and downplayed as much as possible. One would be hard-pressed to find mention of even a single runny nose. Little was said, for example, of certain breaches of discipline. Not only had several members of the expedition been caught hoarding food or selfishly concentrating on saving their personal possessions during the evacuation (a jury-rigged "people's court" was lenient, "sentencing" the guilty parties to be sent back home as soon as possible), but the construction brigade bound for Wrangel Island proved to be an unruly bunch. Only after Shmidt threatened to execute them did they give up their plans to abandon the camp and walk back to the mainland on their own.

Nor was there any hint of the boredom and despair that the

Cheliuskinites certainly felt during their ordeal on the ice. As for fear, only enough to create a sense of drama and danger was injected into the official accounts of the adventure. Any expressions of or anecdotes about doubt or less-than-heroic behavior are included deliberately for specific purposes. One was moral contrast: to highlight the positive behavior of the majority against a few instances of backsliding. Another was to show how, even when the resolve of an individual member of the expedition occasionally flagged, the Cheliuskinites' socialist communitarian ideal prevailed, stiffening his or her determination not just to survive but to labor for the good of the group. Was this the reality? Clearly not, although Shmidt and the Cheliuskinites deserve tremendous credit and admiration simply for surviving the ordeal. It goes without saying that the media's depiction of life at Camp Shmidt was not about trying to capture the reality that existed there. It was about creating a new reality, one in which it was shown that the Soviets could impose civilization anywhere they chose to, no matter how adverse the conditions. Camp Shmidt was intended to offer a microcosmic vision of the model socialist society—an idealized Soviet Union that *should be.*

Nation of Heroes: A Conclusion

Underlying the notion of the Arctic as a mythic landscape was the idea that it was, above all, a land of heroes. The explorers and pilots themselves were positive heroes, the real-life counterparts to the mighty and fearless protagonists who inhabited the pages of the socialist realist novel.[53] But the real significance of the Arctic myth was deeper even than that. The Arctic culture of the 1930s tied the fortunes of every individual in the Soviet Union to the country's exploits in the North. It was no accident, for example, that just as Stalin was portrayed as the father of the USSR's polar heroes, so the *narod,* the Soviet people, was depicted as their extended family. This image was the means by which the socialist realist worldview was able to connect Stalin and the polar heroes with the Soviet population as a whole.

This was a vital rhetorical point, and the *narod* was portrayed as sustaining every one of the Arctic heroes' efforts in the North. According to *Pravda,* the success of the *Cheliuskin* rescue was the "victory of the country's single will."[54] As telegrams from the SP-1 outpost at the North Pole routinely informed nationwide audiences, Papanin and his companions felt no discomfort or isolation during their long months at the top of the world, because the concern and encouragement of the

Soviet people was a palpable force that aided them in their efforts: "We are far from home, far from our fellow countrymen and friends. Thousands of miles of icy waste divide us from our beloved country, but no distance can ever really separate us citizens of the USSR from our country, the first socialist country in the world, from the Bolshevik Party, or from the love and warmth of the people of our country."[55]

The message was clear: the *narod* was meant to be seen as an indispensable factor in the USSR's achievements in the Arctic. For one thing, this reflected the great premium that communist ideology placed on teamwork, community, and collective effort. But more importantly, by providing such an intimate link between the *narod* and the heroes of the Soviet Union—Arctic or otherwise—the socialist realist worldview as a whole spread heroic status outward, into the population at large. It thus united all Soviet people, high and low, in what *Pravda,* not to mention myriad songs, poems, and essays, called the "Stalinist tribe" *(Stalinskoe plemia),* the most advanced and progressive genus of humanity on earth.[56] Polar heroes were inseparable from their fellow countrymen, because every Soviet citizen was joined to every other by the responsibility of making exploits in the North succeed. Hence, every Soviet citizen shared in the rewards as well.

At the heart of the Arctic myth, then, not to mention socialist realist culture in general, lay a fundamental message that the entire Soviet Union was a nation of heroes. Every man, woman, and child in the USSR could—indeed, was called upon to—become a hero. In "March of the Jolly Fellows," the signature song for one of the decade's most popular musical comedies, the poet-songwriter Vasily Lebedev-Kumach spelled out the idea clearly:

> We will achieve, grasp, and discover it all,
> The cold North Pole and the blue vault of heaven!
> When our country commands that we become heroes,
> Then anyone among us can become a hero.[57]

Building socialism was the greatest adventure in the history of humankind, and the heroism celebrated publicly in the press and on Red Square was only the most visible manifestation of the everyday heroism that was needed in the factory, on the collective farm, in the army platoon, or in the classroom.

Throughout the 1930s, the Arctic myth played an indispensable role in creating this landscape of heroism. Metaphorically, public celebrations of the USSR's polar exploits helped to create a mythic image of Stalinist Russia as a shining utopia in which bold Soviet citizens, inspired by the ideology of Leninism-Stalinism and armed with the might of the most advanced technology in the world, were creating the socialist tomorrowland. As Otto Shmidt wrote in *Pravda* after returning from the North Pole in 1937: "Life in our country flies faster than a dream. It is joyous to live and work in a country where bold dreams receive such real support. Here in the Land of Soviets, and only here, are the great and small dreams of humanity fulfilled."[58]

Thus, through its portrayal of Soviet exploits in the Arctic, the socialist realist myth attempted to demonstrate to all that just as the Arctic could be conquered only *by* the Soviet Union, only *in* the Soviet Union could true heroes be made—and only there could the collective and individual aspirations of humanity be realized.

NOTES

1. See Boris Gromov, *Pokhod "Sibiriakova"* (Moscow: Sovetskaia Literatura, 1934), and E. T. Krenkel', *RAEM Is My Call-Sign* (Moscow: Progress, 1978). Otto Iul'evich Shmidt, nicknamed the "Commissar of Ice" by the Soviet media, had one of the most unusual careers in Soviet history. A mathematician and scientist, Shmidt distinguished himself during the Russian Civil War and the 1920s with his work in the People's Commissariats of Food, Finance, and Education. From 1924 to 1941, he served as editor-in-chief of the *Bol'shaia Sovetskaia Entsiklopediia;* in 1928, he led the first expedition to the Pamir glacier. From 1932 to 1939, Shmidt worked in the Arctic, heading the Main Administration of the Northern Sea Route (GUSMP), the agency responsible for the exploration, administration, and development of the two million square miles of Soviet territory that lay east of the Ural Mountains and north of the sixty-second parallel. It was in this capacity that he achieved nationwide fame. Afterward, he served as vice-president of the Academy of Sciences of the USSR (1939–42) and remained active in the Soviet scientific community until his death in 1956. See *Otto Iul'evich Shmidt: Zhizn' i deiatel'nost'* (Moscow: Nauka, 1959) and G. V. Iakusheva, *Otto Iul'evich Shmidt: entsiklopedist* (Moscow: Sovetskaia Entsiklopediia, 1991).

2. See Krenkel', *RAEM Is My Call-Sign;* Boris Gromov, *Gibel' "Cheliuskina"* (Moscow: Goslitizdat, 1936); *Dnevniki Cheliuskintsev* (Moscow: Pravda, 1934); *Pokhod "Cheliuskina"* (Moscow: Pravda, 1934); *Kak my spasali Cheliuskintsev* (Moscow: Pravda, 1934); and *The Voyage of the Cheliuskin* (New York: Macmillan, 1935). The medal of the Hero of the Soviet Union, the highest honor in the USSR, was created in April 1934 especially as a reward for the seven pilots who took part in the *Cheliuskin* rescue: Anatolii Liapidevskii, Mikhail Vodop'ianov, Vasilii Molokov, Ivan Doronin, Nikolai Kamanin, Sigismund Levanevskii, and Mavriki Slepnev.

3. See *Velikii letchik nashego vremeni* (Moscow: OGIZ, 1939); G. F. Baidukov, *Pervye perelety cherez Ledovityi okean* (Moscow: Detskaia literatura, 1987); idem, *Russian Lindbergh: The Life of Valery Chkalov* (Washington, D.C.: Smithsonian Institution Press, 1991); V. P. Chkalov, G. F. Baidukov, and A. V. Beliakov, *Dva pereleta* (Moscow:

Voenizdat, 1938); and idem, *My eshche prodolzhim Stalinskii marshrut* (Moscow: Gosizdat, 1938). On Gromov's flight, see Baidukov, *Pervye perelety cherez Ledovityi okean;* A. S. Danilin, *Cherez Severnyi polius—s mirovym rekordom* (Moscow: DOSAAF, 1981); and M. M. Gromov, *Cherez vsiu zhizn'* (Moscow: Molodaia gvardiia, 1986). In August 1937, shortly after Chkalov's and Gromov's triumphs, *Cheliuskin* pilot Sigismund Levanevskii attempted a third transpolar flight, intending to break Gromov's record by flying to southern California. His aircraft disappeared over the North Pole; no trace of him or his crew has ever been found. See Iu. P. Sal'nikov, *Zhizn', otdannaia Arktike* (Moscow: Politizdat, 1984).

4. See Krenkel', *RAEM Is My Call-Sign;* idem, *Chetyre tovarishcha* (Moscow: Progress, 1978); E. K. Fedorov, *Polar Diaries* (Moscow: Progress, 1983); I. D. Papanin, *Na poliuse* (Moscow: Detizdat, 1939); S. A. Bergavinov, *Arktika i polius zavoevany!* (Moscow: Partizdat, 1937); idem, *Polius nash!* (Moscow: Partizdat, 1937); Lazar Brontman, *Na vershine mira* (Moscow: Detizdat, 1938); and idem, *On the Top of the World* (London: Victor Gollancz, 1938).

5. For the fullest treatment of the Arctic culture of the 1930s, see John McCannon, *Red Arctic: Polar Exploration and the Myth of the North in the Soviet Union, 1932–1939* (New York: Oxford University Press, 1998). Also see idem, "Positive Heroes at the Pole: Celebrity Status, Socialist-Realist Ideals, and the Soviet Myth of the Arctic, 1932–1939," *Russian Review* 56, no. 3 (July 1997): 346–65. One of the first scholars to note the cultural importance of Soviet aviation and polar exploits was Kendall E. Bailes, in *Technology and Society under Lenin and Stalin: Origins of the Soviet Technical Intelligentsia* (Princeton, N.J.: Princeton University Press, 1978). Another major influence on this work has been Katerina Clark, *The Soviet Novel: History as Ritual* (Chicago: University of Chicago Press, 1981). See also Sheila Fitzpatrick, ed., *The Cultural Front: Power and Culture in Revolutionary Russia* (Ithaca, N.Y.: Cornell University Press, 1992); Nina Tumarkin, *Lenin Lives! The Lenin Cult in Soviet Russia* (Cambridge, Mass.: Harvard University Press, 1983); Hans Günther, *Der Sozialistische Übermensch: Maksim Gorkij und der sowjetische Heldenmythos* (Stuttgart: J. B. Metzler, 1993); Hans Günther, ed., *The Culture of the Stalin Period* (New York: St. Martin's, 1990); Richard Stites, *Revolutionary Dreams: Utopian Vision and Experimental Life in the Russian Revolution* (New York: Oxford University Press, 1989); Karen Petrone, *Life Has Become More Joyous Comrades: Celebrations in the Time of Stalin* (Bloomington: Indiana University Press, 2000).

6. Peter Knox-Shaw, *The Explorer in English Fiction* (New York: St. Martin's, 1986), 10–11.

7. Perhaps the best reflection of this image is summed up in the slogan, "From the Kremlin, Stalin cares for each and every one of us." An especially popular poster by V. Govorkov juxtaposed those words with a picture of an avuncular Stalin, sitting in his office and working late into the night on important-looking papers. See *Istoriia strany v plakate* (Moscow: Panorama, 1993), 112.

8. Paul Zweig, *The Adventurer* (New York: Basic Books, 1974), 226–34.

9. For more on this theme, see my article "To Storm the Arctic: Soviet Polar Expeditions and Public Visions of Nature in the USSR, 1932–1939," *Ecumene* 2, no. 1 (January 1995): 15–31.

10. *Sovetskaia Arktika* (August 1938): 7–10.

11. *Izvestiia*, 14 April 1934.

12. H. P. Smolka, *Forty Thousand against the Arctic* (New York: William Morrow, 1937), 169.

13. "Chudnyi stolb," *Sovetskaia Arktika* (November 1937): 96. This image is also found commonly in the state-sponsored folklore of the 1930s.

14. On the psychological and cultural importance of height and high ground, see Simon Schama, *Landscape and Memory* (New York: Knopf, 1995), 385–513, and Roberto DaMotta, "Carnival in Multiple Planes," in *Rite, Drama, Festival, Spectacle: Rehearsals toward a Theory of Cultural Performance*, ed. John MacAloon (Philadelphia: Institute for the Study of Human Issues, 1984), 209–15.

15. Brontman, *On the Top of the World*, 236. Brontman was the *Pravda* correspondent who accompanied the SP-1 expedition to the North Pole in 1937.

16. See Frank Miller, *Folklore for Stalin* (Armonk, N.Y.: M. E. Sharpe, 1990), 37–47, 63–64, 78–82, 144–46; *Velikii letchik nashego vremeni*, 278–80; *Kryl'ia sovetov* (Moscow: Iskusstvo, 1939), 49–50, 62–63, 137–44; and Flora Leites, ed., *Stalinskie sokoly* (Moscow: Khudozhestvennaia literatura, 1939), 55–56.

17. *Pravda*, 22 May 1937. See also "Severnyi polius zavoevan!" *Sovetskaia Arktika* (June 1937), as well as Bergavinov, *Arktika i polius zavoevany!*

18. Jack Zipes, *Breaking the Magic Spell: Radical Theories of Folk and Fairy Tales* (Austin: University of Texas Press, 1979), 43.

19. Ruth Gruber, *I Went to the Soviet Arctic* (New York: Simon and Schuster, 1939), 236. For an examination of the psychic effects the Russian North could have during an earlier era, see Cathy Popkin, "Chekhov as Ethnographer: Epistemological Crisis on Sakhalin Island," *Slavic Review* 51, no. 1 (Spring 1992): 36–51.

20. For cases of clinical depression and other psychological traumas brought on by polar night in the Russian Arctic, see K. S. Badigin, *Na morskikh dorogakh* (Arkhangel'sk: Severo-Zapadnoe Knizhnoe Izdatel'stvo, 1985), 31; and G. A. Ushakov, *Po nekhozhenoi zemle* (Leningrad: Gidrometeoizdat, 1990), 241–42.

21. Mikhail Vodop'ianov, "Sever zovet," *Na kryliakh v Arktiku* (Moscow: Geograficheskaia literatura, 1954), 5. Note that like many other Soviet authors, Vodop'ianov makes explicit reference to Jack London, who was a great favorite among readers in the USSR.

22. Brontman, *On the Top of the World*, 191.

23. *Kak my spasali Cheliuskintsev*, 113; Levanevskii, *Moia stikhiia* (Rostov, 1935), 17–18.

24. Quoted in Krenkel', *RAEM Is My Call-Sign*, 72–73. In a similar fashion, the critic and author Peter Matthiessen encountered the "sickness of infinitude," spoken of by Søren Kierkegaard, in the overwhelming vastness of the Himalayas. See his *The Snow Leopard* (London: Harvill, 1978), 48.

25. *Moscow News*, 17 October 1942; the same interview also appears in Kaverin's personal *fond* in the Russian State Archive of Literature and Art (RGALI), f. 1501, op. 1, d. 151, l. 18.

26. See the Russian State Archive of Socio-Political History (RGASPI, formerly RTsKhIDNI), f. 475, op. 2, d. 446, l. 8.

27. Smolka, *Forty Thousand against the Arctic*, 51.

28. Bergavinov, "Politotdely Severnogo Morskogo Puti," *Sovetskaia Arktika* (January 1937): 19; and A. I. Levichev, "Nekotorye voprosy Sovetskoi torgovli na Krainem Severe," *Sovetskaia Arktika* (April 1937): 22.

29. For example, see V. N. Tarasenkov, "Obskii Sever i ego ekonomika," *Sovetskaia Arktika* (May 1937): 78. Concerning doctors, nurses, and hospitals in the Arctic, the reality was very much at odds with what was said about them. In general, medical care in the North was substandard and in short supply.

30. Russian State Archive of the Economy (RGAE), f. 9570, op. 2, d. 95, l. 238. This statistic did not include children living in large settlements, towns, or cities in the North.

31. Brontman, *On the Top of the World*, 140.

32. Ibid., 154.

33. "Piercing the Arctic," *Literary Digest*, 2 May 1936, 15.

34. *Sovetskaia Arktika* (November 1936): 12–16.

35. Perets Markish, "Stalinskii marshrut," *Kryl'ia sovetov*, 69–75.

36. Ibid.

37. *Sovetskaia Arktika* (April 1939): 89–94.

38. On the theme of Stalin's "Great Family," see Clark, *The Soviet Novel*, 124–29.

39. This motif was used most often in reference to pilots, because it derived from the term "falcon" *(sokol)*, which was the most common epithet employed by the Soviet media in describing aviators during the 1930s.

40. Valerii Chkalov, "Nash otets," *Izvestiia*, 18 August 1938.

41. For descriptions of how Arctic heroes interacted with Stalin, see the various memoirs of the heroes themselves. In addition, see *Sovetskaia Arktika* (December 1939): 17–33; Brontman, *Vladimir Kokkinaki*, 18, 30–32; Baidukov, *Vstrechi s tovarishchem Stalinym* (Moscow: Detizdat, 1940); and, especially, A. A. Fadeev, ed., *Vstrechi s tovarishchem Stalinym* (Moscow: OGIZ, 1939), which contains the remembrances of Ivan Papanin, Mikhail Gromov, Vasilii Molokov, Vladimir Kokkinaki, Georgii Baidukov, Mikhail Vodop'ianov, Valentina Grizodubova, and Andrei Iumashev, among others.

42. Fadeev, *Vstrechi*, 39, 61–62, 161.

43. RGALI, f. 2177, op. 1, d. 57, ll. 3–6.

44. Mikhail Vodop'ianov, "Novogodniaia mechta," *Pravda*, 1 January 1938. In this essay, Vodop'ianov unveiled a suggestion for the USSR to follow up its triumphs at the North Pole with a flight to the South Pole the following year. Nothing came of his spirited, if quixotic, plans.

45. For example, see *Pravda*, 13 January 1934.

46. *My iz Igarki* (Moscow: Detizdat, 1938). The reality behind the book is somewhat dark: most of the children who participated in the creation of *My iz Igarki* were the sons and daughters of deported kulaks who had been exiled to the North during the state's campaign to collectivize agriculture from 1928 to 1932. See the 1988 documentary *And the Past Seems But a Dream* (I proshloe vygliadit snom). Also, the Western journalists H. P. Smolka (*Forty Thousand against the Arctic*, 186–89, 206) and Ruth Gruber (*I Went to the Soviet Arctic*, 183–92) both visited Igarka and reported on this issue.

47. Gruber, in *I Went to the Soviet Arctic*, 81–83, wrote that the population of Igarka hovered between 12,000 and 15,000, depending on the season. According to her, the city had nine schools, attended by 2,329 pupils.

48. *My iz Igarki*, 6, 191–219.

49. *Pravda*, 20 July 1935.

50. *Pravda,* 7 December 1932.

51. The following portrait is compiled from the sources cited in note 2, as well as mass newspapers and participants' memoirs.

52. The presence of Pushkin in the story of Camp Shmidt is not a trivial point. Specifically, it was connected with the lavish celebrations of Pushkin and his work during the 1930s, leading up to the centennial of his death in 1937. Generally, it was linked with the Soviet Union's search for a "Great Tradition"—the effort to construct a national iconography that included ideologically acceptable figures from Russia's past—during the Stalin era. The other books salvaged by the Cheliuskinites were the third volume of Sholokhov's *Quiet Flows the Don,* a translation of Longfellow's *Hiawatha,* and a translation of Knut Hamsun's novel *Pan.*

53. On the synergetic relationship between fiction and reality in socialist realist culture during the Stalinist era, see Katerina Clark, *The Soviet Novel,* 146–47; and Sheila Fitzpatrick, "Becoming Cultured: Socialist Realism and the Representation of Privilege and Taste," in *The Cultural Front,* 217.

54. *Pravda,* 11 April 1934.

55. Brontman, *On the Top of the World,* 241.

56. *Pravda,* 23 July 1936.

57. From "Marsh veselykh rebiat," featured in Grigorii Aleksandrov's 1934 movie musical *Veselye rebiata.* The score for the film was composed by Isaak Dunaevskii, who, with Lebedev-Kumach, formed one of the most successful musical teams in the USSR during the 1930s.

58. *Pravda,* 24 June 1937.

11

"The Best in the World"

THE DISCOURSE OF THE MOSCOW METRO IN THE 1930S

MIKHAIL RYKLIN
Translated by Abigail Evans

> Give us more realistic lighting—these aren't churches, after all, but stations of the underground railway!
>
> —L. M. Kaganovich

In the third volume of his *Aesthetics,* Hegel wrote of an "independent, symbolic architecture." At certain times in history, the entire life of a nation is caught up in the attempt to construct such architectural works, buildings that give expression to the nation's most cherished beliefs—for example, its understanding of spiritual concepts such as God, a higher sovereign, or the ideal society—in an organized and unmediated form of reality. It is for this reason that these architectural works are symbolic, rather than merely products of the "subjective ability to create illusions" from which art ordinarily springs. "Productions of this architecture should stimulate thought by themselves, and arouse general ideas without being purely a cover and environment for meanings already independently shaped in other ways."[1] Their form does not merely signify but symbolizes, "indicating the ideas which their erection aimed at arousing." This leads to the enormous variation among such buildings, something absent from more individualized works, which have become "factors in a *single* consciousness."[2]

If the primary purpose of an independent, symbolic architecture is to unite people, then we might take as examples not only the Tower of Babel (as Hegel did) but also the construction of the Moscow metro from the 1930s to the 1950s. But whereas the discourse surrounding the first of these projects survives only as a few magic formulae carved into stone and the testimonials of several Greek historians, the discourse provoked by the construction of the underground railway in Moscow has been well preserved and can serve as an object of study.

The basis for this discourse was established by L. M. Kaganovich in a speech given on May 14, 1935, at a state function commemorating the opening of the first line of the metro. Many of the positions taken up by Kaganovich in this speech have since been repeated by numerous architects, writers, and builders.

"The Moscow metropolitan [railroad]," the first thesis went, "goes far beyond the ordinary understanding of technical construction. Our metropolitan is a *symbol* [my emphasis] of the new socialist society currently being built . . . and operating upon bases utterly opposed to those upon which capitalist society has been constructed."[3] It is vital to note here the variety of ways in which the phrase "technical construction" may be interpreted, because it is highly ambiguous. In certain contexts it might mean "a technical construction in which everything is ideal—the halls of the stations, the cars, the machinists, the passengers, the wall facings and so forth." It is also possible that "technical" may be set in opposition to "ideal," making the two incompatible. In such cases, the technical represents the "fall" of the ideal, an unavoidable evil that must be surmounted in order to attain the ideal. And there is a third possible reading: the technical as inherently subordinate to the aesthetic, as one of the secondary manifestations of the aesthetic (conceived of as an ideal). It is precisely the ambiguity of this phrase, the equal footing on which fundamentally different interpretive possibilities stand, that is essential. If its meaning were limited to only one of these possibilities, it would lose its symbolic effectiveness. Rather, it employs all of these meanings simultaneously.

In the discourse of the metro, technology ceased to be treated strictly as a professional matter; it was both fetishized (in connection to the ideal) and at the same time debased (made subordinate to the dictates of the aesthetic). It was subsumed by literature as a sort of folktale, a dominant trend in the Soviet culture of the 1930s. Terms that had been in professional use by mine workers, transport engineers, and surface workers were appropriated for mass use, deprofessionalized, and made a part of the master narrative. The engineer's technical assessment was powerless before the pressure of Bolshevik pacing and Komsomol improvisation. The discourse of the metro signaled the twilight of reason, from the engineer's standpoint, reason without which no technical construction, ideal or mundane, could be completed.

The subject of this essay is not the metro as a technical construction but the discourse of the metro, the totality of speech acts surrounding the issue, acts that were to a large extent autonomous and to a degree inaccessible to themselves. The discourse of the metro has a closer relationship to literature than to the professional languages by which utilitarian objects are made. Within this discourse, professional languages lose their specificity, their particular natures, and are totalized; this is how propaganda makes use of them. Although no real construction could ever be created by such a discourse, it does represent, so to speak, a work in and of itself.

The discourse of the metro did attempt to make the metro into an attribute of the new communist state, and in this it was successful—but only within its own confines. As a transportation project, the metro was built by means of a body of knowledge that was free of aesthetic considerations. Another characteristic of the metro discourse of the thirties was its conspiratorial nature. Though it pretended to an epic scale and to complete transparency, it was in fact constantly engaged in a process of selecting from, classifying (in the sense of making secret), and thinning out the field of speech acts, many of which were successfully suppressed and never entered the discourse. From the outset, construction of the Moscow metro was conducted as if it were a military operation; the stations even functioned at times as bomb shelters. Special military objectives were associated with the project that to this day have never been mentioned in print.

This deliberate omission of any mention of the military use of the metro had its own sort of revenge as the war metaphor at the heart of the discourse continued to grow, reaching colossal proportions. The construction of the metro represented a war against what Kaganovich called the "prerevolutionary, old-regime" geology of Moscow, against the old world and the capitalist enemies all around. The discourse of the metro was literally held in the grip of war terminology, its aggressiveness knowing no boundaries. To build was, above all, to do battle. "The Moscow metropolitan is one sector of the great war that we have been carrying on for the last ten years and particularly recently. . . . *We did not simply build the metropolitan, we fought for the victory of our first Soviet metropolitan.*"[4] The metro had to be constructed in the shortest possible time, regardless of the difficulties or sacrifices required, under the sort of imperative theoretically possible only in a state of total mobilization. In building the metro, the state created a language that was later used in talking about military campaigns. The declaration of war against nature, against technical rationalism and the pride of the professional guild, allowed for the possibility (at least in words) of creating a new field of specialization—that of the metro builder. By order of the Party, the metro builder could quickly become a tunnel worker, a plasterer, a tiler, or an electrician.

Another point of pride for those who created this discourse was that the Soviets had built the metro entirely on their own, with no foreign aid. And indeed, much of the work truly was accomplished without foreign help. Moreover, the metro represents the only large-scale construction project of the Stalin era for which practically no prison labor was used. But this claim of complete national self-reliance, too, was part of the conspiracy. Recent publications have revealed that specifications for the construction of the escalators were bought from an English construction firm,[5] a fact no one mentioned in the thirties and forties. Other technical documentation was obtained by means of economic espionage conducted by the NKVD.

The station lighting—a lighting that could be termed illusionist—represents another theme of the discourse. The goal was to create the illusion for passengers that rather than being underground, they were in a sunlit palace in an unknown location. Any architectural plan that could not create this ambience was categorically rejected. Plans that emphasized the pressure of the powerful tectonic mass overhead, the "undergroundness" of the stations, were dismissed alongside "railway station"–type plans that created the "unorthodox" illusion of being beneath the open sky. One architect proposed that station ceilings be painted black so that passengers could not guess their height and would think they were in an ordinary intercity train station.[6] This plan was rejected for its "landedness." The architect should neither hide the undergroundess of the metro nor treat it as a positive quality; instead, he had to create the illusion of a palatial space truly present somewhere on earth but "ideally" away from any specific location: a utopia. Realizing this utopia literally was the architect's task:

> Upon entering a station, a man feels "like [he's] in a palace"—that is how the Moscow workers put it. Indeed, the palaces of our metro are hardly monotonous. There's variety in every station. Where, bourgeois sirs, are the barracks, the destruction of the individual, the obliteration of creativity, of art? On the contrary, we see in the metro the greatest development of creativity, the flowering of architectural thought—every station is a palace, and every palace has been conceived in a completely unique fashion. But each palace is lit by the same light—the light of progressive, victorious socialism.[7]

In Kaganovich's speech, architectural diversity was illuminated by a single, political light, which another orator called "the undying sun of the great Stalinist age." In comparison with such globalism, the struggle by architects for natural, "day-lit" stations seems petty, but without it, such grandiose ideological claims could not have been made.

During the thirties, the metro was the subject of a number of children's books, which, interestingly, appeared both in conjunction with its construction and in advance of it. In one such book, boasting the enthusiastic title *Ready! Stories and Poems of the Metro,*[8] an old peasant visits the metro station where his daughter has been working. The "daylight" lighting throws him into confusion; he thinks that he has somehow entered the tsar's palace and instinctively takes off his hat. His daughter initiates him into the discourse of the metro, which at first he does not understand:

> The walls were of semiprecious stone, the marble columns tall, and everything was lit by a bright light. A cool breeze blew through the halls, and people were going up and down the stairs and escalators.
>
> Nikita Potapov took off his hat.
>
> "What a rich life the tsars lived," he said. "It's like a fairy tale. And the train goes right up to the palaces—so that's how it was set up!"
>
> Katya laughed.
>
> "It isn't the tsars who live so well, papa, it's us. I've brought you underground."
>
> The old man, disbelieving, waved his hat at her.
>
> "There can't possibly be such a place underground!"
>
> "But here it is!" Katya answered and started laughing. "You'll see, we'll go for a ride."
>
> They rode the train in a comfortable car, went on the escalator, and saw all the stations. The old man still couldn't bring himself to put his hat back on, but kept it in his hands, saying, "Who would build such rich palaces for you, Katyasha, underground?"
>
> "Who would build them for us?" Katya answered. "We built them ourselves, we did the digging and we put up the palaces."
>
> Nikita Potakov put on his hat, embraced his daughter, and kissed her soundly, saying, "What a wonder you've shown me, daughter! I'm staying with you, I'm going to live in Moscow."
>
> And the old man stayed in Moscow, and every day he rode the underground.[9]

In this text, entitled "Like a Fairy Tale" and stylized in the manner of a folktale, the basic themes of the metro discourse are all evident. In the metro, day is indistinguishable from night, or it is eternally daytime. These palaces are neither privately owned nor owned by the tsar; they are collectively owned and built by the very people who use them. It is symptomatic that the old peasant puts on his hat—that is, suppresses in himself the manifestation of an age-old submissiveness—when he finds out that these palaces were built by the common people. At first he takes the metro station for an above-ground palace, then for an underground palace built for the new owners by someone else. Only after that is he able to "see" the logic of the new ideology: the people built these palaces for themselves. He no longer has to take his hat off for anybody. He decides that this is a heaven in which he'll stay.

In contrast to above-ground palaces for the rich, the underground palaces of the metro are owned not privately but by the collective, and entrance to them is open to everyone. And unlike in churches, the transcendental is revealed entirely in their structure; it takes neither the form of the spirit nor that of a community of believers who worship the spirit. Individuality has no place in the structures of the metro, nor does the spirit as it has been understood by philosophers from Plato to Hegel: "Individuality is the principle underlying the independent idea of the spiritual life, because the spirit can exist only as independent and personal."[10] The metro represents a structure of ritual and splendor that by definition can be owned by no one individual. Its very existence was seen as the manifestation of "Stalin's concern for the common man." The intensity of this concern was evidenced by the metro's lighting, which was brighter than natural daylight. Only one station on the first line ("Palace of Soviets," now Kropotkinskaia) was supposed to have been illuminated differently; it was intended to serve as the portal to an unprecedentedly large edifice, and illumination was to have issued from the palace itself. These plans were abandoned along with construction of the Palace of Soviets, but the entire project had a monumental influence on the discourse of the Stalin epoch. When builders attempted to dim the lighting at another, more "profane" station, they elicited Kaganovich's outraged cry, "Give us more realistic lighting—these aren't churches, after all."

But these stations did have a sacred quality, which issued from their structure. As soon as workers and peasants learned to see in these structures the features that separated them from ordinary forms of transportation—the manifestation of "concern" for the people, the contribution of the people's own labor, which signified the identity of the new state and its citizens—the stations underwent a change. Their highly prized stylistic diversity disappeared, melted away. They began to be lit by a single light—the light of victorious socialism. The fantasy of difference cancelled itself out, insisted upon the sameness of its own quasi-religious, transcendental light. For this reason, these structures could not take the form of churches in order to become, as Hegel put it, "the surroundings of a meaning that has already taken shape." For the discourse, they first and foremost represented self-sufficient meaning. If, in the discourse of the metro, the stations attained the status of the ideal, it was because they realized the unrealizable—the complete immanence of power in the people and of the people in power. Naturally the metro as a construction and an architectural project was far from being as archaic, "disinterested," or symbolic as were the orthodox speech practices surrounding it. The infinitude of intentions bound up in the metro finds its fullest expression less in the stations than in the discourse of the builders and the entire apparatus surrounding it, including journalists and writers. Indeed, the texts written by the builders give the impression of having been carefully edited and even rewritten by professional writers.

While it was under construction, the metro was the subject of much written work, as if the writers were wrapping it in an enormous ideological cocoon, unwilling to allow it to become simply a place, like Western underground transportation systems, where various professional languages came together. The metro discourse encompassed a constant stream of criticism of metros in the capitals of other countries—Paris, Berlin, London, New York—on the grounds that they were merely ordinary systems of transportation, lacking a symbolic dimension. This dimension was sometimes rather naively understood as a high-quality finish, wall facings of precious materials such as marble, porphyry, and granite, and so on. Western metros gave the impression that they had been built carelessly and opened in haste for merely temporary use. References to other modes of transportation that had developed in the West were deliberately omitted, particularly those catering to the individual, such as the automobile. In those countries, the formation of the individual had come about long before through ownership of property, and so significantly less value was assigned to objects of collective property.

In his "Moscow Diary," Walter Benjamin noted that in postrevolutionary Russia, money as a symbolic quantity could not be exchanged for power.[11] Power, in other words, could not be bought. (This theme was later picked up by and endlessly elaborated upon in the literature of the Stalin age, including children's literature. As early as kindergarten children were acquainted with the poetry of Samuil Marshak, in which the American Mister Twister, "the owner of factories, newspapers, steamships," could not buy a house in Leningrad for his daughter, Susie: "I'd gladly buy a house above the Neva / but they don't want to sell Leningrad.") Those who were creating texts about the metro were particularly proud that the only landowner in the city was the Moscow Soviet, which was actually subordinate to the Party; therefore, no private landowner could become a hindrance to the construction project. In the West, these authors indignantly claimed, the construction of a project like the metro might be dependent upon the whim of the owner of "the measliest trash heap," who might not give permission for the project to cross his land.

> Moscow is not a bourgeois city.
>
> In any capitalist city the owner of the tiniest plot of ground could refuse to allow a metro line to be laid beneath his refuse pit:
>
> "This is my trash, and I won't allow anyone to touch my trash heap."
>
> All of Moscow—the squares, the streets, the alleyways, the courtyards—belongs to one entity alone: the Moscow Soviet. Those who own Moscow have allowed the tunnels to be laid underground because that is what is convenient for the builders and the future passengers of the metro.[12]

There was obviously a related issue of expense; because the Moscow metro was being "built by the whole country," the authorities could afford to spend 750,000 rubles solely on the construction of the first line, a sum that would have been unthinkable for any city budget.

Resources such as these fueled the giantism of the metro's discourse. Because the entire country's resources, including human resources, were concentrated solely in the hands of the Party and could be shuffled limitlessly around the country, the project came into being on an incredible, unprecedented scale. From the viewpoint of the giant collective owner, the project overturned the usual scale of bourgeois values. Precious building materials were being used in enormous quantities for the construction of a public structure, whereas in the West such materials were only narrowly available to the individual for his private use. In one station alone, Kievskaya (on the second line), fifteen different sorts of marble were used. The public came to see it as if to a museum.

How could a bourgeois individual counter such imperial giantism? "At home I have an onyx desk set," one foreigner said, upon visiting Kievskaya station. "It's considered quite a rare material, and my acquaintances look at such a beautiful thing with rapture. And here you have forty-six columns made of onyx from top to bottom. It's positively blinding."[13] Not everyone, however, was as blinded as this owner of an onyx desk set. A few people already recognized that the reverse of such collective grandeur was an invisible process of dispossessing the individual of his property rights, for which the symbolic architecture became a type of compensation.

The discourse insisted that it was unaware of any ugly side to collectivism, such as the enormous doses of violence necessary to maintain it, decreed as it was by the natural state of things. This is hardly surprising, considering that the discourse was itself a particularly violent aggregate of speech acts. Within its confines, total mobilization and war became somehow natural and unavoidable. This naturalizing of war was related to the conspiratorial aspect of the metro discourse, which nurtured violence in its bosom in the form of a metaphor, that it might conceal it from itself.

When placed alongside the grandeur of the project, the daily life of its builders was particularly squalid, at least at the start of the project. According to official accounts, many of the builders lived in barracks with a minimum of conveniences, several people to a room. Some workers allegedly went to bed in their clothes, did not wash their hands, kept vegetables in the places assigned to them for linen, and so forth. What was worse, many of them had come for the "easy money" to be made, something that was also condemned.[14] When talk arose of renovating the barracks, it emerged that there was no money for the plan—it was all being swallowed up by the gigantic construction project.

But that was only how things stood at the beginning of the project. Supposedly, the workers' daily lives were dramatically improved with a wave of the magic wand of that Party sorcerer, Kaganovich, "who applied pressure where it was necessary." The barracks were repaired; curtains were hung on the windows.[15] Did the workers' living conditions actually improve? Or did their poverty open their eyes to the greatness of the project and encourage ideological grace to descend upon them? Because of the systematic limitations and secrecy of the metro discourse, we have no way of answering these questions.

No "ordinary transport system," the Moscow metro had not been intended to be a profit-making enterprise, again in contrast to its Western counterparts, the construction of which had significantly raised land and building values. Kaganovich once more set the tone: "Take a look at our metropolitan. What makes it special? If, in other countries, metropolitans are built primarily to turn a profit, then we've built a metro with the sole purpose of making it easier for the workers of our proletarian capital to get around. . . . A socialist state can allow itself to build structures for the public that might cost more but that afford the population more convenience, a pleasant state of mind, and artistic pleasure."[16] This desire to contrast the ordinary metro with the ideal leads the orator astray here; it is common knowledge that the metros in other countries do not make profits, nor are they private enterprises. Instead, they are primarily funded out of city and state coffers, and much less luxuriantly than the Moscow metro was.

May 15, 1935, brought great rejoicing over the opening of this ideal, aesthetically and culturally perfect construction, which represented the manifestation of Stalin's disinterested concern for the common Soviet man. It was as though the depths of the godless transcendental had opened wide:

> Shaft workers and engineers, architects and marble workers, professors and laborers—everyone squeezed each other tightly by the hand. "To victory!" Everyone knew that the Moscow metropolitan had gone beyond the boundaries of the ordinary conception of a technical construction. . . . That was why the faces of the people were alight. . . . A swarthy girl in a rose-colored blouse climbed on a chair and shouted excitedly: "A Komsomol cheer for Comrade Stalin!"[17]

The Paris metro was widely considered to be Moscow's antithesis. Its "architectural landscape" was disgusting, it had no ventilation whatsoever, and its pursuit of the cheapest way was evident in every detail. The central space of the station was devoted to the trains, while passengers were forced to crowd together on narrow side platforms. The ugliest thing about it was the "staging" of the stations. The aboveground riches of the "capital of the world" gave way within the metro to dirty, poorly lit spaces. "The undistinguished, commonplace, neglected quality of every internal surface, without exception, the dim glow of the occasional light, hanging dismally on a dirty cord, lacking the tiniest hint of any sort of decorative finish . . . and most of all, the oppressive, stuffy air—all of this imparts a feeling of despair, weariness, and bitterness to the passenger of the metropolitan,"[18] wrote the head architect of the Moscow metro, S. M. Kravets. Metros in the United States were little better than those of European capitals; although the ventilation was significantly better than in Paris, the rest was much worse, from an aesthetic point of view. The high level of technology in American subways existed side by side with a poverty of external facings: "one gets the impression at every hand of a project badly done and opened to the public before actually being completed."[19]

Moscow, then, was a sort of anti-Paris. If the beauty of the French capital was concentrated on the surface, in palaces, elegant homes, and public buildings, then in Moscow beauty grew from within, from underground. The ideal transportation system, which consisted of underground palaces, represented a prototype for the future, above-ground image of the new capital of the world. Initially fulfilled below ground, the promise of a bright future would spread upward to the surface.[20]

How can the attitudes of Muscovites toward the metro be characterized today? Has the metro lost its symbolic function completely? Has it finally turned into an ordinary transportation system, a means of locomotion for the least prosperous segments of the population?

An examination of publications from recent years leaves a dual impression. On one hand, no other mode of public transportation has been lambasted as severely as the Moscow metro. On the other hand, it has preserved a certain symbolic prestige, and a purely profane attitude toward its structures is suppressed (and this is true not only for stations of the Stalin era).

The themes that emerge from these articles and observations range from the insufficiency of funds for additional construction to the debt, running into the trillions, for stations and tunnels that have already been built. Strikes are continually threatened and do periodically take place. These problems are particularly dramatic against the backdrop of the former grandeur of the structure. Several writers have called the Moscow metro the worst and most unreliable one in the world, a direct inversion of the metro discourse of the thirties, forties, and fifties. But an inversion, as we know, is a way of repeating the same thing, albeit with a negative symbol. The impression remains that the Moscow metro is either something immeasurably greater than an ordinary transportation system or something immeasurably less. There is no middle road. Its discursive past continues to dominate it, intensifying the trauma of the present, and will not allow the problems of this municipal transportation system to be solved in a profoundly profane way.

The proponents of the metro discourse have not died out and are unwilling to sacrifice a single one of their fundamental positions. "All the oldest metros in the world—in London, New York, Chicago, Budapest—are purely engineering infrastructures, which, with the development of technology, have lost all their uniqueness," opines the architect Natalia Dushkina, granddaughter of Aleksei Dushkin, builder of the Kropotkinskaia, Maiakovskaia, and Avtozavodskaia stations. "Even in this sense the Moscow metro is the antipode of the West. In Russia a completely unique type of artistically conceived, underground space was created, for which there is no analogue in the world."[21]

Hidden in this almost exact replica of Kaganovich's speech is a preservationist, nationalist motive: what earlier was declared a service to the proletariat now becomes Russian. Beyond that, it appears that construction of the metro has helped to preserve the memory of demolished buildings above, serving as a kind of underground memorial to them (the Palace of the Soviets station preserves the memory of the Cathedral of Christ the Savior, torn down and then reerected; the Krasnie Vorota station marks the destroyed Krasnie Vorota [Red Gate]; and so forth). If in earlier times the historic novelty of these "palaces for the people" was emphasized, now it is their "conservationist and preservationist role for the Russian people" that receives more emphasis,[22] which fully coincides with the changed spirit of the times. However, two cornerstone theses of the discourse have remained untouched: the Moscow metro is "not purely an engineering infrastructure" but a "unique type of artistically conceived, underground space," and it is the antipode of the West, rejecting its thoroughly technical rationalism (which formerly was called its bourgeois character). Only in recent times has this "wonder" been nationalized, that is, Russified, although it was constructed by the entire USSR.

Compared with today, there were relatively few passengers on the metro in the Stalin era, which allowed them to be turned more easily into a part of the total artistic production. Today the metro carries not only 9 million passengers a day—the most in the world—but also a fleet of trucks, including oversized ones. It is an indirect sign of the relative poverty of Muscovites, who cannot afford to use taxis.

One of the refrains sounded throughout the discourse was, "There are never accidents in the marble city."[23] And although the most serious accident in the history of the Moscow metro occurred in 1982 in the Aviamotornaia station (an escalator broke, killing eight and injuring thirty), almost no public notice was taken. On the other hand, far less serious accidents not involving casualties have since led journalists to predict the metro's complete breakdown in the near future.

The modern metro continues to be compared in various ways to the ideal construction of the Stalin era. That this construction existed only as part of the discourse of that time, its existence made of words, has been forgotten. This means that the discourse of the metro has not died, though it shows some signs of disintegrating. One would think that the metro's status as the most overloaded one in the world, as well as the slow rate of its renovation, would sufficiently explain the accidents that have occurred (smoke, fires, train collisions), but strangely enough, no one is satisfied with that. It is as though the "Stalinist concern for the common man," which was supposedly embodied in this particular form of city transport, has lasted to the present day, and the mere fact of privatization has not been enough for the public to stop thinking of themselves as the children of some higher maternal being (the motherland, the Party, the land). Instead of an Oedipal triangle that structures the unconscious in the context of the nuclear family, we have, as we always have, a maternal structure of infinite sides that creates frustrated, collective bodies. Attempts to "Oedipalize" them have been fruitless thus far.

The secrecy surrounding the metro continues to develop new layers. In 1995, newspapers published a map of Metro-2, as it is called, a system designed for the exclusive use of high government officials and the needs of specialists.[24] As it turned out, it is significantly longer than the "people's" metro, and its construction is proceeding extremely quickly, unlike the "people's" analogue. The idea of service for the people seems even more intensively "duplicated" than the idea of service for the state itself.

In addition, data continue to emerge about the military's use of the metro and the construction of command centers and bomb shelters within the system. Kaganovich, in order to decide the depth at which stations should be built, actually had test tunnels outside Moscow subjected to aerial bombing. Only after they had "withstood" it did the construction of tunnels in Moscow begin.

Thus the metro discourse of the thirties did not include all speech acts surrounding the construction and use of the metro. What was said was a function of what could not be said directly to the enemy, an enemy who lurked within every atom of the collective body. Furthermore, it has become clear in the post-Stalin era that the construction of these underground palaces was not as disinterested and removed from economic considerations as the metro discourse would have us believe. The cheap stations built during the Khrushchev era, often worse than their counterparts in Paris, have needed almost constant repair. Currently, the asphalt that was used in a number of stations is being replaced by longer-lasting granite. In other words, the total work of art into which the discourse of the period made the metro did not exclude banal economic considerations, which have, after all, kept the metro running successfully to this day. This is not all there was to it, of course. Facing the walls with semiprecious stone was a gesture of symbolic giantism, and some enterprising Muscovites have taken advantage of the opportunities presented by renovations to loot what they could. (This was the case in the Maiakovskaia station.) This looting represents the reverse of the potlatch bestowed by the Soviet state on its citizenry.

Few constructions of the twentieth century correspond to what Hegel once called symbolic architecture. The first Moscow metro stations, rather than being the material incarnations of an independently existing conception (as is a house, for example, or a church), represented above all the attempt to convey a new world philosophy. It was as if they inverted the traditional form of the palace as an above-ground dwelling for the rich and attempted to symbolize the unity of workers and peasants.

Why was it deemed necessary, in the early 1930s, in a capital experiencing a chronic shortage of housing, to build so many underground palaces in the shortest possible time? It is hard from either an economic or a symbolic stance to compare what is called a metro in the West with the project given that name by Party decree at its inception in June 1931. As the authors of the thirties maintained, the concept of the Western metro was circumscribed by a narrow circle of functions. It is more fitting to compare the role of the Moscow metro as an instrument of a new imperial power to the role played by marvels such as the Egyptian pyramids.

The construction of the Moscow metro was one of the first projects that necessitated the mobilization of resources—human, mineral, and energy—from the entire USSR. As a direct result of the metro, Moscow was, with increasing frequency, called "the capital of the world" and "the center of all progressive humanity." Naturally, it was the Bolshevik

Party, as represented by Stalin and Kaganovich, that became the chief architect (the metro was in fact named after Kaganovich). Thus the project was considered part of the war being waged by the Bolsheviks against the "old world."

During this era, metro builders, as a type of "new people," were equated with Bolsheviks. By analogy, the machinists, the ticket takers, the cleaning women, even the passengers of this ideal socialist construction became "new people." The metro itself became the template for Moscow's future above ground. This phantasmagorical Moscow (and one must keep in mind that the first and second lines of the metro were built during the Great Terror) was reminiscent of utopias such as Campanella's *City of the Sun.* Ideology ascribed a compensatory function to the space of the metro in order to soften the impact of the terror—only in words, unfortunately—by using phrases such as "a special climate reigns in the marble city" and "in the marble city there are no accidents." Twelve of the thirteen stations of the first line were constructed with island platforms instead of side platforms, and this relatively minor architectural plus was exaggeratedly recast as a veritable Triumph of Man (and man, in the outlook of the time, was always a collective subject) over the Train, that is, as the triumph of the principle of collective organization over the principle of technical accomplishment, even if perfect. The accomplishments of technology served only to underscore technology's secondary status, its lack of autonomy, and its difference from the Western context, in which man had become an appendage of the machine.

NOTES

1. G. W. F. Hegel, *Aesthetics,* 2 vols., trans. T. M. Knox (Oxford: Clarendon Press, 1975), 2: 636.

2. Ibid., 2: 637.

3. S. Manuil'skaia, ed., *Piat' let moskovskogo metro* (Moscow: Gosudarstvennoe transportnoe zheleznodorozhnoe izdatelstvo, 1940), 3.

4. Ibid., 4.

5. See M. Yegorov, "Kak my stroili metro," *Nezavisimaia gazeta,* 13 May 1995.

6. *Kak my stroili metro* (Moscow: Izdatel'stvo "Istorii fabrik i zavodov," 1935), 233.

7. Manuil'skaia, *Piat' let moskovskogo metro,* 9.

8. M. Cherviakov, ed., *Gotov! Rasskazy i stikhi o metro* (Moscow: Izdatel'stvo detskoi literatury, 1935).

9. Ibid., 106–8.

10. Hegel, *Aesthetics,* 2: 650.

11. Walter Benjamin, *Moskauer Tagebuch,* ed. Gary Smith (Frankfurt am Main: Suhrkamp, 1980).

12. P. Lopatin, *The Metro* (Moscow: Izdatel'stvo detskoi literatury, 1937), 112.

13. Manuil'skaia, *Piat' let moskovskogo metro*, 43.

14. *Kak my stroili metro*, 77, 160–63.

15. *Kak my stroili metro*, 162–70.

16. Manuil'skaia, *Piat' let moskovskogo metro*, 9.

17. Ibid., 41.

18. Ibid., 54–55.

19. Ibid., 55.

20. This theme was frequently elaborated upon: "And the time is not far off when the passenger coming up the granite staircase of the Moscow underground will find himself in a new city, as well made, comfortable, and spacious as the marble city of the metropolitan. Soon it will be as pleasant in Moscow as in the metro beneath Moscow" (ibid., 158).

21. D. Popov, "Samoe prekrasnoe podzemel'e mira," *Moskovskaya pravda*, 18 April 1995.

22. Ibid.

23. Manuil'skaia, *Piat' let moskovskogo metro*, 139.

24. D. Baranets, "Metropoliten spetsial'nogo naznacheniia," *Moskovskie novosti*, 17 December 1995; D. Semenov, "Metro-2: Transport neobshchego pol'zovaniia," *Moskovskaia pravda*, 23 February 1995.

12

Russo-Soviet Topoi

MIKHAIL EPSTEIN
Translated by Jeffrey Karlsen

In attempting to apply the Bakhtinian concept of the chronotope to Soviet civilization, one discovers a curious pattern: *chronos* is consistently displaced and swallowed up by *topos*. Chronos tends toward zero, toward the suddenness of miracle, toward the instantaneousness of revolutionary or eschatological transformation. Topos, correspondingly, tends toward infinity, striving to encompass an enormous land mass and even the earth itself.

This is, to a certain extent, a long-standing Russian tradition. The very history of this nation, as V. O. Kluchevsky wrote, has been one of the continuous colonization of new lands, of the conquest of space on all four sides of the earth and then—as Nikolai Fedorov insisted, referring to the exposure and meteorological capacity, or "skyness," of the Russian plain—in the direction of the cosmos. The very history of Russia is the otherness of its geography; historical periods are marked not by purely temporal changes but rather by dislocations and expansions in space:

> The periods of our history represent the successive stages traversed by our people during that people's occupation and development of such country as it acquired up to the time when natural growth *plus* assimilation of non-Russians brought it about that the Russian population not only overspread the whole plain but passed beyond its boundaries. Also, the periods represent, in sequence, the series of halts or rests which . . . [interrupted] for a time the Russian population's movement over the plain.[1]

This spatial orientation also shapes the eschatological tendency in Russian consciousness, a strange mixture of geography and eschatology that leads toward the topoi of an otherworldly realm. That which resides outside of and above time is itself assimilated as a new region, as an "other" continent (supplementing Europe and Asia) that Russian eschatological consciousness wants to annex to the imperial domain—so that world history might gradually begin to provide glimpses of other, more lofty lands and provinces. Eschatology is the geography of new land and new sky to which the nation, on the basis of its experience and previous territorial conquests, would have the right to migrate.

Because Russia had become accustomed to solving its historical problems geographically, it came to occupy an area so large that finding its place in time became somewhat difficult. Over the last three centuries, Russia fervently strove to enter history, but merely in order to overcome it, to outstrip instantaneously the Western nations, which were proceeding steadily along their historical paths, with the result that Russia would end up on the "other side of history," in the realm of the frozen moment and boundless space. Amid nations conventionally categorized as either historical or ahistorical, Russia chose a special "suprahistorical" path: even as it enters history, it is already preparing its exit.

Time in Russia is displaced by physical and metaphysical space—this is the Archimedean law of the immersion of a large geographical body in history. The vaster Russia became, the more slowly historical time flowed within it; conversely, as it shrank in space, it accelerated in time. Burdened by its new space, Russia would lapse into historical prostration, as it did following its two victorious European campaigns, in 1812 and 1945. Conversely, following unsuccessful wars—the Crimean War, the Russo-Japanese War, World War I—Russia lost portions of its territory and immediately received a stimulus to historical acceleration: reforms and revolution. The failure of the Afghan war exposed the limits of communism's spatial expansion and, having nudged the empire on to internal changes, stimulated its disintegration. In relinquishing its republics and Eastern Europe, Russia, having discarded the unwieldy space of the Soviet Union and the Eastern bloc, became the most dynamic (and perhaps the most volatile) region of the world.

In this chapter I offer some thoughts on the methods of organization of Soviet space. I wrote all of the following sketches in 1982–83 in Moscow, that is, from within the space they describe; they bear the stamp of "intralocality" *(vnutrinakhodimost')*. One of the peculiarities of Soviet space was its topological impermeability, the notion that it could be understood only "from the inside." It was assumed to be impenetrable to those located outside of it. I was able to fulfill this condition—existence within the described space—because I was not allowed to travel outside the USSR until 1986.

Perhaps the chief paradox of Russian-Soviet space, a paradox that in one way or another is examined in all of the following sections, is the striking interrelationship between rarefaction *(razrezheniia)* and condensation *(sgushcheniia).* Reigning over the entire area of the nation is a barely assimilated emptiness, whereas in the settled regions, density attains an improbable concentration, typified by that Bolshevik innovation, the concentration camp. Congestion, density, the overcrowding of communal apartments and second-class train cars, jam-packed public transportation, people jostling each other in line, bags overflowing with groceries, objects piled up in warehouses, even the communist idea of the maximum collectivization of property and of the way of life—all this can be seen as the nation's response to the disproportionate superiority and emptiness of the surrounding space.

Spaciousness and Crowding

The German writer Ernst Jünger, who visited Russia with divisions of Hitler's army, noted: "Just as the earth contains nations filled with wonders, so does it hold a nation that has contrived to avoid even the smallest wonder: Russia." He was unjust; Russia is perhaps not as wondrous as India or Italy, but it has one wonder that is worth all the rest, that incorporates *(vmeshchaet)* them into itself. This wonder is space, capacity *(vmestimost')* in its pure form. It is precisely the absence of smaller, more particular wonders within this space that allowed the wondrous to extend to the point of coinciding with the boundaries of space itself, which is in its true nature boundless.

Many inspired lines and exalted images are dedicated to this main wonder. "What does this boundless space *[neob"iatnyi prostor]* presage?" wrote Gogol. "Will a doughty champion or *bogatyr'* spring up *[rodit'sia]* here, where there is room for him to spread himself and stride about?"[2] Answering and repeating the Russian prophet nearly word for word, a Soviet song sings of the powerful master of the boundless expanse:

O, my homeland is a spacious country:
Streams and fields and forests full and fair. . . .

You can't see the end to all our fields,
Or recall the names of all the towns you've heard. . . .

Man can walk and feel that he's the owner
Of his own unbounded motherland *[neob"iatnaia rodina]*.[3]

This wonder, however, consists not only in spaciousness per se but also in the fact that people within it lead their lives, strange as it may seem, in incredibly close conditions. It is well known that the Soviet norm for per capita living space is five square meters, a figure that was considered "sanitary," sufficient for comfort and health. It would be improper to assume any particular malice here; such a modest living norm is by no means a historical peculiarity of the Soviet period but rather a long-standing, age-old predisposition of the inhabitants of the great plain. People lived thus in Russian villages in the nineteenth century and even in the epoch of Kievan Rus'. Peasants huddled together in their one-room huts, sleeping back-to-back: husband, wife, elders, children, maybe even a heifer and a piglet. The surrounding space is boundless: go ahead, build yourself a forty-room house—material is cheap, the forest is nearby. Yet people stubbornly press closer to each other, as if they are afraid of getting lost in the boundless expanse.

In China, with its giant population, and in Japan, with its small territory, closeness is explainable as a material fact, geographically and demographically conditioned. Closeness in Russia is a metaphysical fact, standing in direct contradiction to the nation's physical properties. Russian closeness is born of a desperate, heroic resistance to an equally Russian spaciousness.

The void is terrifying. Nature, the proverb notwithstanding, does not abhor a vacuum, but humans do. In Russia, we all seem to suffer from a love-hate complex toward space. What is that celebrated "fast driving" that "what Russian does not love"?[4] Is it a flight into space or *from* space? It is both. Having rushed into the void, people try as quickly as possible to hurl themselves out of its invisible surroundings, to prevail, to reach a firm boundary, a crowded refuge. This is why they gather furious *(beshenaia)*, truly furious speed, as if being chased by demons *(besy)*.

A Pushkin poem of the same name ("Besy") depicts not an abstract, fantastic diabolism *(besovstvo)* but the diabolism of a boundless plain, one that moreover has been blanketed by a blizzard, thus having been leveled in both length and height. Here the very same plain arises upright: sky merges with earth in an unbroken, indistinguishable, smooth surface. Diabolism is the game played with humans by this boundless *(bes-predel'noe)*, homeless *(bes-priiutnoe)*, aimless *(bes-predmetnoe)* space, that is, by all these innumerable negations, "demons" in the form of the spirits of emptiness and futility, that circulate through the great plain.[5]

> Terrifying, inexorably terrifying it is
> Within the unknown plains! . . .
> A demon is leading us to the field,
> One can see him whirling on the sides. . . .
> There he flared up
> And vanished in the empty gloom. . . .
> Swarm after swarm of demons rush past
> At a boundless height,
> Their plaintive screeching and howling
> Rending my heart.[6]

Pushkin's poem goes beyond mysticism; it is a grammar of diabolism that, through its numerous negative prefixes and particles—"un-" *(bes)*, "not" *(ne)*, "no" *(net)*—disembodies the entire substance of objects and actions. "In-visible the moon," "in-exorably terrifying," "within the unknown plains," "I have no strength," "the trail is not visible," "an unimagined verst," "we have not the strength to go further," "un-ending, form-less," "at a bound-less height." Perhaps the essence of space qua pure capacity is itself diabolism: it is nowhere, and it is everywhere; it just as easily comes apart as seals itself together; it is not segmented by material boundaries; it cannot be contained in any concrete place or volume; rather, it itself always contains. It is bare totality, encompassing all, itself remaining unencompassed.

Virgin field, unknown plain, empty gloom, boundless heights . . . Such an expanse is the void, total Nothingness, the proximity of which is unbearable. Like a whirlwind within a blizzard, the troika chased by demons has reached some way-station or inn, and the traveler has blissfully taken refuge in this jumble of exhalations and heap of bodies, feeling like the prodigal son returned to the bosom of his mother, in a crowded peasant hut, with his half-brothers and fellow lodgers.

Especially on the Volga, in the steppe region, we sense that desperate expanse that surges in waves into forested central and northern Rus'—the expanse that bore the Razins, the Pugachevs, the Chernyshevskys, the Lenins, all those émigrés from Saratov, Astrakhan,

Simbirsk, that whole mobile army, chased by demons, which Nothingness pursued and before which Nothingness gaped. And where did this furious chase lead? Into the peasant commune, of course, and the smoky peasant hut, the closeness of the Party cell, the collective farm, and, in the most compressed version, into the Stolypin car, into a couchette meant for four people but now *wondrously* holding thirty. In order, using this closeness—one cannot turn around or breathe freely—to rush back through the powerful and free Volga and Siberian expanses. Here, in this rarefied periphery, the art of the greatest concentration was achieved: that of the labor camp, which crammed bodies into plank beds and graves.

Is it not this very combination of spaciousness and closeness—perhaps in less vivid contrast than that of the steppe versus the Stolypin car, but all the same evoking aching feet and chafing sides—that we find in our contemporary cities? How spacious Soviet streets and squares are, sprawling out to encompass a Cossack nomad encampment and a dashing wild whistle, the wanderer's doleful thoughts about his long path and his ever-retreating destination—nowhere else in the entire world are there such intra-urban voids! And how people press close on public transportation and in their living quarters, pressing in until bodies double up and hearts break, to the point of sweet agitation and mortal languor.

Did this "commonism" *(obshchevizm)* come to Russia from Europe, where it remained a pathetic specter? Or did it originate in Russia's own diffused spaces, in the demons that inhabit the rushing plain, herding us into crowded social cells, tightly knit collectives, into the heated breathing of communal apartments and dormitories? This is the true polarity of a national soul that seeks deliverance from the greatest geographical void on the entire earth—in the greatest social conglutination in all world history.

The Journey in Boundless Longing

Boredom, *khandra,* longing . . . these depressive conditions can seize the spiritual life of whole epochs or nations, and then—how are they resolved? By wars? Revolutions? Self-annihilation? In any case, here lies a point of enormous interest not only for psychologists but also for sociologists and historians of culture. And Russian literature, like perhaps no other world literature, offers diverse material for the intensive study of these conditions on whatever social and cultural levels they appear.

A malady, the cause of which
'tis high time were discovered,
similar to the English "spleen"—
in short, the Russian *khandra* . . .[7]

Even these few lines from Pushkin's *Eugene Onegin* reveal a great deal: *khandra*—depression, irritability, yearning—is a specifically national ailment, a problem of ethnic psychopathology.

At the beginning of the nineteenth century, boredom was thought to be an aristocratic illness. A bored visage entered the code of social behavior as a sign of refinement and nobility. Only the plebeian, forever in need, would have a visage inflamed by greedy and unconcealed interest. The satiated man, master of everything and acquainted with all, could not help but be bored. Such was the origin of spleen, the illness of English aristocrats, introduced into poetic fashion by Byron in the image of Childe Harold.

But can one say that it was simply this burden of satiety that crashed down upon Onegin, that all his agitation was the result of a superabundance of leisurely days not filled up by need and labor, and that if he had mingled with the people, working in his native fields, as Dostoevsky conjectured, the desired cure would have taken? Onegin is not Childe Harold; his longing is of another kind, not subtly arrogant. He is afflicted with a different disease, incomparably broader than his class affiliation.

Khandra, in distinction to spleen *(splin),* is not an ailment of satiety. Spleen afflicts aristocrats, whereas *khandra* penetrates deeply into the soul of the whole Russian people, acquiring there another, more potent name: longing *(toska)* or woe *(kruchina).* "Something kindred can be heard in the coachman's drawn-out songs: now bold revelry, now heartfelt longing."[8] The feeling of longing ties the coachman to the nobleman, makes them kin. "From the coachman to the poet, we all sing drearily."[9]

The same motif of longing, born of the road, is later extended by Gogol onto the entire breadth of Russia, whom he addresses in the lyrical ending of *Dead Souls:*

> Everything about you is open, level and desertlike; your lowly towns are like dots, marks imperceptibly stuck upon your plains; there is nothing to captivate or charm the eye. But what then is that unattainable and mysterious force that draws us to you? Why does your

mournful song, which is wafted over your whole plain and expanse, from sea to sea, echo and re-echo without cease in our ears?[10]

The Russian song is mournful *(tosklivaia)*, and this longing *(toska)* is born not of satiety but of the opposite: of some cheerless emptiness of the whole world, whose cities and towns have been brushed away like specks of dust in the wind. Onegin's *khandra*, related on one hand to aristocratic spleen, reveals on the other a proximity to an eternal national longing. What in the novel's first chapter is called *khandra* is the anticipation of another, more all-encompassing feeling. Later, when Onegin leaves St. Petersburg, the European-style, languid and refined city of boredom, and sets off for the countryside, and then for his travels around Europe, this feeling is from time to time called by its real name: *Toska!* "I'm young, life is robust in me, / what have I to expect? Ennui *[toska]*, ennui!"[11]

And as a lyrical commentary to the hero's experiences, the sympathetic voice of the author: the poem "My ruddy-cheeked critic, potbellied scoffer . . .,"[12] written in Boldino at that time, in the fall of 1830, when Pushkin was finishing *Eugene Onegin*. This mournful voice comes not from splendid high-society drawing rooms but from a native rural backwater, as an expression of the nature of the flat plain and the national soul that has become accustomed to it: "Just see if you can cope with the accursed *khandra*. Look what a view you have here: a squalid row of little huts, behind them black earth, the gentle slope of the plain . . . What's wrong, my friend? Now you're not kidding, you're seized with longing—aha!" Longing is the infinite length of space, unfolding from itself and into itself, interrupted by nothing, devoid of qualities, flat and monotonous as the plain. "Squalid row . . . gentle slope." This is an emaciated space, filled by nothing; in fact, the word "longing" *(toska)* has the same root as "emaciated" *(toshchii)*. What is emaciated is physically empty, and longing is a spiritual emptiness. Longing: an emaciated landscape of the soul.

In the Soviet epoch, all ideological power and leadership were conferred upon the ruddy-cheeked critic, who, pointing to the mines of inexhaustible optimism in the hearts of the people, demanded a "little ditty to amuse us for a bit," so that the cheerful melodies would flow from the native pastures and grain fields. He saw the dust of boredom in the eyes of an alien "aristocratic" class and did not notice the heavy sheets of longing in the eyes of his cherished "toiling masses." He repeatedly insisted: boredom comes from satiety; the people are cheerful. But no writer was more of the people and more antiaristocratic than Andrei Platonov, and his characters are perpetually in need—they have barely ripened from bodily vegetation into a consciousness of the world. They are not cheerful; longing is their primary and all-encompassing emotion. All surrounding nature is plunged into some kind of muteness, a curse of bottomless, indifferent boredom. "The air was empty, the motionless trees were carefully hoarding the heat in their leaves, and the dust lay dully on the deserted road—such was the situation in nature."[13]

In Platonov's world, nature exceeds in its capacity everything with which man could possibly fill it; it is eternally alienated from him by the foreignness of its retreating horizon on the never-ending plain. All life in these expanses senses itself to be an idle and unredeemed trifle, the birth of which is not justified by the greatness that surrounds it. "The dog's bored. It's like me—it lives only because it was born."[14] Man, like any other creature, has nothing except his own body, born into the endless expanse, whence "the melancholy in every living breath."[15] What purpose could this petty, mournful swarming serve, when the expanse desires only itself—its perpetual expansion into ever newer lands?

In Dvanov, Kopenkin, Voshchev, Chiklin, in all these Platonovian characters we see the origin of a longing more profound than that of Onegin or Pechorin—a longing not mediated culturally, not busying itself with books, dances, love affairs, amusements. "In front of Zakhar Pavlovich stretched the unprotected lonely life of people who live naked, without the least possibility of deceiving themselves by believing in machines"[16]—or by yielding to any other sort of deceit or cultural-technological temptation. They are emaciated both corporeally and mentally; they are closer to nature; they are not sheltered from the void by a layer of protective fat, of satiating prosperity. The emaciated *(toshchie)* long *(toskuiut)* more strongly; "vainness" *(tshcheta)*, too, is formed from the same old Slavic root meaning "emptiness."[17] The more emaciated the people, and the more deserted the nation around them, the longer the longing—that feeling of vainness and abandonment with which they encompass nonbeing—that stretches between them. More deeply than in the traditional, noble, "superfluous" men, features of a kind of metaphysical superfluity are glimpsed in Platonov's "emaciated" characters. The former are superfluous socially: they do nothing, they do not participate in common life. Dvanov, Voshchev, and the others do act and participate in social life, but this does not arrest the emptiness; it continues to grow beneath their indefatigable hands, just as if it were issuing from a hollow core. And not only while they are cleansing the earth of enemies, but also when they are engaged in peacetime production. "A smell of dead grass and the dampness of recently dug earth hung over the area that had been cleared, making the general sorrow of life and the feeling of the hopelessness of it all *[toska tshchetnosti]* still more palpable."[18]

The foundation pit being dug in the eponymous novel, Platonov's *The Foundation Pit,* is symbolic; as the earth is dug out, the emptiness of the beloved motherland is deepened further. This foundation pit, in which people seem to be planning to build a joyous house, common to all, gradually grows—through heroic, selfless efforts—to such a volume that it can no longer be filled by any structure, and all becomes clear: this is a mass grave. It is not for nothing that the caskets for the dying village are stored in the foundation pit; once the village has been allotted its graves, those villagers still remaining will arrive, having been recruited to the city to dig the foundation pit further and die in it—a ready-made burial refuge.

Voshchev senses that the people are digging toward a kind of secret truth that awaits them behind every successive layer of earth, and that in order to reach it, they will need to dig straight through the entire earth, to supplement the horizontally sprawling motherland with the void of the vertically rent aperture, to spread that void throughout all dimensions, so that they might convince themselves: there is no boundary, up ahead the infinite black hole of the cosmos awaits, and this is also home. "The collective farm had followed him [Chiklin], and they too were digging flat out; the poor and middle peasants were all working with a furious zeal for life, as though they were seeking eternal salvation in the abyss of the foundation pit."[19] And this prolonged disemboweling, as every unearthed layer becomes not the foundation, construction on which is now long overdue, but simply an emptiness that has sprung up, been drawn back, and conveniently stored away, arouses in Voshchev a longing that cannot be compared to Onegin's. For "superfluous" men this longing resided outside, in the social world: there was nowhere to put oneself, nothing with which to occupy oneself. In the busy, the laboring, the emaciated, it resides within, flowing out in unceasing, voiding exertion.

Fair enough; but there is more than longing in the national heart. What about wild abandon? *Privol'e* (free space), *razdol'e* (expanse), *razgul'e* (merrymaking, revelry): unique Russian words that have no precise equivalents in other languages. Do they not, however, contain the same void, at times perceived as maniacal and emancipatory, seeking to be filled?

> What does this boundless space presage? Is it here, from you, that some illimitable thought will be born because you are boundless yourself? Will a doughty champion or *bogatyr'* spring up here, where there is room for him to spread himself and stride about? Threateningly that mighty expanse enfolds me, reflecting itself with terrifying force in the depths of my soul.[20]

Thus in Gogol, too, within the course of several lines, longing turns into heroism *(bogatyrstvo)*, just as in Pushkin, revelry turns to longing. They roll, it is frightening to say, from the empty to the vacant, from vast expanse to wasteland—across the entire range of that Russian thought full of longing and pride.

It is astonishing that such a subtle connoisseur of all things Russian as the academician Dmitry Likhachev failed to detect this interrelationship of longing and the open expanse, instead posing them as a simple antithesis: "*Volia-vol'naia* means the freedom that is joined with the expanse, with the totally unobstructed expanse. The concept of longing, on the contrary, is joined with the concept of closeness, the deprivation of space to man."[21] Of course there is also a longing connected with closeness, bondage, and imprisonment, but this is more the torment of unfreedom and slavery common to all humanity. That peculiarly Russian longing that drifts along the roads and is familiar to all, from the coachman to the first poet, is the child not of closeness but precisely of freedom, of totally unobstructed space. This is the longing not of the prisoner but of the wanderer.

The very limitlessness of this world engenders an aching void in the heart and, along with it, a terrifying storehouse of sweeping energy. When they are combined—daring and longing, the void seeking expansion and the void unsuccessful in its desire to be filled—heroic deeds result. The longing, however, is not only not calmed by these deeds—it expands in the heart. For every step of such a *bogatyr'* is "a journey in boundless longing" (in the words of Aleksandr Blok) and pushes back farther and farther the banks of this longing. Nearly every exploit of this sweeping boldness consists in pushing back the "inhibiting" *(stesniaiushchie)* boundaries; the goal is not to fill them in but to replenish their broadening emptiness, from which no one, least of all those same *bogatyr's*, can be saved. "Embraced by a powerful longing, I roam on a white horse . . ."[22] The freer the horse's flight, the more powerful the horseman's longing. In the excesses of his daring, in the destruction of all boundaries and borders, the enchanted wanderer himself prepares a place for his own future unappeasable longing. "For miles and miles the horizon stretched without a break: grass everywhere, white and tufted, waving like a silver sea and scenting the air on the breeze. . . . there was no end to the steppe, just as there's no end to life's sorrows, and as there was no bottom to my heartache *[toska]*."[23]

Speed is the only thing that gives the soul consolation in the face of these retreating boundaries. Speed is offered to the soul as its last chance for incarnation, for catching up with its retreating border, for reaching the desired limit, where it would be able to stop and define itself, which is its purpose in this world. "What Russian does not love fast driving?" "The versts and steep slopes flash by, turn—stop!" Blok's "mare of the steppe" is galloping along with Gogol's whirlwinds—"whirlwind-horses." But the void always slips away more quickly than it can be overtaken, and closing itself up behind you, it seems to laugh while the sound of the pursuit subsides and fades into obscurity.

This is also the source of the demonic nature of that femininity which is revealed in the body of Russia as an ever-impelling, soul-stinging expanse, unfillable by any *bogatyr'*. You meet this woman by chance, but you cannot stop her—just rush past. It is a long road: a momentarily fleeting glance from behind a kerchief; the muffled song of the coachman with its prison-yard longing. Thus these three motifs—the expanse, femininity, and longing—are unified in Blok's poem "Russia" (1908).[24] For the wandering hero, the void is an insatiable temptation, the Babylonian whore herself, who spreads her legs at every Russian crossroads:

O, my Rus'! My wife!
Our long journey is painfully clear! . . .
Our journey in boundless longing,
In your longing, O Rus'!

The Provinces

"The provinces" as a concept comes to us from ancient Rome, where it took shape within the framework of imperial consciousness. A province was a foreign land that had once been independent, possessing its own capital; but, conquered and annexed to the empire, it had received the stewardship of a Roman deputy and acquired a political and cultural center outside itself, in a distant city and an alien rule. Provinces are located as if not in themselves; they are foreign not to someone or something else but to themselves, because their own center has been extracted from them and transferred to some other space or time.

When a given epoch struggles as a distant stepping-stone to another, great and self-sufficient one, it becomes possible to speak not just of geographical but also of historical provinciality. These dislocations in provinciality become the object of artistic play in a photomontage series, "Play," created by the conceptual artist Eduard Gorokhovsky in the last years before perestroika.[25] The first photograph in the series, which looks as if it has been pulled out of an old album, shows a dignified couple, a man and a woman. Arms locked, they reflect a world of self-sufficient serenity, comfort, familial harmony. But in the ensuing photographs it becomes clear how counterfeit, how pitifully exacting this dignity is. It turns out to have been cast away into the provincial past against the background of a more contemporary environment: microphones, a sports pedestal, an advertisement for Aeroflot. It is surprising, however, that this very environment, contaminated by the finely chiseled faces of antiquity, is also imperceptibly displaced in time; it retreats into the distance, displays its exhaustibility, its lack of topicality, as if, having sunk behind the photograph into the solution of time, it were rapidly beginning to yellow, to warp. On the margins of the photograph, a frayed border is suddenly noticeable. Time develops the photograph in reverse; the image begins to decompose and to fade, in the end returning to the film that originally produced it, in order to undergo a series of disembodying metamorphoses, finally to discover at the end its genuine place, among an infinite series of holes, where the image, just as if it had been laid with land mines on the threshold of the present, reveals its ultimate provinciality: an old-fashioned remoteness and a neglect of art itself (mimesis, imitation). Before our eyes it curls up and rolls on further away. . .

Provinciality thus emerges as the organizational pattern of certain structures that remove their center beyond their own boundaries. This center is located in an unknown space, beyond any visible boundary, and at the same time it is somewhere here, on earth, made of the same substance from which the structure was formed. If the center were in some other world—the realm of pure spirit, or God—then the structure would immediately cease to be provincial, because each of its elements would acquire the potential of unmediated communication with the center, from within its own depths, bypassing everything else. The peculiarity of provinciality is shaped precisely by the fact that it is concentrated on the same horizontal plane as the entire surrounding world, in the same spatio-temporal, malleable and ductile continuum. This is why direct communication with this hidden point is impossible, and one must instead pass through all the intermediate links, in each of which a process of stretching and retreat from the center is occurring in almost the same measure as the process of approach toward it. Each element, however significantly it approaches the center, carries within itself its own provinciality, which surrounds it, whose borders it is impossible to cross, and which undeviatingly moves with it, like the shade of the setting sun.

There exist systems with mobile centers that travel from element to element, so that almost any one of them, while behaving in some sense as a central one, is in another sense peripheral. The provinces are not the same thing as the *periphery,* which always represents something relative, something that is related to the positioning of a given center at a given time. The cultural periphery can simultaneously be the economic center, the religious center can simultaneously be the political periphery, and so forth. Provinces are the fixed, immovable periphery; they correspond to the absolutist qualities of the center. In any structure there are centers and peripheries, but centers and provinces exist only in imperial structures, such as those of ancient China and ancient Rome.

Provinces have a special dimension, their *depth,* which is determined by how distantly and irrevocably the center has been removed beyond the structure's limits. There are structures that are thoroughly provincial, because their core, fundamentally external and foreign, has been consistently removed from every cell. In Russian history, it is not uncommon for even the capital to become provincial, as when a sovereign transferred his throne to a specially created or sparsely populated center. Thus, Ivan the Terrible moved his residence from Moscow to Aleksandrov; Peter the Great went even further, into the north, St. Petersburg; Paul, from St. Petersburg to Gatchina.[26] Russian autocracy is obsessed with the desire to base itself outside its own state, in order to rule that state as if it were provinces, to deprive the centers of self-governance. As a result, even Moscow, and after it St. Petersburg, became provinces in relation to the eternally slippery, transcendental power of the emperor. As soon as the center became populated and merged with the substance of national life, becoming in even the smallest degree self-governing, the governing core would withdraw from it anew and transfer itself without, dramatically provincializing those parts of the world that were now rejected, exfoliated from the capital and the throne.

Russian sovereigns preferred to govern their states not as if they had been inherited, which would have compelled them to observe laws, but as if they had been conquered, which untied their hands and increased their personal power. Having conquered the Tatar kingdom and transformed it into Russian provinces, Ivan the Terrible next conquered Moscow and the whole Russian land as *zemshchina*, symbolizing its foreignness by handing its nominal administration over to the Tatar prince Simeon Bekbulatovich. Russia was continually becoming a province of itself, alienating itself and conquering itself.[27] It offered up even its own sovereigns as something subject to seizure, to be forcibly annexed. It was ruled by deputies, people not born in the regions they ruled, sent there from without, "foreigners," "usurpers." A native of one *guberniia* would rule in another—it had to be another. Moreover, this rule by proxy was standard not only in lands that had been acquired but also in lands that had been Russian from time immemorial, thereby presupposing a kind of provinciality that was no longer Roman or even Chinese but new—a provincialization achieved not through the annexation of external layers but rather one emanating from the deepest core of the culture, engendered by its own intention of development.

At the very core of Russian culture, continually resided a will to isolate and expel its center into a certain opposition to itself, leaving itself ultimately and essentially deeply provincial. Drawn toward and aiming toward the center, longing and envying, it preferred all the same to hold the center outside, and not within itself, not to appropriate the center but to live in painful alienation from it, in a neglected, detached condition.

The same mechanism of extracting cores and forming hollow shells, emasculated provinces, worked with precision in time as well. Thus, Muscovite Rus' became a remote historical province in relation to Petrine Russia, and prerevolutionary, tsarist Russia was provincialized in relation to the postrevolutionary USSR.[28] Within these great epochs, every period also appears as an insignificant, unenlightened backwater as soon as something new, with a quick knockout punch, comes to take its place. But the present, too, lacks its own core—it is but a prologue to the radiant future, a suburb of the future city. Where is it, that central time, in which existence coincides with essence and end?

Provinciality is a special, third condition of the world that can be identified with neither civilization nor barbarism. Barbarism is a force of the periphery, of uncultivated nature, opposing itself to the center and bringing destruction. Civilization is the expertise, skillfulness, moderation, and refinement that are propagated from the center and attached to it. The provinces smooth over these extremes of civilization and barbarism and transform them into something average, intermediary, removing the stark potential difference.

In the provinces, all of civilization is coated with the patina of time; it has faded and yellowed as in an old photograph. Everything has begun to rot, warp, buckle, and settle, submitting to the tendency toward disintegration. Even the newest buildings will look unfinished, undifferentiated from the slime of everyday existence. Time here unfolds in the manner of the past, the world looks older than itself, and things are born into the world tired and wrinkled.

But neither does nature here come forth with that primordial power and purity that is preserved only in obscure villages and nature preserves. It is shot through with civilization: oil stains, felled trees, rusted rails. In the most "untamed" places one finds discarded construction materials, lime, wire, heaps of dirt where the topsoil has been stripped away. The provinces themselves have neither cities nor villages, only a "dwelling zone," tending at times more toward an urban structure, at times toward a rural one, but in principle indeterminate. Civilization here appears to have "sprouted through," and nature to have been "broken up": one necessarily bears an injury inflicted by the other. Civilization hangs with all its weight on nature, sticks to it now on one side, now on the other, and, deprived of its own internal support, keeps it from blossoming or standing up straight. Nothing is complete in itself; things are summoned to give aid to or cause injury in the adjoining sphere.

Self-alienation is the structural principle of the provinces. It is a mechanism of transference: the nucleus is extracted from every cell, as a result of which the cell gets rumpled, it settles. This mechanism acts psychologically as well. A feeling of inadequacy and deprivation forces one to reach out somewhere, to suspect something, to be weighed down by one's incomplete presence and drawn toward what every time turns out to be not here, not in its place, but over to the side, where, of course, there is nothing important either. But for all that, provinciality has its sweetness as well, a languor—an absence of tension, a suspension in a kind of half-dream, where only the debris of former things are met, where souls wander, not having managed to attach themselves to any space or time. The provinces are a world that has been shaken violently, so that everything in it has become rearranged, a test tube of the future social and cultural homogeneity.

The current generation in Soviet art turns more and more consciously to this theme, which is difficult to define and differentiate—to this unbroken cellular tissue made of half civilization, half barbarism. Earlier, in the 1960s and 1970s, we had "urban" and "village" writers. Now that distinction is disappearing as both the city and the country retreat before the much more powerful and unifying reality of The Provinces. Almost all sensitive writers are becoming "provincials," that is, they write both the city and the country as the provinces: Vladimir Makanin, Anatoly Kurchatkin, Aleksandr Eremenko, Oleg Khlebnikov. The last has a poem of two lines, titled "The Holiday":

> It smells of perfume and naphthalene.
> A gangly boy runs with a mandarin.[29]

Here we have it, the exact formula of the provinces. The smell of naphthalene wafts out from the closet onto the street and mingles with perfume: half disinfectant, half perfumery. In all of it there is a nagging incongruity: the holiday is embodied in a gangly boy who runs holding an orange as if it were a furled flag he has pulled out of a gift bag. High semantics are not played out grotesquely within the low; rather, the two merge to the point of indistinguishability in a pitiful and moving scene.

Today Soviet literature continues to see its moral duty and acuteness in battling against philistinism *(meshchanstvo)*—but where is it, this philistinism and parochialism *(obyvatel'stvo),* familiar, concentrated, guarding its place and customs? Provinciality is antiparochial: nothing has its place, everything is bent, fastened to something else; it is impossible to shut oneself up inside something or to lean against something for support. The philistine, with his tenacious psychology of rendering his small cubbyhole habitable, here simply has nothing to grab onto: the provinces are at a radical remove from "bourgeois existence." Those who live in these places could more precisely be called not the local inhabitants *(obyvateli)* but the local *unhabitants (nebyvateli),* the existence of whom is witnessed by nothing save yellowed photographs in gray albums.

Gorokhovsky's "Play" also reveals this antiphilistine, spectral essence of the provinces. Attaching photographs from a family album to an Aeroflot ad is the same thing as taking a dress out of mothballs and scenting it with an abstract perfume. In the final account, all the signs of the twentieth century that rudely encroach upon the serenity of the old couple display the same level of archiveness, yellowedness—both the microphones and the airport. Objects torn from their historical context point to a rupture that distinguishes the provincial subject both from the past century and from the present, from any proper fixation in time. He or she is but a nominal successor and a nominal contemporary, conventionally plotted on the coordinates of time, in order to remove any question of genuineness.

The meaning of provincial existence, lost in these eclectic combinations, becomes an object of secret, esoteric knowledge. From this empirical material someone, having passed through all the levels of initiation, will someday construct a general theory of specters.

The Line

One is compelled to stand in lines so often that a certain mythologeme forms involuntarily in one's consciousness: a dragon devouring its own tail. The line, or the queue, is indeed tail-like, as if a bestial relic had suddenly sprung up in human society.

Why were tails gradually eliminated "in man's process of development from apes"? Humans have continually broadened and animated the space anterior to them, and therefore the posterior sensory organ lost its natural necessity. All communication with and sensation of the world began to occur through the face, through wide-open eyes, through open handshakes. In general a person's front side, like that of all living things, is soft, vulnerable, whereas the back is hard, vertebral, virtually encased in armor. The sum of culture consists in part in humans' beginning to bare their vulnerability, bringing the interior to the surface, exposing the tender to another's gaze. All culture issues from the personality *(lichnost')*, from the face *(litso)*, and is oriented forward.

Now consider the line, where people stand single file, resting their gazes on backs. The line is hostile to culture and to the individual because in it people address each other with, and are joined by, their backs: so that this new breed of person, who spends his or her whole life in lines, is compelled to grow a tail as a product of natural necessity. It is very possible that, in the march of protracted historical evolution founded on the line as a social institution, *Homo sapiens* will again grow tails, now on the order not of biological but of social adaptation: in order to feel the near ones who are behind and to touch the ones in front—not to tap a dumb backside in the thirst for communication but rather amicably to tickle a tail.

Let us probe a bit deeper into the line, which merits at least one mental peregrination. After all, standing in it has consumed so many hours, weeks, years!

The line is pure expectation, which is what makes time spent in it stretch out so languorously: it is not filled up by anything, it lies open in all its emptiness. And meanwhile something is happening, by itself, without your participation or will, so that with every minute, without having moved a finger, you get closer to your goal. The man standing in line is similar in his inactivity to Oblomov but at the same time as businesslike as Shtolz,[30] because all the while he is moving somewhere, simultaneously preserving an inert mass of calm. Time stretches out toward nowhere from the common supply of life, and all this is a necessary expenditure, although it is also obviously a useless one. If queues did not exist, it would be necessary to invent them, because it is there that people find escape from the burden of freedom, acquiring a visual, linearly defined meaning for their existence. What might have been the simple, crude physiological act of eating meat or cheese, which the person in line waits to buy, acquires a socially distant but absolutely attainable perspective, one that with every moment and hour becomes more accessible. Distance imperceptibly decreases, magnifying the pleasurable itch of anticipation. Time flows according to the rules of progress, unswervingly nearing a long-awaited goal. The line is a school of patience and a factory of optimism, because for those who stand in it, it necessarily shortens: patience is rewarded again and again.

In this way, we go beyond the crudely animalistic consumption of food: human feelings are cultivated in the course of acquiring food, instinct is socialized, forces and potentials are systematically distributed, the self is conceived of as a member of a collective. Where else is it so easy, without instructors and capital investments, to realize a program of humanization and socialization of natural needs? What else so fully satisfies the psychological need common to more and more people: to be occupied in an activity that allows one to do nothing but at the same time to be extremely busy? Standing in line, it is easy to make peace with the world and with oneself.

Although a line is a hindrance, obstructing the path to a goal, all the same one values one's place in it highly. It is as if people want to get closer, to destroy the structure and fall on the booty as a crowd, but something acts as a restraint. Everybody is gripped by two feelings at once: superiority over those who are behind and envy of those who are in front. The first impulse gradually wins out: protecting one's position from those nudging from behind is better than grabbing from those standing ahead. Why? The line is moving. The anterior part, and consequently envy, is melting away, while the tail end, and correspondingly superiority, is growing; one's place is becoming increasingly valuable. We might say that society, living in the future to a greater degree than in the present, is modeled on the line.

It is also important that in a line, everyone occupies not only a physical but also a kind of professional position. Everyone is at his post, in this way solving the problem of temporary unemployment in the time spent away from work. Everyone is not only occupying his place but also guarding it, patrolling the Polovtsian steppe, from which at any time audacious invaders might gallop out or ingratiating scouts creep forward. The order of the line as a whole depends upon the vigilance of each person, for a chain broken in one link can no longer unite people and lead to a single goal. Standing in line is also surveillance of the line, a work of monitoring and checking, which, as we know, guarantees the dictatorship of the majority over the minority.

In the same way, the moral principle "one for all and all for one" is realized, acquiring a spatial clarity: "one behind all and all behind one," because each person, by letting no one in front of him, lets no one cut in anywhere in the line. Personal interest guards the social interest.

Another theoretical principle, "equality without egalitarianism," is also realized. Access to the line is open to all, but, having gotten in, each person acquires an ordinal number that distinguishes him or her from all the others. The queue is a social mathematician's dream, the incarnation of the Pythagorean's utopia of a kingdom of embodied numbers, where each person is distinguished from the other only by an ordinal number. Here any entity may actually be conveyed by a number, and its entire peculiarity is solely in the quantitative rank, so that it is precisely the numerical model that engenders the order of the social universe.[31] If the crowd is chaos, then the queue is the cosmos, arranged according to the laws of numerical harmony. But in distinction to the classical cosmos, the modern cosmos is thrust into history, and the number acquires the characteristic of self-propulsion. The one in line continuously changes his or her number; the line is a natural series in movement, from hundreds to tens and ones and then again in the reverse order. For the one who has left the line, or, more precisely, for the one who has reached the end—what's left to do? Go home, eat, lie down, rest, and, having exhausted the goods one stood in line for, get once again into the line, which has not ended but has only been conventionally interrupted for the night.

This is why the line, like a wise serpent-temptress, constantly devours its own tail: anterior continuously becomes posterior. The queue presents itself as a straight line only in appearance; in reality it is a circle, the end of which closes with the beginning. He who exits from the front walks around the line and turns up again behind.

The dialectic of existence is infinite in its circular rotation, in its coupling of causes and effects. Infinite also is our queue—the pharaoh's pyramid, where the stones from below are continuously removed in order to build the upper part; where humanity again and again attempts, using numerical finitude, to produce the infiniteness of the natural series. And everyone has already been in all the lines many times, has been inserted into the first million, and the second, and the third—an innocent shuffling of social daydreamers who have been compelled to strive for infinite goals with finite human means and for that reason have sent these goals out for repeated wear.

Perhaps the queue will remain from our times, as have the pyramids from the Egyptians', a worthy monument to the civilization of the natural sequence, units bridging their path to glory and eternity. The queue is that same pyramid, but a "humanistic" one, formed not from stones but from people, and for that reason flowing in time and not frozen in space. The progress is obvious: that was prehistorical time, whereas ours is historical, which is why the pyramids are arranged not in a sandy desert but in the sands of time. The pyramids are made of innumerable grain-minutes, of the clodded days and years that each person has wrenched from his own life and raised, having passed along the steps of all the lines he has stood in, to the next plateau of this ossified heap of moments. In the construction of this pyramid, every slave raises his stone, his hour—and sets it down in order to hoist upon himself the next one, following in the footsteps of all his predecessors. The queue at times appears as a chain of people uninterruptedly transmitting hand-to-hand something invisible to each other: these are the stones of time, being hoisted onto that common place toward which all queues flow together and which one, remembering the Egyptian prototype, can call the desert of time, or absolute zero. The grandeur of the queue, like the grandeur of the pyramid, is reduced to a zero of the base, to the desert of time and space. The pyramid needs precisely the desert, for any other, positive relief of terrain degrades and softens it. Only absolute zero satiates the striving toward numerical grandeur, toward the consecutive inclusion of all and the repeated utilization of everyone.

I recognize you, Rozanov's last love, eternal Egypt, "well-proportioned, wise, complex,"[32] and how this treacherously loyal writer would have fallen in love with his fatherland anew had he lived to see the pyramids made from the stones scattered in his "apocalyptic" time. For from the seething, demonstrating crowds that flooded the Russian streets in the period between the two revolutions, a new, severely geometric style was crystallized—exactly on the model of the lines that had been stood in. And the highest, most monumental of these pyramids is, with good reason, in the main burial vault, toward which the main queue of the country leads. The mausoleum is the direct descendant of two monumental structures: the tomb at its beginning and the line in the continuation. The Soviet line as superstructure of the Egyptian pyramid.

Thus do I envision a third volume of Rozanov's *Fallen Leaves.* There, instead of the usual hurried notes—"while engaged in numismatics," "selecting cigars," "in the water closet"—would everywhere be one thing only: "in line." And then—unbroken white pages, so that one could leaf through it without reading, ending with an identical postscript: "in line." And under it the date, grandiose in the new fashion: the next-in-line, just-like-the-last millennium of the next-in-line just-like-the-last era *(ocherednoe tysiacheletie ocherednoi ery).*

Urban Nomadism

Usually the line ends in shopping, which leads to a shift in spatial orientation. Horizontal movement gives way to gravitational verticals, to being burdened by booty. The bag *(sumka)* is the most important appurtenance of Soviet urban nomadism. We walk loaded down by our purchases, by groceries, by all that booty which, having procured by hunters' ruses, we then lug home. Our hands are outstretched, at attention, because they are weighed down by edible cargo. Look at the evening throng in the city—how high and aloof the faces and shoulders float by. Hands, which usually shroud the human figure in a haze of gestures, are here eternally lowered and drawn out, like those of porters. They do not gesticulate, signal, or associate—they carry. They are directed not toward the social, horizontal plane of communication but toward the physical, vertical plane of gravitation.

The bag is a sign of our historical destitution and nomadism. In olden times bags were carried by beggars, vagrants, exiles, postmen, soldiers, hunters (according to the Russian lexicographer Vladimir Dal')[33]—that is, people outside the normal way of life. The bag was an appurtenance of social misfits and a few nomadic professions. Now it is general to all strata of society. The spirit of nomadism has spread so widely throughout contemporary life that the bag has appeared in almost everyone's hands. We are all beggars carrying our property with us, hunters wandering through the city in search of rare booty, soldiers making camp in foreign localities (lines in stalls and shops). Humans have become marsupials, bearing on themselves the future contents of their own stomachs.

And after all, how could one overcome the space between store and home if not with the help of the bag full of groceries? We are hardly aware how much our Soviet cities, having extended paths of communication widely but not provided people with private means of conveyance—automobiles—have given rise to a spirit of nomadism, which one would have assumed to be incompatible with the urban environment. Before, workers and domestics, dressed in special clothing, went from store to home with large sacks or carried them by horse. Now these bags are brought out more often (it's impossible to get a month-long supply of food)—yet one buys just as much, and almost every day, and not in soiled aprons but in the same official clothes one wears to the office and the theater. We are not struck by this unnatural confusion of styles in the women floating past us: a light, fluttering raincoat, a dress with frills and lace, and a bag with a load such as a religious wanderer might take on a distant pilgrimage. Here is a genuine mixture of the European and the Asiatic: the appearance of a fashion plate weighed down by her bags—a regular St. Basil's Cathedral. In general, the function of carrying bags in Russia is largely entrusted to women, perhaps because they are believed to be more accustomed to "carrying" by nature: the inflated, "pregnant" womb of the bag seems to enter into the series of their "natural" duties toward the husband and society.

In these bags circulating through the city, there is something undisguisedly rapacious and crudely materialistic. It is as if one's internal organs have crept out onto the surface and are now being held out with one's own hands. One carries a bag on the street like one's own stomach turned inside out. The internal and external strangely interrupt each other in the appearance of Soviet citizens: here they are, dressed respectably, even excessively muffled and tucked in from all sides against the attacks of frost—and suddenly this wide opening of a womb, with bulges of milk packets and pink flashes of sausage. Compared with Westerners, who dress more freely, Soviets are doubly distinguished: they wrap up excessively what could be exposed and expose excessively what ought to be concealed. Tightly hemmed in in their social coverings and bared in their physiological needs. Unfree in one, unduly relaxed in the other.

The very concept of "the bag" *(sumka, suma)* comes from the packs with which animals used to be loaded (from the German *soum,* which meant "the load of a beast of burden"). These packs and wineskins were fashioned from the capacious skins of slaughtered animals or, most often, from their stomachs. Thus the bag by its origin is also a stomach, but one that no longer devours and digests—instead, it carries that which other stomachs will digest. The origin of the bag corresponds to its destiny. Here is the Soviet citizen's hungry belly, which shoppers are doomed to lug along with them, hurriedly cramming it with the offal they have stumbled upon.

The Warehouse

The warehouse, where all objects are arranged in a particular order, could serve as a symbol and prototype of world harmony. Everything there is quantified, distributed according to categories, reflected in lists—the conceptual hierarchy and classification of things acquires a visual incarnation in space. Nowhere besides the warehouse could there be such a strict correspondence between an object's name, fixed on paper, and its real existence. When things are used—brought in, brought out, set in motion—they cannot be precisely fixed in idea and word. In the warehouse they acquire a sacred immobility, the proof of which is the inventory list, where names, unentangled by any grammatical relationships, stand individually, under numbers, in an immobile vertical order.

Numeral-word-object: the ideal correspondence of Pythagorean-Platonic thought. Just as people, in correspondence with a numerical order, arrange themselves in a queue, so things are ordered in the warehouse using the same numerical means. Motion is inherent in people, immobility in things, but in a certain sense one could say that the line is a mobile image of the warehouse, while the warehouse is the immobile image of the line. Common to both is the organization of all units, human and inanimate, in conformity with a sequential number, for, as the Pythagorean Thilolaeus said, "everything knowable has a number. . . . the nature and the force of the number acts . . . everywhere in all human matters and relations."[34]

Is this not the reason that the warehouse acquired a special, highly symbolic meaning in the Soviet state? Is it accidental that church holdings, having lost their sacred purpose, were converted into warehouses?

What occurred was not the abolition of the holy but, so to speak, its replacement. The warehouse is just as ideal an order in the material world as the church is in the spiritual world. The warehouse is a materialist church, but instead of collecting people who are seeking in prayer an exalted form of the soul, it houses a multitude of objects that have found a precise inventoried form. Both the church and the warehouse are like sealed-off refuges of harmony in a fallen, sinful world that has been plundered and pillaged. To sin, to carry off a soul from God—this is stealing, carrying off an object from the warehouse, from the depository of social property, property as incorruptible and impervious to mercenary interest as the conscience.

One of the leading figures in our Soviet reality is the warehouseman. Everyone ingratiates himself with him—not only petty employees but also bosses and managers. Everyone must feel his own inadequacy before him, must be tormented by his own unclean conscience. For the warehouseman stands on the threshold of the sacred world, separating it from the profane. The managers, in all their administrative bustle, are on this side, while the warehouseman is on the other. He is the tsar and the keeper of the immobile kingdom of objects, beyond the limits of which their harmony can only incur losses, deterioration—in the hands of businesslike and anxious factory managers. Sending an object out of the warehouse is the same thing as casting it down into dark, sinful, inconstant earthly life.

This is why warehouse locks are so strong and warehousemen so severe: they are guarding our happy future. There, eternal abundance and the perfect arrangement of all things await us. And because we all live and work in the name of the future, sacrificing our immediate interests to it, the warehouse rank of things is incomparably greater than their production rank. To store and restock things in a warehouse—do we not see here the highest law of a society that aims at an ideal future? For where, if not in the warehouse, is this future already attained, if for now only in a fenced-off space? This is not yet the fully transformed world, but a happy forerunner, where things have found their own measure and number.

The main things in socialism, as Lenin taught, are accounting *(uchet)* and control *(kontrol')*. "Socialism means keeping account of everything. You will have socialism if you take stock of every piece of iron and cloth."[35] But this imperative—"widespread, general, universal accounting and control"[36]—presupposes the existence of things in the warehouse: only there can they be completely "accounted for" and correspond to their exact description. "Every piece of cloth," taken in the perspective of accounting and control, no longer covers the body, no longer serves as clothing, is no longer subject to everyday wear and tear, instead being preserved under its inventory number. All management becomes the warehousing of inventoried things. And the task is not to get things out of the warehouse, releasing them into a dubious, wasteful enterprise, but to bring them into the warehouse, distributing them in their necessary places, in the fullness of control and rational organization. To the extent that all our life is relocated into the warehouse and is formed according the image and model of the warehouse, our happy future will cross into the present, and the nation, under powerful locks and stern warehousemen, will begin to live a severe and orderly warehoused life.

But the problem is that time forces its way even into the eternally peaceful warehouse. From immobility the stock spoils, rots, rusts. Things that are not renewed by time grow old from time. And that is why the more the warehouse approaches its ideal, the quicker it turns into a dump, into a cemetery *(kladbishche)* of untouched things. Touched by no one and nothing, except time. As soon as the warehouse triumphs in our life, we will find ourselves in a cemetery, and our warehouseman, like a cemetery watchman, will unlock the gates himself—there is no longer anything left to take out, anyone to bring it to, any reason to do it.

The Appropriation of Space

In Russia, the four elements are joined in pairs: air with fire, earth with water. Masculine friendship/feminine friendship, but a familial union between them for some reason fails to take shape.[37]

That air gets on well with fire is attested to by the smoke that freely ambles across the Russian heavens: from fires, radiation, friendly skirmishes, smoking breaks, oil spills, and intimate alcoholic exhalations. As far back as Griboedov, the smoke of the fatherland was called "sweet" and "pleasant."[38] "And you, fiery element, go mad, igniting me"—thus Andrei Bely prophetically addressed the motherland as long ago as 1917 ("To the Motherland"),[39] as if foreseeing Lenin's formula of fiery political magic: "Communism is Soviet power plus the electrification of the whole country."[40] When the Soviet government, in accordance with Lenin's plan, GOELRO,[41] had rapidly united with electricity, the air came to smell even more of smoke, which was moreover bitter and acrid, as if from things and bodies burned alive. The plan for electrification is considered to have been fulfilled by the beginning of the 1930s, as the poet Pavel Antokol'skii, in his collection *Great Distances* (1936), already observed: "The entire country lies, growing beautiful from smoke."[42]

The other romantic couple, this time tenderly girlish, is earth and water, which cling to each other in the curves and sobbing of softened matter, of the permanent and omnipresent quagmire. In Russia, earth always and everywhere strives to take in more water and to dampen into a marsh. Rural streets long ago turned into deep channels connecting seas of universal mud. Urban sidewalks have already sucked in the native land and mixed it thickly with heavenly moisture in a marshy layer that stretches like a new geological period over the entire Russian noosphere.

Smoke and mud are two peculiarities of Russian space that warm and soften it. Of course, basic human needs—breathing and walking—are made much more difficult by smoke and mud. The chest burns, knees ache. Space as a whole, however, becomes as if humanized or, more precisely, corporealized. Air is warmed by smoke, approaching the temperature of breath. Earth softens into mud, approaching the consistency of the body. Everything around becomes odorous, acrid, sticky, damp—just as I am. As are my flesh and my soul.

"Let me, O motherland, into your damp, empty expanse, to sob in your expanse," wrote Bely in his poem "Desperation."[43] Could this be the Russian means of mastering space? To sob, to warm with one's breath, to emit smoke, leave dirty traces, leave footprints, in order to inspire in the empty indifferent boundlessness something kindred to oneself? Damply sloshing, hotly breathing. To wrap oneself in space as in the mother's womb, where gases, fluids, and bubbles are all the steady seething and burbling of the gestating bog.

This is what is meant by the smoky air and the dampened earth—this is the effort people make to alter the substance of an enormous nation when they lack the will to give it distinct, well-compartmentalized form. To build over, to pave such an enormous space is impossible. One can only somehow warm it up and dilute it. To let in mud and smoke. One cannot cultivate it—so let us corporealize it. In order to fall not onto hard earth but onto a muttering, chomping mash. In order to choke not on icy wind but on the stifling exhalations of kindred hangovers and glowing embers. Let water and fire propitiate this hard earth, this enormous, cold expanse.

The volitional intuition of space as wide open and faceless corporeality, as maternal womb or as outhouse, grandiose cosmic piss pot . . . To remove the barriers between oneself and nature, to dissolve in it through all the flows and secretions of human manufacture. What from an ecological point of view we describe as the "pollution" of space is, from a mythological point of view, its softening and warming. The child loves to play in its own slobber and other secretions, loves to stomp through mud, to wade in it, just as if delighting in the maternal pliancy of the inorganic body of the earth. Is this not the nature of that initial mythological impulse of corporealization, of the personification of uncontrollable nature, that has determined all of Russia's ecological disasters and monstrosities?

NOTES

1. V. O. Kluchevsky, *A History of Russia,* trans. C. J. Hogarth (London: J. M. Dent and Sons, 1931), 5: 210.

2. Nikolai Gogol, *Dead Souls,* trans. George Reavey (New York: W. W. Norton, 1985), 239.

3. Vasilii Lebedev-Kumach and Isaak Dunaevskii, "Song of the Motherland," in *Mass Culture in Soviet Russia: Tales, Poems, Songs, Movies, Plays, and Folklore, 1917–1953,* eds. James von Geldern and Richard Stites (Bloomington: Indiana University Press, 1995), 271–72. This song was extremely popular from the 1930s through the 1970s and functioned as an unofficial Soviet anthem.

4. Gogol, *Dead Souls,* 269.

5. In Russian, the noun *bes* (devil) resonates with the negative prefix *bez-* or *bes-* (in-, un-, -less).

6. A. S. Pushkin, "Besy" (1830), *Sobranie sochinenii v desiati tomakh* (Moscow: Khudozhestvennaia literatura, 1974), 2: 227.

7. A. S. Pushkin, *Eugene Onegin,* trans. Vladimir Nabokov (Princeton, N.J.: Princeton University Press, 1975), 112. The Russian *khandra* is of the same Greek origin as the English *hypochondria.*

8. A. S. Pushkin, "Zimniaia doroga" (1826), *Sobranie sochinenii,* 2: 92.

9. A. S. Pushkin, "A Small House in Kolomna," in *Polnoe sobranie sochinenii v desiati tomakh* (Moscow: Akademiia nauk SSSR, 1963), 5: 329.

10. Gogol, *Dead Souls,* 239.

11. Pushkin, *Eugene Onegin,* 327.

12. A. S. Pushkin, "Rumianyi kritik moi . . .," *Sobranie sochinenii,* 2: 240.

13. Andrei Platonov, *The Foundation Pit,* trans. Robert Chandler and Geoffrey Smith (London: Harvill Press, 1996), 1.

14. Ibid., 3.

15. Ibid., 54.

16. Andrei Platonov, *Chevenger* (Moscow: Khudozhestviannia literatura, 1988), 62.

17. See Maks Fasmer, *Etimologicheskii slovar' russkogo iazyka v 4 tt.* (Moscow: Progress, 1987), 4: 90–91; N. M. Shanskii et al., *Kratkii etimologicheskii slovar' russkogo iazyka* (Moscow: Prosveshchenie, 1975), 448.

18. Platonov, *Foundation Pit,* 18.

19. Ibid., 161.

20. Gogol, *Dead Souls,* 239.

21. D. S. Likhachev, "Zametki o russkom," *Zemlia rodnaia* (Moscow: Prosveshchenie, 1983), 51.

22. Aleksandr Blok, "Na pole Kulikovom" (1908), *Sobranie sochinenii v vos'mi tomakh* (Moscow: Khudozhestvennaia literatura, 1960), 3: 249–53.

23. Nikolai Leskov, "The Enchanted Wanderer," *Selected Tales,* trans. David Magarshack (New York: Farrar, Straus and Cudahy, 1969), 112. The same link between expanse and despondency was expressed in more generalizing terms by Kluchevsky, who wrote that the Russian landscape was distinguished by "nonvisibility of human habitation on wide spaces, nonaudibleness of sound anywhere in the vicinity: so that there falls upon the traveler, as he beholds this once more, a sense of oppression, a sense of unshakable inertia and unbreakable somnolescence, a sense of desolation and loneliness, a disposition to meditate without clear or precise thought." Kluchevsky, *History of Russia,* 5: 249.

24. Blok, *Sobranie sochinenii,* 3: 254.

25. Eduard Gorokhovsky (b. 1929): an artist working in painting, graphics, and book illustration. Participant in many Russian and Western exhibitions (Kunsthalle Bern, 1988; Phyllis Kind Gallery, New York, 1989; Museum Moderner Kunst, Vienna, 1989). Artistic orientation: photorealism, hyperrealism, conceptualism, sots-art. Much of his work is done at the juncture of painting and photography.

26. This paragraph and the following ones employ several of the contemporary writer and historian Vladimir Sharov's ideas, which he expounds in the novel *Following in Footsteps: The Chronicle of a Certain Race [Sled v sled: Khronika odnogo roda]* (Moscow: Nash dom-l'Age d'homme, 1996).

27. Cf. Kluchevsky, *History of Russia,* 5: 209: "Russia's history, throughout, is the history of a country undergoing colonization and having the area of that colonization and the extension of its state keep pace with one another."

28. In precisely the same way, from the new positions of "perestroika" the entire preceding Soviet structure appears thoroughly provincial, cast aside from the mag-

isterial path of civilization, and the task is defined: to leave the backwater behind and move into the center of the brotherhood of advanced nations, to raise levels to world standards, and so forth.

29. Oleg Khlebnikov, *Pis'ma prokhozhim* (Moscow: Sovremennik, 1982), 52.

30. Oblomov and Shtolz are heroes of *Oblomov,* a novel by Ivan Goncharov (1859). Their respective names are commonly used in Russia to signify, on one hand, laziness and indulgence in revery and, on the other, businesslike activity and efficiency.

31. In Aristotle's words, "since they [the Pythagoreans] saw . . . that the properties and ratios of the musical scales are based on numbers, and since it seemed clear that all other things have their whole nature modeled upon numbers, and that numbers are the ultimate things in the whole physical universe, they assumed the elements of numbers to be the elements of everything, and the whole universe to be a proportion or number." Aristotle, *The Metaphysics,* trans. Hugh Tredennick (Cambridge, Mass.: Harvard University Press, 1956), 1: 33.

32. V. V. Rozanov, "Bibleiskaia poeziia," *Uedinennoe* (Moscow: Politizdat, 1990), 456.

33. Vladimir Dal', *Tolkovyi slovar' zhivogo velikoruskogo iazyka* (St. Petersburg: M. O. Vol'f, 1882), 2d ed.

34. *Antologiia mirovoi filosofii v 4 tt.* (Moscow: Mysl', 1969), 1: 289.

35. V. I. Lenin, "Speech at a Joint Meeting of the Petrograd Soviet of Workers' and Soldiers' Deputies and Delegates from the Fronts, November 4 (17), 1917," in *Collected Works* (Moscow: Progress Publishers, 1964), 26: 294.

36. Lenin, "How to Organize Competition?" in *Collected Works,* 26: 410.

37. The Russian words for air *(vozdukh)* and fire *(ogon')* are masculine; those for earth *(zemlia)* and water *(voda),* feminine.

38. "Returning home after wandering abroad, we find even the smoke of the fatherland sweet and pleasant"—Chatskii's words in Griboedov's comedy *Woe from Wit* (Gore ot uma), 1822–24.

39. Andrei Belyi, "Rodine," *Stikhotvoreniia i poemy* (Moscow: Sovietskii pisatel', 1966), 381.

40. Lenin, "The Eighth All-Russia Congress of the Soviets, December 22–29, 1920: Report on the Work of the Council of People's Commissars, December 23," *Collected Works,* 31: 516.

41. Developed in 1920 under the initiation and leadership of V. I. Lenin as the State Commission on the Electrification of Russia (GOELRO).

42. Pavel Antokol'skii, *Bol'shie rasstoianiia* (Moscow: Goslitizdat, 1936), 78.

43. A. Belyi, "Otchaian'e," *Stikhotvoreniia i poemy,* 159.

Contributors

Oksana Bulgakowa is a visiting professor in the Slavic Department at Stanford University. Among her numerous books and articles are *Die ungewöhnlichen Abenteuer des Dr. Mabuse im Lande der Bolschewiki* (Berlin, 1995); *FEKS: Fabrik des exzentrischen Schauspielers* (Berlin, 1996); *Sergej Eisenstein: Drei Utopien. Architekturentwürfe zur Filmtheorie* (Berlin, 1996); and *Sergei Eisenstein: A Biography* (Berlin and San Francisco, 2001).

Katerina Clark is a professor of comparative literature and Slavic literature at Yale University. She is the author of *The Soviet Novel: History as Ritual* (Chicago, 1981); *Mikhail Bakhtin* (with Michael Holquist, Cambridge, Mass., 1984); and *Petersburg: Crucible of Cultural Revolution* (Cambridge, Mass., 1995).

Randi Cox is an assistant professor of history at Stephen F. Austin State University in Nacogdoches, Texas, where she teaches courses in Russian history and the history of consumerism. She is currently working on a monograph on Soviet advertising agencies of the 1920s.

Evgeny Dobrenko is a professor of Russian and Slavonic studies at the University of Nottingham. He is the author and editor of numerous books including *The Making of the State Reader: Social and Aesthetic Contexts of the Reception of Soviet Literature* (Stanford, 1997) and *The Making of the State Writer: Social and Aesthetic Origins of Soviet Literary Culture* (Stanford, 2001).

Mikhail Epstein is the Samuel Candler Dobbs Professor of Cultural Theory and Russian Literature at Emory University. He is the author of fifteen books and more than four hundred articles and the recipient of numerous national and international prizes. His most recent books in English are *After the Future: The Paradoxes of Postmodernism and Contemporary Russian Culture* (Amherst, 1995); *Russian Postmodernism: New Perspectives on Post-Soviet Culture* (with Alexander Genis and Slobodanka Vladiv-Glover, Providence, 1999); *Transcultural Experiments:*

Russian and American Models of Creative Communication (with Ellen Berry, New York, 1999); and *Cries in the New Wilderness: From the Files of the Moscow Institute of Atheism* (Philadelphia, 2002).

Boris Groys is a professor of philosophy and media theory at the Center of Art and Media Technology, Karlsruhe, Germany. His books include *The Total Art of Stalinism: Russian Avant-Garde, Aesthetic Dictatorship, and Beyond* (Princeton, 1992); *Ueber das Neue* [On the new] (Munich, 1999); and *Unter Verdacht: Eine Phenomenologie der Medien* [Under suspicion: A phenomenology of media] (Munich, 2000).

Hans Günther is a professor of Slavic literatures at the University of Bielefeld, Germany. He is the author of *Die Verstaatlichung der Literatur: Entstehung und Funktionsweise des sozialistisch-realistischen Kanons in der sowjetischen Literatur der 30er Jahre* (Stuttgart, 1984) and *Der sozialistische Übermensch: Maksim Gor'kij und der sowjetische Heldenmythos* (Stuttgart, 1993), as well as the editor of *The Culture of the Stalin Period* (London, 1990).

John McCannon is an assistant professor of history at the University of Saskatchewan. He is the author of *Red Arctic: Polar Exploration and the Myth of the North in the Soviet Union, 1932–1939* (Oxford, 1998). He has written articles about Soviet military affairs and the uses of children's literature by the Stalinist regime, and he is currently working on a biography of the Russian artist-explorer-mystic Nicholas Roerich.

Eric Naiman teaches Russian and comparative literature at the University of California, Berkeley. He is the author of *Sex in Public: The Incarnation of Early Soviet Ideology* (Princeton, 1997).

Jan Plamper is an assistant professor of Russian history at the University of Tübingen, Germany. His recent publications include the articles "Foucault's Gulag" and "Abolishing Ambiguity: Soviet Censorship Practices in the 1930s." He is currently preparing a book manuscript entitled *The Stalin Cult: Studies of Symbolic Power in the Soviet Union.*

Mikhail Ryklin is a senior research fellow at the Institute of Philosophy of the Russian Academy of Sciences, Moscow. He is the author and editor of numerous books including (in Russian) *Terrorologics* (Moscow, 1992); *Art as an Obstacle* (Moscow, 1997); and *Spaces of Exultation: Totalitarianism and Difference* (Moscow, 2002).

Richard Taylor is a professor of politics at University of Wales, Swansea, U.K. He is the author and editor of numerous books and articles on Russian and Soviet cinema. His latest book is *October* (London, 2002).

Emma Widdis is a lecturer in the Slavonic Department, Cambridge University, and a fellow of Trinity College. She has published articles on the cinema, literature, and architecture of the Soviet period in several journals and edited volumes. She is the author of *Visions of a New Land: Soviet Film from the Revolution to the Second World War* (New Haven, 2003).

Index

www.ingramcontent.com/pod-product-compliance
Lightning Source LLC
LaVergne TN
LVHW090804070826
844660LV00022B/1079

* 9 7 8 0 2 9 5 9 8 3 4 1 7 *